Psychology of Learning
for Instruction

Psychology of Learning for Instruction

Marcy P. Driscoll
Florida State University

Allyn and Bacon
Boston • London • Toronto • Sydney • Tokyo • Singapore

Editor in Chief, Education: Nancy Forsyth
Series Editorial Assistant: Christine Nelson
Production Administrator: Ann Greenberger
Editorial-Production Service: Progressive Typographers
Cover Administrator: Suzanne Harbison
Manufacturing Buyer: Louise Richardson
Composition Buyer: Linda Cox

Copyright © 1994 by Allyn & Bacon
A Division of Paramount Publishing, Inc.
160 Gould Street
Needham Heights, MA 02194

Driscoll, Marcy Perkins.
    Psychology of learning for instruction : learning & instructional technology/
Marcy P. Driscoll.
        p.   cm.
    Includes bibliographical references (p. 381) and index.
    ISB N 0–205–13928-0
    1. Learning, Psychology of.   2. Cognitive learning theory.   3. Teaching.
I. Title.
LB1060.D75   1993
370.15'23--dc20   93–1562
                                                                              CIP

Printed in the United States of America

10 9 8 7

This book is dedicated to
Robin, who has always believed in me.

Contents

Preface

I had no real intentions of writing a book about learning theory when I started this one. It was just that, as an instructor of advanced undergraduate and beginning graduate students in education, I have found most other books on learning theory to be unsatisfactory for my purposes. Many focus too much on psychology and not enough on education. Others include either too many theories, which are historically important but not especially relevant to instruction, or only one theory, usually the currently predominating one. Still others illustrate learning theory only as it can be applied in teaching, to the exclusion of other contexts in which learning and instruction routinely occur. Although many of my students *are* teachers (or are in training to become teachers), many are also instructional designers, media specialists, counselors, administrators, and adult educators. They typically do not have much background in psychology, and their concerns are largely applied. I wanted a book that took those things into consideration.

Every time I was visited by publishers' representatives, then, I was accustomed to complaining about the lack of books for courses like mine. It was during just such a visit that the Prentice-Hall representative (who had heard my complaints before) said, "Well, write it yourself, then." She was serious, and the project started there and then.

The result is a book that focuses on learning *and* instruction. Specific implications—and applications—of learning theories are discussed, and examples are drawn from educational situations and educational problems. By education, I mean to include not just teachers of elementary and secondary schools, but also professionals working in higher education and environments outside of formal schooling. To the extent possible, then, I have attempted to illustrate theoretical concepts in concrete terms and with a wide variety of examples—from primary school instruction to corporate training. That I have at least been moderately successful in the breadth of examples can been seen in the following two comments, which occurred during my first try out of the book: "Why have you included so many examples of kids and so few of adults?" asked one student in my class whose background and interests related to adult education and training. "Why have you included so many examples of adults and so few of kids?" asked another student who planned to teach in the primary grades.

Along with its applied focus, the book embodies a theme of "reflective practice." I do not believe that a single learning theory is the answer to all instructional problems. Nor do I believe that we have yet discovered or figured out all there is to know about learning. As a consequence, practitioners can do no more than make informed judgments about what theories have the most to offer them in the solution of their particular problems. My hope is that readers will develop a critical and reflective eye as they progress through this book, keeping in mind the full range of consequences that comes with the adoption of any particular approach. I also hope that they will take this book as a point of departure for continued study about learning and its implications for instruction.

Since the day I was first encouraged to write this book, many other people have helped in countless ways to bring the project to successful completion. To begin with, Gary Shank, Rick McCowen, Neil Schwartz and the other folks at NCIC were willing listeners who reacted to ideas, offered moral support, and generally kept me on-task with their regular queries of "How's the book coming?" Marlynn Griffin produced most of my diagrams and tables; she, Mahnaz Moallem, and Elizabeth Kirby also served as my in-house confidantes, sympathizing when my writing progressed slowly and offering valuable suggestions from their experiences as teachers and designers of instruction.

Two classes of graduate students—one at Florida State University and one at Arizona State University—earned my eternal gratitude for helping me to formatively evaluate the book. They frowned, they praised, they questioned, they criticized, and they suggested. As a result of their feedback, numerous revisions were made that have undoubtedly raised the pedagogical value of this book. I am also thankful to the anonymous reviewers whose comments, as much as I disliked admitting it, were often right on the mark.

Finally, along with my husband, my parents, and parents-in-law have supported me in ways they will never know.

▶ **Part I**

▶ 1

Introduction

Children learn language in a remarkably brief period of time, but an athlete may take years to develop a powerhouse serve in tennis. Students in school learn how to solve complex problems in mathematics, and sales trainees learn how to mollify irate customers. Chess and bridge players learn tactical strategies; preloaders learn efficient strategies for packing milk crates. These are all examples of what we call learning. But what is learning and how does it occur?

Learning is a lifelong activity. Learning occurs intentionally in formal instructional settings and incidentally through experience. Learning encompasses a multitude of competencies, from knowledge of simple facts to great skill in complex and difficult procedures. Learning sometimes requires great effort and sometimes proceeds with relative ease. These are a few of the things we know about learning. But learning is a complex affair. The results of learning are often observable in human performance, but the process of learning is much less obvious. As a consequence, different theories have been developed to explain learning. These theories represent different perspectives, different assumptions, and different beliefs about learning. It is therefore worthwhile to consider both how learning theories develop and what historical roots underlie the specific theories discussed in this book.

WHAT IS A THEORY OF LEARNING?

Most people have an intuitive answer to this question. A theory about learning is a set of laws or principles about learning. But what do these principles involve? What is their purpose? Where do they come from? Let's start with the last question first.

Theories about anything typically originate with questions. Why does the beach remain sunny when afternoon summer thunderstorms are widespread just five miles inland? What makes a person successful in reading? How much do adults know about world geography? How do effective teachers organize their instruction? Some of these questions are prompted by curiosity and a desire to understand the world around us. With the expansion of computers and other high tech equipment in all educational settings, for example, what role will textbooks play? What role do they play now? Are they particularly useful for facilitating learning in certain subject matters? What, in fact, do people learn from reading textbooks?

Other questions may be motivated by problems that require the generation of new knowledge to effect their solutions. For example, should a school or company invest in the latest computer or interactive videodisk technology? Is the cost of this equipment worth the learning gains that might be expected from its use in instruction? To make an informed decision about such a purchase, school or company officials might wish to know what impacts there are likely to be on learning, social processes, and the like.

Finally, many questions are provoked by events which somehow contradict our beliefs about the way things are. For example, consider the following story that I heard recently over National Public Radio. A teacher was describing what happened during a science experiment that his students were conducting, which involved putting empty or partially filled cans of soda into a tub of water and observing the degree to which they floated. To complete their experiment, the students added a couple of unopened cans, one of which happened to be diet soda. Lo and behold, the diet soda floated while the regular soda sank! Both were unopened 12-ounce cans. What could possibly account for the difference in their flotation capability? [The answer appears at the end of the chapter.]

Regardless of how questions arise, they generally lead researchers to conduct systematic observations on the basis of which plausible answers can be constructed. In some kinds of investigations, these observations are conducted without many advance, or a priori, expectations about what will be seen. Certainly, "inquiry demands the selection of a particular set of observations or facts from among the nearly infinite universe of conceivable observations" (Shulman, 1988, p. 5). But this selection may be quite broad and general. In a study examining textbook use and learning, for instance, the researchers might decide to look at grade level, subject matter, and teacher experience as possible variables in textbook use. Although these variables then help in the selection of classes to observe, they would not limit what the researchers observed in those classes.

By contrast, other kinds of investigations require the researchers to generate and test potential answers to the research question. The soda can story described is illustrative. In this case, the students proposed a working hypothesis about one can containing slightly more liquid than the other (therefore, having more volume). An hypothesis, or one's suggested answer to a research question, determines what variables (in this example, amount of liquid) are thought to be important in understanding the event (sinking/floating). The hypothesis also specifies the presumed relationship between the variables and the observed event. That is, the can that sank should contain more liquid than the can that floated.

In order to examine the viability of hypotheses, a set of particular observations must now be conducted, which in this case consisted of the students pouring the contents of each can into a measuring cup and then comparing the amounts in the two cups. The results of these observations would then be compared to the prediction that was hypothesized. The extent to which results and prediction agree determines whether the hypothesis has been verified or refuted. If refuted, then other, alternative explanations must be considered.

The observations made in any investigation enable researchers to construct or verify propositions about what is going on. These propositions form the basis of theories. In the soda can example, the students can be said to have a theory of flotation in which the amount of liquid contained in the can determines whether it sinks or floats. Their subsequent observations, however, revealed that both the regular and diet soda cans contained the same volume of liquid. Therefore, the students were forced to abandon this variable as part of their theory and to consider alternative ones.

Likewise, consider how theory building might occur in an examination of textbook use and learning. Although the investigation would not proceed from specific hypotheses, it is likely that researchers would begin with a question such as, how do textbooks influence learning? In answering this question, they might first examine the degree to which students actually read or studied their textbooks, with the assumption that those who did so would learn more than those who never opened their books. Suppose that observations revealed a general tendency of this sort but that, even among the textbook users, there was considerable variability in performance. This would suggest that the relationship between textbook use and learning involves more than just time spent reading or studying the text. The original assumption must now be amended and might, for example, include the additional variable of what students do when they read or study their textbooks. Eventually, a complex picture, or theory, of textbook use would be drawn.

As can be seen in these two examples, the process of theory building is recursive. The results of each phase of inquiry influence subsequent phases, which eventually feed back to modify original assumptions or hypotheses. In this way, a theory constantly undergoes modifications as new results are accommodated. Figure 1–1 illustrates this process. In the figure we also see the essential purposes of a theory: to explain the occurrence of some phenomenon and to predict its occurrence in the future. A learning theory, then, should explain the results associated with learning and predict the conditions under which learning will occur again. It is obviously the goal of instruction to apply this knowledge in the provision of appropriate conditions for facilitating effective learning.

Although theory building, as I have described it so far, seems orderly and objective, it is not necessarily either. Take, for instance, the problem of choosing what variables are important to investigate. If you assume that learning is a function of student characteristics, such as their motivation or preferred learning style, you could explain the effects of textbook use on performance in terms of how motivated students were to study the information or whether they possessed a verbal learning style. In other words, more motivated students would be expected to learn more than less motivated students, and those with a verbal learning style would be expected to learn more than their counterparts with a visual learning style. Adopting this perspective emphasizes the student and how he or she approaches

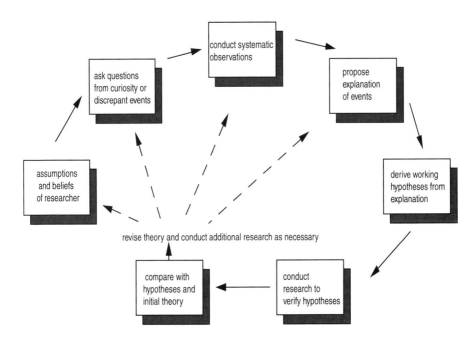

FIGURE   1–1   A Systematic and Recursive Process for Building a Theory

the learning task. Finding support for this explanation would probably involve interviewing students, asking them to think aloud as they read through a text chapter, or administering an instrument to measure motivation and/or learning style. These results would then be correlated with performance.

Alternatively, you could assume that properties of the text itself are responsible for student learning. This might suggest that some textbooks (in the same subject matter) should facilitate learning more effectively than others because they contain objectives, chapter summaries, practice questions and feedback, or other features that influence how students read and study texts. Adopting this perspective emphasizes the textbook, and to find evidence of this explanation would require textbook analyses, with subsequent correlation of text features and student performance. How does one decide which perspective to adopt? Is one more true than the other? Or is there a third alternative that recognizes the importance of both perspectives in providing a more complete understanding of the phenomenon?

Research decisions such as these fundamentally stem from disciplinary assumptions, or beliefs, that investigators have about the phenomena they study. An anthropologist, for example, goes about the study of primitive cultures quite differently from how a psychologist would approach the same investigation. "What distinguishes disciplines from one another is the manner in which they formulate their questions, how they define the content of their domains and organize that content conceptually, and the principles of discovery and verification that constitute the ground rules for creating and testing knowledge in their fields. These principles are different in the different disciplines" (Shulman, 1988, p. 5).

Because the study of learning is not itself a discipline, it has been approached by researchers representing a variety of disciplinary perspectives. You will see this in the resulting theories of learning that have been proposed. Behavioral psychologists, for example, argue that learning can be fully understood in terms of observable events, both environmental and behavioral. Cognitive psychologists, by contrast, believe that learning is mediated by memory processes inside the learner. A third perspective is offered by social psychologists, who contend that learning is a social enterprise, dependent upon interactions between the learner and his or her sociocultural environment. The point is, these beliefs dictate what questions about learning will be investigated and what theoretical constructs will be invented to provide explanations. This also means that two apparently competing theories may not be directed at even the same phenomena. What aspects of learning are obscured by one theory may be illuminated by another.

In the development of a particular theory, research tends to be cumulative, or what Kuhn (1970) called normal science. Investigators ask questions that are logical next steps based on previous findings. They aim to articulate theoretical principles that have already been devised, modifying those principles as necessary to account for unexpected or contradictory findings. Sometimes, however, the predictions that follow from a theory continue to fail, despite whatever modifications are made to the theory. The result is that anomalies are amassed that cannot be explained very easily. When this happens, one or more researchers will propose an alternative, truly competing theory. This is known as extraordinary science and represents a real breakthrough in scientific progress and knowledge development.

To be a worthy competitor, any new theory must reinterpret all the previous findings as well as account for the anomalous ones that prompted its invention in the first place. This can occur on a limited scale within a particular theoretical orientation, as when cognitive psychologists propose new theories of long-term memory to accommodate research results not easily handled by the existing theory. It can also occur on a grand scale when researchers shift theoretical orientations altogether, adopting disciplinary assumptions that are incommensurate with the previous orientation. One cannot, for instance, simultaneously believe that learning is entirely understandable in terms of external, observable events and believe that learning depends on internal memory processes.

This is an exciting time for theory building about learning, because new perspectives are emerging that challenge long-held beliefs about the nature of learning and instruction. Some theorists have even gone so far as to claim that educational practices stemming from some current views of learning are at best misguided and at worst potentially harmful (Cunningham, 1992).

It is important to keep in mind, however, that if we accept Figure 1–1 as a model for the theory building process, then we must also accept the provisional character of theories. As much as we might like to think otherwise, theories do not give us the truth of the matter. They simply provide a conceptual framework for making sense of the data that have been collected so far. Therefore, it is probably wise to view each one critically for what it can contribute to solving important instructional problems. This is what Shulman (1988) called the attitude of a "disciplined eclectic."

A Definition of Learning

Despite the differences among the learning theories discussed in this book, they do share some basic, definitional assumptions about learning. First, they refer to learning as a persisting change in human performance or performance potential. This means that learners are capable of actions they could not perform before learning occurred and this is true whether or not they actually have an opportunity to exhibit the newly acquired performance. Typically, however, the only way a teacher, instructor, or researcher knows that learning has occurred is to ask the learners to demonstrate in some fashion what they have learned. Finding good indicators of learning is as important for designing instruction as it is for building theory.

Second, to be considered learning, a change in performance must come about as a result of the learner's interaction with the environment. This statement has several implications. Some behavior changes, such as the acquisition of fine motor control, can be attributed to maturation and are therefore not considered learned. Other behavior changes, such as searching for food when hungry or becoming garrulous when drunk, are obviously explained on the basis of temporary states. These also do not imply learning. Learning requires experience, but just what experiences are essential and how these experiences are presumed to bring about learning constitute the focus of every learning theory.

A Definition of Learning Theory

A **learning theory**, therefore, comprises a set of constructs linking observed changes in performance with what is thought to bring about those changes. Constructs refer to the concepts theorists invent to identify psychological variables. Memory, for example, is a construct implicated in cognitive perspectives on learning. In other words, we look at the fact that people can demonstrate the same performance time after time and reason that they do so because they have remembered it. We have invented the concept of memory to explain this result.

To build a learning theory requires defining three basic components:

- The results: what are these changes in performance to be explained by the theory?
- The means: what are the processes by which the results are brought about (including any hypothesized structures that these processes are assumed to operate on)?
- The inputs: what triggers the processes to occur? what are the resources or experiences that form the basis for learning?

The answers given to these questions, as well as how the answers themselves are determined, characterize the various perspectives taken on learning and the specific theories that have emerged. You may find it useful to keep these components in mind as you read the chapters of this book. They provide a basis for comparison across theories as well as a means for pinpointing areas in which answers have not yet been attempted.

LEARNING IN HISTORY

How people learn is not a new question in psychology, having been established as a legitimate research pursuit in the late 1800s. But learning is also not the sole territory of psychologist; it has been a matter of deep concern to philosophers for many centuries. What is mind? How does the mind develop? What is knowledge, and how does the mind acquire knowledge? How does the mind come to know other minds? These are just a few of the questions that provide the intellectual and philosophical underpinnings to modern learning theory. It is not my intention to review comprehensively the history of learning theory, but it is useful to trace the major antecedents to today's theories in order to provide a framework for comprehending and evaluating them.

The study of learning derives from essentially two sources. Because learning involves the acquisition of knowledge, the first concerns the nature of knowledge and how we come to know things. What is knowledge? How is knowledge distinguished from opinion or falsehoods? What are legitimate ways of knowing? These are questions of epistemology. How they are answered reflects one's initial assumptions about how the mind acquires knowledge of the world, and these assumptions influence what research methodology is used to conduct investigations on learning.

For example, what does it mean to "know" that density affects an object's weight and therefore its ability to float? [This is a clue to the soda can problem described earlier.] Is it enough to state with conviction that very dense objects will sink while less dense objects will float? Or, does the knowledge lay in one's choice of a stryofoam block to be used for a buoy rather than a rock? Similarly, what counts as legitimate ways of coming to know the relationship between object density and flotation? Must one experience this relationship through actual manipulation of different objects in water, or can one simply be told about it with visual or verbal examples?

As you will soon see, theorists take opposing positions on these questions. Some believe that knowledge is a matter of internally representing the external world and is primarily acquired through experience, whereas others argue that knowledge is a matter of interpretations that learners actively construct by imposing organization on the world about them.

The second source in which modern learning theory is rooted concerns the nature and representation of mental life. When knowledge is acquired, how is it represented in the mind? What are the operations or rules that govern mental phenomena? Although these questions are not considered worth asking by behaviorists, their answers are part of any cognitive, developmental, or biological theory about learning. Mental phenomena have been conceptualized as associations among ideas, complex schemas of organized knowledge, and neurochemical changes in synapses, to name only a few. As you progress through this book, you will see that each of these levels of analysis provides a unique view of learning.

Let us now take a brief look at how these two sources have played out through history in the development of modern learning theory. In later chapters, these foundations will be recalled to help you trace arguments of particular theories.

The Epistemology of Learning

Probably the earliest theory of how the mind acquires knowledge was proposed by Greek philosophers in the fourth and fifth centuries B.C. According to Empedocles, Democritus, and Epicurus, the mind perceives images given off by objects by copying sense impressions into a memory store. Knowledge then becomes a matter of knowing these mental copies, and the earliest copy theories suggested that the mind knew directly what the sensory nerves brought to it (Herrnstein & Boring, 1965). So, for example, a spider on the wall (the object) gives off an image of itself that I perceive and copy in memory, which results in my knowing there is a spider on the wall.

There are obvious problems with this view of knowledge. Why, for example, do we make mistakes in perception? What looks like a spider on the wall turns out to be a dirty fingerprint. Since the sensory input is fixed, the problem must lay in the correspondence between the mental copy and the object. In other words, I am quite sure I saw a spider, but I have to admit that what I saw and what was actually there in this instance did not correspond. The more serious problem for philosophers is that if such a simple mistake can be made, how can we be sure our mental copies of anything are accurate?

A way out of this dilemma is to reject the copy theory and assume that objects can be directly perceived and known. This means that the knower apprehends sensory data corresponding to the features or properties of an object. In the example concerning the supposed spider, I must have perceived properties such as small, black, and perhaps round in shape. Implied in this perspective (known as objectivism) is that reality exists independently of the knower, because an object can exist whether or not it is perceived by anyone (there can be a spider on the wall without my seeing it).

Even phenomena such as atoms that are not directly perceptible to humans are nonetheless assumed to be objectively real and ultimately detectable by the right instrument. Error still presents a problem for this position, however, because in the earlier example I should have perceived dirty fingerprint, i.e., what was really there, rather than spider. Philosophers handled this problem by admitting the possibility of unconscious inference based on a history of experience. In other words, I probably experienced many sensations in the past that were similar to the present one and that always before meant spider. Therefore, I inferred that I saw a spider instead of correctly identifying the sensation as a dirty fingerprint.

With error being explained away by the accumulation of experience, the objectivist position assumes that knowledge of reality is ultimately attainable. Regardless of whether reality (the objectivist view) or copies of reality (copy theory) are known, both positions admit experience as the only valid source of knowledge. That is, I know there is a spider (or fingerprint) on the wall only because I experienced (saw) it. Likewise, it could be argued that knowledge about object density and flotation must come from the experience of dense and heavy things sinking and lighter, less dense things floating. Acquiring knowledge through experience is known as empiricism.

Empiricism is a fundamental element of research, because research is the systematic gathering of data (experiences) that bear on a question of interest. Through research, we attempt to build a body of knowledge that provides answers to this and related questions.

Characteristic features of empiricism include not only the emphasis on sensory experience, but also the thesis that complex ideas are built up from simpler, more elemental ones that become associated through experience. Suppose, for example, you encounter a kitten for the first time. Since all knowledge is derived through sensory experience, you see its size, shape, and color. You feel the softness of its fur, the sharpness of its claws, and the roughness of its tongue. You hear its high-pitched, squeaky meow. Taken separately, these sensory impressions hold little meaning, but together they make up your knowledge of kitten. A complex idea has been formed by connecting together many simpler, more primitive ideas.

In understanding what knowledge is from the objectivist perspective, it is also important to recognize how a history of experiences associated with an object or idea comes to influence later perception. If, in repeated experiences with kittens, your eyes always itched and your nose ran, these sensations would also become part of your knowledge of kittens. For a learning researcher to discover just what knowledge you have about kittens, then, he or she would have to consider not only the objective properties of kittens but also your unique experience of them. Both are represented in your mind, but both are understandable by reference to experience and objective reality.

A very different view of knowledge and learning is offered by a perspective variously known as idealism, subjectivism, interpretivism, or rationalism (Herrnstein & Boring, 1961; Bower & Hilgard, 1981). According to this view, which was suggested by Plato and later developed by Kant in particular, the mind neither copies reality nor apprehends it directly. Rather, reason is considered to be the prime source of knowledge. This implies that all sense data are unstructured and undifferentiated, to be interpreted by the mind according to innate perceptual tendencies. Reality, in other words, is constructed.

The interpretist view of knowledge emphas   s the active and dynamic nature of the cognizing organism. The mind does not passively accept sensory impressions; it actively imposes an organizational and interpretive framework on sense data. This helps to explain why I saw a spider on the wall instead of a fingerprint. As a child, I was afraid of spiders and tended to imagine seeing them at every turn, imposing my concept of spider on all sorts of sensory data from specks of dirt to raisins! Likewise, consider any visual illusion, children's dot pattern puzzles, or the typical test for color vision. You do not see the individual lines and colors on the page, which are the sensations being received by your eyes; you see a red figure 8 or a green figure 5.

Related to the interpretivist view is the idea that at least some knowledge is innate, inherited and present in the mind at birth. There is interesting speculation, for example, that we are genetically predisposed for some fears because of our evolutionary history. It might be that I was predisposed to fear spiders because they were dangerous to the survival of early humans. However, just what knowledge is innate, or what form it takes, has not been brought to consensus, and you will see many different answers proposed by different theorists.

Finally, a third epistemology for learning is pragmatism. In a sense, pragmatism occupies the middle ground between objectivism and interpretivism. Objectivists rejected the copy theory in favor of direct knowledge of reality. Interpretists rejected the copy theory and objective reality to suggest that all knowledge is constructed from within the organism. Pragmatists acknowledge the existence of reality but argue that it cannot be known directly. Thus, they accept the copy theory but with a modified conception of what knowledge means. Knowledge is not absolute, they claim; it is provisional. Sometimes our mental copies or beliefs will accurately reflect reality, but we must be prepared for when they do not. Moreover, we have no way of knowing when they are true. What is true today may indeed be false tomorrow. As a result, although pragmatists hold absolute knowledge as a worthy goal, they emphasize theories of meaning—of what works—in the full recognition that their goal of absolute knowledge may never be reached.

As an example of pragmatic epistemology, consider the often inaccurate mental models we hold about the nature of the world and the things around us that nonetheless enable us to function quite effectively from day to day. How many times have you done something and heard, "That's not the way you're supposed to do it!" Your retort, of course, is "Well, it worked!" Examples of this come to mind every time I work on the computer. My knowledge of how electronic mail works is really quite sketchy, but I am able to send and retrieve messages because I have learned to use certain commands that work pretty faithfully. Only when they fail do I discover that I could be using a more accurate sequence of commands to do what I want to accomplish. My mental model of e-mail, therefore, is neither accurate nor complete, but it generally works. It is meaningful to me.

These three major epistemological traditions—objectivism, interpretivism, and pragmatism—are all evident in the learning theories discussed in this book. Although Leahey and Harris (1989) stated that pragmatism is the working philosophy of most psychologists, others (including myself) have argued that objectivism has been the dominant epistemology in psychology and education (cf. Phillips, 1983; Soltis, 1984; Driscoll, 1984; Cunningham, 1992). Certainly, radical behaviorism (see Chapter 2) and cognitive information processing theory (see Chapter 3) rest on objectivist assumptions.

By contrast, the recently emerging constructivist view of cognition (Chapters 5 and 11) is much more consistent with the interpretist perspective, as is Piaget's genetic epistemology (Chapter 6). Similarly related are the ideas of Bruner and Vygotsky (Chapter 7). Finally, biological theorists (Chapter 8) have raised the nature/nurture question again by proposing that learning is limited and influenced by the evolutionary history of humans. Summarized in Table 1–1 are the assumptions and theoretical implications of the epistemological traditions described above, along with the learning theories most closely associated with them.

Early Experimental Approaches to Learning

Ebbinghaus (1850–1909)

When psychology split off from philosophy to become the "science of mental life" (Bower & Hilgard, 1981), it was largely concerned with sensation and perception. But the research of Hermann Ebbinghaus ushered in a new era of interest in the study of learning. Herrnstein and Boring (1965) attributed the emergence of this interest to a growing faith in scientific research in general and scientific psychology in particular that encouraged researchers to experiment on learning.

By the time of Ebbinghaus, the classical doctrine of associationism which was, in essence, a theory of learning, had already been established in psychology. Recall that the empiricist perspective included the principle of association—that ideas become connected, or associated, through experience. Moreover, the more frequently a particular association is encountered, the stronger the associative bond is assumed to be. This

TABLE 1–1   Three Epistemological Traditions and Their Relation to the Study of Learning

	Objectivism	Pragmatism	Interpretivism
Assumptions about reality	Reality is objective, singular, fragmentable	Reality is interpreted, negotiated, consensual	Reality is constructed, multiple, holistic
Nature of truth statements	Generalizations, laws, focus on similarities	Working hypotheses, focus on similarities or differences	Working hypotheses, focus on differences
Source(s) of knowledge	Experience	Experience and reason	Reason
Types of research designs	Experimental, a priori	Any design may be useful for illuminating different aspects of reality	Naturalistic, emergent
Associated learning and instructional theories	Behaviorism, cognitive information processing, Gagné's instructional theory	Educational semiotics, Bruner's and Vygotsky's views of learning and development	Piaget's developmental theory, constructivism

seemed to account well for learning. For example, the stimulus bread is likely to elicit the response butter more often and more rapidly than the response brown, because the association between bread and butter has been frequently experienced and thus has become well learned.

Ebbinghaus presumed, then, that if ideas are connected by the frequency of their associations, then learning should be predictable based on the number of times a given association is repeatedly experienced. This gave rise to the experimental paradigm used by Ebbinghaus and learning researchers after him. The independent variable was defined as the number of repetitions of a list of associated ideas. The dependent variable to measure learning was the subject's recall of the list.

Because Ebbinghaus wanted to investigate the learning of new associations, untainted by past experience, he invented nonsense syllables to simplify his investigations. These took the form of consonant-vowel-consonant trigrams (e.g., qap, jor, mol, kuw) and were assumed to be inherently meaningless. Then he arranged to present sequences of 16 syllables to himself (drawn from a pool of 2,300 syllables he had constructed; Ebbinghaus, [1885] 1913). With this method, Ebbinghaus had a quantifiable procedure for investigating various laws of association, as well as overall memory and forgetting. In conducting an experiment using six, 16-syllable lists, for example, Ebbinghaus wrote, "If I learn such a group, each series by itself, so that it can be repeated without error, and 24 hours later repeat it in the same sequence and to the same point of mastery, then the latter repetition is possible in about two thirds of the time necessary for the first. The resulting savings in work of one third clearly measures the strength of association formed during the first learning between one member and its immediate successor" (Ebbinghaus, [1885] 1913, 524).

By systematically varying such factors as the number of syllables in the list, the number of lists studied, and the amount of time spent studying each list, Ebbinghaus provided experimental verification of some obvious facts about memory. For instance, the more material there is to learn, the longer learning takes. The longer it has been since something was learned, the harder it is to remember. Ebbinghaus is also credited with establishing the now-classic forgetting curve (Figure 1–2), which shows that forgetting proceeds very rapidly at first and then more slowly as the time from initial learning increases. It pays us to remember, however, that Ebbinghaus' forgetting curve was derived from verbal learning experiments. The forgetting of other types of learned experiences (especially events that may have been personally traumatic) may reveal a quite different pattern (Bourne, Dominowski, Loftus, & Healy, 1986).

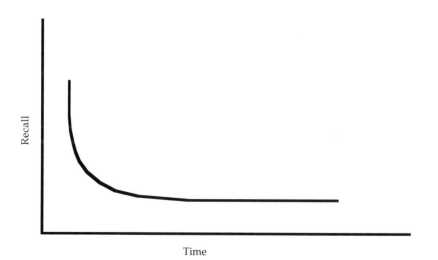

FIGURE 1–2 The Classic Forgetting Curve (After Ebbinghaus [1885] 1913)

Finally, there can be little argument that Ebbinghaus' experiments established a verbal learning tradition that has carried through even to the present day. Although nonsense syllables have given way to meaningful concepts in memory experiments, the principle of association remains a driving force within many modern cognitive conceptions of learning.

Thorndike (1874–1949)

Like Ebbinghaus, Edward L. Thorndike was interested in the doctrine of association, but association between sensation and impulse rather than association between ideas. In other words, Thorndike investigated learning in terms of the associations related to action. For his studies, Thorndike preferred to use animals (mostly cats and chickens), which seemed reasonable at the time on the basis of Darwin's thesis of the continuity of species, and he formulated the first experimental procedures to be used in the study of animal learning. These comprised repeatedly placing an animal in a "puzzle box" and recording, as a measure of learning, the decreasing amount of time it took the animal to operate the latch and escape.

The results of his experiments convinced Thorndike that an animal learned to associate a sensation and an impulse when its action had a satisfying consequence. In other words, the animal formed an association between the sense-impression of the interior of the box and the impulse leading to the successful escape action, because the action led to a satisfying result—namely, escape from the box. This principle Thorndike termed the **Law of Effect**, and it represented a modification of the classical principle of association that would have far-reaching implications for behaviorism.

Finally, Thorndike called into question the existence of mental associations in animals. He argued, albeit tentatively, that the associations which explain animal behavior do not necessarily mean animals feel or think while they act. Nor is it necessary to ascribe mental motives to their actions. Perhaps, said Thorndike, animals have no memories, no ideas to associate. This rather revolutionary notion stands as a second legacy to behaviorism, and behaviorists who followed Thorndike extended it quite boldly.

Pavlov (1849–1946)

A third experimental approach to the study of associations brought together associationism and reflexology. In his investigations of the digestive reflexes of dogs, Ivan Pavlov noticed that the dogs salivated not only to food, but often to a variety of other inappropriate stimuli (e.g., the sight of the trainer who brought the food). Whereas this phenomenon plagued other researchers, Pavlov saw it as an opportunity to experimentally study learning as well as innate reflexes. He called this salivation to the sight of the trainer a learned reflex that is established because of an association between the appropriate stimulus (food) and the inappropriate one (the trainer). In other words, something neutral is paired with something that causes a response until the neutral thing also causes the response. This proved to be the beginning of an extended research program in classical conditioning (or Pavlovian conditioning).

According to the **classical conditioning** paradigm, an unconditioned stimulus (UCS) biologically and involuntarily elicits an unconditioned response (UCR). The dog salivates when food is put in its mouth; you blink when a puff of air hits you in the eye; a child startles when a loud noise is made behind her. Theoretically, this is depicted as follows:

Then, because it is paired with the UCS, a conditioned stimulus acquires the ability to elicit the same response. Because the response is now conditioned to the new stimulus, it becomes a conditioned response. So, for example, ringing a bell does not normally have any effect on salivation, but when it is repeatedly paired with the presentation of food, it can become a conditioned stimulus and will elicit salivation even in the absence of food. This might be depicted in the following way.

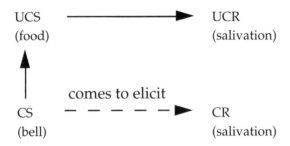

Examples of classical conditioning probably come readily to mind. My dog salivates at the sight of heartworm pills, because dog bones have cus-tomarily been given to him at the same time as the pill. A child cries (CR) at the sight of dogs (CS) after one growled (UCS) menacingly at him. Some years ago, I fell asleep in a church service because the minister turned the lights off. Since darkness had always been associated before with fatigue and going to sleep, it acted as a conditioned stimulus for sleep even though the service was in the morning and I was well rested.

Probably the most widely cited example of classical conditioning in humans is the study conducted by Watson and Rayner (1920) with a nine-month-old baby, Albert B. Interested in the conditioning of emotional responses, Watson and Rayner first sought an unconditioned stimulus that would reliably elicit the unconditioned response of crying in Albert. They eventually discovered that they could trigger the crying reflex with a loud noise, specifically a hammer being struck against a steel bar. Watson and Rayner then presented Albert with a large, tame white rat, and as Albert approached the animal, they hit the hammer against the steel bar. After seven pairings of the noise with the rat, Watson and Rayner presented the rat alone. Immediately, Albert began to cry; the rat was now a conditioned stimulus and crying the conditioned response.

In subsequent tests, Watson and Rayner reported that Albert also cried when exposed to a rabbit and a fur coat. Thus, he exhibited stimulus generalization, a phenomenon that Pavlov had already demonstrated with his dogs. In classical conditioning, stimuli that are highly similar to the CS will also elicit the CR in varying degrees. In addition, Pavlov showed that when a conditioned stimulus is paired with another neutral stimulus, the second stimulus can also become conditioned, resulting in the phenomenon known as higher-order conditioning. Finally, when a conditioned stimulus is presented over a sufficiently long period of time without the UCS, it will eventually lose its ability to elicit the conditioned response. In this way, extinction of the conditioned response to the conditioned stimulus occurs.

So what happened to Baby Albert? Watson and Rayner intended to cure him through extinction and counterconditioning (pairing a pleasant UCS with the rat CS), but they never had the chance, since Albert's mother moved, taking him with her. One can only hope that the conditioned response eventually weakened with time.

The principles of stimulus generalization and discrimination, extinction, and counterconditioning, originally established by Pavlov, became important elements of operant conditioning as well (see chapter 2). Counterconditioning, now known as systematic desensitization (e.g., Wolpe 1958, 1969), is also a standard therapeutic technique for treating various types of fears or anxieties. The question of whether humans truly condition in the Pavlovian sense, however, remains a debatable one. Brewer (1974) reviewed over 200 studies that purported to demonstrate conditioning and concluded that mental processes intervened in most cases. That is, only subjects who were told about UCS-CS pairings tended to acquire the conditioned response. Leahey and Harris (1989) commented that

> *it is interesting to observe that the studies Brewer reviews, almost all of which support the cognitive position, go back as far early as 1919 and were produced in all the following decades up into the 1970s, right through the dominance of behavioral theories in the field of learning. This shows the power of tradition. If research programs are going well, then occasional challenging results are either quietly ignored, called interesting phenomena to be shelved for later study, or explained away. Only when an alternative view emerges, as cognitive theory*

emerged in the 1960s to rival behavior theory, do old problems appear significant. (p. 33)

Although cognitive approaches to learning have only recently come to a position of prominence in American psychology, they had a long-standing tradition in Europe with the Gestalt school.

Gestalt Theory

While the doctrine of association was being articulated in the experiments of Ebbinghaus, Thorndike, and Pavlov, a countermovement developed among German theorists interested primarily in perception. Called the Gestalt school, it was brought to the attention of American psychologists by the publication in English of Wolfgang Kohler's The Mentality of Apes (1925) and Kurt Koffka's The Growth of Mind (1924) (Bower & Hilgard, 1981). Of particular interest are Kohler's experiments with apes, because it was on the basis of these that he struck a dissenting opinion to the associative view of memory. Instead of allowing that the mind learned simple connections between ideas or associations between stimuli and responses, Kohler argued that his apes learned relations among stimuli and could modify their behavior by perceiving stimuli in new ways.

The typical experiment conducted by Kohler involved placing food just out of reach of an ape in a cage. The food could be obtained, on different trials, by moving an obstructing box out of the way, pulling a cord in a particular direction, or putting two sticks together to make a lever long enough to reach the food. Although some of their attempts to reach the food failed, the apes did not behave in a random fashion, asserted Kohler. Nor did learning appear to occur in a regular, continuous way from a pattern of trial and error and a gradual buildup of correct associations. Instead, the apes exhibited what Kohler called insight. After a failed attempt or two and often a period of complete inactivity, the apes employed the correct solution and obtained the food.

According to Kohler, the behavior he observed could not be easily explained by the principle of association alone. Thus, he proposed a "class of inner processes" which enabled the apes to grasp the structure of a situation. That is, they acquired a relation between two things, an "interconnection based on the properties of the things themselves, not a mere 'frequent following of each other' or an 'occurring together'" (Kohler, 1917, p. 578; emphasis his).

Summary

Most of the major issues for learning and the topics of this book have now been established. Ebbinghaus, Thorndike, and Pavlov shared the view that learning depends on associations and proceeded on the assumption that the complexity of thought and behavior can be reduced to simple connections among events. We see the same perspective underlying modern behavioral theory and cognitive information processing theory. In the former, the associations are between environmental stimuli and behavioral responses. In the latter, mental associations mediate between stimulus and response. In both, however, theorists fundamentally assume that they can account for complex behavior in terms of elemental associations.

By contrast, Kohler's view that learning is more than a collection of associations established the treatment of learning and perception associated with Gestalt psychology. This perspective is evident in constructivist conceptions of cognition which are finding voice in schema theory, situated cognition, and education semiotics.

Largely ignored by both behavioral and cognitive information processing theorists have been issues of biology and development in learning. These were of prime concern to Piaget, whose theory has had a tremendous influence on the study of cognitive development, and Vygotsky, whose writings from the 1920s and 1930s are again exerting influence on learning and developmental theories. In addition, neuroscientists have now proposed their own theories of how learning and memory operate and suggested, once more, that evolution may impose constraints on learning.

Finally, motivation has met with a renewed interest in studies of learning. Originally investigated under the notion of "drive" in early behavioral theories, motivation has been reconceptualized as an affective variable mediating cognition and subsequent performance. Along with biological and developmental determinants of learning, motivation as well deserves our consideration.

LEARNING THEORY AND INSTRUCTION

Theories of learning focus on and describe the process of learning. For many learning theorists, this description is their primary goal and whatever applied knowledge may come from it is serendipitous. Cognitive psychologists, for example, largely concern themselves with the structure and processes of the mind and cognition. Development psychologists seek to understand human development from infancy to old age. Neuroscientists hope to discover the secrets of the brain. But some of these researchers, as well as educational and instructional psychologists, think about the implications of learning theories for instruction.

By **instruction** I mean any deliberate arrangement of events to facilitate a learner's acquisition of some goal. The goal can range from knowledge to skills to strategies to attitudes, and so on. The learners can be adults or children of any age, background, or prior experience. The setting in which learning takes place can be formal, school-based, on-the-job, or in the community—wherever programs for learning are being designed and implemented. Those in charge of instruction can include public and private school teachers, training instructors, or instructional designers. The basic assumption, no matter what the particulars of an instructional situation, is that effective instruction is informed by theories of learning.

Reigeluth (1983) distinguished between descriptive and prescriptive learning theory, as well as between learning and instructional theory. As indicated earlier, the very point of learning theory is descriptive—to describe the processes by which observed changes in performance are brought about. On the basis of descriptive theory, however, prescriptive principles can be derived and empirically tested. For example, the behaviorist principle of reinforcement, "pleasant consequences of any behavior increase the probability of the behavior's reoccurrence," can be rephrased in terms of a prescription: "To increase the occurrence of some desired behavior, reward it."

This prescription essentially indicates what conditions of instruction should facilitate learning, but it does not prescribe specific instructional methods. To do this, we might say, "To increase the occurrence of some desired behavior, begin instruction by modeling the behavior, then reward the learner with colored stickers for each succeeding attempt to perform the behavior. Then, when the behavior seems firmly established, reduce reinforcement to every third correct performance." Thus, according to Reigeluth (1983), a learning prescription is not exactly the same thing as an instructional prescription, as might be obtained from an instructional or instructional design theory. As a result, he argued, learning prescriptions may not be as easily applied by the classroom teacher or instructional designer as instructional prescriptions.

Although Reigeluth is undoubtedly right that learning theories are not as readily applied as instructional theories, there are few instructional theories as well developed as most learning theories. One of the few exceptions is Gagné's (1985) conditions of learning (see Chapter 10). But lest we become disheartened, there are instructional implications that can be drawn from the learning theories in this book, and many of these have been independently investigated and have amassed empirical support. To the extent possible, therefore, each chapter not only describes a given learning theory, but also presents instructional implications that either have been, or can be, derived from it. Moreover, questions are included with each chapter that are designed to help you compare and contrast theories and derive instructional implications of your own.

THE GENERAL PLAN AND APPROACH OF THIS BOOK

In Part I, the behaviorist perspective on learning is presented with the radical behaviorism of B. F. Skinner. Although traditional behavioral theorists who preceded Skinner are described briefly, they had relatively little to say about instruction, whereas Skinner had a great deal to say. The cognitive perspective on learning is the subject of Part II, which includes chapters on the information processing model of cognition, the meaningful learning theory of David P. Ausubel, and schema theory and mental models.

Developmental issues related to learning are raised in Part III, beginning with Piaget's theory of cognitive development and information processing theories that have been proposed to cover areas where Piaget's theory seems to be in error. In addition, Bruner's concept formation and inquiry model of instruction and Vygotsky's social formation of mind are discussed.

Part IV offers a chapter on learning and biology, in which the sociobiological and physiological bases of learning and memory are explored. Although these may seem rather far removed from instruction, researchers from a variety of fields have attempted an interdisciplinary discussion on the brain, cognition and education.

Part V focuses on motivation as a mediator of learning and performance. Albert Bandura's social learning theory is presented, along with John Keller's model of motivational design. Finally, in Part VI, learning and instruction are brought together in the contrasting instructional theories of Robert M. Gagné and modern day constructivists.

The book ends with a brief chapter entitled, "Toward a Personal Theory of Learning." Any book on learning necessarily reflects its author's unique perspective and individual beliefs about the nature of knowledge and how we come to know things. My selection of theories to discuss, the sequence in which I have placed them, the examples I have used to illustrate them, and the conclusions I have drawn from them are all clues to my view of learning. So is the pedagogical structure of the book, which is designed to provide you with more instructional support at the beginning than at the end. My assumption is that by the time you finish this book, you will no longer need to rely on either my perspective on learning or any pedagogical strategies that a book can provide.

Also by the time you finish this book, you should have developed or fine-tuned your own informed view of learning. You should be ready to take a stand on the merits or faults of a particular theory as it might be applied to various instructional problems. You should be in a position to identify gaps in theory and to suggest where future research might profitably be conducted. In essence, if this book is effective, you will have become a "reflective practitioner," whether your practice is in the class-room, the training center, or the laboratory.

Answer to soda can problem: Regular soda is much denser than diet soda because of the sugar it contains compared to the very small amount of artificial sweetener contained in diet soda.

SUGGESTED READINGS

Bower, G. H., & Hilgard, E. R. (1981). *Theories of learning* (5th ed.). Englewood Cliffs, NJ: Prentice-Hall.

Soltis, J. F. (1984) On the nature of educational research. *Educational Researcher, 13* (December), 5–10.

REFLECTIVE QUESTIONS AND ACTIVITIES

1. Unger, Draper, and Pendergrass (1986) reported that students may have difficulty understanding epistemologies that clash with their own, tacit beliefs. They suggested, therefore, that students should examine their personal beliefs about knowledge and ways of knowing. Look up Unger et al.'s study, and complete the survey they provide (directions for self-scoring are included). How might your score be interpreted?

   REFERENCE: Unger, R. K., Draper, R. D., & Pendergrass, M. L. (1986). Personal epistemology and personal experience. *Journal of Social Issues, 42*(2), 67–79.

2. Unger et al. (1986) discuss a variety of reasons accounting for different epistemological beliefs among groups of individuals, including gender, for example. Ask your classmates to complete the survey, and then discuss the results. What are possible reasons for the differences in your scores?

   REFERENCE: same as above

3. According to Schommer (1990), the epistemological beliefs learners hold may influence the manner in which they approach a learning task and what they subsequently learn. Specifically, she examined such beliefs as "Knowledge is discrete and unambiguous," "Ability to learn is innate," "Learning is quick or not at all," and "Knowledge is certain." She found that students who believed in learning as a quick, all or none phenomenon generated simple, overly general conclusions from what they read and were overconfident in their own learning. What do Schommer's findings imply for instruction? Should teachers or instructional designers be concerned with their students' epistemological beliefs? How should instruction be modified based on those beliefs?

   REFERENCE: Schommer, M. (1990). Effects of beliefs about the nature of knowledge on comprehension. Journal of *Educational Psychology, 82* (3), 498–504.

▶ Part II

Learning and Behavior

► 2

Radical Behaviorism

Consider the following scenarios.

Scenario 2–1

The third graders at a suburban elementary school reflect the neighborhood in which it is located: most are white, some are black, a few are Hispanic. There are about as many boys as girls, and the range of their abilities is considerable. As in most classes, the students work at different rates, a few rarely participate in any group assignments, and some chronically misbehave. Jesse and Charla, like other students this age, have abundant energy and find it difficult to sit still in class.

Scenario 2–2

An autistic child sits in a chair where she has been placed by her mother. She stares blankly at nothing in particular. Her mother speaks, but the child does not respond. All efforts to get the child to talk or communicate in any way have failed.

Scenario 2–3

Things are set up to run smoothly at the boot camp in Anytown. Soldiers get in shape with daily 5-mile runs and calisthenics. They learn to load, fire, dismantle, and clean their weapons. They are assigned chores, the exemplary performance of which earns them privileges. Breaking the rules, on the other hand, leads to extra pushups, more miles to run, or forfeited time off.

It may not seem at first that these scenarios have much in common. Yet all these situations illustrate (or will, with some fleshing out) the basic tenets of radical behaviorism.

The notion of behaviorism was introduced into American psychology by John B. Watson (1913). Watson promoted the view that psychology should be concerned only with the objective data of behavior. The study of consciousness or complex mental states, Watson argued, is hampered by the difficulty of devising objective and functional indicators of these phenomena. At some point, one is forced to consider the facts of behavior. These, at least, can be agreed upon because they are observable by anyone. To illustrate, suppose in Scenario 2-3 that Private Johnson draws barracks duty one week, which consists of mopping and waxing the barracks floor each day. For completion of the task with no demerits (which means those floors were spotless!), she earns commendations every day and is awarded a pass to go off base Friday night. What can we conclude from this scenario? Did Private Johnson do such a good job because she looked forward to a fine meal at a local Italian restaurant instead of army food for one night? Or maybe she just takes pride in her work. The fact that any number of inferences are possible when we attempt to understand Private Johnson's mental state and the reasons for her behavior is precisely the problem Watson noted. Stick to the facts of behavior: she completed the assigned task, the results were spotless, she earned commendations, she was awarded a pass.

B. F. Skinner, major proponent of radical behaviorism, followed Watson's lead in emphasizing behavior as the basic subject matter of psychology (Skinner, 1938, 1974). But Skinner's work differed in a fundamental way from Watson's and others' work contemporary with and immediately following Watson. In the early days of behaviorism, the concept of association permeated theories about learning. It was assumed that a response (R) came to be established, or learned, by its association with an environmental stimulus (S). Edwin R. Guthrie, for instance, believed that, "Stimuli which are acting at the time of a response tend on their reoccurrence to evoke that response." (1933, p. 365). This has been called one-trial learning because, according to Guthrie, it is the very last stimulus before a response occurs that becomes associated with that response.

Whereas Guthrie's ideas were never fully elaborated, Clark L. Hull's S-R theory of behavior became "fearsomely complex" (Leahey & Harris, 1989). Hull believed that responses become attached to controlling stimuli, but some of these stimuli must be internal because it was not always possible to observe an external stimulus for all responses. Thus, Hull proposed intervening variables such as habit strengths and argued that observed behavior was a function of these as well as environmental variables such as degree of hunger (drive), size of reward (stimulus-intensity dynamism), and so on.

Finally, E. C. Tolman believed that behavior was guided by purpose, which led to his being called a purposive behaviorist. According to Tolman, organisms do not acquire S-R bonds simply by contiguity or reward; they selectively take in information from the environment and build up cognitive maps as they learn. This helped to account for latent learning, in which rats who explored a maze for several trials found the food on a subsequent trial as quickly as rats consistently reinforced in the maze.

Tolman's cognitive maps and Hull's habit strengths, however, smacked of mentalism to Skinner. One cannot directly observe cognitive maps in a rat's mind; they must be inferred from the rat's behavior. Likewise, one cannot directly observe habit strengths; they must be inferred from the rat's persistence in a learned behavior. Skinner argued that such inferences were neither necessary nor desirable.

 B. F. Skinner's approach to the psychology of learning was to set out in search of functional relationships between environmental variables and behavior. In other words, he believed that behavior could be fully understood in terms of environmental cues and results. Cues serve as antecedents to behavior, setting the conditions for its occurrence. Results are the consequences of behavior which make it more or less likely to reoccur. What might go on in the mind during learning, then, is immaterial to understanding or describing it.

Consider Private Johnson again, for example. It may well be that she thought of Italian food while mopping floors, but explaining her behavior does not require making reference to those thoughts. Skinner went so far as to argue that theories of learning simply get in the way of collecting empirical data on behavior change (Skinner, 1950). He denied, in fact, that radical behaviorism should even be thought of as a theory; rather, it is an experimental analysis of behavior (Skinner, 1974).

THE EXPERIMENTAL ANALYSIS OF BEHAVIOR

By systematically observing behavior and manipulating environmental variables surrounding it, Skinner set about to discover the laws that govern learning. He defined learning as a more or less permanent change in behavior that can be detected by observing an organism over a period of time. Suppose, for example, that Jesse in Scenario 2-1 is observed to speak out of turn without raising his hand to be recognized. Over a period of weeks, the number of times he raises his hand increases, while the incidence of speaking out of turn decreases. From observations of Jesse's behavior, it can be said that he has learned to raise his hand to speak in class.

Respondent and Operant Behavior

Skinner distinguished two classes of behavior, respondent and operant, and it is the latter that drew most of his attention. **Respondent behavior**, studied by Pavlov in his famous classical conditioning experiments, refers to *behavior that is elicited involuntarily in reaction to a stimulus*. Pavlov's dogs salivating to food is one example, as is a child's startled reaction to a loud noise. By contrast, **operant behavior** is simply *emitted by an organism*. Skinner contended that all organisms are inherently active, emitting responses that operate on their environment. Most behavior is of this type. Birds pecking at insects in the grass, circus animals performing tricks in the ring, and students raising their hands in class are all examples of operant behavior.

Contingencies of Reinforcement

To understand why some operants are expressed while others are not, Skinner argued that we must look at the behavior in relation to the environmental events surrounding it. That is, we should look at the antecedents and consequences of behavior. Although antecedents set the context for responding, the consequences of a response are critical in determining whether it ever occurs again. If a dog puts its nose in a bee's nest and gets stung, for example, you can be sure the dog will be wary of repeating the behavior. What Skinner proposed, then, was a basic S-R-S relationship, as shown below:

S	—	R	—	S
(discriminative stimulus)		(operant response)		(contingent stimulus)

This relationship provides the framework from which all operant learning laws are derived. Because the nature of the contingent stimulus determines what happens to the response, whether it is reinforced or lost, Skinner referred to learning principles as the contingencies of reinforcement (Skinner, 1969).

The concept of reinforcement, central to Skinner's behaviorism, was initially expressed by E. L. Thorndike as the Law of Effect (1913, p. 4):

> *When a modifiable connection between a single situation and a response is made and is accompanied by a satisfying state of affairs, that connection's strength is increased. When made and accompanied by an annoying state of affairs, its strength is decreased.*

Put simply, behavior is more likely to reoccur if it has been rewarded, or reinforced. Similarly, a response is less likely to occur again if its consequence has been aversive. In order to understand learning, then, one must look for the change in behavior that occurred and determine what consequences of the behavior were responsible for the change. In the case of the dog, for example, the consequence of putting its nose in a bee's nest was aversive, and so it learned not to do that anymore. As for Jesse, he learned to raise his hand in class. What could be the consequence responsible for strengthening that behavior? Suppose the teacher called on Jesse, saying "Good!" each time he raised his hand. It would be reasonable to conclude that the stimulus of the teacher praising him served as a reinforcer contingent upon the response of Jesse's raising his hand.

It is useful at this point to re-emphasize the functional nature of Skinner's contingencies of reinforcement. That is, reinforcement as a consequence of behavior functions to enhance the probability of that behavior reoccurring. But if this probability has not been enhanced, then reinforcement cannot be said to occur. In the same vein, anything that does enhance this probability functions as a reinforcer. To illustrate, consider the following two examples:

1. The teacher calls on Jesse and says "Good!" every time he raises his hand in class, but suppose this behavior fails to increase. After several weeks, Jesse continues to talk out of turn, and rarely raises his hand.
2. Suppose that, instead of saying "Good" each time Jesse raises his hand, the teacher responds with, "Oh, Jesse. You always say such stupid things." And the other children laugh and make fun of him. But after several weeks, Jesse's hand raising behavior has increased.

In the first example, even though praise was contingent upon hand-raising, Jesse did not increase that behavior. Thus, praise in this case did not function as a reinforcer. In example 2, we see a quite different situation. Jesse increased his hand-raising behavior, but because of what consequence? Ridicule by the teacher and other students served as the reinforcer here. This can seem quite contradictory, because we tend to think of reinforcement as reward, and reward has generally positive connotations. The point is, reinforcement is defined in terms of its function, its effect on behavior. Thus, we must be wary of everyday language usage of Skinner's principles, which may not precisely match his scientific meanings.

Through systematic experimental manipulation of the contingencies of reinforcement, Skinner formulated learning principles to account for the strengthening or weakening of existing behaviors as well as the learning of altogether new ones. In addition, he studied reinforcement schedules to determine how learned behaviors are maintained over time. Although Skinner conducted most of his own research with animals, his principles of reinforcement have held equally well where human behavior is concerned. Since these principles are as often applied to the management of learning and behavior as to their understanding, it is perhaps easiest to discuss them in detail from that perspective.

PRINCIPLES OF BEHAVIOR MANAGEMENT

Strengthening or Weakening Operant Behaviors

The basic principles of reinforcement describe the simple strengthening or weakening of a response already in the repertoire of the learner. That is, observation reveals whether the learner is not displaying some desired behavior often enough or is exhibiting some undesired behavior all too often. In the first instance, the desired behavior becomes a target for strengthening; in the second, the goal is to weaken the undesired behavior. As has already been discussed, the nature of the stimulus contingent on the response is an important factor in the behavior's occurrence.

But Skinner discovered a second factor that was also important. The contingent stimulus could be presented immediately after a response to influence the reoccurrence of that response, as in the teacher praising Jesse for raising his hand. Or the contingent stimulus can be removed following a response, with a subsequent effect on the reoccurrence of the response. For example, Jesse's hand-raising could have the effect of silencing his peers' teasing, a positive consequence that strengthens the hand-raising behavior.

Crossing the presentation or removal of the contingent stimulus with the nature of that stimulus—whether satisfying or aversive—yields a set of basic principles for strengthening or weakening behavior, as shown in Figure 2–1. Let us consider, first, those principles which strengthen a response, followed by those which weaken it.

Strengthening a Response: Positive Reinforcement

Positive reinforcement (cell 1 in Figure 2–1) refers to the *presentation of a reinforcer (satisfying stimulus) contingent upon a response that results in the strengthening of that response*. Several examples of positive reinforcement have already been discussed. Praise from the teacher reinforced Jesse's incidence of hand-raising; commendations and an off-duty pass reinforced Private Johnson's completion of her daily floor-mopping task. Other examples of positive reinforcement can be readily observed in classrooms, at home, in social situations, or on the job. Dog trainers, for instance, reinforce "at attention" behavior with dog treats. Employers reinforce beyond quota production on an assembly line with bonus pay. I reinforce my husband with chocolate bars for cleaning the bathtubs each week. One question that all these examples raise, however, is what precisely may serve as reinforcers? And how is one to determine which reinforcer to choose for a given situation?

NATURE OF STIMULUS

	satisfying	aversive
stimulus presented contingent upon response	POSITIVE REINFORCEMENT ① (response strengthened)	PUNISHMENT ② (response weakened)
stimulus removed contingent upon response	RESPONSE COST TIMEOUT EXTINCTION ③ (response weakened)	NEGATIVE REINFORCEMENT ④ (response strengthened)

BEHAVIORAL CONTINGENCY

FIGURE   2–1   Basic Principles of Reinforcement

Types of Reinforcers.   A primary reinforcer is *one whose reinforcement value is biologically determined*. Food, for example, is a biological requirement of all living organisms, and hungry animals will exhibit all sorts of behavior to obtain it. In the well-known Skinner box (Skinner, 1938), food-deprived rats learned to press levers in order to activate a food magazine which dispensed small food pellets. Although primary reinforcement does not function extensively in human learning, it has proven quite useful in some cases. Wolf, Risley, and Mees (1964) reported using bits of food to reinforce wearing his glasses by an autistic boy.

More important in accounting for human learning is the concept of secondary reinforcers. **Secondary reinforcers** are *those that acquire their reinforcement value through association with a primary reinforcer*. Thus, they have been conditioned to be reinforcing. Examples of secondary, or conditioned, reinforcers include gold stars, money, and praise. Praise is a special case of secondary reinforcement, in that it is not a tangible item that can be saved up or used in trade, like money or baseball cards. For that reason, it has been termed a social reinforcer and shown to have powerful effects on human behavior. Ludwig and Maehr (1967), for example, demonstrated that making simple statements of approval regarding students' performance in a physical education class led to their making many more positive statements about themselves.

The Relativity of Reinforcers.   In reviewing the conditions under which positive reinforcement influences behavior, David Premack (1959) demonstrated that behaviors in which learners already engage to a high degree may be used to reinforce low-frequency behaviors. *This procedure of making high-frequency behaviors contingent upon low-frequency behaviors in order to strengthen the low-frequency behavior* has come to be known as the Premack principle. It is simply a type of positive reinforcement, and one effectively exploited by parents everywhere. "You can watch TV (high-frequency behavior) as soon as you finish your homework (low-frequency behavior)."

Choosing a Reinforcer.   The Premack principle illustrates well the need to observe learners in order to determine what reinforcer is likely to be most effective. In the case of the Premack principle, there is an empirical basis for selecting the reinforcer: the behavior serving as reinforcement is one the learner has been observed doing frequently. In other cases, it is often a matter of an educated guess on the basis of what is observed. Young children seem to like colored stickers and gold stars. Soldiers go off base when given the opportunity. Many adults appear to work hard, or take on additional tasks, in order to earn more money. These all have the potential, then, of serving as effective reinforcers. But only by selecting one —whatever seems most appropriate, given the learner and the behavior to be reinforced—and applying it, can one be absolutely sure of its effect. If it works, use it; if it does not, try another.

Strengthening a Response: Negative Reinforcement
Refer to Figure 2–1. Note that in two cells, which are diagonal to one another (labeled 1 and 4), the behavioral principle results in the response being strengthened. Both principles are known as reinforcement, and reinforcement always results in behavior increases. In contrast to positive reinforcement, though, **negative reinforcement** *strengthens a response through the removal of an aversive stimulus contingent upon that response.* Remember that positive reinforcement was the presentation of a satisfying stimulus following a response.

The principle of negative reinforcement was initially discovered in experiments with rats in a Skinner box. The rats learned to press a lever, not for food this time, but to turn off a shock that was being delivered through bars on the floor of the cage. Thus, bar-pressing, a behavior which increased in frequency, was negatively reinforced by removal of the aversive stimulus, shock.

Examples of negative reinforcement are harder to find than examples of positive reinforcement. As a result, its applicability is not as easily evident. Consider, however, one of the principles behind seatbelts. In most cars, a bell chimes or a buzzer sounds until the driver fastens the seat belt. Fastening the belt turns off the sound (which, in my car, is quite irritating). An increase in seatbelt fastening, then, can be said to be negatively reinforced by the removal of the sound.

Other examples of negative reinforcement include the student who sits closer and closer to the front of the room in order to see the blackboard, and the child who finally starts brushing his teeth regularly so that his mother will stop nagging. In the first instance, sitting in front leads to the cessation of fuzzy vision. In the second, teeth-brushing brings an end to nagging.

Weakening a Response: Punishment

While cells 1 and 4 of Figure 2–1 display principles of reinforcement that result in a strengthening of behavior, cells 2 and 3 contain principles for weakening an existing behavior. **Punishment** is *the presentation of an aversive stimulus contingent upon a response that reduces the rate of that response.* No doubt examples of punishment immediately spring to mind. A father spanks a child for taking something which did not belong to him. The drill sergeant hollers, "Twenty more pushups! Let's go!" to the hapless recruit grousing in the back row of the formation. A teacher yells at the student who was talking with a neighbor instead of studying. In all instances, the individual administering punishment for some misbehavior does so with the expectation that the behavior will stop and not be repeated.

Although punishment has the effect of stopping behavior, and in fact is so-called because it has that effect, it also appears to have unfortunate side effects. First, its effectiveness tends to be short-lived. That is, the behavior being punished may come to an immediate halt at the time punishment is administered, but this does not mean it has been necessarily forgotten. The student may quit talking in class when yelled at, only to do it again at another time, perhaps more surreptitiously. A dog I once had provides another good example of this. Shadow was not permitted to jump on the furniture, and she was smacked with a rolled-up newspaper if she tried. My husband and I thought we had stopped this behavior altogether (and proud we were of our success in using behaviorist principles!). But one day when I was home alone, I walked into the living room, and although there was no dog in sight, the rocking chair was rocking furiously!

Azrin and Holz (1966) discussed other, more serious problems with the use of punishment to reduce undesirable behavior. When punishment involves a particularly aversive stimulus or induces pain, it can lead to undesirable emotional responses being conditioned. If fear is elicited, then avoidance or escape behavior may be negatively reinforced inadvertently (Skinner, 1938). Running away and truancy are good examples. A child does poorly in school, is punished severely, and then manages to escape or avoid the punishment by leaving home or cutting class.

The emotional side effects of punishment that is painful are not limited to fear, however. Aggression and anger may result, particularly in individuals who are characteristically aggressive (Azrin, 1967). Moreover, punishment can serve as a model for aggression. In a series of studies examining aggressive behavior in children, Bandura, Ross, and Ross (1961, 1963) demonstrated that those who observed others being aggressive were more likely to be aggressive themselves. This is further supported by evidence from studies of abusive families; by and large, parents who are abusive were themselves abused as children (Steinmetz, 1977; Strauss, Gelles, & Steinmetz, 1980).

Finally, a long history of punishment may cause physical or psychological harm. Especially in situations where the aversive stimuli cannot be avoided or escaped from, the phenomenon of **learned helplessness** may result. This refers to *the passive acceptance of events seemingly beyond one's control*, a phenomenon first demonstrated in a now classic experiment conducted by Seligman and Maier (1967). In their study, conducted in two phases, unpredictable and painful shocks were administered to dogs. For some of the dogs, escape from the shock was possible through a panel in the cage. For the others, escape was not permitted, no matter what they did. In the second phase of the study, the dogs were placed in one of two compartments of a box. A tone sounded to warn of impending shock in that compartment, which the dog could escape by jumping the barrier into the second compartment. The dogs who had been allowed previously to escape the shock learned quickly to jump the barrier each time they heard the tone. The dogs who had previously been prevented from escaping the shock, however, made little attempt to escape under these new conditions.

When individuals perceive that their actions have little effect on aversive events, they, too, begin to exhibit symptoms of learned helplessness. In the context of learning, experiencing repeated failure or constant belittlement of their efforts can lead students to say, "I can't do this. I'm not a good reader" (or writer, or test-taker, or what have you).

With so many problems associated with punishment, under what conditions can it be useful? Azrin and Holz (1966) suggested that punishment has an advantage over other procedures when there is a need to stop a behavior quickly. For example, if a child is about to injure herself by picking up a hot iron, a fast slap on the wrist or loud "NO!" may be the most effective way to gain her attention and stop her in the act. Similarly, Corte,

Wolf, and Locke (1971) found punishment to be the most effective procedure for eliminating self-injurious behavior in retarded children.

Finally, when used sparingly, punishment has the advantage of conveying information about what behaviors are considered appropriate or inappropriate in given situations (Azrin & Holz, 1966; Walters & Grusec, 1977). Sometimes, individuals simply are not aware that their behavior is unacceptable; it may be that the rules are different from what they have been accustomed to. This may happen particularly in multicultural situations, when, for example, ways of interacting that are socially acceptable at home or in one's neighborhood are not acceptable at school. It is for these situations that some behaviorists also recommend a warning precede punishment and reasons accompany it to explain why certain behaviors are not tolerated (Walters & Grusec, 1977).

Weakening a Response: Extinction

Whereas one way to reduce the frequency of behavior is to present an aversive consequence, another, perhaps more effective, way is to take away reinforcement when the behavior occurs (see cell 3 of Figure 2–1). Because this may be done in several ways, three different principles have been named for the possible variations. **Extinction** occurs when *the reinforcement maintaining a response is removed, thereby causing a reduction in the frequency of the response.* In essence, extinction involves breaking an existing contingency relationship between the behavior and whatever stimulus is currently reinforcing it. For example, a pigeon that has been reinforced with food for pecking a lighted circle will eventually stop pecking when food is no longer delivered. Similarly, a student tapping his teacher's arm to get her attention will eventually stop doing it if that attention is no longer given, and a dog will stop whining to be let in if its noise is for naught.

When extinction is used as a procedure for weakening some undesirable behavior, the key to its success is persistence. As most pet owners have undoubtedly experienced, the dog that is being ignored will redouble its efforts for attention at first. Woe to the owner who gives in at this point, however! Delaying attention simply serves as an intermittent schedule of reinforcement, which we will see later in the chapter has the effect of greatly strengthening behavior. With extinction, it is important to consistently withhold reinforcement; eventually the behavior will lessen. As with punishment, it is also useful to reinforce some alternative, desirable response concurrent with extinguishing the undesirable behavior. In that way, learners are being rewarded for something even while they have lost reinforcement for something else. For an example, remember Jesse in Scenario 2–1. The teacher most likely reinforced hand-raising at the same time she ignored talking out of turn, the behavior that was eventually extinguished.

Weakening a Response: Response Cost

Think of the last time you or someone you know got a parking ticket for parking in an illegal spot. The fine imposed by the ticket is what it cost you to park in that spot. It was, in other words, the response cost for the behavior of parking illegally. **Response cost**, like extinction, involves *the removal of reinforcement contingent upon behavior*. But in the case of response cost, this is done by exacting a fine, requiring the offender to give back some previously earned reinforcer. It can have a strong and rapid effect on reducing certain behaviors for some people, depending on the history of the person and the value of the fine (Weiner, 1969). In society, for example, the fine for minor infractions of the law is usually monetary. To be effective, fine amounts should be set high enough to reduce the likelihood of repeat behavior, but it is certainly true that, no matter what the fee, it may have less effect on a rich person or one who has been successful at avoiding payment.

Response cost applied in a school setting can be seen in the following example. On a class field trip, Ms. Johnson was in charge of the six third grade boys most likely to cause trouble. The morning of the trip, she told them what rules of conduct they were to follow, that they would earn stickers for good behavior, but that they would have to give back a sticker every time they broke a rule. After warning one boy twice for the same behavior, Ms. Johnson said, upon the third occurrence, "You know what the rules are, right?" The little boy said yes and tearfully handed her the only sticker he had earned so far. The happy outcome to this story is that the boy behaved without incident the rest of the day and earned the big treat Ms. Johnson had been saving for last.

Weakening a Response: Timeout

The final principle involved in reducing behavior, **timeout**, does so by *removing the learner, for a limited time, from the circumstances reinforcing the undesired behavior*. In some situations, it is very difficult to determine precisely what consequence is responsible for maintaining some behavior. It may be the case, moreover, that several events follow a behavior and all have some reinforcing effect. In a typical classroom, for example, a student's acting out, accompanied by "Watch me!," may cause the teacher to stop class and the other students to laugh, both of which may contribute to its reoccurrence. Stopping the behavior, then, may take more than simply ignoring it (extinction). Yet other conditions may not make response cost an appropriate alternative.

In cases such as these, individuals may be removed altogether from the sources of reinforcement. Wolf, Risley, and Mees (1964) used timeout to virtually eliminate temper tantrums thrown by an autistic boy. Every time a tantrum occurred, they isolated him in a room by himself for slightly longer than the tantrum had been. Solnick, Rincover, and Peterson (1977) added

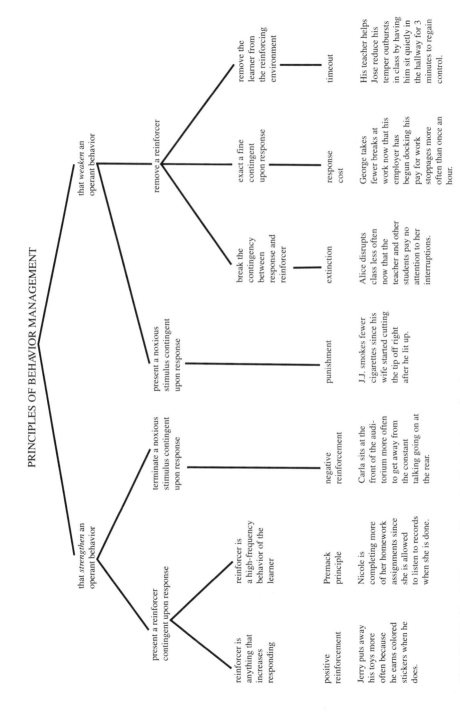

FIGURE 2–2   A Concept Tree for Principles of Behavior Management

further evidence to the effectiveness of timeout, but noted that it can be reinforcing instead of punishing in some circumstances. Imagine, for example, a noisy classroom. The disruptive behavior of one student causes the teacher to put him out in the quiet hallway with his assignment. The next time the class is noisy, this student acts out again, with the same result. What appears to have happened is not timeout at all; rather, the disruptive behavior has been negatively reinforced by the student's escaping the noisy classroom for the quiet hallway.

Sulzer and Mayer (1972) suggested that for timeout to be most effective, the following conditions should be met. Timeout should not be used from an aversive situation (illustrated in the example above). It should provide for removal of all reinforcement, it should be consistently maintained, and the time period should be kept short (a general rule of thumb is one minute for each year of the learner's age). Finally, like extinction and punishment, timeout should be used with other procedures that reinforce alternative, desirable behaviors.

Depicted in Figure 2–2 is a concept tree for principles of behavior management. It illustrates in a visual way what attributes are shared by certain principles (e.g., those that strengthen behavior) and what attributes are unique to each one (e.g., high-frequency behavior as reinforcer is unique to the Premack principle). The tree also includes, for each principle, an example illustrating its use or occurrence.

Teaching New Behaviors

The principles discussed in the previous section concerned behaviors that were already present to some degree in the learner's repertoire. One might say that the learner already knew the behavior; what was learned seemed to be the frequency with which the behavior was to be performed. But how are behaviors learned that are not already present in the organism's repertoire? Bar-pressing, for example, is not a behavior that rats do in their natural environment. Similarly, one could watch a pigeon in a Skinner box for a long time without ever seeing it turn around in a complete circle. Consider also the autistic child described in Scenario 2-2; she sits where she is placed, she fails to respond to any stimuli, and she volunteers no active behavior which could be reinforced. If the child, the rat, and the pigeon never exhibit the behavior targeted for reinforcement, how does it come to be acquired? Behaviorists have defined three principles for teaching new, and in many cases, complex behaviors: shaping, chaining, and fading.

Shaping
Shaping refers to *the reinforcement of successive approximations to a goal behavior*. It involves positive reinforcement, in that a reinforcer is presented

contingent upon desired behavior. But in the case of shaping, the desired behavior reinforced each time only approximates the target behavior. And successively closer approximations are required for the reinforcement to be presented (Reynolds, 1968). To teach a rat to press a bar, then, one might first reinforce proximity to the bar, then raising a paw, extending the paw toward the bar, touching the bar, and finally, pressing the bar. As soon as the rat has made the correct response—in this case, pressing the bar—then the principle of positive reinforcement is followed. That is, each bar press is reinforced until the desired frequency of behavior is exhibited.

Harris, Wolf, and Baer (1967) demonstrated the effectiveness of shaping to teach new behaviors to children. They selected climbing on the jungle gym for shaping in a little boy who spent no time on it. Teacher attention was the contingent reinforcer. Thus, teachers paid attention to the little boy first when he went near the jungle gym, then when he touched it, climbed on it, and finally, climbed on it extensively.

Shaping has also been found to be particularly effective in teaching autistic children. Wolf, Risley, and Mees (1964), for example, trained an autistic boy in speech acquisition, using bits of food to reinforce making eye contact, producing any sound, producing specific sounds, and finally saying complete words and sentences. In this example, however, as in the previous ones, it could still be argued that the learners were capable of producing the desired response; they just did not. Bar-pressing, in other words, is not a difficult response. Climbing on a jungle gym was well within the capabilities of the small boy. Even the autistic boy could produce sounds that were then shaped into language. Is shaping as effective with truly difficult responses, which are not initially within the capabilities of the learners?

That the answer is yes can be illustrated with the following example. A waiter at a Moroccan restaurant served tea with dessert by raising the teapot high above his head and pouring the tea into tall, narrow glasses on a very low table, where we diners were sitting on floor cushions. He spilled nary a drop, and so, of course, we marvelled at his skill and asked how he had learned to pour tea in such a manner. His reply went something like this. "Well, naturally, I couldn't do it at first without spilling tea all over the place. So, I tried holding the teapot only slightly above the glasses. When I could pour without spilling, I moved the teapot up a few inches. And I kept repeating this process until I could do it with the teapot over my head." Successive approximations had been reinforced until the goal behavior was achieved. In this case, the ability to make the response at one level of approximation served as the reinforcer to attempt the next approximation.

The above example also illustrates a factor critical to the success of shaping. The waiter did not attempt a more difficult approximation until he had mastered the easier one. Similarly, in shaping any new behavior, a closer approximation to the goal should not be reinforced until the previous

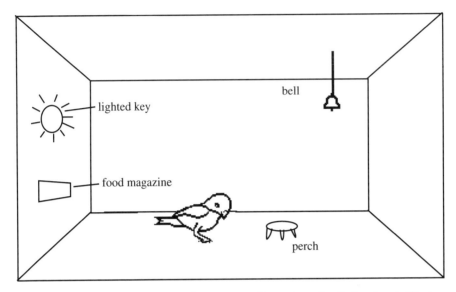

FIGURE   2–3   **A Pigeon in a Skinner Box Learning the Behavioral Chain: Climb Perch, Peck Bell, Turn Circle, Peck Key**

one has been firmly established. If too large a step is expected of the learner at once, the behavior may break down and shaping may have to resume at the point where the learner has repeatedly demonstrated success. Finally, it is also important in shaping to ensure that reinforcement is delivered immediately contingent upon the desired response. Any delays can result in some random behavior being reinforced and becoming conditioned.

Skinner (1948) called this superstitious behavior and demonstrated its inducement by delivering noncontingent reinforcement to pigeons. That is, he offered food at random intervals, not dependent upon the animal's behavior. Whatever the pigeon happened to be doing at the moment reinforcement arrived, however, became more likely to reoccur because of the reinforcement. As a result, Skinner observed the inadvertent conditioning of all sorts of weird behavior, and he argued that the simple contiguity between response and stimulus could account for the learning of superstitious behavior in humans. For example, you buy a new pen with which to take a particular test, and you score well on the test. Scoring well rewards your use of that pen, and so you begin to attribute good performances to the causally irrelevant pen when, in fact, good performance was contingent upon your study behavior.

Chaining
Whereas shaping is used to teach new behaviors that are relatively simple and continuous in nature, **chaining** serves to *establish complex behaviors made*

up of discrete, simpler behaviors already known to the learner. Consider, for example, a typical conditioning experiment conducted with pigeons. In a Skinner box, pigeons can be taught to peck a lighted key on a wall at one end of the box (Figure 2–3). They can also be shaped to turn circles, to peck a bell hung at the other end of the box, and to climb on a perch. All of these behaviors can be independently established through shaping and then strung together in a behavioral chain through backward or forward chaining.

Suppose that the desired behavioral chain is the following:

climb perch — peck bell — turn circle — peck key

To establish this through forward chaining would require a sequence of contingent reinforcement in which "climb perch," as the first step in the chain, is reinforced first. Then, "climb perch, peck bell" would be the required performance for reinforcement, and so on until the entire chain must be performed in order for reinforcement to be administered. With backward chaining, the last step in the chain is reinforced first, with each immediately preceding step successively required before reinforcement is given. Thus, a backward chain of contingent reinforcement would look like this:

reinforce peck key
reinforce turn circle, peck key
reinforce peck bell, turn circle, peck key
reinforce, climb perch, peck bell, turn circle, peck key
(the entire chain)

A typical example of chaining in human behavior is learning a new dance. Each dance step may be acquired through shaping, but then the steps are strung together in sequence through forward or backward chaining. Memorizing long passages of prose is another typical example of forward chaining. Sentences are added in succession until the entire passage can be repeated without error. Finally, reassembling their weapons after cleaning is a behavioral chain that is probably acquired through forward chaining by the soldiers in Scenario 2–3.

Discrimination Learning and Fading

To this point very little has been said about the control the setting has over learning except in terms of the consequences of behavior. Behaviors are acquired and exhibited because they are reinforced; nonreinforced behaviors tend not to occur, at least in the setting where they have been ignored or punished. This is an important distinction. Individuals are clearly able to distinguish between settings in which certain behaviors will or will not be reinforced. A playful slap on the back may produce grins from the guys in the gym, but it is likely to have a quite different effect on one's commanding officer or teacher. Thus, something besides the behavior itself must be learned, and these are the cues, or discriminative stimuli (S^Ds), which signal to the learner when and where the behavior is to be performed.

Most learning in formal instructional situations is accompanied by cues. School bells signal the end of classes; getting up to leave before they ring is a behavior likely to be punished. Thus, staying in one's seat is reinforced before the bell rings; moving about the halls is reinforced after it rings. The bell simply acts as a cue to indicate what behavior is appropriate and will be reinforced (or conversely, what behavior is inappropriate and will be punished).

Discriminations are often learned, then, by a behavior being reinforced in the presence of one stimulus and being punished in the presence of another. Alternatively, a different behavior may be reinforced in the presence of the second stimulus. Motor vehicle drivers, for example, must learn to stop at a red light and go on the green light. Thus, the S^D for stopping is a red light, and the S^D for going is a green light. In either case, however, errors can sometimes be extremely costly, so that applying the simple principles of positive reinforcement and punishment may not be the most effective for establishing the discrimination.

In his studies with pigeons, Terrace (1963a, 1963b) demonstrated that almost errorless discrimination performance could be achieved with fading. He first taught the pigeons to peck a red key, so that red became a discriminative stimulus for pecking. Then he turned off the key, which caused the pigeons to stop pecking, and gradually lengthened the intervals during which the key was dark. The darkened key then became the discriminative stimulus for not pecking. Finally, Terrace slowly faded in a green light in place of the darkened key. Since the pigeons never pecked the dark key, and the fading was so gradual from darkened key to well-lit green key, the green key came to be established as the S^D for not pecking.

The concept of fading as it has been applied to human performance has come to refer to the fading out of discriminative stimuli used to initially establish a desired behavior (Sulzer & Mayer, 1972). In other words, the desired behavior continues to be reinforced as the discriminative cues are gradually withdrawn. A classic example of fading used in instruction can be seen in Skinner and Krakower's (1968) *Handwriting with Write and See* program. In this program, children trace letters in an instructional workbook. Gradually, portions of the letters, which serve as the discriminative stimuli for forming the right shapes, are faded, thus requiring the children to compose increasingly more of each letter. Reinforcement is accomplished through a special chemical reaction between the pens used by the children and the paper. They form a black line when their letters are correct, but the paper turns orange when the pen moves from the prescribed pattern.

Other examples of fading can be seen in the gradual reduction of verbal cues given by a laboratory instructor as students work through a set of procedures for staining slides or in the withdrawal of physical cues given by a golf pro showing a beginner how to hold and swing a golf club. Job aids in industrial settings are also good examples of fading. As employees become more proficient in their assigned duties, they rely less and less on the cues provided by the aid.

Maintaining Behavior

If we consider that the job of instruction is not only to bring about desired changes in behavior, but to maintain them as well, then we must determine what conditions will be most effective for behavior maintenance. A typical behaviorist approach to the question would be to find some high-frequency, persistent behavior occurring naturally and to study the consequences responsible for its maintenance. One good example is people playing the slot machines at Las Vegas or Reno. Some will stand there for hours, doing nothing but pumping coins or tokens into the machines and pulling the handle. Every so often, the player receives a payoff, accompanied by flashing lights and ringing bells. So what is going on here?

According to Leahey and Harris (1989), Skinner was in search of a means to economize on the costs of feeding his experimental subjects when he made an interesting discovery. When he reinforced only some of the bar-pressing responses made by his rats, rather than reinforcing every response, the behavior became much more resistant to extinction. In other words, continuous reinforcement, while necessary to establish a response in the first place, was not essential to maintaining that response. In fact, intermittent reinforcement worked much better for that purpose. By systematically investigating schedules of reinforcement, Ferster and Skinner (1957) were able to determine what pattern of reinforcement gave rise to what sort of behavior maintenance.

Although behaviorists have investigated reinforcement schedules and invented new ones since Ferster and Skinner's original experiments, four basic schedules remain. These are determined on the basis of whether reinforcement is contingent upon a given response (called a ratio schedule) or upon the passage of time (called an interval schedule). In addition, reinforcement can occur regularly, after a fixed amount of time or number of responses, or it can occur irregularly, after a variable amount of time or number of responses. Taking these characteristics together, we have four

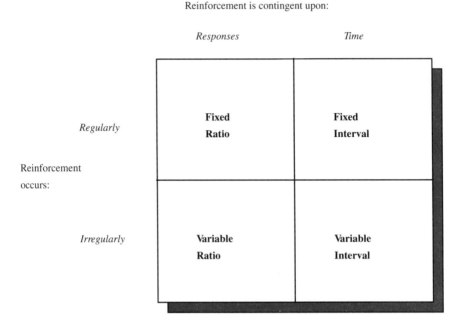

FIGURE   2–4   Types of Reinforcement Schedules

possible schedules, as shown in Figure 2–4: fixed ratio, fixed interval, vari-able ratio, and variable interval.

Fixed Ratio Schedules

Continuous reinforcement, i.e., reinforcing every desired response, amounts to the same thing as a fixed ratio schedule of one (FR1). Ratio schedules of reinforcement are those in which the reinforcer is delivered contingent upon the response made by the learner. A fixed ratio schedule, therefore, requires the learner to make so many responses before reinforcement is delivered. Quota systems on factory assembly lines are examples of fixed ratio schedules. For every 15 widgets produced (FR15) or for every 300 chickens inspected (FR300), employees earn a standard wage credited toward their pay. This type of reinforcement schedule tends to produce a response pattern like the one shown in Figure 2–5A. In other words, responding occurs at a high and steady rate, since the more employees pro-duce, the quicker they earn more money. Animals responding on a fixed ratio schedule also show a tendency to pause immediately following rein-forcement. While this phenomenon has not been demonstrated consistently with humans, studies have shown that it can occur. For example, I typically

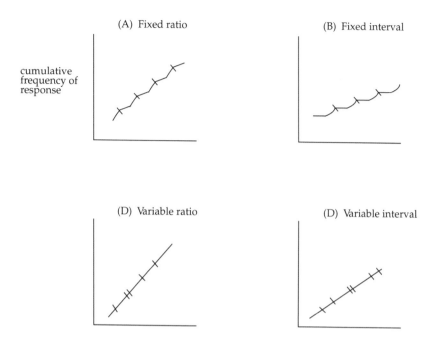

∖ indicates that reinforcement occurs at this point on the curve

FIGURE   2–5   Response Patterns Produced by Different Types of Reinforcement Schedules

put myself on a FR15 schedule when grading undergraduate assignments, getting up for a snack or a short walk after each 15 papers graded. Getting started again after the break, however, generally entails a pause before I am fully focused on the task once again.

Fixed Interval Schedules

As indicated, time is the determining factor for an interval schedule of reinforcement. For a fixed interval schedule, then, reinforcement is delivered after some fixed period of time, such as five minutes (FI 5 min) or ten days (FI 10 days). A commonly cited example of this type of schedule is the procedure by which many professors are tenured and promoted. Although tenure and promotion are ostensibly tied to performance, they are typically awarded, or become available for award, at particular times, such as after so many years in rank. As a result, performance over time may take on the characteristic "scallop" typically produced by a fixed interval schedule (Figure 2–5B). In other words, responding becomes more frequent as the time for reinforcement nears. Weekly quizzes can produce a similar pattern of performance, in that students will study more often and for a longer time the closer quiz day is.

Variable Ratio and Variable Interval Schedules

In variable schedules, the time or number of responses required for reinforcement is varied from reinforcement to reinforcement. Thus, a VR5 schedule means that, on the average, reinforcement is delivered for every five responses, but one time it may be given after the second response and the next time after the eighth response. Similarly, a variable interval schedule of five minutes (VI 5 min) means that reinforcement may be given after three minutes, then after seven minutes, then after four minutes, and so on, creating an average interval of five minutes.

Variable schedules typically produce the highest and steadiest rates of responding, with variable ratio schedules producing the highest of all (Figure 2–5, C and D). The slot machine example provided earlier demonstrates the effect of a variable ratio schedule; typically, payoffs are scheduled to occur after some average number of pulls on the lever. (This average, by the way, is set high enough so that the money taken in is always more than the money paid out.) In a classroom setting, teachers can assure steadier rates of studying or homework completion by administering pop quizzes on the average of once a week (VI 5 days), or by collecting and spot-checking assignments (e.g., every third assignment, on the average, for a VR3 schedule).

Planning a Program of Behavior Change

To this point, principles have been discussed that relate the incidence of behavior to its environmental cues and consequences. Learning has been described as a relatively permanent change in behavior, and schedules of reinforcement have been presented that are useful for maintaining such changes. The question that remains is, How can these principles be systematically applied in order to bring about specific, desired changes in behavior? What follows are five essential steps in implementing a behavior change program (see Table 2–1 for a summary). Evaluating the success of such a program will be discussed last.

Step One: Set Behavioral Goals

In order to go about changing behavior, one must determine what behavior is to be changed and what the change is. Questions to consider in this step are: What is desirable behavior? How often should the behavior occur? Does the change in behavior involve its being strengthened or reduced? Is some new behavior to be taught? What are the requirements for behavior maintenance? Also essential to setting behavioral goals is knowing to what extent the targeted behavior is being exhibited relative to its desired

TABLE 2–1   Implementing a Program of Behavior Change

Step 1:   Set behavioral goals

Step 2:   Determine appropriate reinforcers

Step 3:   Select procedures for changing behavior

Step 4:   Implement procedures and record results

Step 5:   Evaluate progress and revise as necessary

strength. In other words, is the learner not doing enough of something, or is some behavior being exhibited too often?

In order to have an accurate answer to the question of what learners are actually doing in any given situation, they must be observed. For example, the teacher in Scenario 2-1 at the beginning of this chapter could have the impression that Charla is "always acting out," which disrupts class and wastes valuable instructional time. Observation may reveal, however, that Charla acts out only three or four times a day. The results of her behavior are so severe in terms of lasting impact on the class that it just seems she is acting out more often. Similarly, Jesse could be raising his hand to be recognized at a reasonable rate, as often as any other student in the class. But if he is a particularly active child and talks out as often as he raises his hand, one behavior could easily mask the other in what the teacher perceives.

Observation, therefore, provides a baseline of behavior, a measure of behavior incidence as it occurs before any intervention is implemented. From this baseline, goals for change can be determined. The teacher may still decide, for example, that Charla's acting out behavior should be reduced because of its adverse impact on the class. A reasonable goal may be to reduce the incidence of acting out to no more than once a day. As we will also see, the baseline provides a basis against which the success of the intervention can be measured.

Step Two: Determine Appropriate Reinforcers

The choice of reinforcers for use in a behavioral change program depends on the learner, the instructor, the behavioral goals, and the practical circumstances surrounding the implementation of the program. Behavior in young children, for example, may be reinforced with colored stickers or gold stars that would clearly not be appropriate or effective with older students or adults. Some teachers are opposed to the use of tangible rewards, preferring instead to use praise, attention, and other social reinforcers. A behavioral goal that involves reducing a behavior may call for a procedure such as response cost, which means that appropriate fines rather than reinforcers must be determined.

Finally, there will always be pragmatic considerations in choosing reinforcers. It is not always easy to determine what will be the most effective reinforcer for a particular individual, or, once a reinforcer is identified, it may not be within the control of the program designer. Peer approval, for example, can be a particularly potent source of reinforcement for teenagers (Sulzer & Mayer, 1972), but it is not something easily controlled by teachers or parents. Moreover, an ethical dilemma may arise in some situations as to whether the program professional has a right to control an effective reinforcer. In a community mental health facility, for example, money to buy cigarettes or candy has been found to have powerful reinforcing effects on the residents (Mulligan, Oglesby, & Perkins, 1980). But should the mental health professionals have control over the residents' money in order to use it as reinforcement?

Step Three: Select Procedures for Changing Behavior
The decision as to what procedure should be used obviously depends on what behavior change is desired. To strengthen an existing behavior, positive and negative reinforcement and the Premack principle are possibilities. To teach a new behavior, one might select from shaping, chaining or fading. To maintain behavior, some schedule of reinforcement should be selected to produce the desirable pattern of performance. And finally, to reduce or weaken a behavior, punishment, response cost, timeout, or extinction could be implemented. To choose from among the options, where more than one procedure may be appropriate to a given goal, one should consider such questions as, How important is it that I effect this change in behavior quickly? How permanent is the result of this procedure likely to be? What other unintended effects might this procedure have that I would like to avoid? Are there any additional factors that should be taken into consideration?

Step Four: Implement Procedures and Record Results
Once a plan for behavior change has been generated, it may be implemented and its results monitored. Observation again becomes important at this step, since only by looking at the behavior can any change from baseline be detected. Recording behavior incidence also helps to ensure that real, rather than imagined, changes are monitored. It is easy to engage in wishful thinking, hoping for changes or thinking that changes must have occurred by virtue of the program being in place.

Step Five: Evaluate Progress and Revise as Necessary
Based on the records kept in Step Four, it should be easy to see whether, in fact, any change from baseline behavior has occurred. If the program was designed to reduce some behavior, it should have had that effect, or if it

was designed to teach some new behavior, then that behavior should now be in evidence. Assuming that the desired behavior has been achieved, no change in the program may be warranted. However, after a new behavior is taught or a behavior is established at a desirable rate, some alteration in the reinforcement schedule may be required to sufficiently maintain the behavior.

What if, on the other hand, the program has not produced the intended results? Any number of possibilities could be the problem, but according to Skinner, simple observation and systematic alteration of the program should enable you to find out which one is the culprit. It may be that another procedure would be more effective, or that a different reinforcer should be selected. Perhaps a combination of procedures should be tried, as in reducing one behavior while at the same time reinforcing an alternative to take its place. Whatever the problem, the program should be modified appropriately and implemented again. This process of monitoring results and revising as necessary should be repeated until success has been achieved.

Since radical behaviorism is the experimental analysis of behavior, and behavior is assumed to be reliably, functionally related to environmental events, a behaviorist would not necessarily be content with showing that a behavior change had occurred following the implementation of some pro-gram. It would also be necessary to reverse the procedure, or remove the implementation, to see whether the behavior reverted to baseline levels. Only in this way can we be sure that it was the program, and not some con-founding, random set of variables, that was responsible for the change in behavior.

To take an example, suppose that the teacher decides to implement timeout in order to reduce Charla's acting out behavior. During baseline, conducted over a week's period, observations revealed that Charla acted out about four times each day, for an average duration of five minutes each. The typical results of the acting out included the teacher stopping class, paying attention to Charla to get her under control, and then spending some minutes trying to regain the attention of the rest of the students. At the beginning of week 2, the teacher implements the timeout procedure, iso-lating Charla for eight minutes each time she acts out. The teacher does this by taking Charla by the hand without saying a word and putting her in a chair just outside the classroom door. At this point, the teacher says, "When you can be quiet, you can return." The teacher continues class and after eight minutes allows Charla to return to her seat.

Suppose that timeout appeared to be effective, and Charla's acting out dropped to once a day by the end of the week. To be sure that it was time-out, and not something else going on in class having the desired effect, the teacher would institute a reversal in procedure and stop using timeout

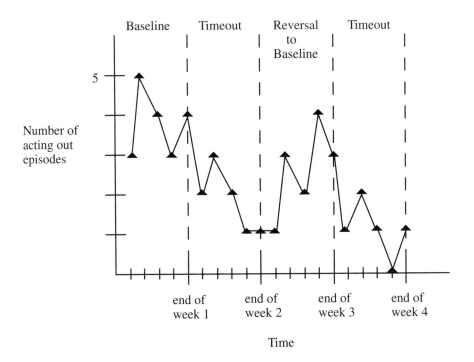

FIGURE 2–6 Occurrences of Acting Out Behavior in Relation to Timeout: A Hypothetical Case

during week 3. Thus, she would go back to her original reaction to Charla's behavior, which should have the effect of increasing its incidence. Finally, at week 4, timeout would again be reinstituted and its results monitored. If timeout is indeed an effective procedure for reducing the undesired behavior of acting out, then the record of results should resemble that displayed in Figure 2–6.

Although this reversal process has the advantage of demonstrating the functional relationship between any behavioral procedure and behavior, it also has several disadvantages in a practical, rather than experimental, context. First, it is time-consuming to establish a reasonable estimate of baseline and to carry out each phase long enough to demonstrate a procedure's effectiveness. More importantly, however, once a behavior change has been effected, it may be extremely counterproductive, or even unethical, to return that behavior to its original rate. Consider the autistic child in Scenario 2-2, for example. If her mother was successful in shaping verbal behavior, would it be desirable to extinguish talking simply to show that shaping, and not something else, was responsible for getting her to talk in the first place? Similarly, performing tasks without demerits is desirable behavior in boot camp whether or not earning off-base passes is the only factor responsible for its occurrence. As such, most applications of behaviorist principles are considered to be successful when the goals for behavior change have been met.

CONTRIBUTIONS OF BEHAVIORISM TO INSTRUCTION

Few would argue that radical behaviorism has had a profound impact not only in psychology but on instruction as well. And its influence continues to be felt in fields ranging from clinical therapy to instructional design. Although many applications and new developments in behaviorism go beyond the scope and purpose of this book (e.g., biofeedback, treatment of clinical depression), others bear examining. The ones I have chosen to discuss here might be characterized on a continuum of emphasis on individual behavior to behavior within an instructional system. The technology of behavior modification, for example, represents one end of the continuum. Behaviors of a particular individual are targeted for change and a program is devised to fit the unique needs of that person. On the other end are instructional applications of behaviorism in computer-assisted instruction, where the behavior of all learners is managed in essentially the same way.

It should also be noted that applications of behavioral principles generally work best in settings where reinforcers can be controlled. It seems likely, then, that they may be more applicable in elementary school than in high school, more relevant to instructional programs in jails than those in the workplace. In any setting, however, behaviorism can be a valuable tool for interpreting and understanding (as opposed to controlling) behavior.

Behavior Modification

Application of behavioral principles in the way described so far in this chapter is essentially the same as behavior modification (also known as behavior therapy or contingency management). Typically, behavior modification is used to treat problem behaviors in social, personal, or school situations. Clinical applications include treatments for phobias, or obsessions, or eating disorders, to name a few (Bower & Hilgard, 1981). Instructional applications involve treatment of school-related problems, such as inattention, hyperactivity, temper tantrums, or any behavior that interferes with learning and the normal conduct of classroom activities. Special education teachers are typically well-trained in the use of behavior modification, since they regularly deal with children who have special problems and special needs. As part of the individual education plans for individual students, teachers may target problem behaviors, devise and implement interventions, and keep records to monitor student progress and inform changes to the original plan.

For all of the applications mentioned so far, control of the behavior modification process resides with the behavioral specialist, therapist, or teacher. In recent developments, however, behavior modification methods are taught to individuals, who then use them to change their own behavior. This is an application of behavior modification known as self-control, and it has been successfully demonstrated with people who wish to lose weight, quit smoking, or improve their social skills, study habits, or concentration. Bower (Bower & Hilgard, 1981) reported that he taught a college seminar in which students teamed up with a cooperative friend in order to change some aspect of their own behavior. One of my own favorite examples of self-control came from a friend whose husband enlisted her help to quit smoking. Given his propensity toward saving money, they decided an appropriate punishment would be sending money to fly-by-night charities. Therefore, the husband wrote a series of $25 checks and handed them to his wife with instructions to mail one every time she saw him smoking. Three checks later, he had quit smoking altogether and, to my knowledge, has never smoked since.

Classroom Management

Whereas behavioral therapists and special education teachers generally focus on the needs of individuals, teachers in regular classrooms may have twenty to thirty students or more to manage at one time. To a limited extent, they may apply behavior modification to change the problem behaviors of one or another student. More often, teachers set up group contingencies, i.e., a standard reinforcement given to individuals or the group as a whole for following certain rules of conduct. A kindergarten teacher, for example, may reward his class for picking up their things by taking them to the playground ten minutes sooner than usual. A middle school teacher may award bonus points to students because they all worked so hard on a particularly difficult assignment. My high school biology teacher allowed us to be exempt from turning in homework assignments if our biweekly quiz scores were high enough.

One means of applying group contingencies in the classroom that some teachers find useful is the token economy (Ayllon & Azrin, 1968). In this system, tokens serve as conditioned reinforcers that can later be exchanged for objects or privileges. Tokens are earned for good conduct—whatever behaviors have been identified by the teacher for strengthening. But since tokens operate much like money, students may be fined for breaking the rules or engaging in behavior the teacher has deemed undesirable.

In one of the first formal uses of a token system for reinforcing and maintaining desired behaviors, patients at a mental hospital earned tokens for appropriate behaviors in the ward (Ayllon & Azrin, 1968). With their tokens, patients could buy candy, soda, trips to town, movies, and the like. Bushell, Wrobel, and Michaelis (1968) demonstrated the effective use of a token system with preschool children to strengthen school-related behaviors. The study took place in a regular classroom setting, and children earned tokens for such behaviors as attending to assigned tasks, being quiet, asking questions, and so forth.

When tokens can be exchanged for objects, such as books or toys, keeping a steady supply of such things can become rather expensive. Sulzer and Mayer (1972) therefore recommended that teachers consider using a variety of activities for which students can exchange tokens. In one study they reported (Campbell & Sulzer, 1971) that no less than forty-two activities were available to be earned, including: turn filmstrip projector, feed fish for a week, pass out paper, spend extra time at the library, or spend time in the science laboratory.

Management of Instruction

Behavioral principles have proved useful not only for managing student behavior in the classroom, but also for managing the way instruction is carried out. To this point, behavior of students has been conceived in terms of how they conduct themselves in and out of class. Learning has meant learning how to behave appropriately. But what about learning how to add or learning what is contained in the Articles of the Constitution? What about learning content as opposed to discipline?

Instructional Objectives

According to the behavioral perspective, just as we can set goals for appropriate behavior, so can we express in behavioral terms the instructional outcomes we desire students to achieve. In fact, behaviorists would argue the only evidence we have of learning comes from the students' behavior; they can do something after instruction that they could not do before. It is important, therefore, to specify desired instructional outcomes in terms of clear, observable behavior. These goal statements are variously called behavioral objectives, instructional objectives, or performance objectives.

Mager (1962) made popular the three-component objective, which states the behavior to be acquired, the conditions under which the behavior is to be demonstrated, and the criteria governing how well the behavior is to be performed. Typical Mager-type objectives, for example, would include the following:

1. Given the values of two sides of a right triangle, students will be able to correctly solve for the value of the third side.
2. Handed the pieces of an unassembled M-16, the soldier will be able to assemble the weapon in no more than two minutes.

Although other objective formats are used (for example, the five-component formats used in the instructional design models of Merrill [1983] and Gagné, Briggs, & Wager [1988]), all specify essentially the same information.

The effectiveness of instructional objectives for enhancing academic performance has been debated since the 1960s, primarily because research studies have yielded mixed results. Gagné (1985) argued for informing learners of objectives, since doing so readies them for learning. Objectives also provide a framework for studying what will eventually be tested. In a meta-analysis of research on objectives, Klauer (1984) provided evidence of a small, positive effect of objectives on learning, but also noted that objectives tend to focus learners' attention on certain information and away from other information. This would suggest that, to enhance learning, objectives must be written for all information considered important to learn.

As will be discussed again in Chapter 10, many educational and training programs today are based on objectives. However, they probably do not include objectives for each and every skill or piece of information that students might expect to learn. Rather, objectives are written for critical skills or the minimum information deemed acceptable for a graduate of the program to know. In addition, some educators (e.g., Popham, 1988; Dick & Reiser, 1989) suggest that students be given simpler, perhaps more general, statements of objectives to guide their learning, since these are easier to understand and yet still keep students and teachers alike on the same track toward particular goals.

Contingency Contracts

An instructional application that may make use of both behavior modification and instructional objectives is the **contingency contract**. Used with individual students, the contract sets out the terminal behavior the student is to achieve, along with any conditions for achievement and the consequences for completion (or noncompletion) of the assigned task(s). The contract is negotiated between teacher and student, and both agree to its terms.

Contingency contracts are particularly useful in open educational systems, where students from several grade levels participate together in learning activities. Since students are not all at the same achievement levels, they negotiate individual contracts each week indicating their expected progress in accomplishing objectives in subject areas such as math or read-ing, for example. Instructors at all levels of schooling have also found con-tingency contracts to be a useful means of managing independent study projects. Instead of simply giving an assignment such as, "write a ten-page research paper on a topic related to behavioral psychology," instructors may negotiate with individual students on what should be included in the paper and how well it should be written.

Personalized System of Instruction (PSI)

In 1968, Fred Keller proposed a whole new approach to college instruction that was based on behavioral principles (Keller, 1968). Keller noted prob-lems with typical group instruction in the classroom—delays in reinforcing achievement, students progressing to more difficult instruction when they have not mastered basic material—that he believed could be solved with the personalized system of instruction (PSI), also known as the Keller Plan. PSI calls for course material to be broken up into units, or modules, each with a set of behavioral objectives specifying what is to be learned in that unit. Units generally correspond with chapters in a textbook, so that they are taken up in sequence. What makes PSI unique are the following charac-teristic features:

1. Emphasis on individual study. Students tackle course material on their own, often aided by study guides which provide practice on unit objectives (e.g., Johnson & Perkins, 1976). The teacher and any course aides serve as resources to students when they encounter difficulty understanding information or answering questions in the textbook or study guide.

2. Self-pacing. Students work at their own pace, and report to class only when they are ready to take a unit quiz. As a result, some students work quickly, finishing the course in half the semester or less, while other stu-dents, who require more time to master concepts, take the entire semester to finish.

3. Unit mastery requirement. Students are required to meet a prespeci-fied mastery level on each unit. When they take a unit quiz, they receive feedback immediately, and if unit mastery has not been achieved, they may take the quiz again with no penalty. Typically, three or four versions of a unit quiz are available to students, and individual records are kept, noting which version a student took at a given time.

4. Use of proctors. The requirement to provide immediate feedback to students regarding their quiz performance obviously means considerable work for the teacher. To alleviate this problem, proctors are used to score quizzes and provide feedback. Proctors may be advanced students who have already taken the course, or they may be students in the class who

have mastered the unit they are now proctoring. Advantages to the latter arrangement include students solidifying their own knowledge of the material as well as getting to know their fellow students better.

5. Supplementary instructional techniques. Since the primary mode of instruction in a PSI course is self-study, lectures, demonstrations, and other modes of delivery may be used in a supplementary way to enhance motivation and transfer. Students may be motivated to reach a particular unit, for example, because mastery of the unit is their ticket to attend a special demonstration related to the next unit.

In the decade following Keller's proposal, PSI was tried in literally thousands of college courses. Kulik, Kulik, and Cohen (1979) reported that students generally liked PSI better than traditional courses, course grades were higher in PSI than in traditional courses, and student achievement on course final examinations was higher in PSI than traditional courses. There are several reasons, however, why PSI is not more popular currently.

Offsetting its effectiveness are the costs of PSI in time and resources. Preparation time is likely to be great initially, because study materials must be generated and multiple versions of quizzes written. Some arrangement for quiz-taking and proctoring must be made, and in the days before computers, this often meant scheduling two rooms for a significant number of hours each week (which is not looked upon kindly by college administrators). Record-keeping can also be burdensome, since individual records must be kept on the progress of all students, and copies of all quizzes and keys must be accounted for.

Although problems of record-keeping and quiz-taking may be ultimately solved through the use of computers, other disadvantages of PSI are not so easily counteracted. Some students, for example, are simply unable to meet the mastery criterion set for passing quizzes, despite repeated testing (e.g., Sussman, 1981). It may be that more moderate levels of mastery should be set (cf, Reiser, Driscoll, & Vergara, 1987), or that some students would better profit from alternative instructional presentations. Finally, self-pacing permits procrastination, which means that some students will not finish the requirements of a PSI course within the designated semester-long period. After several semesters of experience with a PSI course that I taught, I learned to reduce procrastination by limiting self-pacing. That is, quizzes were made available for a three-week window, which essentially forced students to maintain a reasonable rate of progress.

Teaching Machines to Computer-Based Instruction

"Educational toys with feedback are to be found in patent files reaching back at least a hundred years," said Sydney Pressey in 1964 (Pressey, 1964,

p. 354). So perhaps it is not entirely accurate to attribute teaching machines and programmed instruction solely to the influence of behaviorism, but certainly automation has been viewed as the solution to the problem of providing immediate reinforcement for correct responses in instruction. Although contingency contracts allow for reinforcement at task completion and PSI provides for immediate feedback on quiz performance, neither provides for sufficient reinforcement during learning. An automated teaching machine, however, has this capability.

After the early teaching machines of Pressey (1926, 1927), Skinner (1958) proposed applying behavioral principles to teaching academic skills through programmed instruction. In an instructional program, content is arranged in small steps, called frames, which progress from simple to complex and require a response from the learner to go on. Since the steps are small and increase gradually in difficulty, learners respond correctly most of the time, which means their responses are reinforced frequently. What this amounts to is shaping of complex academic skills.

A typical example of a programmed text can be found in Holland and Skinner's (1961), *The Analysis of Behavior*, an excerpt of which is shown in figure 2–7. It should be obvious from this excerpt that early programmed instruction, despite providing immediate and frequent reinforcement, suffered from one serious flaw: it was boring. The small steps, for some students, were too small. Furthermore, all students had to work through the frames in the same order.

To improve on this linear style of program, Crowder (1960) introduced the notion of branching. In branching programs, frames are larger and are typically followed by questions with several possible answer options. Depending on how students answer a given question, they are branched to another segment of the program. In this way, students who know the material already may skip quickly ahead to new material. Likewise, students having difficulty with the instruction may be branched to remedial segments, which provide additional information and practice.

Computer-based instruction, as originally conceived, is simply programmed instruction presented via computer. The computer provides obvious advantages over text-based programmed instruction, which can be very cumbersome for both the writer of the program and the student. The computer allows for complex branching sequences and can automatically record a student's responses (corrects, errors, even the particular sequence followed through the instruction). Increased computer technology has also enabled program designers to include complex graphics and synthesized speech along with text. As a result, instructional software is increasingly available that provides drill and practice on various academic skills, simulations to enhance problem-solving, or tutorials in various subject matters.

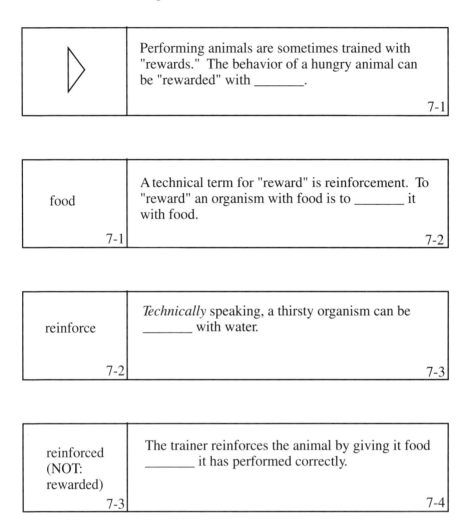

FIGUREN2–4MA **Typical Example of Programmed Text (Holland and Skinner, 1961, pp. 42–45)**

Behaviorism has obviously contributed to a number of instructional innovations, and behavioral principles continue to be useful to educators in maintaining classroom discipline, solving behavioral problems, and planning instruction. The emphasis in this chapter has been on what behaviorism offers for understanding human learning, and how that understanding can be applied toward effective instruction. But the picture would not be complete without some discussion of behaviorism's shortcomings. What aspects of learning does it fail to account for readily? What problems can be seen in the behavioral paradigm that suggest alternative theories should be explored? This chapter will conclude with examination of those questions.

THE BEHAVIORAL PERSPECTIVE ON LEARNING: ISSUES AND CRITICISMS

Verbal Behavior

The astute reader may have noticed that nowhere in this chapter has the learning of language been mentioned. Skinner maintained a long-standing interest in language, publishing an extensive operant analysis of language learning in 1957 with *Verbal Behavior* (Skinner, 1957). Skinner treated language as he did any other set of complex operant responses. He proposed that the verbal behavior of children is shaped, with appropriate verbal labels for objects and events being maintained through reinforcement as inappropriate ones are extinguished.

Skinner's position on language learning met with heavy criticism (e.g., Chomsky, 1959), and, indeed, accounting for certain kinds of utterances is difficult. Although a child's learning to call only cows by that label may hold up under operant analysis, consider a sentence such as, "I am looking for my glasses" (Leahey & Harris, 1989). Our immediate reaction to such a statement is to explain it in terms of what the person is thinking. He has an image of his glasses, which he has misplaced and is now trying to find. But Skinner, not permitting references to thought or mind, would argue that the stimulus in control of the verbal statement is the person's observation of his own searching behavior. That is, searching behavior in the past has resulted in the person finding his glasses and stopping the behavior; so he has learned to say, "I am searching for my glasses" as a response to this stimulus situation (Leahey & Harris, 1989).

This account of language learning not only seems a bit weird (Malcolm, 1964), but it also has been difficult to prove. Empirical tests, by and large, have failed to demonstrate that verbal behavior can be conditioned in the same way as other behavior (Leahey & Harris, 1989).

Reinforcement and Human Behavior

While Skinner was interested in deriving functional laws of learning, i.e., the probability of behavior is increased when it is followed by reinforcement, some researchers wondered why reinforcement operates as it does. Why are some consequences of behavior reinforcing when others are not? Shedding light on this question are results summarized by Leahey and Harris (1989) on the use of different sorts of reinforcement schedules with humans. In order for human learners to exhibit the response patterns characteristic of certain reinforcement schedules, they had to be instructed as to the schedule in effect. Moreover, when given false information about what schedule would be in effect, human subjects responded according to what they believed was going on and not according to the actual manipulation (cf., Brewer, 1974).

In attempting to explain why reinforcement works, Estes (1972) provided an important link between behaviorism and later cognitive conceptions of motivation. Estes reviewed studies indicating that humans must have an expectation of being rewarded in order for reinforcement to work, and they must value the reward. As we will see in later chapters, the concepts of expectancy and value will play major roles in social learning theory (e.g., Bandura, 1986) and motivation (e.g., Keller, 1983).

Intrinsic Motivation

Finally, problems cropping up with the behaviorist conception of reinforcement were only further exacerbated by investigations into the notion of intrinsic motivation. It seems obvious to the casual observer that learners sometimes do things without ostensibly being reinforced. Some children spend hours reading, for example, because they "like to read." Others will spend days putting together jigsaw puzzles "just for the fun of it." Skinner would explain this behavior by referring to the reinforcement history of the individual. Some time ago, he would argue, the sources of reinforcement for that behavior were undoubtedly external (e.g., the child's parents praised her for reading and spent time reading with her). Over time, however, internal referents became associated with the behavior and became conditioned reinforcers to sustain it.

Skinner's account of motivation, like his ideas about language, met with criticism. Bates (1979) reviewed studies which demonstrated how intrinsic satisfaction can even be undermined by extrinsic reinforcement. When rewards were given to learners for behavior in which they had already engaged on their own (e.g., puzzle solving or creating artwork), their response rate went down. This supports the notion that reinforcement is not necessarily a straightforward affair.

In recent reviews of the function of reinforcement in motivation, Keller (1983) and Dweck (1986) suggested that a distinction be made between endogenous and exogenous task rewards. That is, endogenous rewards are what typically follow from successful completion of a task (e.g., increased competence). Exogenous rewards, on the other hand, represent an arbitrary relationship between task and reward, such as the grade assigned to a completed project. Since exogenous rewards tend to reduce intrinsic interest in the task, Dweck (1986) recommended setting goals that reflect an endogenous emphasis, whereas Keller (1983) suggested using unexpected, noncontingent rewards to enhance performance. In chapter 9, the topic of motivation is taken up in greater detail.

CONCLUSION

Perceived problems and limitations with radical behaviorism as an explanatory paradigm for learning have led many investigators to propose cognitive, neurological, developmental, and other theoretical constructs as alternative ways of understanding learning. To Skinner, reliance on internal mechanisms of learning has led psychology away from a science of behavior to "questions that should never have been asked" (Skinner, 1987, p. 785). And he argued for a return to consideration of behavior "as a subject matter in its own right" (Skinner, 1987, p. 780).

Yet, "all psychological research is essentially behavioral," claimed Bornstein (1988), "in that psychological data inevitably take the form of observable, measurable behaviors, whether those are conditioned responses, responses to questionnaire items, verbal reports of stimulus recognition, or descriptions of inkblots. Because behavioral data must ultimately serve as the dependent variable in all psychological research, however, it does not necessarily follow that internal states, causes, and motivations are inappropriate or misleading constructs" (pp. 819–820). In the chapters that follow, these constructs will be examined, as behaviorism was in this chapter, for their explanatory value in understanding learning and their usefulness for planning effective instruction.

SUGGESTED READINGS

Bijou, S. W., & Ruiz, R. (Eds.) 1981. *Behavior modification: Contributions to education.* Hillsdale, NJ: Erlbaum.

Sulzer, B., & Mayer, G. R. (1972). *Behavior modification procedures for school personnel.* New York: Holt, Rinehart and Winston.

In addition, two journals—*Journal of Applied Behavior Analysis* and *Journal of Experimental Analysis of Behavior*—routinely publish articles dealing with some aspect of radical behaviorism.

REFLECTIVE QUESTIONS AND ACTIVITIES

1. Consider the principles of behaviorism in light of the epistemological traditions described in chapter 1. To what view of knowledge is behaviorism most closely aligned? What evidence supports your choice?

2. View the movie, *A Clockwork Orange*, which was produced by Stanley Kubrick in the 1970s. Analyze the procedures used in terms of classical and operant conditioning.

   a. What image, or metaphor, of conditioning is presented in this movie?
   b. How do you think B. F. Skinner would have reacted to the procedures used in the movie?
   c. What alternative procedures might Skinner have proposed for altering Alex's violent behavior?
   d. What events were occurring in the 1970s that might have influenced Kubrick's decision to portray conditioning in this light?

3. Read B. F. Skinner's *Beyond Freedom and Dignity* or *Walden Two*. Consider the following questions.

   a. What is Skinner's vision of a "perfect" society?
   b. Do you think such a society could ever be realized? Why or why not?
   c. Do you think such a society is desirable? Why or why not?

4. Describe a learning situation in which you (or someone of your acquaintance) had (or are currently having) difficulty achieving some desired performance. Analyze the event in terms of the principles of behavior modification. Then, develop a plan to overcome the difficulty. Finally, describe how implementation of the plan should be monitored, including what you would do if it seemed to be ineffective.

5. As you will see in the following chapters, many theorists have rejected the concepts of behaviorism, believing that an understanding of learning is better served by other concepts. Take an initial position on the usefulness of behavioral principles, both for practitioners and for researchers.

▶ Part III

Learning and Cognition

▶ 3

Cognitive Information Processing

Consider the following scenarios.

Scenario 3–1

This is a story about two adult readers. Sarah lives in a small rural community and participates nightly in the county's adult literacy program. She reads aloud haltingly, sounding out unfamiliar words. The selection she reads is a simple tale about village life, so that she is able to easily comprehend the gist of it.

When she decided to go back to graduate school, Rita purchased her first home computer, complete with modem. She is typical of many computer users, experienced in word processing but not especially knowledgeable about how the machine works. An operating problem has sent her to the manual about the modem, where she attempts to make sense of sentences like, "The primary application for the local digital loopback is to permit a modem that is not CCITT V.54 compatible to engage in a remote digital loopback test with your modem."

Scenario 3–2

Two music students, one a mediocre trombone player and the other a talented clarinetist, attend a school concert together as part of a class assignment. Afterward, they compare notes. "Did you hear the clarity of tone and absolute precision of the clarinet solo?" raved the clarinetist. "No," replied the trombone player, "but did you see what the trombone section was up to? For some reason, all the players had their shoes off."

Before proceeding further, reflect momentarily on the behaviorist perspective discussed in the previous chapter. How might a behaviorist account for the behaviors exhibited in these two scenarios? How is a complex behavior such as reading acquired? Why did the two music students see and hear different things at the concert? Questions similar to these pose problems for behaviorism. And although behaviorism had dominated American psychology for half a century, it was to be supplanted by cognitive challenges.

Remember that the study of cognition was not new to psychology. Before radical behaviorism had gained such a stronghold on psychological research and theory, Tolman used cognitive maps to explain purposive behavior in rats, and Hull relied on a number of cognitive mediators between stimulus and response. Pavlov, as well, had introduced the concept of the "second signal system" to account for language learning. Vygotsky had launched his theory of how inner speech functions as a cognitive mediator explicitly in reaction to American behaviorism. Moreover, Gestalt psychologists in Germany had proposed that organizational processes in cognition were important to perception, learning, and problem solving. What was new in American psychology was the computer metaphor adopted for conceptualizing cognition.

The birth of computers after World War II provided a concrete way of thinking about learning and a consistent framework for interpreting early work on memory, perception, and learning. Stimuli became inputs; behavior became outputs. And what happened in between was conceived of as information processing. Today, what is known as cognitive information processing (CIP) is in reality an integration of views developed from a variety of perspectives. "Like the traditional cognitive view, the CIP model portrays the mind possessing a structure consisting of components for processing (storing, retrieving, transforming, using) information and procedures for using the components. Like the behavioral view, the CIP model holds that learning consists partially of the formation of associations" (Andre & Phye, 1986, p. 3).

OVERVIEW OF THE INFORMATION PROCESSING SYSTEM

According to the cognitive information processing view, the human learner is conceived to be a processor of information in much the same way a computer is. When learning occurs, information is input from the environment, processed and stored in memory, and output in the form of some learned capability. Adherents of the CIP model, like behaviorists, seek to explain how the environment modifies human behavior. But unlike behaviorists, they assume an intervening variable between environment

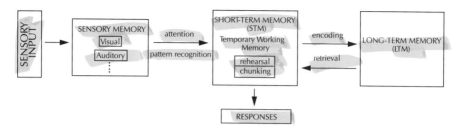

FIGUREN3–1M The Flow of Information as Generally Conceptualized in Information Processing Theory

and behavior. That variable is the information processing system of the learner.

Most models of information processing can be traced to Atkinson and Shiffrin (1968), who proposed a multistore, multistage theory of memory. That is, from the time information is received by the processing system, it undergoes a series of transformations until it can be permanently stored in memory. This flow of information, as it is generally conceived, is shown in Figure 3–1. Displayed in the figure are the three basic components of the proposed memory system—sensory memory, short-term memory, and long-term memory—along with the processes assumed to be responsible for transferring information from one stage to the next. Let us briefly consider what these components are and how they are believed to function.

The Components of Memory

Sensory memory represents the first stage of information processing. Associated with the senses (vision, hearing, etc.), it functions to hold information in memory very briefly, just long enough for the information to be processed further. For example, imagine yourself in a dark, unfamiliar room. You strike a match, which flares briefly and then goes out. In the split second after the match has gone out, you retain a visual after-image of the room, which stays with you just long enough for you to determine where the door or light switch is located. There is a separate sensory memory corresponding with each of the five senses, but all are assumed to operate in essentially the same way.

The short-term memory functions as a temporary working memory (Atkinson & Shiffrin, 1968, 1971). This is the stage at which further processing is carried out to make information ready for long term storage or a response. Working memory has been likened to consciousness. When we are actively thinking about ideas and are therefore conscious of them, they are in working memory. As an example, you may keep in mind the phone number of a local restaurant in order to call immediately for dinner reservations (i.e., make a response). Or, you may devise a means to help you remember the phone number at a later time, in which case you are preparing the information for storage.

Working memory not only holds information for a limited amount of time (e.g., you quickly forget the phone number upon dialing unless you have devised a way to remember it longer), but it also holds a limited amount of information. In other words, you can think about only a few ideas at one time or read and understand relatively few phrases at once. With very long and complex sentences, for example, the reader has typically forgotten the beginning of the sentence by the time the end of it is reached. You can well imagine the effect on comprehension and recall that this limited capacity for keeping things in mind will have.

The long-term memory represents our permanent storehouse of information. Anything that is to be remembered for a long time must be transferred from short-term to long-term memory. Although forgetting is a phenomenon we have all experienced (and will be discussed in detail later in the chapter), it is assumed that once information has been processed into long-term memory, it is never truly lost. As for capacity, despite the protests of many children, long-term memory cannot be filled up. As far as we know, long-term memory is capable of retaining an unlimited amount and variety of information.

The Flow of Information during Learning

As indicated earlier, information is transformed—or processed—as it passes from one stage of memory to the next. What are the processes assumed to be responsible for these transformations? Let's examine a particular example from Scenario 3–1 to trace what may happen during learning. Suppose Sarah comes to this sentence in the story she is reading: "Visitors to the town are always struck by the beauty of its wide, azalea-lined avenues." The letters on the page stimulate Sarah's visual sensory register, which receives and briefly records a representation of the information as it originally occurred. Then, familiar shapes of letters and words are perceived as pattern recognition takes place. It is at this point that the process of attention also exerts an effect. An unfamiliar word may cause processing to slow, because added attention must be paid to individual letters rather than whole words.

Upon entering working memory, the information is coded conceptually, i.e., takes on meaning. Meanings of the individual words are retrieved from long-term memory to assist Sarah in constructing a representation of the whole sentence. Since the sentence is more than a few words, internal rehearsal may also occur to preserve the first few words in memory while the end of the sentence is being perceived.

Finally, in order for the information to be processed into long-term memory, Sarah must encode its meaning. This means that the representation she constructs of the sentence must be meaningful and make connections with related knowledge already in long-term memory. For example, her previous experience with azaleas and wide streets may allow her to construct an image of what this sentence describes. Her image then becomes a useful retrieval cue when she is asked to recall what she has read.

It may be evident from this example that processing does not truly occur in the unidirectional, linear way in which it is often depicted (e.g., in Figure 3–1). Instead, the representation Sarah constructs of the sentence is determined both by the information itself (data-driven, bottom-up processing) and by her prior knowledge (conceptually driven, top-down processing). The degree to which either type of processing dominates seems to depend on the nature of the learning task itself and the amount of prior knowledge the learner brings to it.

Little has yet been said about the control processes influencing information flow. Whether these are thought of as comprising a system component (e.g., Gagné, 1985; Andre & Phye, 1986) or as processes modifying information flow within and between components (e.g., Atkinson & Shiffrin, 1971), they have the same effect. In some way, an executive monitor keeps track of the information flow and makes decisions about processing priorities. This may occur in a conscious, strategic fashion or in an unconscious, automatic way. For example, Sarah may have very deliberately chosen to associate an image with the sentence she read, because she has found imagery to be a very effective study strategy. On the other hand, suppose the story had previously described only camellias adorning villagers' lawns. Sarah may then have developed an expectation that could cause her to mistakenly perceive "camellias" instead of "azaleas" in the target sentence. In either case, a control process has modified the information flow and what was ultimately understood and learned.

The sections that follow focus on each of the major components and processes of the human processing system. As you read them, keep in mind two things. First, the computer provided a concrete metaphor for human information processing and, thus, a language for describing and integrating a variety of learning phenomena. Second, for instruction to be meaningful and relevant, it must build upon learner prior knowledge and help learners to construct cognitive connections between what they already know and what they are being asked to learn. The chapter concludes with a brief glance at alternative cognitive conceptions to the information processing view.

SENSORY MEMORY

The existence of some sort of perceptual store in the information processing system that registers information and holds it very briefly was demonstrated in a series of experiments conducted by Sperling (1960). Sperling presented subjects with a visual array of twelve letters (arranged in three rows of four letters each) such as the one shown in Figure 3–2. He flashed the array on a screen for 50 milliseconds (one-twentieth of a second) and then asked subjects to report what letters they had seen. Even with such a brief exposure, subjects could consistently report three or four letters accurately.

Although this result seemed to indicate a limited processing capacity, Sperling was able to show that, in fact, all of the letters had entered sensory memory. He did this by using a partial report technique. That is, he used a high, medium, or low tone to signal to subjects which row of the array they were to report. Instead of a relatively poor performance (three or four of twelve letters), subjects showed remarkably good performance, reliably reporting three or four letters in the row (so, three or four of four) no matter which row was signaled. It appears, then, that sensory memory is temporally, rather than visually, limited. In other words, a great deal of visual information registers, but it decays very rapidly without further processing, within a quarter of a second according to Sperling's experiments.

Relatively little is known about the sensory memories corresponding to the other senses, but they are presumed to function in a similar way. Darwin, Turvey, and Crowder (1972) replicated Sperling's results with the auditory system. They found, however, that the auditory sensory memory (or echo) lasted longer than the visual sensory memory (or icon), typically up to 4 seconds under partial report conditions. An explanation for this difference is thought to lie in the requirements for speech perception. In other words, sounds must remain in sensory memory long enough for them to be combined with other sounds so that speech may be understood.

FIGURE   3–2   Visual Displays Similar to Those Used by Sperling (1960)

Sperling's use of the partial report technique also illustrates the effect that attention has on information processing. The tone served as a cue to focus attention on a particular part of the display so that it could be processed further and recalled. Attention is a process that has been conceptualized in a variety of ways. Instructors admonish students to pay attention in class, but they also adopt measures to focus students' attention on particular features of instruction. Either way, a student who is not attentive misses some of the information to be learned.

Cognitive psychologists, noting that some information always seems to be lost in processing, initially thought that attention acted as a bottleneck or filter preventing information from entering the system (e.g., Broadbent, 1957). Treisman (1960) showed, however, that attention is not an all-or-none proposition and suggested that it serves to attenuate, or tune out stimulation. Her ideas are easily illustrated by thinking about what happens at parties. You may be attending to one conversation, ostensibly unaware of what else is being said around you. But when you hear your name spoken or someone else talking about a topic that interests you, your attention shifts. Apparently enough information was being processed to prompt you to react and pay closer attention to the secondary source.

More recently, researchers have come to view attention as a resource with limited capacity to be allocated and shared among competing goals (cf, Kahneman, 1973; Grabe, 1986). This suggests that learners have some control over the process and may selectively focus attention to meet certain ends. It is also true, however, that some tasks require relatively little attention and may be accomplished effortlessly and automatically. The concepts of selectivity and automaticity are important aspects of attention that hold implications for instruction. Let us consider each in turn.

Selective Attention

Selective attention refers to the learner's *ability to select and process certain information while simultaneously ignoring other information.* The two music students in Scenario 3–2, for example, selectively attended to different sources of information at the concert. Even the type of stimulation to which each attended differed. The clarinetist listened to the sound of the clarinet solo, while the trombone player watched the antics of the players in the trombone section. Notice that the clarinetist also focused attention on particular features of the solo. For any student to learn about such concepts as tone quality and precision fingering, they must attend to, and learn to discriminate, variations in stimuli that relate to these concepts.

The extent to which individuals can spread their attention across two or more tasks (or sources of information) or focus on selected information within a single task depends upon a number of factors. The most obvious, perhaps, is the meaning that the task or information holds for an individual. Your name spoken in a crowded room catches your attention because it is highly meaningful to you. Likewise, the clarinet solo is meaningful for the clarinetist and therefore likely to be selectively perceived at the expense of other aspects of the performance.

Second, similarity between competing tasks or sources of information makes a difference. It is hard to listen to two conversations at the same time when both speakers are the same sex and are speaking in a similar tone and volume. Imagine the poor student, for example, who is trying to listen to the teacher at the same time a classmate talks in her ear. Similarly, a learner may enjoy studying classical music but find her concentration slipping when vocal music is played.

Task complexity or difficulty is a third factor that influences attention. Simple tasks, such as winding yarn into a ball, require relatively little attention and are easily done at the same time as other things. Watching a light-hearted TV comedy, putting together a jigsaw puzzle, and talking to your family about tomorrow's schedule are probably all tasks that can be accomplished simultaneously. But reading a medical history for purposes of diagnosis or assembling an intricate set of electrical circuits demands more complete and focused attention. A task may also demand more attention when it is something about which the learner has little prior knowledge. For example, a post-baccalaureate student taking his first course in learning theory is likely to find it necessary to pay close attention to both his instructor and the textbook.

Finally, the ability to control attention, in both a general and specific sense, appears to differ with age, hyperactivity, intelligence, and learning disabilities (Grabe, 1986, p. 66). For example, attention deficit disorder is a condition afflicting a small proportion of preadolescent children. They seem to be unable to focus attention or to turn off irrelevant stimulation. As a result, their school performance typically suffers.

How, then, is attention best managed in instructional situations? To influence attention or alertness of students during the course of a classroom lesson, Good and Brophy (1984) recommended that instructors employ standard signals (e.g., "let's begin," "back on task!," turning the lights on or off). A third grade teacher of my acquaintance uses a maraca to gain the attention of all students when they are working in pairs or small groups. Because he has used that signal from the first day of class, students know when they hear it that they are to stop whatever they are doing and look at him for direction.

When it is important to focus students' attention on certain aspects of the instructional materials, stimulus features can be highlighted through the use of color or type of print (in textual materials), voice inflections or gestures (in classroom presentations), and novelty. To emphasize the different sorts of roles that computer consultants often play, for example, a community college teacher wears different hats during his lecture, each one representing a different role.

Finally, Grabe (1986) reviewed ways in which learners themselves may be taught to stay on task and selectively attend to important features of instruction. He indicated that two things appear to be important: (1) learners should be taught to take more time in responding to a learning task (to reduce impulsiveness), and (2) they should be given a strategy for focusing attention and allowed to practice that strategy (p. 74). Certain games that require attention, e.g., *Concentration* or *Simon Says*, can be used to help students develop better attending skills.

Automaticity

When tasks are overlearned or sources of information become habitual, to the extent that their attention requirements are minimal, **automaticity** has occurred. Driving a car provides a good example of the distinction Shiffrin and Schneider (1977) made between automatic and controlled processing. For the most part, the driving task is automatic, enabling the driver to listen attentively to a radio program, for example. But when traffic is heavy or something unusual occurs to demand the driver's attention, driving shifts to a controlled process. The driver then must pay much closer attention to driving and fails to hear what is being said on the radio.

LaBerge and Samuels (1974) have developed a theory to account for automatic processing in reading. They believe decoding words should be so automatic for readers that they can concentrate their attention on comprehending the meaning of what is read. In Scenario 3–1, for example, Sarah has learned to decode but has not yet learned the skill to the point where it is automatic. As a result, her reading is slow and fraught with difficulty. Rita, on the other hand, may decode automatically most of the time, but here faces unfamiliar information that makes her comprehension of the meaning difficult. As a result, she, like the driver in traffic, must shift from automatic to controlled processing in order to decode the unfamiliar words.

To develop automatic decoding skills in readers, researchers have explored a number of possibilities, including extended word identification practice as part of the regular text-reading curriculum (e.g., Beck, 1981, 1983). More recently, researchers have become encouraged by the potential of the computer for providing many different types of word tasks in an engaging environment (Perfetti & Curtis, 1986). It may also be useful for teachers to include read-aloud activities (such as reading and answering questions) after learners have read silently. Readers' sensitivity to different kinds of scripts can impair their comprehension, but such impairment seems to be obviated by reading aloud during rereading (Jacoby, Levy, & Steinbach, 1992).

Once reading is automatic, however, what readers will comprehend and remember from text depends upon how they allocate their attention as they read. Readers will generally allocate greater attention to important elements in a text (Anderson, 1982). They determine importance based on the purpose for which they are reading as well as features of the text that signal something is important.

As noted in the previous section, the reader's attention can be directed by typographical cues in the text (e.g., boldface print, capitalization [Glynn & Divesta, 1979]), as well as the presence of titles (Kozminsky, 1977), specific phrases (e.g., "an important cause of . . . " [Armbruster, 1986]), and idea unit structure (Kintsch & van Dijk, 1978). Idea unit structure refers to the placement of main ideas and supporting details within a paragraph. Ideas that appear high in the structure are more likely to be attended to and remembered than details buried deep within a paragraph. Writers of instructional texts, then, are well advised to employ these features to direct learner attention to the important, to-be-learned information.

Readers, on their own, also differentially allocate attention according to the purpose for which they are reading. Reading a novel, for example, typically involves reading for the gist of a story, and readers may be hard pressed to recount very specific details when they are finished. Reading a textbook or technical manual, on the other hand, is done with a specific purpose in mind—to locate and learn important information. Assigning instructional objectives (Klauer, 1984) or inserting questions in the text (Andre, 1979) has proven effective for helping students focus their attention on specific text information.

Automatization of other basic skills besides reading (such as the rules of arithmetic operations and grammar) is considered to be a desirable educational goal for the primary grades (Gagné; 1983, Bloom, 1986). By extension, one can also see the usefulness of learning certain tasks as adults to automaticity. Pilots must react automatically to a variety of information sources in the cockpit. Astronomers automatically process patterns of stars in the search for anomalies that might be signs of new stars or other astral phenomena. And detection of signs of abuse is probably automatic for skilled therapists.

Pattern Recognition

Just attending to information is not enough to ensure its further processing, however. One might say that attention is necessary but not sufficient; information must also be analyzed and familiar patterns identified to provide a basis for further processing. **Pattern recognition** refers to the

A a a A A a a A a

FIGURE   3–3   Variations of the Letter A

process whereby *environmental stimuli are recognized as exemplars of concepts and principles already in memory*. This recognition is preconceptual, something like finding a shape that matches a stencil without identifying what the shape or stencil pattern actually represents.

Pattern recognition is a particularly difficult process to model in the human information processing system, and, consequently, several different models have been proposed. Each carries particular implications for how the process operates and for what form information is represented in memory. Briefly, **template matching** assumes that *mental copies of environmental stimuli, or templates, are stored in memory*. Pattern recognition, then, consists of simply matching the incoming information to the appropriate template in memory. Although this seems intuitively appealing, look at Figure 3–3 and consider what this means for a template-matching model of pattern recognition. In order for you to recognize all of those figures as representations of the letter *A*, you would have to have templates in memory to match each one. For obvious reasons, this model fails as a reasonable account of human pattern recognition.

According to an alternative, **prototype** model, *what is stored in memory is not an exact copy of a stimulus, but rather an abstracted, general prototype*. Pattern recognition in this case involves comparing the incoming information with the prototype. If a close enough match is found, then the incoming stimulus is recognized as an example of the class of objects or events represented by the prototype. Thus, all of the letters in Figure 3–3, for example, are similar enough to the assumed prototype to be recognized as *A*s.

The prototype model has become popular for explaining pattern recognition, primarily because of evidence that suggests we tend to store prototypic concepts in memory (see, in particular, Eleanor Rosch's work [1973, 1975]). For example, asked to indicate what color comes to mind in response to the verbal stimulus *red*, you are likely to choose a color that is close to fire-engine red. Similarly, reading about Olympic athletes or shore birds tends to evoke general ideas about these concepts rather than specific, previously encountered examples.

A third model of pattern recognition, called **feature analysis**, presumes that *specific, distinctive features are stored in memory*. Incoming information is then analyzed for the presence of these features. To consider the letter *A*

---

ntifying the colors of the words, tending instead to read the
es. Knowledge of color words, coupled with reading skill,
one's ability to perceive the colors. The same would hold
ading; one has a tendency to read the words as they should
than as they actually are.

oblems can also require overcoming the effects of past
erception. In other words, some problem situations must be
new way in order for a solution to be reached. In Kohler's
ents with a chimpanzee, for example, bananas were placed
himpanzee's reach with a stick near at hand. In order to get
the chimpanzee had to perceive the properties of the stick as
se as a tool to knock the bananas within reach. Similarly,
ght problem such as "If the lily pads on a pond double every
ond is completely covered on the 100th day, on which day is
?" requires thinking of the problem in terms of logic rather

little is known about how people come to be proficient at
ms in a new light in order to solve them, there is evidence to
practice on many different kinds of problems may help
Davidson, 1983). Practice with a variety of problems can make
aware of the role of context in problem solution and thus
the consideration of alternate assumptions.

ences of past experience and context on perception can also
er in our expectations about students. It has been well
that teachers' expectations of students may affect their
f student achievement, as well as their own behavior toward
., Good, 1987). In other words, expecting a student to be a
lass can predispose the instructor to perceiving more problem
imilarly, a student with a reputation for high achievement is
o be perceived in that light.

ectations themselves may develop from previous experiences of
from the immediate context, or both. For example, the teacher
to associate, and therefore comes to expect, certain behaviors
nd low achieving students, males and females, or well and
ved children. But context also plays a part. Teachers may expect
ame individual in a generally high achieving class than in a class
ns less well overall.

gh the self-fulfilling prophecy (Rosenthal and Jacobson 1968) has
siderable influence in schools over the past 20 years, recent
as shown that what teachers do (or fail to do) matters more than
ers expect with regard to student achievement. Goldenberg
cribed two cases of paradoxical expectancy in which the
first-grade, year-end achievements were in marked contrast to

one more time, its defining features might include the two sides, the angle at which they are joined, and the horizontal connecting line. All stimulus letters would be analyzed for these features and, if found, would be identified as *A*s.

Feature analysis, like the prototype model, is supported by experimental evidence and together, the two models have influenced pedagogical recommendations for concept learning. Tennyson and Cocchiarella (1986) proposed a model for teaching concepts that calls for presenting, first, a best or prototypic concept example followed by a variety of examples that differ from the prototype in systematic ways. The examples help learners to abstract the meaningful dimensions of the concept and determine which features are critical and invariant and which are nonessential and variable across examples.

To see how this model might work, consider one of the concepts from the previous chapter: positive reinforcement. A best or prototypic example might be one in which positive reinforcement is shown with animals and the use of a primary reinforcer. Then, additional examples could be explored in which positive reinforcement is demonstrated with children in school or adults at work and the use of secondary or social reinforcers. Or consider how a medical student might learn to distinguish diseased from normal cells. With stained slides showing clear examples of each for comparison, the student could examine other slides bearing cells that show a range of what is considered normal characteristics and a range of what is identified as diseased.

Although the feature comparison and prototype models account well for most instances of pattern recognition, they also are unable to account for why certain patterns are recognized even though all the features are not present or they fail to resemble their prototype. For example, a degraded copy of the letter *A*, as might be seen on a badly eroded tombstone or a poorly produced overhead transparency, is still recognized as an *A*.

To explain this and other perceptual phenomena not easily handled with the prototype or feature analysis models, we rely on principles of organization, context, and past experience. Gestalt psychologists, in studies dating from the early twentieth century, demonstrated that human perception tends to involve "going beyond the information given" in order to construct a meaningful interpretation. That is, the way in which stimuli are organized will prompt the viewer to see them in certain ways, apart from what is actually there. For example, look at the pictures displayed in Figure 3–4. What do you see? Chances are, you did not say, "just a bunch of dots." The principle of closure prompts us to close up the spaces between the dots in Figure 3–4 (left) and to perceive the figure as an "*A*". Due to proximity, we view the dots in Figure 3–4 (center), not as *nine dots*, but as *three sets of three dots*. Finally, similarity dictates that similar units will be perceived as

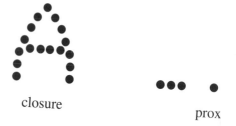

closure   prox

FIGURE   3–4   Gestalt Principles of (

one, so that we do not see black and w
a black *X*.

The effect of context on patterr
reference to the tombstone and overhea
those instances, why is it likely for the
A? Presumably, the reason is that clue
which surrounds it. Other, more eas
words are on the tombstone and transp
the degraded letter has been determ
obvious. Figure 3–5 illustrates how
perceptual ambiguity. The figure in the (
the number 13. Which will be perceive
letters in the row or the figures in t
contextual clues.

Past experience, or prior learning, is
its effect on pattern recognition. This refe
been learned or experienced previously v
perceived in later situations. A good illus
Stroop effect. An individual is shown a :
green, or red) that are printed in different
colors as quickly as you can." What happ

12

A   13

14

FIGURE   3–5   Context Effects on Perception

difficulty in ider
words themselv
interferes with
true for proofre
be typed rather

Solving pr
experience on
perceived in a
(1925) experim
just out of the
at the bananas
affording its
solving an ins
day, and the p
it half-covered
than math.

Although
casting proble
suggest that
(Sternberg &
learners mor
more open to

The influ
come togeth
documented
evaluations
students (e.
problem in
behaviors. S
more likely

The exp
the teacher,
has learned
with high
poorly beha
less of the s
that perfor

Althou
had a con
evidence h
what teac
(1992) de
children's

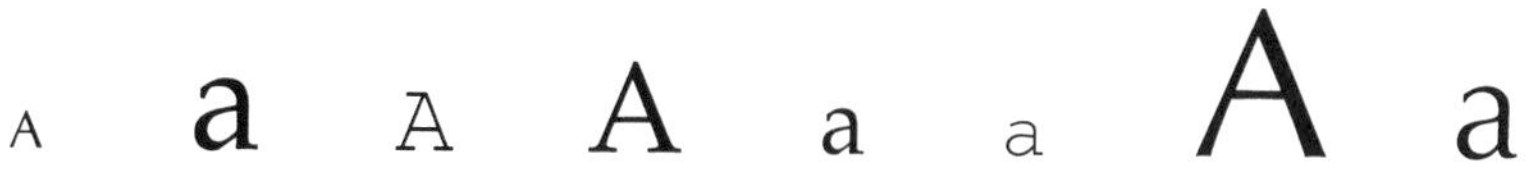

A a A A a a A a

FIGURE   3–3   Variations of the Letter A

process whereby *environmental stimuli are recognized as exemplars of concepts and principles already in memory*. This recognition is preconceptual, something like finding a shape that matches a stencil without identifying what the shape or stencil pattern actually represents.

Pattern recognition is a particularly difficult process to model in the human information processing system, and, consequently, several different models have been proposed. Each carries particular implications for how the process operates and for what form information is represented in memory. Briefly, **template matching** assumes that *mental copies of environmental stimuli, or templates, are stored in memory*. Pattern recognition, then, consists of simply matching the incoming information to the appropriate template in memory. Although this seems intuitively appealing, look at Figure 3–3 and consider what this means for a template-matching model of pattern recognition. In order for you to recognize all of those figures as representations of the letter *A*, you would have to have templates in memory to match each one. For obvious reasons, this model fails as a reasonable account of human pattern recognition.

According to an alternative, **prototype** model, *what is stored in memory is not an exact copy of a stimulus, but rather an abstracted, general prototype*. Pattern recognition in this case involves comparing the incoming information with the prototype. If a close enough match is found, then the incoming stimulus is recognized as an example of the class of objects or events represented by the prototype. Thus, all of the letters in Figure 3–3, for example, are similar enough to the assumed prototype to be recognized as *A*s.

The prototype model has become popular for explaining pattern recognition, primarily because of evidence that suggests we tend to store prototypic concepts in memory (see, in particular, Eleanor Rosch's work [1973, 1975]). For example, asked to indicate what color comes to mind in response to the verbal stimulus *red*, you are likely to choose a color that is close to fire-engine red. Similarly, reading about Olympic athletes or shore birds tends to evoke general ideas about these concepts rather than specific, previously encountered examples.

A third model of pattern recognition, called **feature analysis**, presumes that *specific, distinctive features are stored in memory*. Incoming information is then analyzed for the presence of these features. To consider the letter *A* one more time, its defining features might include the two sides, the angle at which they are joined, and the horizontal connecting line. All stimulus letters would be analyzed for these features and, if found, would be identified as *A*s.

Feature analysis, like the prototype model, is supported by experimental evidence and together, the two models have influenced pedagogical recommendations for concept learning. Tennyson and Cocchiarella (1986) proposed a model for teaching concepts that calls for presenting, first, a best or prototypic concept example followed by a variety of examples that differ from the prototype in systematic ways. The examples help learners to abstract the meaningful dimensions of the concept and determine which features are critical and invariant and which are nonessential and variable across examples.

To see how this model might work, consider one of the concepts from the previous chapter: positive reinforcement. A best or prototypic example might be one in which positive reinforcement is shown with animals and the use of a primary reinforcer. Then, additional examples could be explored in which positive reinforcement is demonstrated with children in school or adults at work and the use of secondary or social reinforcers. Or consider how a medical student might learn to distinguish diseased from normal cells. With stained slides showing clear examples of each for comparison, the student could examine other slides bearing cells that show a range of what is considered normal characteristics and a range of what is identified as diseased.

Although the feature comparison and prototype models account well for most instances of pattern recognition, they also are unable to account for why certain patterns are recognized even though all the features are not present or they fail to resemble their prototype. For example, a degraded copy of the letter *A*, as might be seen on a badly eroded tombstone or a poorly produced overhead transparency, is still recognized as an *A*.

To explain this and other perceptual phenomena not easily handled with the prototype or feature analysis models, we rely on principles of organization, context, and past experience. Gestalt psychologists, in studies dating from the early twentieth century, demonstrated that human perception tends to involve "going beyond the information given" in order to construct a meaningful interpretation. That is, the way in which stimuli are organized will prompt the viewer to see them in certain ways, apart from what is actually there. For example, look at the pictures displayed in Figure 3–4. What do you see? Chances are, you did not say, "just a bunch of dots." The principle of closure prompts us to close up the spaces between the dots in Figure 3–4 (left) and to perceive the figure as an "*A*". Due to proximity, we view the dots in Figure 3–4 (center), not as *nine dots*, but as *three sets of three dots*. Finally, similarity dictates that similar units will be perceived as

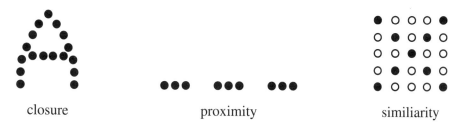

closure   proximity   similiarity

FIGURE   3–4   Gestalt Principles of Organization

one, so that we do not see black and white dots in Figure 3–4 (right), we see a black X.

The effect of context on pattern recognition can be illustrated by reference to the tombstone and overhead transparency mentioned earlier. In those instances, why is it likely for the degraded letter to be perceived as an A? Presumably, the reason is that clues to its identity exist in the context which surrounds it. Other, more easily perceived letters suggest what words are on the tombstone and transparency. Once the word containing the degraded letter has been determined, the identity of the letter is obvious. Figure 3–5 illustrates how context is used to resolve some perceptual ambiguity. The figure in the center could be either the letter B or the number *13*. Which will be perceived depends on whether the other letters in the row or the figures in the column are used to provide contextual clues.

Past experience, or prior learning, is the last factor to be considered for its effect on pattern recognition. This refers to the simple fact that what has been learned or experienced previously will have some impact on what is perceived in later situations. A good illustration of this can be seen in the Stroop effect. An individual is shown a series of color words (e.g., blue, green, or red) that are printed in different colors and is asked to "name the colors as quickly as you can." What happens is that the person has great

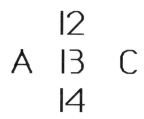

FIGURE   3–5   Context Effects on Perception

difficulty in identifying the colors of the words, tending instead to read the words themselves. Knowledge of color words, coupled with reading skill, interferes with one's ability to perceive the colors. The same would hold true for proofreading; one has a tendency to read the words as they should be typed rather than as they actually are.

Solving problems can also require overcoming the effects of past experience on perception. In other words, some problem situations must be perceived in a new way in order for a solution to be reached. In Kohler's (1925) experiments with a chimpanzee, for example, bananas were placed just out of the chimpanzee's reach with a stick near at hand. In order to get at the bananas, the chimpanzee had to perceive the properties of the stick as affording its use as a tool to knock the bananas within reach. Similarly, solving an insight problem such as "If the lily pads on a pond double every day, and the pond is completely covered on the 100th day, on which day is it half-covered?" requires thinking of the problem in terms of logic rather than math.

Although little is known about how people come to be proficient at casting problems in a new light in order to solve them, there is evidence to suggest that practice on many different kinds of problems may help (Sternberg & Davidson, 1983). Practice with a variety of problems can make learners more aware of the role of context in problem solution and thus more open to the consideration of alternate assumptions.

The influences of past experience and context on perception can also come together in our expectations about students. It has been well documented that teachers' expectations of students may affect their evaluations of student achievement, as well as their own behavior toward students (e.g., Good, 1987). In other words, expecting a student to be a problem in class can predispose the instructor to perceiving more problem behaviors. Similarly, a student with a reputation for high achievement is more likely to be perceived in that light.

The expectations themselves may develop from previous experiences of the teacher, from the immediate context, or both. For example, the teacher has learned to associate, and therefore comes to expect, certain behaviors with high and low achieving students, males and females, or well and poorly behaved children. But context also plays a part. Teachers may expect less of the same individual in a generally high achieving class than in a class that performs less well overall.

Although the self-fulfilling prophecy (Rosenthal and Jacobson 1968) has had a considerable influence in schools over the past 20 years, recent evidence has shown that what teachers do (or fail to do) matters more than what teachers expect with regard to student achievement. Goldenberg (1992) described two cases of paradoxical expectancy in which the children's first-grade, year-end achievements were in marked contrast to what the teacher had expected. He concluded in one case that "The teacher had failed to take corrective action when she should have *because she had expected* [the student] to do well on her own" (Goldenberg, 1992, p. 539). In the other case, "*in spite of the teacher's low expectations* for [the student's] success, the teacher took actions that appear to have influenced [her] eventual first-grade reading achievement. . . . Low expectations were clearly evident, but they were irrelevant in determining the teacher's actions" (p. 539). Although expectations can have an influence on teacher behavior, then, they do not always matter. What appears to be more important is whether the instructor monitors student achievements and takes corrective action as necessary.

Sensory memory, attention, and pattern recognition, while important, obviously tell only part of the story. When learners have paid sufficient attention and pattern recognition of selected portions of the stimulus has occurred, a great deal more processing is still required for the information to become a meaningful and permanent part of memory. The next stage of activity occurs in working memory.

WORKING MEMORY

Information selected for further processing comes to the working memory, also known as the short-term memory or short-term store. At this stage, concepts from long-term memory will be activated for use in making sense of the incoming information. But, as indicated earlier in the chapter, there are limits to how much information can be held in working memory at one time and for how long information may be retained there, unless, of course, something is done to increase capacity or duration in some way.

In a now classic study of short-term memory, George Miller (1956) demonstrated that about 7 ± 2 numbers could be recalled in a digit-span test. This test consisted of reading subjects a list of numbers and asking them to immediately repeat what they had heard. With seven items being the typical memory span, is it any surprise that local phone numbers are exactly seven digits? Miller also whimsically wondered whether there are magical qualities to the number seven; after all, there are "the seven wonders of the world, the seven seas, the seven deadly sins, the seven daughters of Atlas in the Pleiades, the seven ages of man, the seven levels of hell, the seven primary colors, the seven notes of the musical scale, and the seven days of the week" (Miller, 1967, pp. 42–43).

Despite Miller's whimsy, seven bits of information have been shown to constitute the memory span for a great variety of materials. Moreover, each bit of information can vary tremendously in size. A ten-letter word, for example, may be one bit, along with a six-word sentence. Discovery of this fact has led to the notion that *working memory capacity may be increased through creating larger bits*, known as the process of **chunking**. Take, for example, the span of letters shown below.

JFKFBIAIDSNASAMIT

As individual letters, they more than exceed working memory capacity. But as five chunks—JFK, FBI, AIDS, NASA, and MIT—they are easily processed.

What this has been taken to mean for instruction is that learning tasks should be organized so that they can be easily chunked by the learner. This may be as simple as breaking complex tasks into manageable steps, as in a science experiment, or presenting discrete bits of information to be studied and practiced, as in the frames of a computer-based tutorial lesson. In addition, issues in political science that involve very complex arguments, for example, will be better understood if the arguments are broken down and examined bit by bit.

How chunks of information are actually stored in working memory has been likened to a series of slots, with each chunk taking up one slot. As new chunks come into memory, they push out those that were previously occupying the available spaces. This is now the accepted explanation for the serial position effect known as recency. In the serial position task, subjects are given a list of words or nonsense syllables to learn. Typically, fifteen or twenty items are presented at a rapid rate, and immediately following the last item subjects recall as many as they can. You can guess which ones they recall best—the items at the end of the list or those seen most recently. It was assumed, then, that later items on the list pushed out of memory those which had been seen first. There was simply not enough room for them all.

To determine the duration of working memory, Brown (1958) and Peterson and Peterson (1959) presented subjects with sets of three letters they were to recall after brief intervals. What seems like an easy task becomes much more difficult when rehearsal is prevented during the retention interval. That is, subjects had to count backwards by threes from a given number until the retention interval was up. Results indicated that memory for the letters was still good after only 3 seconds, but after 18 seconds decay was nearly complete. Given individual differences, it is generally accepted that unrehearsed information will be lost from working memory in about 15 to 30 seconds. In the days of the rotary dial, this is about the same amount of time it took to dial a number and get a busy signal!

In order to prevent the loss of information from working memory, and to ensure its being transferred to long-term storage, two processes are necessary: rehearsal and encoding.

Rehearsal

When you repeat a phone number to yourself over and over while waiting to use the phone, you are engaged in rehearsal. Some would call this maintenance rehearsal because the repetition serves to maintain the information in the working memory for some designated period of time. Once you have made the call and reached your party, you no longer have the need to maintain the phone number in the short-term store.

Rehearsal has been used to explain the primacy effect of the serial position curve. When items are presented as described earlier, but at a slower rate, subjects remember not only the last items on the list, but the first ones as well (Figure 3–6). You can imagine why. With only a few items in memory at the beginning of the list, subjects have time between items to rehearse all the items they have seen. As more items crowd in, however, the rehearsal task becomes more difficult, so that items in the middle of the list receive less practice. As before, items at the end are recalled well because they are still in working memory at the time of recall.

Whereas recency and primacy effects are ostensibly associated with short-term memory, there is anecdotal data to suggest that something similar goes on even after information should be in long-term memory. For example, if a pop quiz is given after a typical 50-minute lecture, chances are students will remember best what was discussed in the first 10 minutes of class and in the last 10 minutes before the quiz. Likewise, most journalists adhere to the maxim that important information should go at the beginning and end of their articles, because these are the paragraphs best remembered

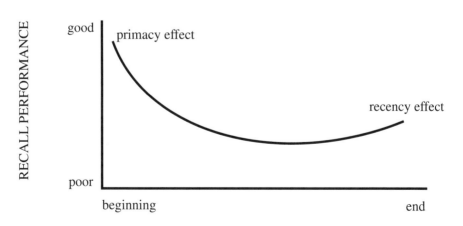

POSITION OF ITEM IN LIST

FIGURE   3–6   Serial Postion Curve

by readers. These phenomena have led some researchers to question the dual stage nature of memory and to propose instead some sort of intermediate memory or a continuum from short-term to long-term memory.

Finally, for information to reach a relatively permanent state in long-term memory, maintenance rehearsal is not enough. Learners will argue that simple repetition is an effective means for them to remember something for a long time. In the case of highly overlearned material, such as arithmetic facts, spelling words, or a memorized script, they are probably right. But repetition of more complex and meaningful information will not ensure its being fully processed into long-term memory. Elaborative rehearsal, or encoding, will.

Encoding

Encoding refers to the process of relating incoming information to concepts and ideas already in memory in such a way that the new material is more memorable. Left to their natural inclinations, humans will always try to make things meaningful, to fit some new experience into the fabric of what they already know. We have already seen the evidence of this in perception and attention. Encoding serves to make permanent what these processes have initiated.

Studies demonstrating the various ways in which encoding may take place are too numerous to review in any comprehensive fashion here. But it is useful to consider briefly the major types of encoding schemes that have been investigated. The concept of organization, to begin with, has long been of interest to psychologists and educators alike. Bousfield (1953) found that people will group related pieces of information into categories in order to learn and remember them better. Even when information is seemingly unrelated, learners will impose their own, subjective organization on the material in order to learn it (Tulving, 1962). To assist learners in organizing material meaningfully, outlines (Glynn & Divesta, 1977), hierarchies (Bower, Clark, Lesgold, and Winzenz, 1969), and concept trees (see the examples provided in Chapter 2 and later in this chapter [Tessmer & Driscoll, 1986]) have all proven effective.

Mnemonics and mediation (Matlin, 1983) provide other effective means for encoding. Learning a list of unrelated words, for example, is facilitated by linking the words together in the form of a story (Bower and Clark, 1969). The story then serves as a mediator to make the words on the list, which are meaningless by themselves, more memorable. This can be a helpful strategy for young children to use while learning to read. By themselves, single words may not have much meaning at first. But when children write stories incorporating certain words, they often find it easier to read and recognize these words later. Similarly, mnemonics such as ROY G BIV or "My Very Earnest Mother Just Showed Us Nine Planets" serve to aid in the learning and recall of the colors in the spectrum and the planets in our solar system (see reviews of mnemonic strategies by Higbee [1979] and Bellezza [1981]).

Finally, imagery can be a very effective means of encoding information. Studies have shown that pictures suggesting visual images (Levin & Kaplan, 1972) or simply instructions to form images related to text material (Kulhavy & Swenson, 1975) are effective in facilitating learning. Some teachers now find that combining this method with story creation as described can be a very powerful means for facilitating not only learning but motivation (D. Cooper, personal communication, September, 1992). Children "publish" their stories by drawing illustrations to accompany them. In so doing, they strengthen their understanding of words in a very personal, meaningful way.

Before leaving this topic, it is perhaps wise to point out that nearly any method of elaborative encoding is better for learning than mere repetition of information. But which approach is best depends upon the learners and the material to be learned. Moreover, learners who have developed idiosyncratic but effective encoding strategies will not necessarily benefit from some strategy imposed by the instruction. For this reason, there has been considerable interest recently in determining how learners may be taught to develop and use their own strategies effectively (cf. Pressley & Levin, 1983; Levin & Pressley, 1986; Segal, Chipman, & Glaser, 1985).

Learners may be encouraged to invent their own mnemonics, for example. Instructors in a driving under the influence program who attended a workshop I presented invented the acronym VOMIT to remind themselves of the effects of drinking on the driving task. (I no longer recall what the individual letters stand for, but no doubt they do! This just illustrates how individually effective mnemonics can be; what works for one learner may not for another.)

Self-questioning has also been investigated as a means for learners to encode information they hear in lectures or read in printed instructional materials. Sometimes learners ask themselves questions to aid in comprehending material, such as, "How does the meaning of this concept differ from what was discussed on the previous page?" Other questions, which call for drawing inferences, should help learners to integrate new information with what they have already learned.

In reviewing research on self-questioning as an encoding strategy, Snowman (1986) pointed out that some learners must be taught how to frame good questions if the strategy is to be effective. Some teachers do this as early as the second grade by asking their students, "What could you ask yourself to be sure you understand ___ ?," and then providing feedback on the students' responses (S. Briggs, personal communication, October, 1992). But Ormrod (1990) speculated that it might be just a matter of students asking fact-based, low-level questions because they have learned to expect such questions on class examinations. Perhaps requiring learners to demonstrate inferential thinking in class and on assessments will prompt them to generate more inferential self-questions at encoding.

It may seem, in this discussion of working memory, that some aspects of permanent memory have already been touched upon, and indeed they have. It is virtually impossible to divorce the processes of working memory from those of long-term memory completely, because they are intimately related. Encoding, for example, by virtue of its role in transforming information as it passes from working to long-term memory, could be as easily discussed under the framework of the latter as the former. Encoding will continue to play an important role as we now consider what happens to information when it reaches long-term memory.

LONG-TERM MEMORY

Do you remember what you had for dinner last night? Or what you did on your birthday last year? Perhaps you recall a visit to another country where the most memorable events were your donkey ride down a steep embankment, the shopkeeper who offered you ouzo at nine o'clock in the morning, and the hotel manager who kept repeating, "So sorry. No reservation." Now consider how these memories differ from your knowledge that Albany, not New York City, is the capital of New York and that reading a weather map will tell you whether to expect rain in the next few days. Although these are all examples of information you retain in long-term memory, they differ in whether they represent specific experiences unique to you or general knowledge of the world that is shared by others.

Tulving (1972) was the first to make the distinction between episodic and semantic memory. He conceived of these as two information-processing systems, each selectively receiving information, retaining certain aspects of that information, and retrieving the information as required. Episodic memory is memory for specific events, as when you remember the circumstances surrounding how you learned to read a weather map. Semantic memory, on the other hand, refers to all the general information stored in memory that can be recalled independently of how it was learned. For example, perhaps you cannot remember how you learned to read a weather map, because the circumstances surrounding the event were not particularly memorable. But you do remember the skill.

Although the two systems are related, it is semantic memory that most concerns educators. Generally, what is supposed to be learned in school, or indeed in any instructional situation, is semantic in nature. Before 1972, Tulving argued, most memory research concerned episodic learning. Since then, however, researchers have focused primarily on semantic memory, devising theories for how semantic information is represented in memory, how it is retrieved for use, and how it is forgotten. These questions provide the basis for discussion in the next several sections.

The Question of Memory Representation

How information is represented in semantic memory is a central issue in the study of long-term memory (LTM) and one that has concerned researchers for centuries. Consider the difficulty of the task. Questions must be answered such as, What is the nature of the knowledge unit that is stored in memory? How are relations among these units represented? How can we account for individual differences in memory? Is there only one kind of knowledge unit, or are visual images substantively different from verbal propositions? Try to keep these questions in mind as some of the proposed answers are presented.

Network Models of LTM

One way to conceive of long-term memory is to think of it as a sort of mental dictionary (Klatzky, 1980), but instead of words being represented alphabetically, concepts are represented according to their associations to one another. For example, if I say "black," what comes to mind? I expect you said "white," which is closely associated with *black* by virtue of being its opposite. Other kinds of associations are obviously possible. A *canary* is a kind of bird, while *has gills* is a property of fish.

Network models assume the existence of nodes in memory, which correspond to concepts, i.e., things and properties. These nodes are thought to be interconnected in a vast network structure that represents learned relationships among concepts. Collins and Quillian (1969) proposed one of the earliest network models, but others are still being refined (e.g., Anderson & Bower, 1973; Anderson, 1976, 1983).

Network models have the advantage of representing individual differences among learners, because individual learning histories presumably lead to different memory networks. These models also enable predictions, which can be easily verified by the performance of learners on certain memory tasks. For example, look at the partial network shown in Figure 3–7. That memory might be structured this way can be ascertained by asking subjects to respond to sentences such as, "A bird has wings," or "A blue heron is a fish." Since the concept *bird* points to the property *has wings*

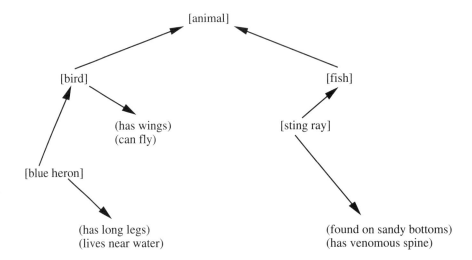

FIGURE   3–7   A Partial Network Representing Concepts Associated with Animal, in the Tradition of Collins and Quillian

(assuming this was a learned relationship), the subject should say the first sentence is true. In the case of the second sentence, however, *blue heron* and *fish* cannot be directly connected, because the search process can only proceed in the direction indicated by the arrow. Thus, this sentence must be false.

In a similar fashion, predictions can be made about the speed at which subjects should be able to verify sentences as true. For example, learners should be faster in recognizing the truth of "A blue heron has long legs" than "A blue heron is an animal." In the first case, search had to proceed across only one pointer; in the second case, two pointers, or levels of memory, are searched.

Predictions such as these were, in fact, confirmed by Collins and Quillian (1969), providing experimental support for the network models. But they also encountered some troubling findings. Subjects more quickly recognized a canary as a bird, for example, than a penguin as a bird, yet recognition times should be equal since the distance in both cases is the same. Typicality of concepts, then, presented a real difficulty for network models, which was to be overcome by feature comparison models of long-term memory.

Feature Comparison Models of LTM

Smith, Shoben, and Rips (1974) proposed that concepts in memory were not stored in interconnected hierarchies, as suggested by network models, but with sets of defining features. Association to other concepts is then accomplished through a comparison of overlapping features, hence, the label feature comparison models. For example, to verify "A blue heron is a bird," an individual would search all the characteristics of *blue heron* and all those of *bird*, and finding a sufficient overlap, would say the sentence is true.

Feature comparison models nicely explained the typicality effects so troubling to network models. Some concepts simply do not have clearly defined members; they are "fuzzy sets" in which some members are better examples of the concept than others. Thus, feature comparison models distinguished between defining and characteristic features. Defining features are those that a bird, for example, must have in order for it to be classified in that category. Characteristic features, on the other hand, are those that are usually associated with typical members of the category. That most birds fly is an example. Thus, canaries are more quickly recognized as birds than penguins because they are more typical than penguins, which swim instead of fly. In a similar way, it takes longer to say that a bat is not a bird, because bats share features characteristic of birds even while the match on defining characteristics is poor.

Since there are a great many real world concepts of the fuzzy type (Kintsch, 1974), feature comparison models can seem very attractive. But they are not particularly economical, i.e., large collections of features would be required for learning, and the models make no claims about how such collections would be organized. Finally, semantic comparison models have been criticized for their failure to account for semantic flexibility. That is, context can cause certain aspects of a concept's meaning to be more or less prominent. If you hear, "Help me move the piano," you will probably think of it as a heavy piece of furniture, but the sentence, "You play the piano beautifully" emphasizes its musical aspect (Barclay, Bransford, Franks, McCarrell, and Nitsch, 1974).

Propositional Models of LTM

How different from one another are network and feature comparison models? In posing this question, Klatzky (1980) cited evidence that feature comparison models may in fact be rewritten as enhanced network models. Perhaps for this reason, the network has remained the primary metaphor for long-term memory. Propositional models, however, offered a new twist to the network idea. Instead of concept nodes comprising the basic unit of knowledge that is stored in memory, propositional models take this basic unit to be the proposition (Anderson & Bower, 1973). A proposition is a combination of concepts that has a subject and predicate. So, for example, instead of the concept *bird* representing a node in memory, the propositions "A bird has wings," "A bird flies," and "A bird has feathers" are stored.

There appears to be some psychological reality to the notion of propositions, because subjects will take longer to read sentences containing many propositions than those containing few, even when the number of actual words is the same (Kintsch, 1974). In addition, recall tends to reflect propositional structure rather than sentence structure. For example, suppose you read the following sentence as part of a passage on shorebirds: "The blue heron, a tall bird with a long neck and long legs, can usually be found in the marshy areas near water." Asked to recall later what you had read, you would be unlikely to reproduce this sentence. Instead, you might recall some of the ideas, or propositions, expressed in it, such as: "The blue heron is a tall bird. It has long legs and a long neck. It lives near water." For this reason, propositions have been used as a measure of recall in some memory experiments (e.g., Royer & Cable, 1975; Royer & Perkins, 1977).

One of the most well-developed network models that emphasizes propositional structure is adaptive control of thought (ACT) (Anderson, 1976). Based on an earlier model called human associative memory (Anderson and Bower, 1973), ACT has undergone extensive testing and modification to reach its present configuration ACT* (Anderson, 1983).

Parallel Distributed Processing (PDP) Models of LTM

One of the newest approaches to modeling long-term memory takes as its driving force the notion of parallel processing. Parallel processing is distinguished from serial processing in that parallel processes occur more or less simultaneously while serial processes occur sequentially, in a linear fashion. As an example of the difference, think back to the sentence verification task used to test network models. If the test sentence was, "A blue heron is an animal," serial processing dictates that the search would start at *blue heron* and proceed along the pathways connected to the concept, one pathway at a time. In parallel processing, however, all possible pathways would be searched simultaneously. It should be obvious that parallel processing predicts much faster verification times than serial processing.

The assumption of parallel processing has been popular with recent network models (e.g., Anderson, 1983), but it becomes central to parallel distributed processing (PDP), or connectionist, models of memory. (Connectionist models refer to a class of models, some of which—including the PDP models—attempt to describe cognition at a behavioral level while others seek to describe the actual neural patterns of the brain, as in chapter 6.) The PDP models have been primarily developed by McClelland, Rumelhart, and the PDP Research Group (1986) and are reviewed by McClelland (1988) and Estes (1988).

PDP models propose that the building blocks of memory are not concept nodes, not semantic features, not propositions, but units and connections (McClelland,1988). These are subsymbolic in nature, which means that they do not correspond to meaningful bits of information like concept nodes or propositions do. Instead, the units are simple processing devices, and connections describe how the units interact with each other. They form a vast network across which processing is assumed to be distributed. When learning occurs, environmental input (or input from within the network) activates the connections among units, strengthening some connections while weakening others. It is these patterns of activation that represent concepts and principles or knowledge as we think of it. This means that knowledge is stored in the connections among processing units.

Bereiter (1991) offered a "rough physical analogy" for understanding how a connectionist network might operate:

> *Imagine that in the middle of a bare room you have a pile of a hundred or more frisbees, which are connected among themselves by means of elastic bands that vary in thickness and length. On each wall is a clamp to which you fasten a frisbee. Take any four frisbees and clamp one to each wall. There will be an oscillation set up as those four frisbees pull on the other ones, and those pull on each other. In time, the oscillations will cease, and the frisbee population will settle into a pattern that reflects an equilibrium among the tensions exerted by the elastic bands. (p. 12)*

If one were to change which frisbees are clamped to the wall or the lengths or thicknesses of the bands connecting the frisbees, oscillation would reoccur and a new pattern would settle out.

Because connections among units are assumed to carry different weights of association, learning occurs in the continual adjustment of the weights. Moreover, since processing occurs in parallel, many different adjustments can take place simultaneously, and there can be continuous error adjustments as a function of new information.

Perhaps an example will bring some level of concreteness to this discussion. Consider, once again, the canary as bird and penguin as bird knowledge that we acquire. PDP models claim that experience with birds will activate a great number of units and connections, in order to represent the various aspects about birds. Experience with canaries will strengthen certain connections—those, for example, that represent the typical characteristics of birds. Experience with penguins will inhibit some bird connections, primarily those that deal with flying. So at a later time, subjects will be faster to recognize a canary as a bird than a penguin, because its connections to bird are stronger.

PDP models offer a number of advantages over the other models in terms of what they explain about human information processing. First, they seem to account well for the incremental nature of human learning. With constant readjustment of connection weights, they provide a more dynamic picture of human learning than has been suggested heretofore (Estes, 1988). PDP models also offer "for the first time a convenient way of incorporating goals into the dynamics of information processing systems" (Estes, 1988, p. 207). That is, connection weights in most PDP systems are adjusted to reduce disparity between their output and some target output, which may be viewed as a goal.

Finally, there is potential in PDP models to explain cognitive development (McClelland, 1988). Some knowledge, in terms of prewired connection weights, can be built into the network. Exploring different configurations of initial memory architecture may lead to breakthroughs in determining just how much of human memory is "hard-wired."

Estes (1988) sounded some cautionary notes, however, concerning the conclusions over the long term to which PDP models may lead. He cited the lack of forthcoming evidence to support PDP models as a mirror of neural processes in the brain. He reminded us that there is little reason to believe a single processor model will be sufficient to model brain functions. After all, "the evolution of the brain has not yielded a machine of uniform design like a digital computer but rather a melange of systems and subsystems of different evolutionary ages" (Estes, 1988, p. 206). He concluded that the final test of any theory will come in the record of extended research that follows from it.

Representation of Imagery

To this point, only verbal information and its representation have been discussed. Yet, ask anyone what imagery is, and the response is likely to be, "pictures in my mind." Does this mean that imaginal information is represented in some way different from verbal information? How do we account for the variety of imaginal information, especially since there is more to imagery than just visual representations? We can imagine the tune of a favorite song, or the feel of a kitten's fur against our skin—examples of auditory and tactile imagery, respectively. In the same way, it is possible to generate examples of olfactory imagery ("Is that a hot apple pie I smell?") as well as kinesthetic imagery, which is often used in relaxation training.

Despite our subjective impressions of imagery, not all psychologists have been convinced of its existence as a separate form of information storage (e.g., Pylyshyn, 1973). Some investigations of visual imagery, for example, have shown that people remember a picture's meaning, rather than its visual attributes (e.g., Bower, Karlin, & Dueck, 1975; Light & Berger, 1976). This supports a unitary view of visual and verbal coding, which means that information about pictures is assumed to be represented in the same way as verbal information.

Other research, however, has challenged the unitary view. In a series of experiments conducted by Shepard and his associates (reviewed in

Shepard, 1978), subjects appeared to mentally rotate images of three-dimensional figures in order to find their match among sets of distractors. That is, the amount of time it took to find a match was directly related to the number of turns required to rotate the test figure to the position of its match. This result held true even when subjects were given verbal instructions so that they had to rely on information in memory to generate the images.

The superiority of memory for concrete words over abstract words also poses problems for a unitary view of memory representation. People find it much easier to remember words like *sailboat*, *apple*, and *zebra* when they appear on a list than words such as *liberty* and *justice* (see, for example, Paivio, Yuille, & Rogers, 1969). If a dual-code or dual-systems approach is taken, however, these results are easy to explain. According to the dual-systems view (Paivio, 1971), there are two systems of memory representation, one for verbal information and the other for nonverbal information. Thus, for input such as concrete words, two codes are possible. The meaning of the words can be represented by the verbal system, but images of the words can also be represented by the imaginal system. With two memories available at recall, as opposed to one for abstract words, subjects should remember concrete words better.

Exactly how the imaginal system operates to store visual or other imaginal information is not known, although dual code theorists agree that mental images are not exact copies of visual displays. Images tend to be imprecise representations, with many details omitted, incomplete, or, in some cases, inaccurately recorded. They also require effort to maintain and have parts that fade in and out (Kosslyn, 1980). Think of someone you know well, for example, and try to visualize that person's face. Does he or she wear eyeglasses, and can you remember what they look like? Chances are you may remember verbally whether your friend wears glasses and then try to reconstruct visually what he/she looks like.

Researchers assume a strong connection between the verbal and imaginal systems, and for this reason, directions to form images and visual aids to instruction are both likely to enhance learning of some verbal material. Kosslyn (1980) suggested that images may be important to learning in enabling learners to represent what is not depicted in the instruction and then to transform these representations to facilitate comprehension and problem solving. Visual aids can function in the same way, particularly for learners with poor verbal skills (cf. Levin 1983).

Retrieval of Learned Information

Once information has been stored in long-term memory, no matter in what form, it can be retrieved for use, retained over time, or forgotten. The process of **retrieval** from long-term memory is relatively simple to understand. Previously learned information is brought back to mind, either for the purpose of understanding some new input or for making a response. Using previous knowledge to understand and learn new material has already been discussed as encoding. But making a response based on previous knowledge raises the question, What kind of response? Consider the two questions below. Which question is likely to be more difficult to answer?

1. What does the word *esoteric* mean?
2. Which of the following words is the best synonym for *esoteric*?
   a. essential
   b. mystical
   c. terrific
   d. evident

Clearly, the first question is harder than the second because it provides fewer clues as to what the answer might be. This distinction between cued and noncued retrieval is the same as the difference between recall and recognition. To recall information, learners must both generate an answer and then determine whether it correctly answers the question. In recognition, however, potential answers are already generated, and the learner must only recognize which one is correct.

Recall
In free recall situations, learners must retrieve previously stored information with no cues or hints to help them remember. Subjects in many memory experiments, for example, are exposed to target information and then told to "write down everything you can remember about what you just read." Similarly, instructors ask such recall questions on tests as, "Write an essay about America's involvement in World War II," or "Describe the connectionist view of human memory." Because there are no cues present to potentially bias retrieval, the output of free recall is assumed to represent accurately what is in memory. However, researchers have found that the amount subjects recall under these conditions tends to be low. Providing them with cues raises the overall amount subjects are able to remember.

Cued recall tasks, then, are those in which a hint or cue is provided to help learners remember the desired information. This happens, for example, when teachers add qualifiers to their essay questions, such as "Be sure to discuss the role Pearl Harbor played in changing America's war policies." Leahey and Harris (1989) also cited the example of an actor learning lines as a cued recall task. Each line serves as a cue for remembering the next line.

Recognition

Recognition, in contrast to recall, involves a set of pregenerated stimuli presented to learners for a decision or judgment. In some cases, learners are asked to determine whether the stimulus information has been seen before, as in old-new recognition tasks. Tasks of this nature are common in memory experiments, but are becoming increasingly popular for assessing reading comprehension (e.g., Royer, Lynch, Hambleton & Bulgareli, 1984). For example, students read a target passage and then complete a sentence verification test. On the sentence verification test are test sentences of four types: (1) an original sentence from the passage; (2) a paraphrase of the original sentence in which the words are changed but the meaning is retained; (3) a meaning change sentence in which one or two words in the original sentence are replaced to alter its meaning; and (4) a distractor sentence which is consistent with the gist of the passage but unrelated to the original sentence. Students who comprehended the passage should be able to recognize the original and paraphrase sentences as old and classify the meaning change and distractor sentences as new. Those who fail to comprehend the meaning of the passage, on the other hand, are likely to think that the meaning change and distractor sentences are old on the basis of their similarity to sentences in the passage.

Two factors appear to influence old-new recognition. The most obvious is the strength of the memory trace, in that stronger memories will be more accurately recognized than weaker memories. But regardless of the strength of a memory trace, a decision must still be made about its match to the test stimulus. Imagine, for example, that you are choosing drapes to match the color of your living room carpet. You must make a decision concerning a particular set of drapes from your memory of the carpet's color. Now consider two possible scenarios: (1) the drapes are inexpensive, and besides, you can return them if the color is a poor match, (2) the drapes are expensive, must be paid for in advance, and cannot be returned. In which scenario are you more likely to make a yes decision?

The second factor influencing yes-no or old-new recognition is a decision criterion based on the context surrounding the recognition task. High-risk conditions lead to a more stringent criterion than low-risk conditions, even though the memory trace in both situations is equivalent in strength and match to the test stimulus.

Besides yes-no recognition, there is also forced-choice recognition as exemplified in multiple-choice tests. As before, memory strength plays a role in the decision to choose a particular answer. The decision criterion, however, is determined not only by risk conditions surrounding the overall task, but by the distractors in each test item. That is, a severe penalty for wrong answers will decrease guessing overall, even though, in a four-distractor item, the chances of getting an item right by pure guessing is 25 percent. But suppose, in question 2, you could eliminate two of the distractors immediately. This increases to 50 percent the chances of getting the answer right, high enough odds, perhaps, to offset the penalty. An obvious implication of this for test construction is to write distractors that have equal probability of being chosen if the learner is forced to guess.

Retrieval Cues

Regardless of expected response type, the process of retrieval can be greatly influenced by the cues available to learners at test time. Two different principles have been investigated by researchers that suggest a relationship between conditions at encoding and conditions at recall.

The **encoding specificity** principle states, in essence, that *whatever cues are used by a learner to facilitate encoding will also serve as the best retrieval cues* for that information at test time (Thomson & Tulving, 1970; Tulving & Thomson, 1973). To illustrate, Anderson and Ortony (1975) gave subjects the sentences, "The container held the apples" and "The container held the cola." What images come to mind when you read those sentences? Most likely, you encoded an apple basket and a cola bottle. In fact, Anderson and Ortony found that *basket* served as an effective retrieval cue for the first sentence but not the second, while *bottle* served as a good cue for the second sentence but not the first.

Retrieval, then, is very much influenced by the context of encoding. This suggests for instruction that many different contexts or examples may be important to discuss during the presentation of new concepts. In this way, students will have many cues available to assist in encoding that may later be used for recall. If new information is presented in only one context, students may not find sufficient cues in test questions to support retrieval of information that is actually in memory.

Related to encoding specificity is the concept of state-dependent learning. Some years ago, a study was conducted in which subjects learned lists of paired words in one situation and recalled the lists in a different situation (Bilodeau & Schlosberg, 1951). The situations differed in the rooms in which the sessions (whether learning or testing) took place, whether the subjects were standing or sitting, and the method of list presentation. Results indicated that recall was best for those who were instructed and tested in the same situation. When the instructional situation differed from the testing situation, recall suffered. More recent studies on the effects of drugs have suggested that these recall differences can be explained in terms of the subjects' state of mind during learning and testing. Information learned in a particular state of mind (e.g., free from the influence of alcohol or other drugs) will be remembered best in the same state of mind (Goodwin, Powell, Bremer, Hoine & Stern, 1969).

Bower (1981) has demonstrated a similar phenomenon with moods. Words learned under a happy mood were better recalled under a happy mood than a sad mood, and words learned under a sad mood were best recalled in that state. Bower argued that emotions, just like information, are coded in memory. And indeed it seems likely that chemical changes in the brain induced by drugs, strong emotions, and learning may all be similarly explained.

Forgetting

At some point, all theories of memory must address the phenomenon of forgetting. We all forget things, but we may do so for many different possible reasons. The most common explanations for forgetting are failure to encode, failure to retrieve, and interference.

Failure to encode simply means that *the information sought during retrieval was never learned in the first place*. Learners often have the illusion of knowing. Poor readers, for example, typically do not monitor their reading very well and so believe they have read and understood something when they have not done so. Learners with ineffective study strategies face the same problem. They tend to equate effort with learning rather than monitor the actual effects of their learning strategies. A student in one of my classes, for example, could not understand why she had achieved such a low score on one of the examinations. "But I studied for hours!" she wailed. When I asked how she had studied, she looked back at me blankly—by rereading her notes and the book, of course. Repetition can only go so far. Elaboration may have helped to ensure that course material was solidly encoded in memory.

Failure to retrieve information that has been encoded in memory is a second cause of forgetting and refers to *the inability to access previously learned information*. This is something like losing the directory to your computer's hard drive. The files are still there, but without the appropriate cues (i.e., file names), they cannot be accessed and retrieved. Issues of encoding specificity and state-dependent learning have obvious relevance here. The more cues that are used in encoding, the more likely one or another of them will be available to facilitate retrieval. In addition, assuming the validity of the dual-code theory, the more often encoding cues are generated in both the verbal and imaginal systems, the more likely retrieval will be facilitated.

A common strategy for enhancing retrieval is note-taking (Gagné & Driscoll, 1988). This is sometimes known as an external retrieval strategy (Kiewra, 1985; Kiewra & Frank, 1988; Kiewra, DuBois, Christian, McShane, Meyerhoffer, & Roskelley, 1991) because its product—notes—serves as memory storage external to the learner. Students who elaborate on their notes also tend to perform better than those who simply reread them (Peper & Mayer, 1978), in essence optimizing the effects of encoding together with external retrieval.

Finally, long before the development of information processing theory, interference was proposed as a cause of forgetting, which meant that *other events or information got in the way of effective retrieval*. McGeoch (1932) described forgetting of verbal materials in terms of two major laws. According to the first, forgetting was considered to be a function of the similarity between the circumstances of learning and testing, much as encoding specificity accounts for retrieval and forgetting now. The second set forth the conditions of interference, i.e., that numerous events and competing information can interfere with the retrieval of target information. Moreover, interference can occur from information learned either before or after the to-be-remembered information is learned. For example, retroactive interference has occurred when you read this chapter, read the next chapter, and then have difficulty recalling information from this chapter. Later learning interferes with the recall of earlier learned material, particularly as practice on the later material increases. This makes sense when we consider that information learned later is more recent and thus probably yields stronger memory traces than information learned earlier.

It is also possible, however, for previous learning to interfere with later learning. This is known as proactive interference, and the degree of interference is related to the amount of practice on the original task. Take, for example, the case of a long-time tennis player trying to learn racquetball. Since both are racket sports, it seems reasonable to believe that knowing one would facilitate learning the other. Instead, the well-learned skill of swinging a tennis racket interferes with the recently learned response of swinging a racquetball racket. Many players will find themselves swinging with the entire arm, as in tennis, rather than with just the wrist.

Proactive interference of a kind has also been demonstrated in the learning and memory of verbal materials by aging adults. Rice and Meyer (1985) investigated so-called memory deficits among older adults. Results of some studies had indicated that older adults remember less from a prose passage than younger adults. In the series of experiments Rice and Meyer conducted, however, they found no evidence to support a memory deficit. Instead, they found that older adults, because they had so much more experience and prior knowledge, tended to get caught up in the details of the passage (which prompted reminiscing) and lose sight of the main ideas they were to recall. In other words, proactive interference had occurred. When main ideas were signaled, however, the effects of the interference were averted, and older adults remembered just as much as younger readers.

In a recent review of studies conducted with aging adults, Fry (1992) reached similar conclusions, and he suggested several concrete ways in which practitioners can help older adults learn and remember. For instance, visual displays of how the subject matter is structured and concepts related can provide useful encoding and retrieval cues. Similarly, because problems in the learning and remembering of adults seem to be a function of declining speed rather than declining mental powers, allowing adults to work at their own pace is a desirable instructional strategy. Finally, like children, adults can be taught more effective strategies for encoding and retrieval (Fry, 1992).

There is no denying that memory failure can also be caused by other conditions, such as amnesia or Alzheimer's disease. These causes, however, have relatively little relevance to instruction and are therefore beyond the scope of this chapter.

Implications of LTM for Instruction

Reflect for a moment on the characteristics and processes of long-term memory that have been discussed to this point. What might they imply for various features of instruction? Three general recommendations emerge. First, instruction should present or encourage multiple representations of material to be learned. Whether imagery is represented in the same or a different system from verbal information, it appears to enhance learning and retrieval. Second, instruction should be organized to maximize retrieval possibilities. Since retrieval and encoding are intimately linked, this means that the possibilities for encoding should also be maximized. Numerous ways to do this exist, a few of which will be reviewed here. Finally, instruction should employ or encourage strategies for minimizing or counteracting interference.

There are two ways to approach these recommendations, and they provide a reasonable framework for discussing in greater depth some of the instructional implications of LTM that researchers have investigated. The first way is to consider the organization of the instruction itself. The second is to examine how learners themselves have control over memory storage and retrieval processes.

Organization of Instruction

How might instruction be organized to provide for multiple representations of information, to enhance encoding and retrieval, and to counteract the effects of interference? There are doubtless many answers to this question, but let me suggest a few.

In his model for designing instruction, Merrill (1983) proposed a type of instructional presentation form he called "representational elaboration" or "alternate representation" (p. 308). Following the presentation of initial primary information, an instructor or designer may wish to present additional information. This information, according to Merrill, is designed to facilitate learning but is secondary to the major purpose of the instruction. It consists of elaborations of the primary information, and one way to provide this elaboration is to present the primary information in some form other than the way it was originally presented. So, for example, a diagram, chart, or formula that is redundant with the primary information is considered to be an alternate representation.

Alternate representations have effectively facilitated encoding and memory storage of verbal information (refer to the discussion on imagery in the previous section) and conceptual information. Wilcox, Merrill, and Black (1981) found, for example, that a visually displayed conceptual hierarchy facilitated students' concept learning. Assuming a hierarchical network structure of memory, they reasoned that the conceptual hierarchy helped students to better encode concepts.

Taking a similar approach, Tessmer and Driscoll (1986) argued from Anderson's (1976) ACT model that students would better learn concepts if the propositional relationships among a set of concepts were displayed. They devised the concept tree (see Figure 3–8 for an example; refer also to Figure 2-2), which was found to enhance learning, especially for students with poorer reading skills.

As a means of assisting learners to abstract the meaningful dimensions of the concepts and develop the procedural knowledge required to make effective use of conceptual information, Driscoll and Tessmer (1985) also developed the **rational set generator**. It combines into one procedure the instructional criteria for teaching concept discrimination (i.e., distinguishing a given concept from other, similar ones) with those for teaching concept generalization (i.e., appropriately using a given concept in a number of contexts). The result is a rational set of examples that can be used in instruction or in testing (Figure 3–9). When used in testing, the examples can help to diagnose particular misconceptions where additional instruction may be warranted. The rational set generator has been applied by teachers in presenting examples for practice and in printed instruction. It has also recently been adapted for use as a template for presenting concept examples in computer-based instruction (Dempsey, 1986; Litchfield, Driscoll, and Dempsey, 1990; Dempsey, Driscoll, and Litchfield, in press).

Finally, if forgetting is caused by interference, especially when similar materials must be learned, "it stands to reason that interference would be reduced if the distinctive features of similar materials were emphasized. Emphasizing distinctive features and deliberately comparing and contrasting similar materials should help the student avoid confusion" (Anderson & Faust, 1973, p. 465). This recommendation may seem dated,

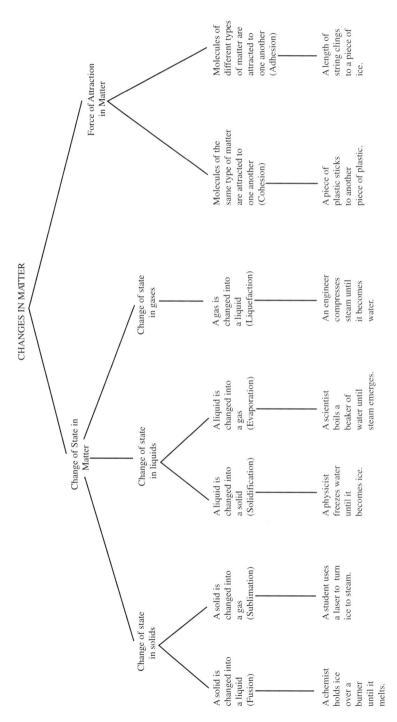

FIGURE 3–8 A Concept Tree for Changes in Matter

Source: Tessmer and Driscoll 1986, 197. Reprinted from *Educational Communication & Technology Journal* by permission of the Association for Educational Communications and Technology. Copyright 1986 by AECT.

SUBJECT MATTER CLASSES

	Science Physics Chemistry	Technology Industry Engineering	Art Homemaking Business Recreation
Fusion	A physicist uses an oven to convert aluminum to molten aluminum.	A blast furnace converts iron ore to molten steel.	A burning candle heats its wax until the wax runs down the side in drops.
Sublimation	A chemist electrifies a mound of sulfur, which releases sulfur fumes.	A steel factory burns 10 tons of coal a day, which creates a lot of coal fumes.	A ranger burns a bunch of tree limbs to make a smoke signal.
Solidification	A physics student puts some molten lead into the freezer to harden.	A blob of mud poured on a hot sidewalk soon becomes a pile of dirt.	After a volcanic eruption, lava cools to form lava rock.
Evaporation	A bottle of alcohol is heated to release alcohol fumes.	A drill engine burns gasoline while it runs, which ends up as exhaust.	A glass of soda left outside soon will dry up and become part of the atmosphere.
Liquefaction	A scientist sends electric jolts through a chamber of hydrogen and oxygen to create water.	An engineer uses a compressor to convert alcohol fumes back into alcohol.	When the sky is hit by lightning bolts, rain is often created.
Cohesion	A scientist discovers that glass plates can be joined by sliding one plate over another.	A doctor closes a small wound by pressing one piece of skin onto another one.	After a snowfall, a fresh layer of snow will cling to old layers of snow on the ground.
Adhesion	When a chemist pushes a piece of steel next to a piece of aluminum, they stick together.	A mechanic notices that oil clings to his rubber gloves.	A teacher runs a piece of chalk across a blackboard, which leaves a white mark on the board.

FIGURE   3–9   Examples of Changes in Matter From a Ratioal Set Generator

Source: Tessmer and Driscoll 1986, 199. Reprinted from *Educational Communication & Technology Journal* by permission of the Association for Educational Communications and Technology. Copyright 1986 by AECT.

but it still holds today. When instruction can be organized so that similarities and differences among similar concepts and ideas are made evident, interference should be minimized and learning facilitated.

Metacognition and Study Strategies

When we shift the focus from instruction to learners, different aspects of long-term memory become prominent, suggesting different sorts of instructional implications. Earlier in the chapter, executive control processes were mentioned that enable the learner to modify information flow within and between components of the memory system. These processes have been investigated under the rubric of metacognition (Flavell, 1979; Brown, 1980; Duell, 1986). **Metacognition** refers to *one's awareness of thinking and the self-regulatory behavior* (also known as conditional knowledge [cf. Prawatt, 1989]) *that accompanies this awareness*. "In the course of learning and problem solving, representative kinds of regulatory performance include: knowing when or what one knows or does not know; predicting the correctness or outcome of one's performance; planning ahead and efficiently apportioning the outcomes of one's cognitive resources and one's time; and checking and monitoring the outcomes of one's solution or attempt to learn" (Gagné & Glaser, 1987, p. 75).

What is currently known about metacognitive skills and their acquisition goes well beyond the scope of this chapter, and the interested reader is referred to Derry and Murphy (1986) and Duell (1986) for their excellent reviews on the topic. Research results generally indicate, however, that metacognitive ability depends on person variables, task variables, strategy variables, and the interaction among all three (Duell, 1986).

With respect to person variables, older learners seem to have a better understanding of their memory abilities and limitations than younger learners. Although students of all ages appear capable of learning various memory strategies, older learners are more planful and purposeful in their use of these strategies. Additionally, there is evidence that learning-disabled children are less efficient and less planful than normal children (Torgeson, 1977). This suggests that instructors should frequently remind younger and less planful learners when and how to use memory strategies.

Task variables refer to differences in instructional content that influence use of metacognitive strategies. For example, information that is new to learners will be approached with quite general learning strategies. As learners become more proficient in a subject or if the material they are to learn relates to a subject they know quite well already, they employ more domain-specific strategies (Gagné & Driscoll, 1988). For instructors to use or suggest the use of particular strategies, then, they should have some idea as to how much their students already know about the material to be learned.

Finally, strategy variables have to do with the metacognitive strategies themselves, the various ways in which learners may go about encoding, storing, and retrieving information. Some strategies are so simple that learners can acquire them easily by being told what to do. Breaking a complex or long learning task into manageable segments is one example. Other strategies, however, require extensive practice before they can be used easily and effectively. Taking notes or self-questioning with inferential questions may be examples of this type.

Educators generally agree on the importance of self-regulatory skills in learning, as will be especially evident in chapter 10. Successful learners seem to acquire and refine these skills throughout their school and learning history. But what about the less successful and proficient learners? Teaching learners to assume an active and purposeful role in their own learning has been a growing concern among instructors and researchers alike. Programs now exist to train students in metacognitive or study skills (e.g., Weinstein, 1982; Feuerstein, Rand, Hoffman & Miller, 1980; Dansereau, Collins, McDonald, Holley, Garland, Diekhoff, & Evans, 1979; De Bono, 1985; Wang & Palincsar, 1989). Some are aimed at college students, others at younger learners. Some concentrate on domain-specific skills pertaining to a particular subject, such as reading comprehension; others train more general strategies that may be useful across a broad range of tasks. And some programs are embedded within school curricula, while others exist as separate, study skills courses.

Despite the variety among these programs, those that are effective seem to have at least two criteria in common. First, students must have a base of prior knowledge that may be related to the strategies they are learning. Domain-specific strategies, in particular, are virtually useless when students know little about the subject to which they pertain. Second, students must know when and why various self-regulatory strategies may be effectively employed (e.g., Pressley, Borkowski, & O'Sullivan, 1984; Prawatt, 1989; Sawyer, Graham, & Harris, 1992). Knowing how to be planful is not enough to guarantee that one will be planful. Having such conditional knowledge does not guarantee that one will always use it. But realizing when and why such behavior will be useful in furthering learning goals helps to motivate students to engage in metacognitive, self-regulatory ways.

ALTERNATIVE CONCEPTIONS OF COGNITION

It is common practice to cast unfamiliar ideas and phenomena into more familiar terms and ways that are better understood. The same holds true in scientific endeavors, and Roediger (1980) reviewed the various metaphors that have been used by psychologists to understand and explain memory. He argued that the prominent metaphor in information processing theory is one of "actual, physical space, with memories and ideas as objects in that space" (Roediger, 1980, p. 232). For example, working memory has limited *room*, information in long-term memory is *organized*, we *search for* memories that have been *lost,* and so on. "Memories or memory traces are considered to be discrete objects in particular locations in the mind space" (Roediger, 1980, p. 232).

Although the spatial metaphor has served as a general and powerful explanation of human information processing, what happens when an alternative metaphor is adopted? According to Roediger, "perhaps the main argument for alternative theories is simply that competitors to the dominant theory may lead to interesting new experiments and facts that would not be discovered following the predominant way of thinking" (p. 239). There are, in fact, several alternative conceptions to the spatial metaphor that deserve our attention.

The Levels (Depth) Metaphor

Craik and Lockhart (1972) (see also Craik & Tulving, 1975; Jacoby & Craik, 1979) criticized the notion of memory components (sensory memory, short term memory, and long-term memory) and proposed instead a levels of processing model. According to this model, memory traces are a function of the depth to which incoming information is processed. When information is processed more deeply, it is more likely to be remembered.

The notion of depth was defined roughly in terms of three types of processing: physical, acoustic, and semantic. For example, if the word *heron* was a test stimulus, subjects might be asked to verify if it contains the letter *e* to prompt physical processing. To prompt acoustic processing, subjects could be told to find a word that rhymes with *heron* or be asked if there is an *n* sound in the word. Finally, semantic processing would involve storing the meaning of the word, so that subjects might be told that herons are long-legged shore birds or be asked to form an image of the bird. When researchers actually employed manipulations of this kind to test the theory, results were supportive. Learners remembered best items that had been semantically processed.

Unfortunately, a second prediction of the model failed to hold up. If depth of processing is the critical variable, then more processing at the same, shallower level should not improve memory. Nelson (1977) gave subjects two presentations of an item, accompanied by the same encoding task at the acoustic level. In other words, subjects would see a word such as *heron* and be asked, "Does the word have an *n* sound?" He found, contrary to the levels prediction, that subjects remembered more after two presentations than after only one. This means that factors other than depth must be taken into account in explaining memory performance.

Baddeley (1978) also criticized the levels of processing theory for its failure to provide an objective measure of depth. What is really meant by deep processing, however intuitively appealing the idea seems? Because there is consistency between the levels metaphor and elaborative encoding in the spatial metaphor, Klatzky (1980) and others have suggested that the two might be profitably reconciled. That is, both metaphors may serve in a complementary fashion to describe different aspects of memory. And as their predictions fail, or prove inadequate, modifications to both must be made.

The Construction (and Reconstruction) Metaphor

Earlier in the chapter, encoding was referred to as the process of relating new information to information already in memory. Little was said about the nature of this process except that elaboration involving the incoming material and prior knowledge serves to facilitate learning and remembering the new material. Concurrent with the development of dominant information processing concepts were arguments that initial perception and encoding of information is a **constructive** process, while remembering is a **reconstructive process**.

Bartlett (1932) was responsible for introducing the construction metaphor, when he argued that, "remembering is not the re-excitation of innumerable fixed, lifeless and fragmentary traces. It is an imaginative reconstruction, or construction" (Bartlett, 1932, p. 213). Bartlett asked his students to read the story, "The War of the Ghosts," and to recall it several times over a period of months. He found that students' recall of the events of the story was incomplete, as might be expected given the time lag. But more than that, in their recollections, the students tended to distort aspects of the story to make them more consistent with their own experience.

Neisser (1967) likened the process of remembering to a paleontologist reconstructing a dinosaur. That is, from bone fragments and some knowledge as to how they must go together, the paleontologist may build a model of a dinosaur that is presumed to closely resemble the real thing. So it is with remembering, said Neisser.

> The present proposal . . . is that we store traces of earlier cognitive acts, not the product of these acts. The traces are not simply 'revived' or 'reactivated' in recall; instead, the stored fragments are used as information to support a new construction. It is as if the bone fragments used by the paleontologist did not appear in the model he builds at all—as indeed they need not, if it is to represent a fully fleshed out, skin-covered dinosaur. The bones can be thought

of, somewhat loosely, as the remnants of the structure which created and supported the original dinosaur, and thus of sources of information about how to reconstruct it. (pp. 265–86)

The question of what exactly is constructed and stored to serve as a basis for later reconstruction has been answered by some researchers as schemata and mental models. These ideas have become well enough developed in the research literature to merit discussion in greater detail (see chapter 5).

THE RHIZOME (OR SEMIOTIC) METAPHOR

Imagine the rhizome—a mass of roots, a tangle of tubers with no apparent beginning or end. It constantly changes shape, and every point in it appears to be connected with every other point. Break the rhizome at any point and the only effect is that new connections will be grown. Eco (1984) proposed the rhizome as a metaphor for the structure of knowledge in human understanding. This metaphor lies at the heart of the semiotic conception of cognition.

Inherent in all models discussed in this chapter so far is the basic assumption that knowledge is an internal representation of some kind of external reality. Information is out there, to be received and stored by the human information processing system. Many recommendations for instruction capitalize on this assumed isomorphism between the external reality and the internal representation. Semiotic theory claims, however, that no such isomorphism is possible. Rather, all knowledge of the world is mediated through signs, which are jointly determined by the physical world and the cognizing organism (Cunningham, 1987, 1992). A sign is anything that stands for something else, and semiosis is the process of constructing sign systems and negotiating meanings. What makes humans unique is our ability to create and use signs that go beyond our immediate experience. So what is learning in semiotic theory and what is knowledge?

Learning is essentially equivalent to semiosis, and knowledge is "better thought of as knowing, or as a process. Through our experience in the world, we build ways of knowing, structures that determine our current understanding. And via these structures, we literally construct our knowledge dynamically as we interact with the world" (Cunningham, 1992, p. 169). The rhizome models the unlimited potential for knowledge construction, because it has no fixed points (no nodes or basic representational units) and no particular organization (my own mental image of a rhizome resembles a plateful of spaghetti; Eco [1976] also spoke of a jarful of marbles which, when shaken, will produce a new configuration and a new set of connections among marbles).

For purposes of illustration, think once again about herons. Network models suggest that your knowledge of herons is stored in terms of a heron concept node, with various features connected by association. Propositional models suggest that the features are part and parcel of your understanding of herons, since propositions, rather than concept nodes, are stored. PDP models refer to the patterns of activation related to your understanding of herons. But now think of herons and air traffic control. Shank (1988) argued that, through the method of juxtaposition, any two things may be linked, with meaningful relationships generated between them. In fact, interesting insights can occur in the juxtaposition of disparate ideas. But the relationships you have now generated between herons and air traffic control are not easily accounted for in current memory models, which do not adequately capture the dynamic nature of knowing. The rhizome metaphor, however, allows for infinite juxtaposition.

If the rhizome is limitless in possibility, and therefore indescribable at a global level, then we are forced to consider cognition at a more local level, as "transitory systems of knowledge" (Eco, 1984, p. 84). Particular slices of the rhizome reveal a person's knowledge at that time in that context, with no assumption of invariability over time or across contexts. This presumes that neither knowledge nor the ways in which we use to describe it are stable. Rather, "the rhizome concept alerts us to the constructed nature of our [environmental understanding] and the possibilities of different meaning, different truths, different worlds" (Cunningham, 1992, p. 171).

What semiotic theory means for instruction is only now being explored, along with similar efforts under the rubric of constructivism (see Chapter 11) Adopting a new metaphor for cognition and learning implies new metaphors for instruction. These call into question the nature of teaching and the teacher's role, the instructional strategies to support learning, the product of knowledge acquisition, and the assessment of learning (see Cunningham and Shank, 1984; Cunningham, 1987, 1992; Driscoll & Lebow, 1992).

"Michael Roth (1990), for example, makes sure that his science students experience multiple ways of representing their experiences while conducting laboratory experiments (e.g., verbal description, equations, pictures and diagrams, demonstrations, tables of numbers, graphs, etc.), all the while encouraging them to point out the strengths and weaknesses of each mode and what is foregrounded in one representation but obscured by another" (Cunningham, 1992, p. 180). Although this sounds comparable to recommendations consistent with the dual-code theory, it also goes beyond them to facilitate reflection on the part of learners. In other words, Roth's students are not only learning science, they are also learning signs—what it means to represent information by means of one kind of sign or another.

A semiotic approach to instruction also puts emphasis on the affective domain and motivation, because an expected outcome of examining multiple perspectives in a reflective way is the learner's commitment to views compatible with self-chosen values (Cunningham, 1992; Driscoll & Lebow, 1992). And providing students with greater autonomy in learning—for example, in lengthy, integrated projects where students assume different roles—is a strategy consistent with this emphasis.

In chapter 11, a collection of new approaches to instruction that have evolved from these and similar notions of learning as a constructive process will be discussed further.

CONCLUSION

As noted in the previous chapter, B. F. Skinner continued to argue against the necessity for inventing mental fictions to account for learning. At first, Roediger (1980) seemed to side with Skinner when he pointed out the proliferation of mental entities in current models of human memory and questioned what we have really learned from them. His conclusion, however, was not that mental constructs are useless, but that we should be cautious in what we take them to mean about learning and memory. "Advances in theories of human memory parallel, and perhaps depend on, advances in technology. . . . The information processing approach has been an important source of models and ideas, but the fate of its predecessors should serve to keep us humble concerning its eventual success. . . . Unless today's technology has somehow reached its ultimate development, and we can be certain it has not, then we have not reached the ultimate metaphor for the human mind either" (Roediger, 1980, p. 244).

Cognitive information processing theorists have not been the only ones interested in learning and memory from a cognitive perspective. In chapter 4, the ideas of educational psychologist David P. Ausubel will be explored, and in chapter 5, schema theory and mental models, with their corresponding implications for instruction, will be presented.

SUGGESTED READINGS

Dillon, R. F., & Sternberg, R. J. (1986). *Cognition and instruction.* Orlando: Academic Press.

Educational Psychology Review. (1992). Special issue on semiotics and education, 4(2), 165–269.

Gagné, E. D. (1985). *The cognitive psychology of school learning*. Boston: Little, Brown.

Phye, G. D., & Andre, T. (1986). *Cognitive classroom learning*. Orlando: Academic Press.

REFLECTIVE QUESTIONS AND ACTIVITIES

1. Consider cognitive information processing theory in light of the epistemological traditions described in chapter 1. To what tradition do CIP theorists seem most closely aligned? What evidence supports your choice?

2. Look for examples of the computer metaphor for learning and memory in popular culture and literature. Early episodes of *Star Trek* are likely sources. Analyze the characters' actions in terms of the information processing model. Are any of the model's assumptions or characteristics violated in the name of science fiction? If so, consider the implications for learning and instruction if those violations were indeed true.

3. Using the same learning episode you described in Question 4 of Chapter 2, generate a plan for improving performance that is based on cognitive information processing theory. How does this plan differ from your behavioral plan? What aspects of learning are highlighted by each plan? Are they mutually exclusive, or might a combined plan be more effective than either alone?

4. Prepare a list of metaphors that have been or could be used to describe and understand learning (e.g., learning is information processing [a computer metaphor]; learning is growing [an organicist metaphor]; learning is making progress toward some goal [a travel metaphor], etc.) For each metaphor, describe the implied roles of the learner, the instructor, and the instructional materials. For each metaphor, consider what assumptions are being made about the nature of knowledge and ways of knowing. Add to your list as you complete the chapters of this book.

▶ 4

Meaningful Reception Learning

Consider the following scenarios.[*]

Scenario 4–1

The place is a public school seventh grade social studies classroom. It is seventh period, and a lesson on democracy has begun, with a focus on American history. The students have brainstormed a list of characteristics describing their understanding of government, and from their answers, their teacher Mr. Amaya has written a simplified definition of the term on the board. With this, the students prepare to discuss different forms of government (including oligarchy, democracy, fascism, etc.), following which they will focus in on democracy and all its related concepts.

Scenario 4–2

The students in Accounting I must understand basic concepts in record keeping for financial management before they will be prepared to keep books and balance budgets. As a way of introducing students to these ideas, Ms. McGee decides to include a visual display of the Accounting Cycle, which is an overview of the entire process of record keeping and the purpose for keeping records in financial management. This should serve as a basis for understanding the specific forms and procedures which make up the steps in the financial management process.

---

[*] My thanks to Mark Brewer and Tony Cuevas, who supplied the instructional examples upon which these scenarios are based.

In these two scenarios, the students share a common instructional goal. They must learn a body of information that is presented during class. Although many students may approach this goal by memorizing, learning should mean more than reproducing information on a test. It should imply understanding, or what David P. Ausubel called meaningful learning.

The twofold question of what is meaningful learning and how it takes place greatly interested Ausubel, an educational psychologist who continued a verbal learning tradition begun by Ebbinghaus (1885) (see chapter 1). Ausubel (1965) argued that knowing, meaning, and understanding—all cognitive operations—can provide significant data for a science of psychology and for a theory of learning. Although he regarded the human nervous system as a "data-processing and storage mechanism" (Ausubel, 1965, p. 8), Ausubel did not consider as cognitive theory the computer models of cognition being developed at the time by Newell, Simon, and Shaw (1958). As a result, his theory developed on a parallel course to the information processing theory discussed in the previous chapter.

Whereas Ebbinghaus (1885) believed that human learning and memory should be studied uncontaminated by old associations or meaning, Ausubel thought that meaning was at the very core of cognitive experience. It therefore made no sense to Ausubel to study learning with materials so bereft of meaning as the nonsense syllables invented by Ebbinghaus and adopted by many cognitive psychologists. Ausubel preferred to use prose, or textual, materials of some length. These, he argued, more closely approximate the kinds of learning materials children encounter in actual classrooms. It is interesting to note that Ausubel was the first investigator since Bartlett (1932) to use lengthy prose passages, rather than individual words or sentences, in his studies on learning.

Meaning, however, was not something Ausubel thought resided "in the text" and outside the learner. Textual materials, like anything else learners might experience, were only to be considered "potentially meaningful." Meaning occurred when learners actively interpreted their experience using certain internal, cognitive operations. To account for these cognitive operations and how they interact with experience to give rise to learning, Ausubel proposed a theory of meaningful reception learning (Ausubel, 1962, 1963a, 1968; Ausubel, Novak, & Hanesian, 1978).

Although Ausubel's theory is no longer particularly current, it had a substantial influence on both learning research and educational practice. Theoretically, Ausubel's ideas predated the schema theories discussed in the next chapter. And practically, many of Ausubel's suggestions for pedagogy have been incorporated into current models of instructional design.

COGNITIVE STRUCTURES AND MEANINGFUL LEARNING

According to Ausubel (1963b), his entire theory and research program were predicated on the premise that "existing cognitive structure, that is, an individual's organization, stability, and clarity of knowledge in a particular subject matter field at any given time, is the principal factor influencing the learning and retention of meaningful new material" (p. 217). In other words, prior knowledge is the most significant determinant of what new learning will occur. Given the importance Ausubel placed on prior knowledge in learning, then, how does he conceive of memory structure?

Cognitive Organization in the Learner

"The model of cognitive organization proposed for the learning and retention of meaningful materials assumes the existence of a cognitive structure that is hierarchically organized . . . " (Ausubel, 1963b, p. 217). As indicated earlier, Ausubel acknowledged the existence of neurophysiological events underlying learning, but he expressed his theory in terms of hypothetical constructs of memory structure and learning processes. He proposed **cognitive structure** as the learner's *overall memorial structure or integrated body of knowledge*. This cognitive structure is made up of sets of ideas that are organized hierarchically and by theme. Moreover, within any given hierarchy, the most inclusive ideas are the strongest and most stable. Except for its emphasis on a hierarchy of ideas, this structure is similar to those proposed by the propositional model of memory that was discussed in the previous chapter.

For an example of cognitive structure, consider what you know about banks. You have sets of ideas associated with banking, such as a bank offers certain services, a bank has certain types of personnel working there, and so forth. More specifically, you might remember precisely what services are offered. There are certain types of accounts, safety deposit boxes, loans, etc. Even more detail could be remembered with respect to accounts, for instance. There are personal checking accounts, personal savings accounts, and business checking accounts, to name several. Perhaps at the lowest level of the hierarchy would be the features defining each type of account. Figure 4–1 displays the hierarchy that might represent this knowledge about banks. According to Ausubel, the general ideas high in the hierarchy (e.g., offer certain services) would be more stable and therefore more easily remembered than specific ideas low in the hierarchy (such as, what minimum balance is required in a personal checking account).

The cognitive structure provides an overall framework into which new knowledge will be incorporated, but to describe how specific linkages occur, Ausubel proposed the notion of anchoring ideas. **Anchoring ideas** are the *specific, relevant ideas in the learner's cognitive structure that provide the entry points for new information to be connected*. They are what enable the learner to construct meaning from new information and experiences that are only potentially meaningful.

For example, if you knew nothing whatever about banks, to have someone talk about characteristics of checking accounts would be quite meaningless to you. You would have no anchor with which to connect the new information. Likewise, making sense of a sentence such as, "The notes were sour because the seams split" (Bransford, 1979), is difficult to understand without the anchoring idea, bagpipe. However, if you knew that banks offered a variety of services, such as different types of accounts, this might serve as a suitable anchoring idea for learning more about personal checking accounts.

Cognitive structure and specific anchoring ideas within the cognitive structure, then, are prerequisites to meaningful learning. They describe the memory structure within which new knowledge will be integrated. But we have yet to see how the processes of learning occur, i.e., how the new knowledge is actually connected with and incorporated into the learner's existing knowledge.

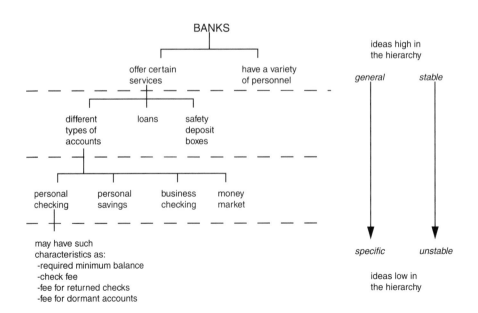

FIGUREN4–1   Basic Principles of Reinforcement

Meaningful Reception Learning

As a means of differentiating the types of learning that go on in typical classrooms, Ausubel (1961, 1963b) made two important distinctions. First, he distinguished between reception and discovery learning, a distinction he considered important because he contended that most school learning is of the reception type. In reception learning, Ausubel (1961) stated, "the entire content of what is to be learned is presented to the learner in its final form" (p. 16). The learner is therefore required to internalize the information in a form that will be available for later use. In discovery learning, on the other hand, learners are required to "rearrange a given array of information, integrate it with existing cognitive structure, and reorganize or transform the integrated combination in such a way as to create a desired end product or discover a missing means-end relationship. After this phase is completed, the discovered content is internalized just as in reception learning" (Ausubel, 1961, p. 17).

Reception learning, then, is essentially the same as what commonly occurs in expository instruction, where learners are told information rather than discovering it for themselves. Science textbooks, for example, state principles (often with a description of the research conducted to arrive at these principles) and provide examples of their application. From the principle's definition and examples, along with practice in its application, students are expected to understand what it means. By contrast, science teachers often facilitate discovery learning by having students conduct experiments from which they derive their understanding of scientific principles.

Although discovery learning methods certainly have a place in instruction (e.g., in laboratories or everyday problem solving) (see also discussions in Chapter 7 and Chapter 11), Ausubel believed that such methods "hardly constitute an efficient *primary* means of transmitting the *content* of an academic discipline" (Ausubel, et al., 1978, p. 26, emphases theirs).

The second distinction made by Ausubel (1961, 1963b) and Ausubel et al. (1978) is between rote and meaningful learning. Rote learning is the same as verbatim memorization, and to Ausubel, that means the learner has made no real connection between what was already known and what was memorized. What was memorized stands as an arbitrary piece of information in isolation from the rest of cognitive structure. Children frequently memorize the Pledge of Allegiance, for example, and cannot tell you what the pledge means. By contrast, meaningful learning refers to the process of relating potentially meaningful information to what the learner already knows in a nonarbitrary and substantive way. This means that, in the previous example, the children would have some notion as to what the flag means as a symbol of the United States. With this prior knowledge, they can construct an understanding of what is entailed by pledging allegiance.

It is important to realize, said Ausubel, that either rote or meaningful learning can occur in reception and discovery learning situations. Students may attempt to memorize the results of a science experiment, for example, instead of understanding what the results suggest about the principle under study. Likewise, in reception learning, just because the learner is in a position of receiving information does not mean the learner must be passive. Quite the contrary, meaningful reception learning implies that the learner is cognitively active.

Two conditions are therefore essential to meaningful learning. One is that the learner must employ a meaningful learning set to any learning task, and the other is that the material to be learned must be potentially meaningful. In other words, if the learner intends to memorize, then meaningful learning will not result, no matter whether learning is by discovery or reception. On the other hand, the learner may approach the task with a meaningful learning set but be stymied by the lack of potential meaning in the learning task itself.

Assuming that the two conditions for learning have been met, Ausubel et al. (1978) further distinguished among three types of meaningful learning. In essence, these types amount to different types of possible outcomes that may result from meaningful learning. The first, representational learning, refers to learning the meanings of unitary symbols or words. This is the most basic form of learning and, according to Ausubel et al. (1978), serves as the foundation for all other learning to occur. As an example, think of a young child viewing a picture of a robin for the first time. Before then, the sound of the word *robin* was only potentially meaningful. Making a connection between the sound of the word and what the word stands for, or represents—i.e., the robin in the picture—is representational learning. The child has learned a meaningful correspondence between a particular sound and a particular experience.

Through actively relating this representation to other relevant experiences, the child soon comes to reliably call all robins by that name, including those which have not been experienced directly. When this happens, Ausubel contended that concept learning has occurred. With concept learning comes not just knowing that the word *robin* stands for that particular bird, but what *robin* means in general. Its criterial attributes—what makes this bird a robin and that bird not a robin—are understood.

Finally, in propositional learning, the meanings of new ideas expressed in verbal propositions are acquired. By this Ausubel meant that individual words or concepts are combined in such a way to form a new idea, which is more than the sum of the meanings of the individual words (Ausubel, et al., 1978). Making inferences, or reasoning from knowledge of particular concepts, would be considered propositional learning. So, to take the robin once again, a student might observe a robin hopping and bowing before another robin. Given the time of year and general knowledge about birds, the student might conclude, "Oh, those robins must be engaged in a mating ritual." New knowledge about the mating habits of robins has just been acquired.

Both concept and propositional learning are likely to occur in Scenario 4–1, and this is typical of most subject matter learning beyond the earliest stages. Concepts such as democracy and oligarchy are being learned, along with their criterial attributes (e.g., what makes the government in America an example of democracy). If we assume that Mr. Amaya's goals extend beyond knowledge about government to reasoning from that knowledge, students will also learn new propositions concerning democracy. For example, they might generate logical reasons for constitutional decisions made by the founding fathers or argue differing points of view in recent civil rights cases.

Scenario 4–2 parallels Scenario 4–1 in the types of learning most likely to occur. Students acquire concepts of financial management such as credit, debit, income, and expenses. But they are also likely to learn propositions related to balancing a budget such as, expenses greater than income will produce a deficit in spending.

It should be obvious that Ausubel considered representational, concept, and propositional learning to be themselves hierarchically related. For propositional learning to occur, students must know what the component concepts mean in a verbal proposition. Similarly, for concept learning to occur, learners must have established the initial representation between the concept name and the object it represents. Aside from some minor variations owing to the age and experience of the learner, all three types of meaningful learning proceed in much the same way. Learners relate new information to what they already know in a nonarbitrary and substantive fashion. Just how this takes place is discussed next.

KNOWLEDGE ACQUISITION AND RETENTION

For the purposes of discussion, it is useful to make a distinction between what takes place during initial learning and what takes place over time in retention. In Ausubel's theory, learning is conceived as a building process, consistent with the construction metaphor described in the previous chapter. New information is added to and integrated with an existing cognitive structure. Retention, on the other hand, involves maintaining the availability of acquired information, as well as cementing and reorganizing that information in order to permit efficiency of access. Ausubel recognized the importance of both aspects to his theory of learning and believed that they entailed different processes.

Processes of Meaningful Learning

Recall for a moment the hierarchical structure of cognition that Ausubel proposed. If memory is actually organized in this fashion, then how is new information likely to be added to an existing structure? There are three possible ways: new information can be subordinate to (lower in the structure), superordinate to (higher in the structure), or coordinate with (at the same level in the structure) an existing idea. Consistent with each of these ways, Ausubel proposed a process of learning.

Derivative and Correlative Subsumption

The principal way of adding information to cognitive structure, in Ausubel's view, is to attach new ideas and details in a subordinate fashion to the anchoring ideas already present. This is the process Ausubel called subsumption (Ausubel, 1962, 1963a, 1968; Ausubel, et al., 1978). That is, *new, incoming ideas are* **subsumed** *under more general and inclusive anchoring ideas already in memory.* Another way to think of subsumption is to consider the anchoring ideas as hooks that snag those incoming details and modifiers pertaining to them.

Because incoming details can relate to anchoring ideas in two possible ways (both still subordinate), subsumption is said to occur in two ways. **Derivative subsumption** refers to the *learning of new examples or cases that are illustrative of an established concept or previously learned proposition*. If we consider A below to be the anchoring idea in a learner's cognitive structure, with examples a1, a2, and a3 associated in a subordinate fashion, then new example a4 will be derivatively subsumed under A.

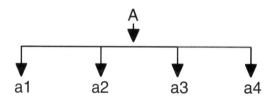

For example, if A is the general concept, dog, and collies, cocker spaniels, and labradors are known as examples, then it is relatively easy to learn the example, whippet, and subsume that information under the general concept. The criterial attributes of the concept A remain unchanged; simply, new examples are recognized as relevant.

Other instances of derivative subsumption include learning in geography that Texas and India are both places where rice is grown. Or in

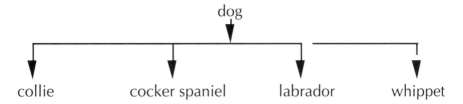

law, cases may be found that were all decided based on the same legal precedent. Finally, a teacher or instructional designer might encounter numerous examples where a particular principle of learning has been employed.

More typical of the way most learning occurs, according to Ausubel, is **correlative subsumption**. This process refers to the *elaboration, extension,* or *modification of the previously learned concept or proposition by the subsumption of the incoming idea.* Instead of simply adding a new example, then, the new information adds a new characteristic or feature to the existing idea. In so doing, it interacts with the existing idea to change the learner's understanding of it in some way. The original A becomes A' as shown below.

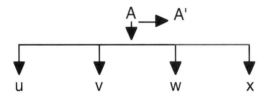

For example, suppose A above represents the concept positive reinforcement in an education student's cognitive structure of behavioral management. The student knows that positive reinforcement increases behavior (attribute u) through the presentation of a reinforcer (attribute v) that is contingent upon the desired response (attribute w). When the student now learns that the reinforcer can be a high-frequency behavior (new attribute x), his or her understanding of positive reinforcement has now been extended to include the special circumstances surrounding the Premack principle. The criterial attributes of the concept have been modified. As indicated above, A has also been replaced by A', because the student's understanding of the positive reinforcement principle is no longer the same as it was.

Examples of correlative subsumption can also be readily seen in the content being taught by Mr. Amaya in his social studies class. As the students learn about different aspects of government, they correlatively subsume these characteristics under the inclusive concept, government.

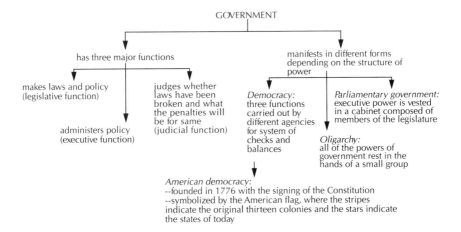

FIGURE   4–2   Basic Principles of Reinforcement

(They may also derivatively subsume the labels, democracy and oligarchy, for example, under the label, government.) Then when discussion turns to expressions of patriotism, for example, such as displaying the American flag to commemorate the founding of America's democracy, students correlatively subsume this information under the anchoring idea of democracy (Figure 4–2).

Superordinate and Combinatorial Learning
Not all learning can be explained through the processes of derivative and correlative subsumption, because not all learning occurs in a subordinate fashion. In discovery learning, for instance, students may be working with examples to discover the more general concept or proposition. Thus, learning must be occurring in a superordinate, rather than subordinate, way. Similarly, what about instances in which students learn about similar concepts at the same level in the hierarchy as the anchoring idea? Learning in that case must be neither subordinate nor superordinate, but coordinate, or lateral. To account for learning that is not subordinate in nature, Ausubel et al. (1978) proposed the processes of superordinate and combinatorial learning.

Superordinate learning occurs through a synthesis of established ideas. That is, a *new, inclusive proposition or concept is learned under which already established ideas can be subsumed.* If ideas x, y, and z are already established in the learner's cognitive structure and their association is discovered, then new idea A is learned under which they are all subsequently subsumed, as in the diagram on the following page.

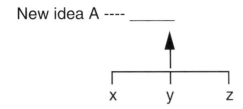

An example of subordinate learning is evident in my experience with purchasing my first home computer. At the time, I knew virtually nothing about microcomputers except that I wanted one with which to do word processing. A slick salesman sold me a computer with monitor, word processing package, and dot matrix printer. I took it all home, hooked it all up, and nothing worked. To make a long story short, the word processor was not configured for the computer (event x); it was adjusted. The printer did not work with the computer (event y); a different printer card solved the problem. The word processor was not compatible with the printer (event z); the designers of the word processor never could figure this one out, so I sold the printer. What did I learn (new idea, A) from these events? Make sure all components of the system work together before leaving the store!

When new concepts or propositions are neither more inclusive of nor subordinate to relevant anchoring ideas in the cognitive structure, they are meaningfully learned in a combinatorial way. In other words, **cominatorial learning** occurs when *the new idea is not relatable in a specific sense to an existing anchor but is generally relevant to a broad background of information,* which may contain a number of similar ideas sharing criterial attributes, as shown in the diagram below.

An example of combinatorial learning can be seen in the relationship between the flow of heat and the conducting of electricity through metals. Heat flow and electrical conductivity are not specifically related, in a subordinate or superordinate sense. Yet to understand each, a learner must have some previous knowledge of how metals are structured. Moreover, since the processes are analogous, having already learned about how heat flows through metals can facilitate understanding how electricity is conducted and vice versa (cf. Royer and Cable, 1975; Royer and Perkins, 1977; Driscoll, 1985).

Concepts exist in most subject matter disciplines that are coordinate to one another. And even though many coordinate concepts are also subordinate to some inclusive idea, their relationships to one another must be learned as well as their relationships to the subsuming idea. To take the government example again, democracy, oligarchy, and fascism all bear a coordinate relationship to one another. Thus, learning about one can provide a general background of information, which may be useful in learning the others. Ausubel and Fitzgerald (1961) found, for example, that knowing a lot about Christianity aided learners in acquiring new knowledge about Buddhism. Like the types of government in the previous example, these types of religion bear a coordinate relationship to each other, appropriate to combinatorial learning. According to Ausubel et al. (1978), "Most of the *new* generalizations that students learn in science, mathematics, social studies, and the humanities are examples of combinatorial learnings, for example, relationships between mass and energy, heat and volume, genic structure and variability, demand and price" (p. 59).

The Processes of Meaningful Learning: Assimilation Theory

By 1978, Ausubel had adopted the label assimilation theory to describe the meaningful learning processes of subsumption, superordinate learning, and combinatorial learning. In earlier versions of the theory (Ausubel, 1963a, 1968), assimilation referred primarily to the process of retention, whereby new information tends to be reduced to (or assimilated by) the meaning of the stable, more established anchoring idea. Although Ausubel's notions of what happens in retention changed little, which will be discussed in the next section, he came to use the concept of assimilation more broadly. Taking together learning and retention, "The result of the interaction that takes place between the new material to be learned and the existing cognitive structure is an *assimilation* of old and new meanings to form a more highly differentiated cognitive structure" (Ausubel, et al., 1978, pp. 67–68).

Retention of Meaningful Learning

As indicated earlier, retention involves maintaining the availability of acquired information so that it may be accessed for use at a later time. Immediately following initial meaningful learning, new information is easily accessible, its stability enhanced by virtue of its anchorage to relevant concepts in the cognitive structure (Ausubel, 1963b). Over time, because it is more economical to remember a single inclusive concept than a large number of specific details, subsumed ideas become less and less distinguishable, or dissociable, from the inclusive anchor. When they can no longer be retrieved as entities separate and distinct from the anchoring idea, they are said to be forgotten.

This trend toward reduction in memory and an ultimate loss of knowledge bears two different labels, depending upon how the information was originally acquired. When examples or extensions of concepts and propositions acquired through subsumption can no longer be retrieved, obliterative subsumption has occurred. The student who has learned many different breeds of dogs, for example, simply will not remember them all when asked to name as many as she can. Or the geography student may remember that rice is grown in India but forget that it is grown in Texas. Unless there is continued practice with or use of the examples, there is no reason to keep them all available in memory. Similarly, consider what happens when mathematical concepts such as standard deviation are learned. Undoubtedly a definition, component concepts, and a formula for calculating standard deviations were part of initial learning. But without continued practice in its use, the formula will be rapidly forgotton.

Since superordinate or combinatorial meanings are not acquired through subsumption, to say they are forgotten through obliterative subsumption would be something of a misnomer (Ausubel, et al., 1978). Therefore, Ausubel adopted the label, obliterative assimilation, to denote the forgetting process involving information learned in superordinate or combinatorial ways. In all cases, the basic forgetting process is the same, but Ausubel believed the consequences of forgetting can be far more serious for correlative, superordinate, and combinatorial learning than for derivative learning (Ausubel et al., 1978). It is probably immaterial, for instance, if a particular example of dog or rice-growing place cannot be remembered. But suppose not enough about standard deviation is recalled to enable the learner to reconstruct the formula for its calculation. Since correlatively subsumed details should have modified the learner's overall understanding of the concept, forgetting them to this degree would be a true loss of knowledge.

Finally, it is important to note the difference between forgetting after rote learning and forgetting after meaningful learning. Despite the fact that information in both cases becomes irretrievable, there is still a net gain in the cognitive structure following meaningful learning. The concept or proposition that provided anchorage for meaningful learning is generally more differentiated than it was previously. Thus, as Ausubel (1963b) put it, there is "memorial residue of ideational experience" which enables the concept or proposition to be "more functional for future learning and problem-solving occasions" (p. 218).

Readiness for Learning

In the generally accepted sense of the word, learning readiness refers to a learner's developmental level of cognitive functioning. It is this cognitive maturity that is assumed to determine the extent to which learners are capable of learning at various levels of abstraction within a subject matter discipline. While not discounting the impact this type of readiness may have on learning, Ausubel (1963b) and Ausubel et al. (1978) emphasized readiness as a function of previously acquired subject matter knowledge. "If [Ausubel] had to reduce all of educational psychology to just one principle, [he] would say this: The most important single factor influencing learning is what the learner already knows. Ascertain this and teach him accordingly" (Ausubel et al., 1978, p. 163).

Readiness in this sense, then, depends upon both the substantive content in the learner's cognitive structure and its organizational properties. In the first place, experts in a subject matter simply have a lot more extant knowledge than do novices in the subject. The idea that extensive background knowledge facilitates subsequent learning has been consistently demonstrated (e.g., Ausubel & Fitzgerald, 1961, 1962; Tobias, 1976; Glaser, 1984). But the organization of knowledge also influences subsequent learning. "If cognitive structure is clear, stable, and suitably organized, accurate and unambiguous meanings emerge and tend to retain their dissociability strength or availability. If, on the other hand, cognitive structure is unstable, ambiguous, disorganized, or chaotically organized, it tends to inhibit meaningful learning and retention" (Ausubel et al., 1978, p. 164).

It follows from the previous argument that learners with poorly organized cognitive structures in a subject matter should be aided in learning by materials that make clear similarities and differences among concepts to be learned. In fact, early studies conducted by Ausubel and his associates (e.g., Ausubel & Fitzgerald, 1961; Ausubel & Youssef, 1963) provided evidence that this was true. When learners already possessed organized and stable cognitive structures, however, such materials made no difference in what else they learned (Ausubel & Fitzgerald, 1961).

Royer, Perkins, and Konold (1978) provided evidence of a different sort to support Ausubel's claim that cognitive organization influences learning. They gave students passages to read, labeled with either the name of a fictitious person or the name of a famous person (e.g., Adolf Hitler). After studying the information, students rated sentences as to whether the sentences were old (i.e., from the passage) or new (i.e., never seen before). Subjects' judgments were quite accurate when the passage they read was ostensibly about a fictitious person. Having no anchoring information into which to meaningfully subsume the new information, students essentially learned the new ideas by rote. When they thought the information was about Adolf Hitler, however, learners typically had prior knowledge about Hitler to which they could attach the new ideas. As a result, they tended to misidentify as "old" sentences that were new but were thematically related to Hitler, such as "He hated and persecuted the Jews."

To be ready for learning new material, then, learners of all sorts must possess a relevant, stable, and organized cognitive structure. Ausubel acknowledged, however, two additional influences on readiness that it is important to mention. The first has to do with age differences among learners, and the second concerns culturally disadvantaged learners.

According to Ausubel et al. (1978), "the cognitive organization of children differs mainly from that of adults in containing fewer abstract concepts, fewer higher order abstractions, and more intuitive-nonverbal than abstract-verbal understandings of many propositions" (p. 140). Children, in other words, learn proportionately more through representational learning than do adults, and more of their own learning is representational than conceptual or propositional. This simply means that children have a greater reliance during learning on concrete-empirical experience. Perhaps more so than adults, then, children should be taught in concrete ways. By extension, adults should be taught concretely when they know very little about the subject matter, because in those circumstances, representational learning must occur to provide a basis for concept and propositional learning.

Accounting for the effects of culture on learning, Ausubel claimed, can be done within the same theoretical framework established for learning in general. That is, children who are culturally disadvantaged relative to their classmates have different cognitive structures owing to the differences in their life experiences and prior learnings. This means that some learning tasks are likely to exceed the cognitive readiness of these children (Ausubel et al., 1978). What should be done about it? According to Ausubel, the basic principles underlying appropriate teaching strategies are essentially the same, regardless of who the learners are. To repeat the principle he considers most important: Ascertain the cognitive structures of your learners and teach accordingly. How one might do this most effectively is discussed next.

MEANINGFUL LEARNING AND CLASSROOM PRACTICE

With Ausubel's background as an educational psychologist, he maintained a steadfast interest in the educative process as well as the learning process. Instruction, he contended, should proceed in accord with established principles of learning. Ausubel conceived of learning principles within a type of transfer paradigm—transfer in the sense that the clarity, stability, generalizability, inclusiveness, and discriminability of prior knowledge will influence subsequent learning. Similarly, he conceived of instruction in the same way. The acquisition of adequate cognitive structure depends upon "(a) using for organizational and integrative purposes those substantive concepts and principles in a given discipline that have the widest explanatory power, inclusiveness, generalizability, and relatability to the subject matter content of the discipline; and (b) employing those methods of presenting and ordering the sequence of subject matter that best enhance the clarity, stability, and integratedness of cognitive structure for the purposes of new learning and problem solving" (Ausubel, 1963a, p. 218).

So, if the broadest concepts are best taught first, and methods are used to make them clear and stable for later learning, what exactly does this mean for instruction? The instructional solutions Ausubel proposed effectively parallel three aspects of cognitive structure that he came to call cognitive structure variables (Ausubel, et al., 1978). Rephrased in terms of functions or purposes of instruction, they are:

1. Instruction should facilitate the linkage between the new information to be learned and that which is already in cognitive structure. In other words, relevant cognitive structure should be activated, or made available, when new learning commences.

2. Instruction should facilitate discriminability of new ideas in the learning material from both similar and different (but potentially confusable) anchoring ideas in the cognitive structure.

3. Instruction should increase the stability and clarity of anchoring ideas in order to facilitate their availability for later learning and problem solving.

Let us examine the instructional strategies that Ausubel proposed to serve those purposes.

Advance Organizers

To help accomplish the first function of instruction, Ausubel (1963a, 1968) and Ausubel et al. (1978) proposed the advance organizer. Advance organizers are relevant and inclusive introductory materials, provided in advance of the learning materials, that serve to "bridge the gap between what the learner already knows and what he needs to know before he can meaningfully learn the task at hand" (Ausubel et al., 1978, pp. 171–172). In other words, just having relevant cognitive structure is not sufficient to ensure meaningful learning. Learners must apply what they know to the learning task.

It has been found, for example, that participants in many conventional memory experiments tend to view information they are asked to learn as separate and distinct from their prior knowledge (Spiro, 1977). They adopt an experiment set, which means that they approach the learning material in a rote fashion and fail to assimilate the information into related prior knowledge. Unfortunately, all too often learners tend to approach learning tasks in much the same way, regardless of whether they have prior knowledge to apply to the task. I have seen this happen in my graduate courses in which former teachers fail to use what they know about teaching to help them in learning about formal theories of learning and instruction. The advance organizer, then, was suggested by Ausubel as a means to avoid rote learning by specifically activating relevant prior knowledge.

As a definition, Ausubel et al. (1978) stated, "organizers are presented at a higher level of abstraction, generality and inclusiveness than the new material to be learned" (p. 171). Consider why this might be so. For one thing, learners are likely to have somewhat idiosyncratic cognitive structures, and while it might be desirable to construct advance organizers for each and every learner to meet their unique needs, that is not a very practical strategy. Thus, organizers should be sufficiently general to function for a variety of learners. In addition, remember Ausubel's call for using the most inclusive and relatable concepts of a discipline to guide learning. Constructing organizers more abstract and inclusive than the learning materials is one way of doing this.

The effectiveness of advance organizers for enhancing learning and retention of verbal materials has been a subject of great debate in the research literature. Some studies (e.g., Ausubel, 1960; Ausubel & Fitzgerald, 1961; Ausubel & Youssef, 1963; Kuhn & Novak, 1971; West & Fensham, 1976) confirmed the positive effects of advance organizers on learning. Others suggested that the facilitating effect might be limited to learners with low verbal or analytic ability (e.g., Ausubel & Fitzgerald, 1962). But research reviews conducted by Barnes and Clawson (1975) and Hartley and Davies (1976) pointed to even more equivocal findings.

Some of the problems cited in the research concerned methodological flaws in conducting the studies. For example, researchers may have failed to ascertain whether the organizers in their studies contained relevant concepts that would activate existing subsumers. In the absence of analyses of the learners' cognitive structures and the concepts to be learned, Ausubel et al. (1978) argued, it is unlikely that an appropriate organizer could be constructed. Moreover, if criterion tests are either too easy or too hard, or if they are designed to measure verbatim recall, then no organizer effects should be expected.

A more serious criticism of advance organizers is that their definition is vague (Hartley & Davies, 1976). If researchers operationalize the concept of advance organizers in different ways, then it should come as no surprise that their results do not agree. Ausubel et al. (1978) countered this criticism by pointing to the volume of space in an earlier work (Ausubel, 1968) devoted to the "nature and definition of an organizer and how it affects information processing" (p. 175).

Focusing on the conditions under which advance organizers might be expected to facilitate learning, Mayer (1979a) reported the results of a set of experiments he conducted to test the claims and criticisms regarding advance organizers. From his results, Mayer suggested that advance organizers should exhibit the following characteristics:

1. Have a short set of verbal or visual information,
2. Be presented prior to learning of a larger body of to-be-learned information,
3. Contain no specific content from the to-be-learned information,
4. Provide a means of generating the logical relationships among the elements in the to-be-learned information, and
5. Influence the learner's encoding process. The manner in which an organizer influences encoding may serve either of two functions: to provide a new general organization as an assimilative context that would not have normally been present or to activate a general organization from the learner's existing knowledge that would not have normally been used to assimilate the new material. (Mayer, 1979a, p. 382)

Think back for a moment to Ms. McGee in Scenario 4–2. Recall that she has decided to use a visual display of the Accounting Cycle at the beginning of a lesson on financial management. Will this serve as an advance organizer for accounting students as they learn the specific forms and procedures that comprise the financial management process? Does it contain the necessary characteristics specified by Mayer? It is a short visual display (1), it comes in advance of the learning materials (2), it is a big picture overview of the process and so does not contain specifics about financial forms or procedures (3), and it provides an assimilative context for the new information (4). Whether it permits logical relationships to be developed among elements of the to-be-learned information is beyond the scope of this brief example. But on the face of it, we may reasonably conclude that Ms. McGee's Accounting Cycle display will effectively function as an advance organizer.

Mayer (1979a) went on to suggest that further research is required to determine what analogies, images, and examples in various subject matters may best serve as effective advance organizers. In order for advance organizers to work with particular students as well, they should probably be constructed by the teacher or instructional designer who has specific knowledge about what the learners already know. Mayer concluded with the following checklist for producing organizers to be used in research, suggesting that organizers that generate a yes for each question should be explored further:

1. Does the organizer allow one to generate all or some of the logical relationships in the to-be-learned material?
2. Does the organizer provide a means of relating unfamiliar material to familiar, existing knowledge?
3. Is the organizer learnable, i.e., is it easy for the particular learner to acquire and use?
4. Would the learner fail to normally use an organizing assimilative set for this material, e.g., due to stress or inexperience? (Mayer, 1979a, p. 382)

Research on the advance organizer since Mayer's recommendations were published has resulted in greater emphasis on the learners' prior knowledge (e.g., Sui, 1986; Mannes and Kintsch, 1987). Learners must have necessary prior knowledge for the organizer to activate, and the organizer must draw explicit connections between old and new topics (West, Farmer, and Wolff, 1991). Synthesizing Ausubel's ideas with the results of more recent research, West et al., (1991) suggested the following procedures for constructing advance organizers:

1. Examine the new lesson or unit to discover necessary prerequisite knowledge. List.
2. Reteach if necessary.

BOX   4–1   Advance Organizer for a Lesson on the Government of the United Kingdom

Assume that Mr. Amaya's class from Scenario 4–1 has now completed their lesson on the democratic government of the United States. As a part of that unit, they eventually discussed the three branches of government—executive, legislative, and judicial. In the following advance organizer, these branches are mentioned as a bridge to the next unit on the government of the United Kingdom.

In our unit on the U.S. government we learned that there are three branches in the federal government: the executive, the legislative and the judicial. The primary function of the legislative branch, the Congress, is the passage of laws, whereas the major task of the judicial branch is the protection of citizens' rights under the national Constitution. In this next unit on the United Kingdom we will learn that there are also these three branches: executive, legislative and judicial, with similar functions.

(West, Farmer, and Wolff, 1991, p. 116)

3. Find out if students know this prerequisite material.
4. List or summarize the major general principles or ideas in the new lesson or unit (could be done first).
5. Write a paragraph (the advance organizer) emphasizing the major general principles, similarities across old and new topics. Examine examples in this text. Use them as models.
6. The main subtopics of the unit or lesson should be covered in the same sequence as they are presented in the advance organizer. (p. 125)

BOX   4–2   An Advance Organizer for Theories of Learning

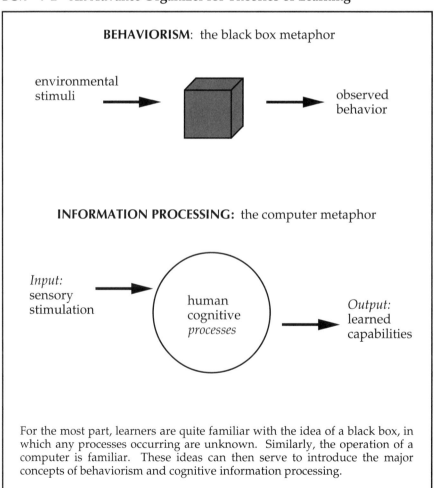

BEHAVIORISM: the black box metaphor

environmental stimuli ⟶ ⟶ observed behavior

INFORMATION PROCESSING: the computer metaphor

Input: sensory stimulation ⟶ human cognitive *processes* ⟶ *Output:* learned capabilities

For the most part, learners are quite familiar with the idea of a black box, in which any processes occurring are unknown. Similarly, the operation of a computer is familiar. These ideas can then serve to introduce the major concepts of behaviorism and cognitive information processing.

As can be seen in Step 5 and in the example provided in Box 4–1, West et al. have also emphasized the verbal (as opposed to visual) nature of advance organizers. Box 4–2, however, illustrates how visual material may serve effectively as an advance organizer. In this example are two diagrams I have successfully used to introduce different learning theories. These two metaphors tap what individuals know about black boxes and computers and maps these onto the major concepts of behaviorism and cognitive information processing. In the former, for example, no reference is made to events or processes inside the learner. In the latter, by contrast, specific hypotheses are made to suggest that such processes are akin to what computers do with information.

Comparative Organizers and Integrative Reconciliation

To improve discriminability among concepts, the second function of instruction, Ausubel (1963a) and Ausubel et al. (1978) recommended the use of comparative organizers and the principle of integrative reconciliation. To take the latter concept first, Ausubel (1963) deplored the common practice of textbook writers to compartmentalize ideas or topics into separate chapters without exploring their relationships. The result, he claimed, is "incalculable cognitive strain and confusion" on the part of the learner. Students may not see, for example, how new propositions differ in substance from what they already know, causing them to dismiss the new information as unimportant. Or, they may fail to see inherent similarities or differences among concepts in the learning material itself. In this case, misconceptions are likely to result.

Consider, for example, the principles of behavior management that you studied in chapter 2. Because there are similarities among principles that result in behavior increase (e.g., positive reinforcement, Premack principle), and among those that result in behavior decrease (e.g., punishment, extinction), these principles can be easily confused. Moreover, many learners experience confusion with negative reinforcement, which sounds like an oxymoron. The concept negative is closely associated in everyday life with aversive events, which seems to connote punishment, whereas reinforcement positively influences behavior.

A strategy to ameliorate the situation just described is for instructional programmers to employ the principle of integrative reconciliation. That is, related ideas should be explicitly cross-referenced. Their relationships should be explored to point out significant similarities and differences and to reconcile real or apparent differences. Multiple terms for equivalent concepts should also be signaled. When this is done, learners may effectively integrate new information with existing cognitive structure, maintaining discriminability between old and new information and among similar concepts.

A way to achieve integrative reconciliation, particularly where teachers or designers have no control over how text materials are written, is to provide learners with comparative organizers similar to the concept tree presented in chapter 2. Remember that Figure 2–2 displayed the principles of behavior management in a diagram that illustrated their unique as well as shared features. Comparative organizers have much in common with advance organizers (and can themselves be presented in advance of the learning materials), but they differ in content and use. They function to compare and contrast potentially confusable ideas in order to increase the discriminability of those ideas. As such, they should expressly point out areas of similarity and difference.

In Mr. Amaya's social studies class, for example, a comparative organizer might be useful in helping students determine differences and similarities between the governments of the United States and the United Kingdom. For example, a chart or frame (West et al. 1991) could be constructed like that shown in Figure 4–3.

	Executive	Legislative	Judicial
Description of function			
United States			
Great Britain			

FIGURE   4–3   **A Comparative Organizer, or Frame, for a Unit on Government**

Although research concerning the effectiveness of comparative organizers is somewhat scanty, it is generally positive. Ausubel and his colleagues have successfully used comparative organizers to facilitate meaningful learning of unfamiliar information about Buddhism (Ausubel & Fitzgerald, 1961; Ausubel & Youssef, 1963) and about the Civil War (Fitzgerald & Ausubel, 1963). In addition, Reigeluth (cf. Reigeluth & Stein, 1983) has incorporated the notion of comparative organizer into his Elaboration Theory of Instruction. In this model, synthesizers are recommended as a strategy for relating and integrating ideas both within a particular lesson or topic and across lessons and topics.

Progressive Differentiation

"When subject matter is programmed in accordance with the principle of progressive differentiation, the most general and inclusive ideas of the discipline are presented first and are then progressively differentiated in terms of detail and specificity." (Ausubel 1963a, p. 219). To Ausubel, the significance of this principle for instruction is self-evident. Because cognitive structure is hierarchically organized and most learning occurs by correlative subsumption, progressive differentiation as an instructional strategy simply parallels the learning process. It therefore provides an efficient and easy way to learn, enhancing the stability and clarity of anchoring ideas in the cognitive structure.

Evidence of progressive differentiation can be seen in Mr. Amaya's approach to teaching his students about democracy. He started with the more inclusive concept, government, which will furnish (in Ausubel's terms) the ideational anchorage for the more specific concept of democracy. In turn, democracy will anchor relevant details about the practice of democracy in America and other places.

Although Ausubel, et al. (1978) claimed that textbooks and teaching procedures rarely follow the principle of progressive differentiation, it contributes to the basis for sequencing prescriptions in the Elaboration Theory (Reigeluth, 1979; Reigeluth & Stein, 1983). Progressively more detail is to be elaborated in each level of instruction (from the most general, inclusive content to the most specific) until the desired level of detail is reached. Empirical support for the Elaboration Theory (and thus, progressive differentiation) is hard to come by, partly owing to the difficulty and expense of conducting long-term studies of semester or year long courses that have been designed according to the theory. But Reigeluth & Stein (1983) noted the popularity of the approach with experienced teachers, who use sequences of instruction very similar to that prescribed by the Elaboration Theory. They concluded, "Such intuitive appeal to experienced educators, although not experimental data, does nevertheless provide important support for the Elaboration Theory" (Reigeluth & Stein, 1983, p. 379).

Consolidation

Finally, in order to increase the stability of cognitive structure, instruction should be designed to assure consolidation, or mastery of ongoing lessons. "By insisting upon consolidation . . . before new material is introduced, we make sure of continued subject-matter readiness and success in sequentially organized learning" (Ausubel, et al., 1978, p. 197). For this recommendation, Ausubel drew on the results of experimental studies that showed overlearning was required for transfer of prior learning to new learning tasks (e.g., Morrisett & Hovland, 1959).

Ausubel had relatively little else to say about consolidation as an instructional principle. He noted that it may be achieved through "confirmation, correction, clarification, differential practice, and review of repeated exposure, with feedback, to learning material" (Ausubel et al., 1978, p. 197). But he also suggested that additional research would shed light on what degree of consolidation is most economical and what means are best for achieving it.

Summary

Judging from the number of studies and amount of controversy it has generated, the advance organizer is probably Ausubel's most well known contribution to instruction. And it continues to have an influence on pedagogy and research. With increased evidence of the very strong impact prior knowledge has on subsequent learning, the advance organizer offers intuitive appeal for activating that knowledge. Ormrod (1990) recommended it as a strategy in expository teaching to show students how instructional material is organized and how that material relates to what they have previously learned. West et al. (1991) suggested its use when students see no obvious connections between topics. Gagné and Driscoll (1988) discussed organizers as a means for satisfying one of the conditions for verbal information learning. Namely, a meaningful context must be provided for effective encoding of information, and both advance and comparative organizers may accomplish this. Finally, researchers are exploring the efficacy of graphic organizers for promoting learning and metacognition (cf. Barron & Schwartz, 1984; Bean, Singer, Sorter & Frazee, 1986).

Accounting for the effects of advance organizers, however, has had additional, opposing consequences for Ausubel's theory. On the one hand, Mayer (1977, 1979b) has proposed the concept of assimilation-to-schema (also known as Mayer's assimilation theory), which brings together Ausubel's ideas, the cognitive notion of schema, and other research on sequencing of instruction. On the other hand, Anderson, Spiro, and Anderson (1978) claimed that schema theory can provide a more precise treatment of Ausubel's ideational scaffolding. Although "Ausubel's thinking about the role of abstract knowledge structures in learning from text generally was on the right track" (Anderson et al., 1978, p. 439), research inspired by Ausubel, they contended, has generally proved inconclusive. Examining both sides of this issue should simultaneously provide a meaningful conclusion to this chapter and an advance organizer for the next.

MEANINGFUL LEARNING AS ASSIMILATION TO SCHEMA

Most modern cognitive conceptions of schema harken back to Bartlett (1932). In a study investigating the nature of remembering over a long period of time, Bartlett used the term schema to mean an organizing and orienting attitude which involves active organization of past experiences. Bartlett found that his subjects' recall of "War of the Ghosts" contained inaccuracies that could be directly related to their own interests and attitudes. He theorized that they invoked a relevant schema for understanding the story, and then, at recall, reconstructed in accord with the schema details about the story that they had forgotten.

Ausubel et al. (1978) acknowledged a similarity between anchoring ideas and Bartlett's notions of schema, but then they dismissed Bartlett's position as being fundamentally different from Ausubel's. Schemata are perceptually based, they argued, whereas anchoring ideas are cognitive. Bartlett theorized about the reconstructive nature of retention; Ausubel was interested in the constructive nature of learning. Ausubel et al. (1978) suggested that recall is really not reconstructing original meanings, it is reproducing information that has undergone memorial reduction.

As the concept of schema has developed in the cognitive literature, it is similar to both Bartlett's and Ausubel's positions. In 1977, Mayer proposed the concept of assimilation-to-schema, with which he synthesized verbal learning research from a variety of perspectives. According to the assimilation-to-schema view—or assimilation theory, as it has since been called—meaningful learning depends upon reception, availability, and activation. First, the to-be-learned material must be received by the learner. Then, a meaningful structure of familiar ideas, or relevant schemata, must be available to the learner, which can be used to organize and assimilate the new information. Finally, this meaningful structure must be activated during learning. Moreover, depending upon what aspect of cognitive structure is activated by an instructional procedure, different learning outcomes may result (Mayer & Greeno, 1972).

For example, suppose the parents of one of Mr. Amaya's students had emigrated to the United States from another country that had a different form of government than the United States. It is likely that the student would have heard his parents discussing life in the old country and would therefore have a potential set of relevant schemata available for understanding types of government. It is just as likely, however, that the student may not make the connection between what he is currently studying and his parents' experience without some sort of prompt from the teacher. Mr. Amaya, however, could activate these schemata by having his students read a short story about emigrés to the United States.

Note the obvious similarity between Mayer's model and Ausubel's theory, on which it is based. In contrast to Ausubel, however, Mayer put his model to the test by examining not only studies of advance organizers (Mayer, 1979b) but also cognitive research on instructional sequencing and memory organization (Mayer, 1977). He concluded that assimilation theory offers a sufficient framework for understanding the results of all these studies as well as for suggesting ways the conditions for meaningful learning may be met.

While Mayer offered evidence to support Ausubel's basic ideas, Anderson et al. (1978) found the theory vague and inconclusive. To bring some preciseness to Ausubel's ideas, they relied on the concept of schema as a generic characterization of things and events. Thus, "to interpret a particular situation in terms of a schema is to match the elements in the situation with the generic characterizations in the schematic knowledge structure. Another way to express this is to say that schemata contain *slots* or placeholders that can be *instantiated* . . . with certain particular cases" (Anderson et al., 1978, p. 434).

As an example, consider a class reading a text about a dairy farm. Assuming they have a farm schema (i.e., general knowledge about farms), they are likely to encode the details of the passage in terms of the available slots in the schema. There are usually animals on a farm, so into the farm animal slot will be encoded dairy cows, and so forth. Similarly, once the seventh graders in Mr. Amaya's class have acquired a government schema, they will instantiate the details of different types of governments according to the higher order schema. If no schema exists, however, verbal material will be meaningless to a reader. "A general implication for education is that the schemata a person already possesses are a principal determiner of what will be learned from a text" (Anderson et al., 1978, p. 438).

Does this conception of schema instantiation lend precision to Ausubel's ideational scaffolding? Ausubel himself did not think so. In a reply to Anderson et al. (1978), Ausubel (1980) argued "(1) that their theory of schemata is substantively almost identical . . . with my more inclusive theory of anchoring ideas in cognitive structure . . . , and (2) that in their actual research . . . , their schemata, unlike mine, do not facilitate *meaningful* learning (i.e., the acquisition of *new* meanings [e.g., concepts, facts, and principles] such as characterize school or subject matter learning) but rather *rote* learning . . . " (p. 401). In the next chapter, schema theory will be discussed in greater detail, along with other recent theories of mental representation. Perhaps then, these competing claims may be better judged.

SUGGESTED READINGS

Ausubel, D. P., Novak, J. D., & Hanesian, H. (1978). *Educational* *psychology: A cognitive view.* New York: Holt, Rinehart and Winston.

REFLECTIVE QUESTIONS AND ACTIVITIES

1. Consider Ausubel's meaningful reception learning in light of the epistemological traditions described in Chapter 1. To what view would he most likely subscribe? What evidence supports your choice?

2. How is Ausubel's conception of cognitive structure similar to or different from the models of long-term memory presented in chapter 3? To illustrate your answer, select a concept (or set of concepts) that might be the focus of instruction. Indicate how, once learned, it would be represented in memory, according to Ausubel versus information processing theorists.

3. Using your example from 2, describe what recommendations Ausubel would make for teaching those concepts. Contrast his ideas with the recommendations for instruction implied by information processing theory. How are they similar? How are they different?

4. Describe a possible study that investigates the differential effects of instruction designed from the perspectives of meaningful reception learning versus information processing. What variables might be important to examine? What differences might you expect between the two perspectives on those variables?

5. Many current textbooks on learning mention Ausubel's work only briefly. Take a position on the probable impact of his ideas on educational theory and practice. In your opinion, does his theory of meaningful reception learning provide new or additional insights into learning and/or instruction?

Schema Theory and Mental Models

Consider the following scenarios.

Scenario 5–1

The study of cooking provides a useful example of the difficulty of learning complex subjects. To a noncook, the combination of ingredients in mayonnaise is not at all an obvious one. It is for this reason that it is interesting to ask naive subjects just what they expect mayonnaise to be made of:

Protocol of the experimenter (DAN) and CN, an 8-year-old female

DAN: How do you make mayonnaise?

CN: How you make mayonnaise is you look at a cookbook.

DAN: OK, but without looking at a cookbook, can you guess what it is that's inside of mayonnaise?

CN: Uh.

DAN: How would you make it?

CN: Uh Butter—uh let me think (5–sec pause) hmmm (10-sec pause) whipped cream very very very fine-ly whipped so it's smooth. That's probably how you make it, just with whipped cream, very very very very fine and smooth.

DAN: Anything else?

CN: You might add a little taste to it.

DAN: Taste of what?

CN: (10-sec pause) Sort of a vanilla taste.

DAN: Suppose I said that mayonnaise is made from egg yolk—and oil. What would you say?

CN: I would say it's very very wrong.

DAN: Why?

CN: You can't make mayonnaise out of egg yolks and water—I mean oil.

DAN: Why not?

CN: Because of taste and smoothness and stuff like that.

Protocol of the experimenter (DAN) and GB, an adult male psychology professor

DAN: How would you make something like mayonnaise?

GB: Mayonnaise? How do you make mayonnaise? You can't make mayonnaise, it has to be bought in jars. Mayonnaise. Um. You mix whipped cream with, ummm, some mustard. (Norman, Gentner, & Stevens, 1976, p. 185)

Scenario 5–2

Without recourse to mechanical or electrical or even magnetic devices the navigators of the Central Caroline Islands of Micronesia routinely embark on oceanic voyages that take them several days out of the sight of land. Their technique seems at first glance to be inadequate for the job demanded, yet it consistently passes what Lewis (1972) has called "the stern test of landfall." Of the thousands of voyages made in the memory of living navigators only a few have ended with the loss of a canoe. Western researchers travelling with these people have found that at any time during the voyage the navigators can accurately indicate the bearings of the port of departure, the goal island, and other islands off to the side of the course steered even though all these may be over the horizon out of the sight of the navigator. These navigators are also able to tack upwind to an unseen target keeping mental track of its changing bearing, something that is simply impossible for a Western navigator without instruments. (Hutchins, 1983, pp. 191–192)

These two scenarios were excerpted from research studies conducted by cognitive scientists (a new breed of investigator representing the intersection of psychology, computer science, linguistics, and often, the neurosciences). In the first, the primary aim of the study was to understand how individuals approach novel problems for which they may have little relevant knowledge. In the second, the goal was to understand Micronesian navigation; how do these navigators function? Reflect for a moment on the nature of these research goals. How adequate are the theories of behaviorism, cognitive information processing, and meaningful reception learning to accomplishing them? Can the reinforcement contingencies be specified to account for a navigator's skill in tacking for an unseen target? How is the information represented that a child calls upon to figure out how mayonnaise is made?

It is useful at this point to make a distinction held by most cognitive researchers regarding the types of knowledge acquired by learners. Making mayonnaise requires knowing not only what its ingredients are but also how they are mixed together. Similarly, Western navigators may know all the same facts as the Micronesian navigators but not be able to demonstrate the same navigational skill without instruments to aid them. This distinction between knowing that and knowing how has led theorists to assume that two different types of knowledge are acquired: declarative knowledge and procedural knowledge.

Ausubel (see chapter 4) did not make the same distinction in so many words, but it is implicit in the difference he described between meaningful and rote learning. Meaningful learning implies that learners can use their conceptual knowledge; it is not simply memorized to be recited later.

Information processing theorists also recognized a difference between declarative and procedural learning. Because any adequate theory must account for both types, most recent formulations of memory models include explicit procedural directives that act upon memory units. Anderson (1983), for one, referred to condition-action pairs underlying human cognition that he called productions. When something like concepts are learned, declarative knowledge is acquired about the concepts, but productions are also acquired that specify conditions for classifying new examples as concept instances. These are something like if-then statements. If the new example contains certain features, for instance, then it must belong to this concept classification. Or, more concretely, if I witness a teacher praise a student for offering a good idea in a class discussion, and she speaks out more in class as a consequence, then I have seen positive reinforcement in action. I can not only describe the concept of reinforcement, I can recognize its application.

The declarative-procedural distinction is basic to the research and theory-building to be discussed in this chapter, and there is assumed to be an integral relationship between the two. Developments in schema theory and mental modeling came on the heels of cognitive information processing theory, perhaps to better account for procedural behavior. How is it that people use their knowledge to make inferences, to solve problems, to deal with novel circumstances? In this chapter, schema theory will be discussed first, followed by mental models research, which has been conducted to understand how learners conceptualize their knowledge within specific subject matter domains. Although these approaches independently contribute implications for instruction, together they also suggest strategies for thinking and learning in context. These will be discussed last.

SCHEMA THEORY

According to Rumelhart (1980), "schemata truly are the *building blocks of cognition* . . . the fundamental elements upon which all information processing depends" (p. 33). As noted in both chapters 3 and 4, the concept of schema is generally attributed to Bartlett (1932), but schema theorists agree that their notions about schemata more closely parallel Kant's (1787/1963) conception. In Kant's view, schemata are category rules, which make up one's understanding and which are applied to experience and knowledge acquisition. Despite the claim of Kantian roots, schema theory developed in the mid-1970s as a way of accounting, within a parsimonious system, for findings that proved difficult for other memory models. These resulted from investigations into the effects of prior knowledge on new learning and are worth reviewing briefly.

Antecedents to Schema Theory

Comprehension and Memory for Gist

When you read a set of related sentences about a single topic, what happens? Do you pay much attention to the content of each sentence independent of the others? No, you do not. Besides, sentences often contain references to information spelled out in other sentences, so that you know "he" in a later sentence, for example, refers to the same man described earlier in the paragraph. These intersentence references allow you to comprehend the gist of the message. Later, if asked to recall what you read, you would also be likely to remember the gist, rather than each of the actual sentences that you read.

Many studies demonstrated the intertwined nature of comprehension and memory; what is remembered is largely a function of what was understood to begin with. But studies also revealed that both are driven by meaning, rather than by the structure of the stimulus information. Bransford and Franks (1971), for example, presented the following sentences to subjects:

> *The house was in the valley.*
> *The house was little.*
> *The valley was green.*
> *The house burned down.*

Instead of constructing multiple representations in memory as anticipated—one for each of the four sentences—subjects appeared to construct only one, namely: "The little house in the green valley burned down." Remember the research findings cited in chapter 3 to support propositional models of memory. There, it was argued, subjects appeared to store individual propositions from a complex input sentence. Here, the opposite phenomenon has occurred.

Effects of Theme on Comprehension and Memory
Learners not only read for gist, they appear to read for theme. If a relevant theme is not available, comprehension is inadequate and recall suffers. To illustrate, read the following passage.

> *The procedure is actually quite simple. First you arrange items into different groups. Of course one pile may be sufficient depending on how much there is to do. If you have to go somewhere else due to lack of facilities that is the next step; otherwise you are pretty well set. It is important not to overdo things. That is, it is better to do too few things at once than too many. In the short run this may not seem important but complications can easily arise. A mistake can be expensive as well. At first, the whole procedure will seem complicated. Soon, however, it will become just another facet of life. It is difficult to foresee any end to the necessity for this task in the immediate future, but then, one never can tell. After the procedure is completed one arranges the materials into different groups again. Then they can be put into their appropriate places. Eventually they will be used once more and the whole cycle will then have to be repeated. However, that is part of life. (Bransford, 1979, pp. 134-135)*

None of the sentences in the above paragraph seems particularly difficult to understand, but together they do not make much sense. Bransford and Johnson (1972, 1973) and Dooling & Lachman (1971) found that without benefit of the theme, "washing clothes," subjects had difficulty comprehending and remembering the passage. Similar effects also have been demonstrated with pictures providing the theme (Bransford & Johnson, 1972), and Bransford (1978) argued that appropriate verbal knowledge can support the understanding of physical features of stimuli as well. For example, the flat blades of a dressmaker's shears might go unnoticed without the knowledge that they enable cutting on a flat surface. Finally, new, thematically consistent information is often falsely recognized as having been previously presented (Sulin & Dooling, 1974; Royer, Perkins, & Konold, 1978). This phenomenon was discussed in the previous chapter as providing evidence for meaningful learning. Recall that learners are assumed to integrate new information within a related cognitive structure.

Prior Knowledge and Perspective
Certainly, the work conducted or inspired by Ausubel (see chapter 4) is relevant to the development of schema theory. Ausubel argued that the activation of relevant prior knowledge was critical to meaningful learning, since

existing cognitive structure provided the foundation for learning new things. Notice how consistent Ausubel's terminology is with the construction metaphor presented in chapter 3. Anchoring ideas provide the ideational scaffold for new information in cognitive structure.

Researchers interested in the role of prior knowledge in thinking and solving problems hypothesized that changes in a learner's knowledge base can produce sophisticated cognitive performance (Glaser, 1984). A first step to affirming this hypothesis was to examine differences in learning and memory between those with high and low knowledge in a particular area. Chiesi and co-workers (Chiesi, Spilich, & Voss 1979; Spilich, Vesonder, Chiesi, & Voss, 1979) demonstrated that subjects who knew a lot about baseball were able to remember much more from a summary of a baseball inning than subjects who knew little about the game. Similarly, Chi (1978) replicated the results of Chase and Simon (1973a, 1973b) with findings that expert chess players outperformed novices at recalling the positions of chessmen on the board.

Strongly associated with prior knowledge are people's interests and past experiences, which have also been shown to affect a learner's interpretation and recall of information. Anderson (1977) reported a study in which an ambiguous passage that could be interpreted in terms of playing cards or playing music was read to music students. As might be expected, students with an interest in music interpreted the passage to be about music and were unaware that the passage could be interpreted any other way.

This effect of perspective on learning and memory was also demonstrated by Pichert and Anderson (1977) and Anderson and Pichert (1978). In their studies, individuals were asked to read a passage describing two boys playing in front of a house. Half the subjects were told to read the story from the perspective of a real estate agent, while the other half were to adopt the perspective of a burglar. As predicted, perspective affected recall. That is, the real estate agent subjects remembered details about the number of rooms and condition of the house, whereas the burglar subjects remembered details about valuable objects and the isolation of the house from surrounding neighbors. But there was an unexpected finding as well. When asked to adopt the alternate perspective, without rereading the story, subjects remembered information that they did not report the first time! How was this notion of perspective to be explained in theories of memory? The answer to this, and indeed the way to incorporate the results of all these studies of prior knowledge, can be found in schema theory.

What Is a Schema?

A schema is "a data structure for representing the generic concepts stored in memory" (Rumelhart, 1980, p. 34). Schemata are packets of knowledge, and schema theory is a theory of how these packets are represented and how that representation facilitates the use of the knowledge in particular ways. Thus, there are schemata "representing our knowledge about all concepts: those underlying objects, situations, events, sequences of events, actions, and sequences of actions" (Rumelhart, 1980, p. 34). To illustrate these various aspects of schemata, Rumelhart presented four different analogies.

First, schemata are like plays, in that a schema has variables that can be associated with different aspects of the environment, just as a play has characters, settings, actions, and so forth. Suppose, for example, that a playwright has written a very simple play about beating egg yolks in order to make mayonnaise. There must be a person to do the beating, an implement that person will use, a container for the eggs, and an overall setting in which the action will occur. Rumelhart would argue that our schema for egg-beating is very much like this description. And when the playwright specifies who will do the beating, what implement will be used, and where the action will take place, this amounts to the same process as schema instantiation. In other words, the schema variables take on specific values. Moreover, these values are typically constrained. Only certain tools are used to beat eggs, for example, and egg-beating generally takes place only in kitchens.

Schemata are like theories. Theories enable us to interpret events and phenomena surrounding us. To the extent that our theories work, they also allow us to make predictions about unobserved events. So it is with schemata. "The total set of schemata instantiated at a particular moment in time constitutes our internal model of the situation we face at that moment in time" (Rumelhart, 1980,. 37). In addition, schemata provide the basis for making inferences about unobserved events. Consider the egg-beating event, for example. If you read a description of someone beating eggs that never mentioned what tool was being used, your egg-beating schema would fill in that gap with the default value (cf. Minsky, 1975) for egg-beating implement. Asked later what tool was used to beat the eggs, you are likely to reply, "Oh, an egg beater, hand mixer, something like that. ... " Default values are our initial guesses for variables whose values have not yet been observed.

While plays and theories are passive, schemata are active, so that schemata are like procedures, such as computer programs. They actively evaluate incoming information for the quality of fit, and they may involve a network of subprocedures. For example, the egg-beating schema undoubtedly has a subschema for how hard and how long to beat for given purposes. Schemata such as these that direct one's actions in a given situation have come to be called scripts. Finally, schemata are like parsers, in that they break down and organize incoming information to fit appropriate schema structures.

Schema-Based Processing

How do schemata operate to influence information processing? At the least, schema theory must deal with how schemata are acquired in the first place, how they are initially selected to use on a processing task, and how they are instantiated, combined, changed, and maintained throughout the course of processing (Spiro 1980). Let us first consider the simplest of these aspects, selecting and using schemata to comprehend or interpret some incoming stimulus.

Rumelhart (1980) described how readers construct interpretations of the following brief passage:

> *Business had been slow since the oil crisis. Nobody seemed to want anything really elegant anymore. Suddenly the door opened and a well-dressed man entered the showroom floor. John put on his friendliest and most sincere expression and walked toward the man. (p. 43)*

Sentence by sentence readers appear to invoke and evaluate schemata for their relevance to the story and ability to account for the available facts. So, for example, a business schema is selected with the first sentence, which suggests hypotheses about what is being sold. Encountering the word *elegant* in the second sentence causes readers to modify their interpretation; perhaps people do not want to buy large, elegant cars. *Showroom* is consistent with the car-selling schema, so that *well-dressed* signals money and buyer schemata, and so on. You can see the interaction between bottom-up and top-down processing that occurs in schema theory accounts of processing. An incoming stimulus activates a schema (bottom-up), which, by virtue of its variables, sets up expectations (top-down) for additional information as to the values of these variables. To the extent these expectations are met, that schema is instantiated. Information contrary to expectation, however, leads to alternate schema activation or modification of the current schema.

What about learning, then? How does experience contribute to the permanent modification of schemata? Three different processes have been proposed to account for changes in existing schemata and the acquisition of new schemata due to learning. They are accretion, tuning, and restructuring (Rumelhart & Norman, 1978; Rumelhart, 1980; Vosniadou & Brewer, 1987). **Accretion** is roughly equivalent to fact learning in that *information is remembered that was instantiated within a schema as a result of text comprehension* or understanding of some event. For example, remembering from the description of mayonnaise making that a blender was used to beat the eggs is indicative of accretion. The egg-beating schema remains unchanged, but the variable for implement has been filled with blender.

When existing schemata evolve to become more consistent with experience, then **tuning** has occurred. Rumelhart and Norman (1978) suggested that this process accounts for the minor schema modifications that come with new exemplars of concepts and principles. Adding to one's egg-beating schema the information about how long to beat for mayonnaise versus omelets is an example of tuning.

Finally, **restructuring** involves *the creation of entirely new schemata which replace or incorporate old ones*. This may occur through schema induction (Rumelhart, 1980), in which a new schema is configured from repeated consistencies of experience. Or, as Rumelhart and Norman (1981) argued, restructuring occurs most of the time through learning by analogy. In this case, a new schema is created by modeling it on an existing schema and then tuning it to fit the new situation. What typically occurs, according to Rumelhart and Norman, is that learners will try to use an existing schema to interpret the new situation, as did the child who initially applied her understanding of whipped cream to the mayonnaise problem. Areas of mismatch suggest ways in which the new schema must differ from the old, while areas that were not contradicted are carried over into the new schema.

Evidence for Schema Theory

As indicated earlier, researchers initially conceptualized knowledge structures in terms of schemata to explain effects of prior knowledge on learning and memory. Parallel efforts developed on several fronts to incorporate schema notions into models of text comprehension as well as artificial intelligence. Minsky (1975) proposed that conventionalized world knowledge was represented in frames, and Schank and Abelson (1977) investigated the role of scripts in accounting for human actions. Although these early investigations were largely conjectural, the restaurant script developed by Schank and Abelson (1975) provided a basis for later empirical testing that supported the psychological reality of scripts and schemata.

The restaurant script contains information about what it is like to go to a restaurant. There are roles to be filled (customer, waiter/waitress, cashier), certain props (such as table, menu, food, check, or tip), and certain activities (sitting down, ordering, paying the bill, tipping, and so on). This general script is also likely to vary depending upon the type and location of the restaurant. For example, fast food restaurants differ in predictable ways from five-star restaurants, and restaurant customs in the West are likely to differ from those of other cultures.

Several studies (e.g., Anderson, Spiro, & Anderson, 1979; Bower, Black, & Turner, 1979) demonstrated that such a restaurant script served as the context for understanding and remembering information from stories taking place in restaurants. Subjects used their general knowledge about restaurants to comprehend particular events described in the stories. But now consider a story such as the following:

> *Jim went to the restaurant and asked to be seated in the gallery. He was told that there would be a one-half hour wait. Forty minutes later, the applause for his song indicated that he could proceed with the preparation. Twenty guests had ordered his favorite, a cheese souffle. (Bransford, 1979, p. 184)*

Because this story violates your general restaurant script, there seems to be something wrong with it. Bransford (1979) made two points with this illustration. First, the fact that schema violations impede comprehension and memory argues for the very existence of knowledge structures like schemata. Second, suppose you subsequently learn that Jim went to a very special type of restaurant, where customers who can cook are allowed to compete for the honor of preparing their specialties for other customers. The competition involves the customer entertaining the crowd, by singing, dancing, or whatever. Now, the target passage probably makes more sense when you reread it. But Bransford contended that you must have a general restaurant schema in the first place in order to construct a modified one in which to incorporate this story.

Evidence for schema-based processing and the constructive nature of memory comes from another source as well. Elizabeth Loftus and her colleagues conducted a series of studies examining eyewitness memory (see Loftus, 1979, for a review). The typical procedure followed in these studies was to show subjects a videotape of a crime or automobile accident and then to ask them questions about what they remembered seeing. The type of question had significant implications for recall. In one study (Loftus & Palmer, 1974), for example, students viewed a film of an auto accident and were asked either, "About how fast were the cars going when they smashed into each other?" or "About how fast were the cars going when they hit each other?" Subjects' memory for the speed of the cars differed significantly depending on which question they were asked. Moreover, subjects asked the question with the word *smashed* reported having seen broken glass significantly more often than subjects asked the question with the word *hit*. These results suggest the possibility of a smash schema being activated and used to reconstruct memory for the auto accident event; a hit schema activates slightly different knowledge.

Although the results of Loftus' research provide support for schema theory, they should be viewed with caution when considered for their application to eyewitness testimony in a court of law. The biasing effects of questions that have been produced in the laboratory do not necessarily hold when witnesses are actively involved in a real crime or accident. Yuille and Cutshall (1986) interviewed witnesses to an actual shooting in which one person was killed and another seriously injured. Subjects showed highly accurate memory for the event over a period of five months, and they resisted attempts to mislead them through the wording of questions.

Applications of Schema Theory

Schema theory has proved useful in understanding a variety of phenomena related to learning. It also suggests specific implications for instruction. As these have been investigated in the literature, they relate to comprehension of text material, textbook design, arithmetic problem solving, and understanding of cultural differences.

Comprehension of Text Material

Because reading involves using schemata to comprehend what is read, it is important to determine what schemata readers possess and whether these match the requirements of the reading task (Kintsch, 1976, 1977; van Dijk & Kintsch, 1983; Rumelhart, 1975; Mandler, Johnson, & Deforest, 1976). Many stories in Western culture, for example, share a common abstract structure which includes an initial setting, adventures of a main character, and resolution of some problem that faces the main character. This story grammar or narrative schema guides both comprehension and later recall of story events.

People may also develop schemata to guide their understanding of scientific or technical articles (Bransford, 1979; cf. Brooks & Dansereau, 1983). Most of the research articles cited in this book, for example, follow a standard schema: introduction to the problem under study, method used to conduct the investigation, results, and discussion. Moreover, schemata can be reflected in text structures as well as types of content (Armbruster, 1986). Basic text structures can include simple listing, comparison/contrast, temporal sequence, cause/effect, and problem/solution (Armbruster, 1986, p. 255). Finally, different schemata may be developed for various literature genre—newspaper stories, detective fiction, etc.

In all cases, it is assumed that comprehension and memory are facilitated when learners both know and can access a relevant schema. It is also safe to assume that, when readers undertake a subject entirely new to them, they must acquire a new text schema before comprehension of the content will occur readily. Therefore, instructors may find it useful to alert students to the schematic structures of text materials in order to facilitate their learning. Poor readers, in particular, can comprehend more of what they read if they are taught to focus on the structure of the text (Varnhagen & Goldman, 1986).

Schema Theory and Textbook Design

In chapter 3, the recommendation was made to signal a text's organization to readers. Not only should this help readers pay more attention to important information, but it also provides a foundation for more effective encoding. On the basis of schema theory, this recommendation must be both qualified and expanded. "Authors can help readers access the appropriate textual schemas by (a) organizing the textbook using conventional text structures—the basic text structures and/or more genre- or content-specific text structures and when these are known and appropriate, and (b) clearly signalling the text organization" (Armbruster, 1986, p. 258).

Armbruster reviewed research in which certain types of signals appeared to be effective in emphasizing certain types of text structures. For example, additive conjunctions (e.g., also, likewise) can be useful in signaling compare/contrast text structures, whereas causal conjunctions (e.g., consequently, as a result) are likely to be effective with cause/effect text structures. To help readers access or construct relevant content schemata, Armbruster (1986) concluded that current research suggests (1) the "judicious use of analogies or comparisons" (p. 261), and (2) the presentation of "well-developed concepts and thorough explanations that make explicit the important relationships among ideas" (p. 264). Once again, it is worthwhile to note the similarity between these recommendations and the notion of comparative organizers as suggested by Ausubel.

Arithmetic Problem Solving

Many researchers interested in how students solve word problems in arithmetic have lately adopted schema theory as a guiding framework (e.g., Greeno, 1980; Sweller, Mawer, & Ward, 1983; Cooper & Sweller, 1987; Derry, Hawkes, & Tsai, 1987). Assumptions are made that learning mathematics consists of acquiring a large number of schemata and that solving problems requires accessing relevant schemata regarding problem types. Sweller (1989) asserted that a schema, if available, provides for rapid and relatively effortless problem solving. Moreover, in the absence of an appropriate schema, or in the case of incorrect classification of a problem, an inappropriate schema will still be used. This suggests that a major aspect of learning to solve problems is learning to recognize what problems match which schema.

Evidence for schema-based problem solving can be seen in studies of good problem solvers who appear to have schemata for meaningful problem types (e.g., Schoenfeld & Herrmann, 1982) and in studies indicating that students' errors on word problems stem from misclassification of the problem rather than computational errors (e.g., DeCorte, Verschaffel, & De Win, 1985). A possible implication of these results is that, to improve arithmetic problem solving, students should receive training and practice in recognizing and representing problem types. Lewis (1989), for example, taught students a diagramming method for representing compare problems in arithmetic. Fuson and Willis (1989) demonstrated that classroom teachers could successfully teach children to use schematic drawings to represent the structure of addition and subtraction problems. In both instances, the representational strategy benefited students in conceptualizing and solving a variety of problems.

Schema-Based Cultural Knowledge

The concepts of schemata and scripts have also been useful beyond the confines of cognitive psychology. Social behavior, sex-role stereotyping, and responses to mass media or advertising can be framed in terms of schemata (Leahey & Harris, 1989). Harris, Schoen, and Lee (1986) conceptualized cultural knowledge as acquired scripts. Although similarities may exist among cultures in a restaurant script, for example, there will be differences in some of the roles, activities, or conditions. These can easily lead to misunderstandings when a member of one culture visits another.

Cultural schemata may not seem to be directly related to instruction, but they can affect how students will behave in particular instructional situations—sometimes with disastrous results. One of my doctoral graduates from Taiwan, for example, found his schema for multiple-choice tests to be inappropriate for taking tests in the United States. He was accustomed to selecting more than one response on multiple-choice items and did not realize, on his first test in graduate school in the United States, that only one answer would be considered correct. Needless to say, he quickly modified that schema. Given our increasingly multicultural society and the increased demands for training in international settings, it is probably wise to keep in mind the cultural schemata learners may bring to instruction.

MENTAL MODELS

Research on the processes of problem solving has shown that when learners lack relevant prior knowledge, they may be forced to use general problem solving strategies rather than specific, schema-based ones. Because this leads to inefficient, often unsuccessful solutions to problems, a growing number of researchers have been concerned with how large bodies of knowledge are acquired and conceptualized by learners. Mental models research, as it has been called, attempts to explicitly lay out human understanding within specific subject matter domains. The point of this research, for many, is simply to figure out human knowledge about the world. But clearly, there are applied consequences of these models as well. Mental models of liquids, for instance, "would be relevant to understanding why operators of nuclear plants do not always correctly interpret their instruments. Similarly, in order to train seamen about how a steamship works, the better our models of exactly what kind of knowledge is involved in liquid flow and phase transitions, the better we would be able to simulate, teach, and test for this knowledge" (Stevens and Gentner, 1983, p. 1).

What Are Mental Models?

When people interact with the environment, other people, or the artifacts of technology, they develop interpretive representations that drive their performance (Norman, 1983; Johnson-Laird, 1983, 1988; Gagné & Glaser, 1987). These representations are mental models, schema-based but also including perceptions of task demands and task performances. Norman (1983) made the following observations about mental models (p. 8):

1. Mental models are incomplete.
2. People's ability to control their models is limited.
3. Mental models are unstable.
4. Mental models do not have firm boundaries.
5. Mental models are unscientific.
6. Mental models are parsimonious.

What this means is that people bring to tasks imprecise, partial, and idiosyncratic understandings that evolve with experience. Additionally, these understandings are utilitarian for the most part, rather than necessarily accurate.

As an illustration of a mental model in action, consider this brief description provided by Norman (1983). He observed people using hand-held versions of several types of calculators and questioned them about their methods and understanding of the calculator.

> One of the subjects I studied (on a four-function calculator) was quite cautious. Her mental model seemed to contain information about her own limitations and the classes of errors that she could make. She commented, "I

always take extra steps. I never take short cuts." She was always careful to
clear the calculator before starting the problem, hitting the clear button several
times. She wrote down partial results even when they could have been stored in
the machine memory. (Norman, 1983, p. 8)

In trying to describe subjects' mental models of calculators, Norman speculated that most develop a rule to hit the clear button excessively because the action is functional across all kinds of calculators. The rule enables generalization to occur and thus makes the mental model work in a variety of situations. Note that the model is not accurate for all calculators, since some require only one press of the clear button to clear all registers.

An important aspect of mental models is their predictive power. That is, they provide a basis for making inferences, or reasoning. When children have previously constructed concrete models of the logical arguments underlying a given set of problems, for example, they can learn to solve more abstract problems. Falmagne (1980) trained children to solve "if p, then q; *not q*, therefore *not p*" problems by presenting them with concrete premises, such as "If it is Tuesday, then Mary has gym. Mary does not have gym; therefore, it is not Tuesday."

Adults also have difficulty with abstract problems if they are unable to construct a mental model of the problems. D'Andrade (cited in Rumelhart, 1980) told participants they were to imagine themselves as quality control experts in a label-making factory, and their task was to determine whether labels were incorrectly constructed. A label was correctly constructed if, when there was a vowel on one side of the label, there was an odd number on the other side. Only 13 percent of the subjects were able to appropriately apply this rule. But then D'Andrade had subjects imagine themselves as store managers inspecting store receipts with the rule, if any purchase exceeds $30, the signature of the store manager must be on the back of the receipt. This rule is formally identical to the previous one with which subjects had difficulty, but now 70 percent were able to apply it appropriately.

Evidence for Mental Models

Johnson-Laird (1983) used the following illustration as evidence of the need for, and existence of, mental models. Excerpted from Arthur Conan Doyle's (1905) story, "The Adventure of Charles Augustus Milverton," is this account of how Sherlock Holmes and Dr. Watson set out to burgle the house of a blackmailer, "the worst man in London."

With our black silk face-coverings, which turned us into two of the most
truculent figures in London, we stole up to the silent, gloomy house. A sort of

tiled veranda extended along one side of it, lined by several windows and two doors.

"That's his bedroom," Holmes whispered. "This door opens straight into the study. It would suit us best, but it is bolted as well as locked, and we should make too much noise getting in. Come round here. There's a greenhouse which opens into the drawing room."

The place was locked, but Holmes removed a circle of glass and turned the key from the inside. An instant afterwards he had closed the door behind us, and we had become felons in the eyes of the law. The thick, warm air of the conservatory and the rich, choking fragrance of exotic plants took us by the throat. He seized my hand in the darkness and led me swiftly past banks of shrubs which brushed against our faces. Holmes had remarkable powers, carefully cultivated, of seeing in the dark. Still holding my hand in one of his, he opened a door, and I was vaguely conscious that we had entered a large room in which a cigar had been smoked not long before. He felt his way among the furniture, opened another door, and closed it behind us. Putting out my hand I felt several coats hanging from the wall, and I understood that I was in a passage. We passed along it, and Holmes very gently opened a door upon the right-hand side. Something rushed out at us and my heart sprang into my mouth, but I could have laughed when I realized that it was the cat. A fire was burning in this new room, and again the air was heavy with tobacco smoke. Holmes entered on tiptoe, waited for me to follow, and then very gently closed the door. We were in Milverton's study, and a portiere at the farther side showed the entrance to his bedroom.

It was a good fire, and the room was illuminated by it. Near the door I saw the gleam of an electric switch, but it was unnecessary, even if it had been safe, to turn it on. At one side of the fireplace was a heavy curtain which covered the bay window we had seen from the outside. On the other side was the door which communicated with the veranda. A desk stood in the centre, with a turning-chair of shining red leather. Opposite was a large bookcase, with a marble bust of Athene on the top. In the corner, between the bookcase and the wall, there stood a tall, green safe, the firelight flashing back from the polished brass knobs upon its face.

In order to understand this passage in the first place, you very likely activated relevant schemata having to do with burglaries, creeping through darkened rooms, etc. Readers familiar with Sherlock Holmes will also have activated prior knowledge about his famous deductive powers. But now Johnson-Laird posed the following question. On the next page is a simple plan of the house with the veranda running down one side of it.

Which way did Holmes and Watson make their way along the veranda —from right to left or from left to right?

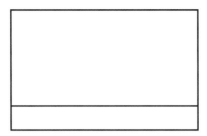

According to Johnson-Laird (1983), about one in a hundred people can spontaneously give the right answer to this question. Upon rereading the passage with the question in mind, most people can answer it correctly. This suggests two conclusions. (1) There appear to be different levels of comprehension, perhaps governed by task requirements. Reading for pleasure may result in only partial representations of passage information. (2) In order to make the required inference about Holmes' and Watson's direction, one must construct a mental model of the spatial layout. (The solution, by the way, can be found at the end of the chapter.)

Johnson-Laird (1988) also pointed out that people must have spatial mental models of their homes in order to navigate them successfully in the dark. Imagine walking blindfolded through your kitchen or dining room. You could do it with little difficulty because you have a mental picture of where the furniture is located. Suppose now that you hear the warning, "Watch out, I've moved the table to the end of the room." You would still be able to avoid it because you can form an image of the table in its new location (Johnson-Laird, 1988, p. 99).

Other evidence for mental models can be found in the expert-novice studies, a few of which have already been cited to support schema-based processing. In this tradition, it has been amply demonstrated that experts in a domain structure their knowledge in ways different from novices (e.g., Chase & Simon, 1973a, 1973b; Chi, Glaser, & Rees, 1982; Larken, McDermott, Simon, & Simon, 1980). When attempting to solve problems, then, experts and novices build different mental models to guide their efforts. "Our research suggests that the knowledge of novices is organized around the literal objects explicitly given in a problem statement. Experts' knowledge, on the other hand, is organized around principles and abstractions that subsume these objects. These principles are not apparent in the problem statement but derive from the knowledge of the subject matter" (Glaser, 1984, pp. 98–99).

Researchers have attempted to model people's mental models in a variety of subject domains using a host of different methodologies. Hutchins (1983), for example, in the study cited in Scenario 5–2, used both field observation and protocol analysis to compare the mental models of

Western and Micronesian navigators. diSessa (1983) adopted field observation in an artifical domain. That is, he presented subjects with a simulation of a Newtonian world in order to observe the extent to which physics students understand ideal Newtonian laws. DeKleer and Brown (1983) are representative of researchers who build computer simulations of human mental models. They relied on interactions with expert circuit analysts to produce a simulation of expert knowledge in electronic circuit analysis. Finally, McCloskey (1983) conducted laboratory experiments to examine how experts and novices solve problems involving mechanics. He then compared the results of his experiments to historical differences found in naive theories of mechanics in the sixteenth century.

Mental Models and Instruction

What are the implications of mental models research for instruction? "As designers, it is our duty to develop systems and instructional materials that aid users to develop more coherent, useable mental models. As teachers, it is our duty to develop conceptual models that will aid the learner to develop adequate and appropriate mental models" (Norman, 1982, p. 14). Conceptual models are any of the models invented by teachers, designers, scientists, or engineers to help make some target system understandable.

Before instruction even takes place, however, teachers and designers should identify the mental models that learners bring to the instructional situation (Glaser, 1984; Gagné & Glaser, 1987). Studies in physics, for example, have shown that many learners have naive theories of physical phenomena (e.g., Lewis, Stern, & Linn, 1993; Champagne, Klopfer, & Anderson, 1980; McCloskey, Caramazza, & Green, 1980). Such naive theories may contain contradictory, erroneous, or unnecessary concepts, with the result that learning and problem solving become difficult and ineffective.

Tracking the development of learners' mental models through the transition from novice to expert can be a means for determining what next steps in instruction should be taken (Gagné & Glaser, 1987). In a developmental study, Carey (1985a) documented changes in children's concept of alive as they gained domain-specific knowledge about biological functions. Likewise, Siegler and co-workers (Siegler & Klahr, 1982; Siegler & Richards, 1982) found that children's reasoning about balance-scale problems was greatly influenced by experience with new information. Using a task analysis procedure to determine what theory guided children's performance, Siegler was able to match their current knowledge state with learning events that helped them move to a new level of reasoning.

Teachers' knowledge of students' problem solving knowledge has also been associated with problem solving achievement. In a recent correlational study, Peterson, Carpenter, and Fennema (1989) concluded that more knowledgeable teachers appeared to pose problems to students, question their problem solving processes, and listen to their solutions. These actions were related to problem solving achievement. Less knowledgeable teachers, by contrast, tended to explain problem solving processes to students, "thereby also doing the thinking for students" (Peterson, et al., 1989, p. 568).

How can teachers ascertain the mental models of their students? There are at least four possible ways to do it: (1) observe them; (2) ask them for an explanation; (3) ask them to make predictions; and (4) ask them to teach another student (Jih & Reeves, 1992). A mathematician who does research on math instruction, Schoenfeld (1985) often asks his students without warning to explain their reasoning on a problem or to justify the approach they are taking to solve it. Not only does this enable him to judge their mental models, but also the tactic encourages students to monitor their own mental models. "By the end of the term, I don't need to ask questions anymore. Students have gotten into the habit of analyzing where they are" (Schoenfeld, quoted in *A Mathematician's Research on Math Instruction*, 1987).

By understanding what models learners are currently using to guide their performance, teachers and designers can build upon them by specifying what Glaser (1984) called pedagogical models. These may be the same as conceptual models that have been invented to make some system understandable, or they may be a series of approximations that may be thought about and debugged in the course of instruction. diSessa (1982) referred to a kind of task analysis for identifying components of preexisting theories that can be involved in developing more sophisticated theories. Collins and Stevens (1982, 1983) offered a model of inquiry instruction that provides strategies for helping learners make predictions from and debug their current models of understanding (see chapter 7 for more discussion of this model). For example, Anderson (cited in Collins & Stevens, 1983) assisted learners in formulating models of what geographic factors affect average temperature by getting them to form and test hypotheses about the locations and temperatures of specific places. In addition, diSessa (1982), Champagne, Klopfer, Fox, & Scheuerman (1982), and Lewis, et al. (1993) have designed computer simulations that allow physics students to explore the implications of their own theories and compare these results to the predictions of other theories.

Finally, mental models may be explicitly taught to facilitate performance (Gagné & Glaser, 1987) . These conceptual models provide an important supplement to teaching strategies. "We have found that students make up their own conceptualizations anyway, and if we don't give them guidance, their models can be bizarre and difficult to overcome" (Norman, 1982, p. 108). Choosing an appropriate conceptual model to use in instruction, however, can be a difficult task. In studies of how computer-ignorant students learned to use a text editor, Norman and his colleagues faced a choice between providing an incomplete model or spending a great deal of time conveying a complete model. They found their way out of this dilemma by providing different conceptual models at different points in the instruction, each designed to elucidate a different aspect of the editor (Norman, 1982).

In a similar fashion, instruction on the specific concepts that underpin a model can be verbally presented to supplement a diagrammatic presentation of the model. In teaching inferential statistics, for example, Hong & O'Neil (1992) found that most intermediate performers (those who could not match the performance of experts but who knew much more than novices about statistics) represented problems in diagrams like the one shown in Figure 5–1, because these helped them to solve the problems. Teaching these diagrammatic models to novices after they had had some instruction on the underlying concepts facilitated both conceptual and procedural understanding (Hong & O'Neil, 1992).

For pedagogical or conceptual models to effectively facilitate learning, they should meet three basic criteria: learnability, functionality, and usability (Norman, 1983). A good model is easy to learn, most likely drawing upon information that is highly familiar to learners. A good model is functional, in that it corresponds to important aspects of the target system it is designed to clarify. For example, the components making up a system might be identified as well as how these components function together to enable the system to operate (Mayer & Gallini, 1990). A good pedagogical model may not necessarily be a complete model, in the sense of representing all important aspects of the target. If this is the case, then several

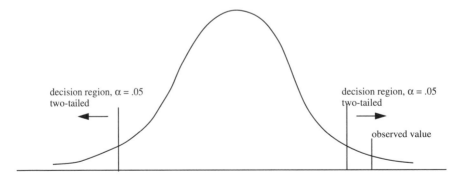

FIGURE   5–1   A Diagram of the Normal Curve with Areas of Statistical Significance Drawn

When the observed statistic occurs with a probability less than α (as shown), then the decision is to accept that value as statistically significant.

models may be required to fully conceptualize the desired information, and learners should be told that each one is not a perfect representation of the system being learned (Jones, 1988). Finally, a good model is easily used, given the limitations of the human information processing system. Again, this argues for a series of incomplete models over a complete one that taxes learners' processing capabilities.

SITUATED LEARNING AND A QUESTION OF TRANSFER

At the beginning of this chapter, I distinguished between procedural and declarative knowledge, in part because the thrust of schema theory and mental models research has been to account for procedural behavior. But it should be obvious that declarative knowledge has played a major role in this account, and it is now time to reintegrate the two under a single framework. As Brown, Collins, and Duguid (1989) put it,

> *Many methods of didactic education assume a separation between knowing and doing, treating knowledge as an integral, self-sufficient substance, theoretically independent of the situations in which it is learned and used. The primary concern of schools often seems to be the transfer of this substance, which comprises abstract, decontextualized formal concepts. The activity and context in which learning takes place are thus regarded as merely ancillary to learning—pedagogically useful, of course, but fundamentally distinct and even neutral with respect to what is learned.*
>
> *Recent investigations of learning, however, challenge this separating of what is learned from how it is learned and used. (p. 32)*

A growing number of researchers and educators are arguing that learning must be situated in authentic tasks for knowledge to be useful and therefore used in similar situations. In mathematics, for example, it is unlikely that students will effectively use what they know if their only experience of mathematics involves solving computational or word problems that are presented devoid of some meaningful context.

As an illustration, consider the following problem that Schoenfeld (1988) cited as an example of students mastering computational skills without understanding. "An army bus holds 36 soldiers. If 1,128 soldiers are being bused to their training site, how many buses are needed?" Although 70 per cent of 13-year-olds nationwide correctly performed the long division that is required to answer this question, only 23 per cent actually gave the correct answer. Almost a third said "31 remainder 12" (Schoenfeld, 1988, p. 150). "That [students] failed to connect their formal symbol manipulation procedures with the 'real-world' objects represented by the symbols constitutes a dramatic failure of instruction" (Schoenfeld, 1988, p. 150).

In this final section of the chapter, knowledge as situated cognition will be introduced. Initial implications of this view for instruction will also be discussed. However, these ideas will be taken up again in later chapters, because they are consistent with aspects of a variety of other theories. That knowledge is situated in action is a central tenet of Piaget's theory (chapter 6). That learning is situated in a cultural context is an important facet of both Bruner's and Vygotsky's theories, which will be developed more fully in chapter 7. Finally, the instructional theory known currently as constructivism draws on all of these ideas and will be discussed in chapter 11.

A QUESTION OF TRANSFER

Think back for a moment to the findings of expert-novice studies. Experts appear to structure their knowledge differently from novices. They employ domain-specific or schema-based problem solving strategies, whereas novices employ more general tactics. Their mental models are more complete, richer in information and connections to related material. But what do these findings mean for transfer? Do experts bring to bear relevant aspects of this rich knowledge structure when they encounter entirely new problem domains or atypical problems within their domain of expertise?

Transfer is routinely taken to be one of the most important instructional goals. Teachers want students to transfer the arithmetic skills they learn in school to everyday activities such as balancing a checkbook and judging good buys at the supermarket. Or, they hope learners will use their knowledge of science to make wise choices about the use of energy and other environmental resources. Bank executives want manager-trainees to transfer to the job the knowledge and skills they acquire in training programs. And fighter pilots must be able to solve problems in the air similar to those they have encountered in simulators or printed instructional manuals.

For years, debate has raged as to whether transfer is highly limited in scope or whether it is broad and ranges across diverse domains. The question of transfer has been tackled by behaviorists as generalization, and by verbal learning theorists and cognitive information processing theorists as interference/transfer. From these diverse efforts has come evidence of at least some general cognitive skills that transfer broadly. But these typically appear to be weak in their power to solve problems or advance understanding (cf. Newell and Simon, 1972). Breaking a problem into subproblems is one example. So-called strong cognitive skills, on the other hand, are context-specific and show little transfer across subject domains (e.g.,

Pressley, Snyder, & Cariglia-Bull, 1987). In other words, effective strategies for solving problems in mathematics do not transfer to solving problems in science or literature. And despite arguments by Papert (1980) that computer programming is a powerful vehicle for teaching general problem solving, these claims have generally gone unsubstantiated (e.g., Salomon & Perkins, 1987; Allocco, Coffey, Dalton, Dariano, Dioguardi, Galterio, & Monahan, 1992).

Even when two tasks require the same underlying knowledge, transfer can fail to occur. Situated learning is thought to be the reason (Singley & Anderson, 1989). Recall the study by d'Andrade in which subjects were given the rule, "If a label has a vowel on one side, it should have an even number on the other." They performed poorly unless problems were couched in the context of a familiar schema (i.e., store receipts in amounts greater than $30 must have the manager's signature on the reverse side). In a similar study, individuals trained in the logic of the conditional were expected to perform well on problems involving this rule (Cheng, Holyoak, Nisbett & Oliver, 1986). Results indicated, however, that knowledge of logic did not transfer. Like d'Andrade's subjects, the individuals in the study of Cheng et al. (1986) performed much better when the rule was phrased in more familiar terms (e.g., "if a person is drinking alcohol, then he must be over 21" or "if a person enters this country, she must have had a cholera shot"). Cheng et al. (1986) explained their findings in terms of a permission schema, which has a limited range of transfer. According to Singley and Anderson (1989), then, people use knowledge only in situations where it is obviously relevant. Thus, for them, the fundamental issue is not just the acquisition of knowledge, but the acquisition of a particular use of knowledge and the range of circumstances over which that use is applicable.

Context-Bound Learning and Instruction

"Thinking is intricately interwoven with the context of the problem to be solved" (Rogoff, 1984, p. 2). "Situations might be said to coproduce knowledge through activity. Learning and cognition, it is now possible to argue, are fundamentally situated" (Brown et al., 1989, p. 32). "The meaning of a concept is always situation specific and context dependent" (Kintsch, 1988, p. 165). From diverse sources come these remarkably similar pronouncements, and associated with this view of knowledge and learning are at least two fundamental assumptions.

First, concepts and other cognitive skills are conceived as tools (Brown et al., 1989; Perkins & Salomon, 1989; Tessmer, Wilson, & Driscoll, 1990). This means "they can only be fully understood through use, and using them entails both changing the user's view of the world and adopting the belief system of the culture in which they are used" (Brown et al., 1989, p. 33). Culture here can refer to different academic disciplines, professions, or trades as well as to communities in different countries. So, for example, just as carpenters and cabinet makers use chisels differently, so do engineers and physicists use mathematical principles differently (Brown et al., 1989).

Conceiving of concepts as tools also means that they, like tools, can be acquired but not used. Students everywhere have been known to acquire inert knowledge—definitions, formulas, etc.—that they do not really know how to apply meaningfully. For that to occur, and this is the second assumption, learning must involve authentic activity. For the situated learning theorist, then, how should instructional activities be structured to make them authentic and therefore likely to facilitate knowledge in use? A few answers to this question are explored here; others will be suggested in later chapters.

In a general way, authentic activities are those "coherent, meaningful, and purposeful activities" within which knowledge and skills are embedded (Brown et al., 1989). For example, estimating is a skill that many grocery store employees use daily. A customer asks for two pounds of sliced turkey or ground beef, and the deli clerk or meat packer extracts an amount of meat to put on the scales that approximates this weight. The closer the estimation, the more efficient the clerk or packer will be. The point is, for school children to learn estimating in a meaningful way, they should do so in the context of some activity within which estimation has a purposeful function.

Mathematics learning is one area in which evidence has continued to mount emphasizing the importance of authentic, situated instructional activities. Analysis of a tenth grade class in geometry, whose students performed well on a statewide test of mathematics performance, led Schoenfeld (1988) to argue that students will develop erroneous beliefs about mathematics if they are not exposed to authentic activities. He found, for instance, that the teacher taught students how to construct geometric figures without discussing why certain constructions were right or wrong, that is, without making reference to geometric proofs. As a result, the students saw no relevance to the proofs and made no use of their knowledge about proofs when they were faced with a construction task.

Likewise, students develop the belief that math problems can be solved quickly (if they truly understand the material) when most of the problems they do in class and for homework can be solved relatively quickly (Schoenfeld, 1988; Doyle, 1988). "Over the period of a full school year, none of the students in any of a dozen classes we observed worked mathematical tasks that could seriously be called problems," lamented Schoenfeld (1988, p. 159). In his view, however, learning mathematics means thinking mathematically, and to do that requires problems that are more like what mathematicians endeavor to solve and an approach to problem solution that is more like what mathematicians do.

As an example, Schoenfeld (1982, 1985) has taught heuristics to college students like those used by mathematicians. As a class, students tackle problems using such strategies as "focusing on key points that give leverage" and "exploiting extreme cases." Although these may seem to be quite general strategies, they are learned in a highly contextualized fashion. In addition, the teacher takes an active part in the problem-solving process, not declaring strategies or answers but jointly developing them with the class, much as a team of mathematicians might work together to solve a common problem.

In a similar vein, Lampert (1986) taught multiplication by first posing problems to students that deploy their knowledge of coins (e.g., "using only nickels and pennies, make 82 cents"). In so doing, she built upon students' intuitive knowledge about multiplication. Then learners made up their own problems to solve and eventually derived the standard algorithm for solving them, thus acquiring computational knowledge. Finally, principled knowledge came from tackling a variety of other problems that involved the same algorithms. Throughout their class activities, Lampert questioned students in ways to reveal their assumptions about mathematics and to extend their thinking into new, unfamiliar domains. She emphasized the link between conceptual and procedural knowledge and encouraged reflective thinking during problem solving.

By extension, one can see the usefulness of authentic activity for developing skills and knowledge in other subject matter domains. Learning science, for example, may require doing science, that is, tackling problems of the sort that interest scientists and in a manner akin to their ways of seeking information about those problems. Similarly, a course in learning to design instruction should engage students in the activities of instructional designers. Across all these examples, however, there still seems to be one thing in common, despite the emphasis on context-dependent learning. In all cases, students are engaged in solving problems.

Revisiting Transfer

When the question of transfer was raised some pages back, the answer was not particularly encouraging. Problems with demonstrating transfer have been taken as evidence for the situated, contextual nature of cognition. Researchers argued against the existence of general, context-free cognitive skills and for learning in highly contextualized ways. In a sense, the dichotomy between procedural and declarative knowledge has been eschewed by situated learning theorists. Since declarative knowledge is, by definition, inert, it fails as an important goal for learning. What is important, to paraphrase Singley and Anderson (1989), is the acquisition of the uses of knowledge. The emphasis for instruction, it seems, falls squarely on the process of learning, rather than the product of learning.

Two additional views are emerging that perhaps offer some synthesis between the traditional cognitive view of learning and that promoted by situated learning theorists. First, recent results appear to "challenge the picture of expert performance as driven primarily by a rich knowledge base of highly context-specific schemata" (Perkins & Salomon, 1989, p. 20). As a consequence, there is increasing interest once more among cognitive scientists in the nature of general cognitive skills. Taken as evidence for such skills are the heuristics learned by Schoenfeld's (1982, 1985) college math students, as described in the previous section, and general problem-solving strategies demonstrated by physics experts in studies conducted by Clement (1982). These are general skills, but they operate in contextualized ways to access extensive domain knowledge (Perkins & Salomon, 1989).

In addition, transfer of specific skill and knowledge appears to take place under two conditions: (1) with much practice, in a large variety of situations, leading to a high level of mastery and near-automaticity, or (2) with deliberate, effortful abstraction of a principle (Perkins & Salomon, 1989; Salomon & Perkins, 1989). Thus, Perkins and Salomon assert that transfer does occur, but in more situationally specific ways than previously believed. Regarding instruction for general cognitive skills, their conclusion is very similar to that recommended by situated learning theorists: cultivate general strategic knowledge together with context-specific knowledge.

Finally, the semiotic approach to cognition introduced in Chapter 3 offers a position of synthesis. On the one hand, semiosis, or the construction of signs and sign systems, is potentially limitless, with context playing a critical role in its results. As such, our models of cognitive representation must reflect flexibility and the importance of context on sign constructions. On the other hand, there are also broad and general constraints upon those constructions. For example, Cunningham (1992) noted that no two snowflakes are alike, but we have no difficulty recognizing snowflakes. Their infinite variation still operates within broad constraints. So it is with knowledge and cognition, claimed Cunningham, and these consistencies are as important to understand as the context-specific differences.

CONCLUSION

The question of how knowledge is acquired, represented, accessed, and used is a complex one, for which there are no easy answers. This chapter has presented several contemporary approaches to knowledge representation for learning, thinking, and problem solving that provide insights beyond those of traditional cognitive theory. But they, along with this chapter, have only scratched the surface.

> *"The solution to the riddle of Holmes and Watson is that they must have walked along the veranda from right to left. After*

> *they broke into the house round the corner from one end of the veranda, they passed through various rooms and along a corridor, and then they turned right into Milverton's study and saw a door that communicated with the veranda" (Johnson-Laird, 1983, p. 166)*

SUGGESTED READINGS

Hyde, A. A., & Bizar, M. (1989). *Thinking in context: Teaching cognitive processes across the elementary school curriculum*. New York: Longman.

Educational Psychologist (1988). Special Issue: Learning mathematics from instruction, 23(2).

REFLECTIVE QUESTIONS AND ACTIVITIES

1. Consider the tacit assumptions about knowledge and knowing that theorists make in this chapter. To what epistemological tradition do they seem to fit most appropriately? What evidence supports your position?

2. At the end of the previous chapter, Anderson, et al. (1978) were quoted as claiming that schema theory adds precision to Ausubel's ideas about cognitive structure. Do you agree with their claim? Why or why not? Draw specific comparisons between schema theory and meaningful reception learning.

3. How do notions about schemata and mental models differ from the

models of memory proposed by information processing theorists? What kinds of learning performances are accounted for by each?

4. How would a schema theorist analyze a situation in which learners are experiencing difficulty achieving some instructional goal? What recommendations might be suggested for ameliorating the situation?

5. Select an instructional goal which involves the learner developing a mental model. Describe what instruction you would design to ensure that learners acquired the desired model.

▶ Part IV

Learning and
Development

6

Cognitive and Knowledge Development

Consider the following scenarios.

Scenario 6–1

In a typical Piagetian assessment for number conservation, the experimenter aligns two rows of blocks (or pennies, or some other object familiar to young children) so that they contain the same number and appear to be the same length. The experimenter now questions Aaron, a preconserver.

E: Do both these rows have the same number of blocks or does one have more than the other?

Aaron: They're the same.

E: How do you know?

Aaron: Because I can count them.

When the experimenter pushes one row of blocks closer together and repeats the series of questions, Aaron responds that one row has more blocks because it "sticks out more." Even after he recounts the blocks in each row, he maintains that the longer row has more blocks.

Now the experimenter questions Michele, who conserves numbers. Regardless of how the lines of blocks are arranged, she insists that each has the same number of blocks, because "I counted them, and you haven't added any or taken any away!"

Scenario 6–2*

Between the ages of 4 and 10, children's understanding of many concepts can change dramatically. Asked to name some things that are alive, Nan, who is 5 years old, listed a button (because "it holds my shirt together") and a table (because "you can see it"). Bernard, a 6–year–old, didn't think a table was alive, but neither did he think plants were alive. To the query, "Can a flower starve?", he replied, "Nah. That's silly. Only people can starve."

Billy, who is 10 years old, judged animals and plants, but not inanimate objects, to be alive.

How can we account for the differences in behavior among the children described in these two scenarios? Take Aaron in Scenario 6–1, for example. He knows how to count, and the evidence of his senses (he sees 8 blocks in each row; he counted 8 blocks in each row) should be enough to convince him that there are the same number of blocks in each row. Yet, he steadfastly maintains they are different when one appears longer than the other. In a similar way, Nan (Scenario 6–2) believes that buttons are alive and Bernard that plants are not alive. Where did they get these beliefs? Can we discover events in their experience sufficient to explain their misconception of alive as having been learned this way?

Evidence of this nature presents problems for many learning theories, which do not always distinguish between the learning of children and the learning of adults. That distinction, in itself, is an open question. Do children learn in a manner significantly different from that of adults? Or can whatever differences are observed be attributed to the greater experience of adults rather than a qualitative difference in the process of learning between adults and children? Issues related to these questions will be examined in this chapter and the next.

If something more than learning as it has so far been described is responsible for behavioral and conceptual differences across the life span, then just what is it? And precisely what role does learning play? For many psychologists, cognitive development provides the answers. "The idea of development entails the existence of an endpoint: the child moves, steadily or erratically, toward a goal" (Kaplan; 1967, cited in Kessen, 1984). Werner (1957) saw this goal as the result of differentiation, articulation, and integration whereby a nonspecialized cell gradually becomes an efficient, fully functioning organism. Werner also distinguished development from both change and growth, since change can be regressive and growth can mean quantitative improvement without necessarily involving qualitative improvement. For humans, then, cognitive development is the transformation

---

* This scenario is based on the findings of Carey (1985a).

of the child's undifferentiated, unspecialized cognitive abilities into the adult's conceptual competence and problem-solving skill.

Two fundamental questions must be answered for development to be understood (Sternberg, 1984a). One, what are the psychological states that children pass through at different points in their development? And two, what are the mechanisms by which they pass from one state to another? It is particularly in answer to the second question that issues of learning become relevant. Although the Piagetian approach to cognitive development has provided the most complete account, recent information-processing analyses may supplement the Piagetian account where it appears, if not wrong, at least incomplete (Sternberg,1984a; Siegler, 1986). Let us now turn to Piaget's theory of development, cognitive alternatives to this theory, and their combined implications for learning and instruction.

JEAN PIAGET'S GENETIC EPISTEMOLOGY

Jean Piaget (1896–1980) has been variously characterized as a biologist, philosopher, and child psychologist. In fact, he was all of these. But while spanning all three fields, Piaget's work was directed at elaborating a theory of knowledge, of how the child comes to know his or her world (Gruber & Voneche, 1977). This study of the origins (genesis) of knowledge (epistemology) led to Piaget's calling his view genetic epistemology.

If you recall from chapter 1, empiricists argue that knowledge results from an accumulation of experience, whereas nativists believe that the organism is born with an innate set of ideas that form the basis for knowledge. Interpretists, some of whom are also nativists, assume that all knowledge is actively constructed within the organism, rather than being received passively from the environment. Piaget was highly critical of empiricism, but he was not particularly comfortable in presuming that knowledge is entirely innate (the nativist position). Instead, he evolved a view, consistent with interpretivism, that suggested a compromise between nativism and empiricism. He sometimes labeled his view interactionism, since cognition was assumed to be an interaction between heredity and environment.

Piaget also called his view constructivism, because he firmly believed that knowledge acquisition is a process of continuous self-construction. That is, knowledge is not out there, external to the child and waiting to be discovered. But neither is it wholly preformed within the child, ready to emerge as the child develops. Instead, knowledge is invented and reinvented as the child develops and interacts with the world surrounding her. This point cannot be overemphasized. Piaget believed that children actively approach their environments and acquire knowledge through their actions. Moreover, such actions are neither random nor aimless. Very young infants, for example, immediately suck upon any object placed in their mouths. And they mouth objects as a way to learn about their worlds. Piaget called these goal-directed behaviors schemes and contended that schemes evolve as children develop.

Finally, Gruber and Voneche (1977) apply the label logical determinism to Piaget's theory. This label captures Piaget's emphasis on the functioning of logic in each stage of development. He proposed, in other words, that certain logical structures develop at each stage, and how these structures operate during a particular stage determines the structure of the stage to follow. This is something like the unfolding of a logical argument (Leahey & Harris, 1989). At any stage, the child's cognitive structures are like the premises of the argument. Experience provides information on which to base deductions from these premises, deductions which then yield a new set of premises or cognitive structures. At any point in the process, however, whatever logical structures currently exist will dictate the schemes children will employ to find out more about the world. The sucking scheme, for example, rapidly gives way to other actions, and when children acquire the ability to mentally represent symbols, imitation becomes a widely initiated scheme.

Types of Knowledge

Piaget distinguished among three types of knowledge that children acquire: physical, logico-mathematical, and social-arbitrary knowledge (Piaget, 1969; Wadsworth, 1978). **Physical knowledge**, also called empirical knowledge, has to do with *knowledge about objects in the world, which can be gained through their perceptual properties*. Aaron and Michele in Scenario 6–1, for example, undoubtedly know that blocks are solid and cube-shaped and come in different colors and sizes. These are inherent properties of blocks, and children acquire knowledge of these properties by seeing and handling the blocks. Objects themselves and a child's physical actions on objects are therefore the source of physical knowledge.

The acquisition of physical knowledge has sometimes been equated with learning in Piaget's theory (Gruber & Voneche, 1977). That is, thought is fit directly to experience. The child experiences the hardness of blocks and learns, for example, that blocks cannot be easily crushed themselves but can crush softer or more brittle objects. Internally representing these experiences results in cognitive schemas, or concepts, which stand as organized collections of properties of objects. Schemas are essentially passive modes of organization (Brainerd, 1978), and learning occurs when new information is added to them.

It is useful at this point to mention the differences in meaning associated with Piaget's (and others') use of the terms *scheme, schema* and *schemata*. In an edited collection of Piaget's writings, Gruber and Voneche (1977) consistently used the term *scheme* to refer to units of generalized behavior (or actions) that provide the basis for mental operations. Piaget (1969) clearly intended the same meaning when he spoke of the "schema of an action" being the generalizable quality in the action.

Brainerd (1978), however, distinguished between schema (as a passive mode of organization) and scheme (as an active organizational principle). In justification, Brainerd cited Piaget (in Piaget & Inhelder, 1969), who noted that schema was often a mistranslation for scheme, the preferred term. Finally, Siegler (1986) and Wadsworth (1978) avoided the issue altogether, Siegler by referring only to mental structures and Wadsworth by using the plural schemata to represent the totality of children's logical structures. Both, however, consistently emphasized the active nature of children's thinking.

What can we conclude from this discussion? It is apparent that Piaget strongly believed in the active role of the child during development. Cognition is rooted in action, and actions (I will use the term, *schemes*) evolve to become increasingly internal as children acquire rudimentary physical knowledge.

The second type of knowledge, logical-mathematical, goes beyond simple physical knowledge and is therefore not available from the perceptual properties of objects. **Logical-mathematical knowledge** *is abstract and must be invented*, but through actions on objects which are fundamentally different from those actions enabling physical knowledge. For example, to acquire physical knowledge of blocks, a child may pick one up, feel it, taste it, hit another object with it, or throw it. But to understand how two rows of blocks are in some way the same when they look physically different requires a different kind of action scheme. To acquire what Piaget called conservation of number, children must experience many different arrangements of blocks and other objects, with the number of objects remaining invariant. Such actions make possible, claimed Piaget, a new construction of thought which is evidence of development. Thus Michele, because she reasons beyond her perceptual information, is thought to be at a later point in development than Aaron.

The abstract character of logical-mathematical knowledge gives it an advantage over physical knowledge in its greater range of application. Physical knowledge of blocks, for instance, can be extended only to other blocks, but conservation of number applies to blocks, pennies, people, or what have you. The cognitive result, therefore, of schemes enabling the invention of logical-mathematical knowledge is a coherent set of mental operations. These operations exist within relational structures or networks

TABLE 6–1   Three Types of Knowledge

	Physical Knowledge	Logical-Mathematical Knowledge	Social-Arbitrary Knowledge
Defined	Knowledge about the physical properties of objects	Abstract knowledge	Knowledge made by people
How acquired	Discovered by actions on objects; objects are the source	Invented from actions on objects; actions are the source	Obtained from actions on and interactions with others; people are the source
Reinforcer	Objects	Objects	Other people
Examples of areas of knowledge	Size, color, texture, thickness, taste, sound, flexibility, density	Number, mass, area, volume, length, class, order, time, speed, weight	Language, moral rules, values, culture, history, symbol systems

From *Piaget for the Classroom Teacher* by Barry J. Wadsworth. Copyright © 1978. By Longman Publishing Group. Reprinted by permission of Longman Publishing Group.

of operations that are considered to be the highest order mental organizations (also called schemata; Wadsworth, 1978).

Finally, much of Piaget's own work, and the work of others his theory has stimulated, concentrates on the development of logical-mathematical knowledge. But in acknowledging the social aspect of children's development, he distinguished a third type of knowledge. **Social-arbitrary knowledge** is *culture-specific and can be learned only from other people within one's cultural group.* Actions again hold the key to the acquisition of this kind of knowledge—that is, actions on, or interactions with, other people. Presented in Table 6–1 is a summary of the types of knowledge proposed by Piaget.

The Stages of Development

The concept of stage has already been implicated in the discussion of physical versus logical-mathematical knowledge. Knowledge about blocks as physical objects, for example, precedes a child's ability to reason or solve problems using blocks. Thus, reasoning is evidence of a later stage in development. Piaget believed that children progress through an invariant sequence of four stages. These stages are not arbitrary, but are assumed to reflect qualitative differences in children's cognitive abilities. Piaget's criteria for defining true developmental stages can be summarized as follows, based on Brainerd (1978) and others:

1. Each stage must represent a qualitative change in children's cognition. Significant quantitative improvements in intelligence with age are not enough to satisfy this first criterion. Children must demonstrate qualitative leaps as well, which imply that changes have occurred in the underlying logical structures of cognition. Conservation of number, for example, seems to represent such a change; preconservers behave very differently from conservers.

2. Children progress through the stages in a culturally invariant sequence. This means that every child passes through the stages in exactly the same order of necessity, not just on the average. Moreover, once a higher stage has been entered, regression to a lower stage is not possible, and all normal children reach the last stage. Now that Michele demonstrates number conservation, she will never again act as a nonconserver.

3. Each stage includes the cognitive structures and abilities of the preceding stage. This is known as the hierarchization requirement and is closely related to the second criterion. The more primitive structures of early stages are not lost as a child progresses to a later stage. Rather, they form the foundation for more sophisticated abilities, becoming integrated and coordinated with the more complex structures of the later stage. This also means that each stage is more adaptive, more adequate, than the one preceding it.

4. At each stage, the child's schemes and operations form an integrated whole. As mentioned earlier, what schemes a child employs to explore her world depend upon her stage of development. These, in turn, provide information to be integrated within the existing logical structures of the present stage. If Michele and Aaron are in different stages, for example, they would each employ different schemes and exhibit different cognitive capabilities. But their behavior would be logically consistent with the cognitive structures presumed to exist at their respective stages.

Before turning to a description of Piaget's four stages, it is important to remember that some variability is apparent in the ages at which children attain each stage. That is, Michele and Aaron might be the same age but appear to be in different stages. But whether she is precocious for her age or he is slow does not invalidate the stage concept. Both will ultimately be expected to exhibit the characteristics of every stage at some point and to reach the last stage.

ܟܢ **Stages of Cognitive Development According to Piaget**

Stage of Development	Typical Characteristics
Sensorimotor (birth to approximately age 2)	Modifies reflexes to make them more adaptive
	Becomes goal-directed in behavior, with goals moving from concrete to abstract
	Begins to mentally represent objects and events
Preoperational (2 to 7 years)	Acquires the semiotic function. Engages in symbolic play and language games
	Has difficulty seeing another person's point of view. Thought and communication are egocentric
	Reasons from a focus on one perceptual dimension of problems
Concrete operational (7 to 11 years)	Performs true mental operations (conservation, reversibility) and solves concrete problems in a logical fashion
	Has difficulty thinking hypothetically and systematically considering all aspects of a problem
Formal operational (11 years on)	Solves abstract problems in systematic and logical fashion
	Reasons hypothetically and often develops concerns over social issues

What are Piaget's stages of development? In order of appearance, they are: the sensorimotor period (birth to approximately age 2), the preoperational period (roughly age 2 to age 6 or 7), the concrete operational period (age 6 or 7 to age 11 or 12), and the formal operational period (age 11 or 12 through adulthood). Table 6–2 presents a summary of the characteristics typical at each stage.

The Sensorimotor Period (Birth to 2)

Siegler (1986) wrote of his questioning students in a developmental psychology class about aspects of intelligence in infancy. "A number of students commented that they found it odd to describe infants as having intelligence at all. By far the most frequently named characteristics of infants' intelligence were physical coordination, alertness, and ability to recognize people and objects. It was evidence of Piaget's genius that he perceived much more than this" (Siegler, 1986, p. 30). In fact, immense cognitive changes occur from immediately after birth to approximately age 2.

Newborns come into the world with a variety of innate reflexes (e.g., sucking, reacting to noises, focusing on objects within their view). Within a short time, they begin to modify these reflexes to make them more adaptive (e.g., sucking a finger becomes a different action from sucking a nipple). Initially, infants' actions are directed primarily at their own bodies, but they increasingly center on the external world. In addition, infants' behavior begins to reflect clear goals, and these goals progress from concrete to abstract. Piaget (1951) described his son deliberately dropping objects (a concrete goal) and then varying the heights from which he dropped them (an abstract goal).

Toward the end of the sensorimotor period, children begin to mentally represent objects and events. To that point, they can only act, and during the transition to mental representation, they may use simple motor indicators as symbols for other events. Piaget (1951) described his daughter Lucienne, for example, playing with a partly open matchbox in which a watch chain has been placed. Apparently aware of what the opening represented and wanting it to become wider, Lucienne opened her mouth wider and wider!

The Preoperational Period (2 to 7 Years)
Early in the preoperational period, children acquire what Piaget called the semiotic function. This means they are able to mentally represent objects and events, as evidenced in their imitation of some activity long after it occurred. Pretending, or symbolic play, is highly characteristic of this stage, and language acquisition proceeds rapidly.

Also characteristic of preoperational intelligence are children's egocentrism and centration, which are thought to place limits on their thinking. First, preoperational children have difficulty in seeing points of view other than their own. A conversation between two preschoolers, for example, sounds less like a conversation than like two monologues; children typically talk past one another rather than to one another. This egocentrism is also evident in children's inability to mentally rotate spatial arrangements in order to identify a different perspective. As for centration, preoperational children focus solely on one dimension of a problem, as Aaron focused on the length of the two rows of blocks. He was unable to reconcile the dimension of number with the dimension of length, thus failing to conserve number.

The Concrete Operational Period (7 to 11 Years)
Children overcome the limitations of egocentrism and centration when they enter the stage of concrete operations. It is at this stage that they

demonstrate logically integrated thought. In other words, through actions which have become increasingly internalized, they invent logical-mathematical knowledge resulting in operations. Operations are reversible and maintain some invariant property through a series of transformations. In the number conservation task, for example, the rows are rearranged, but the number in each row stays the same. Moreover, any new arrangement can be reversed so that the rows again look the same. Solving number conservation tasks, then, is evidence that a child has acquired these operations.

Despite their ability to solve many different kinds of problems, concrete operational children still cannot think hypothetically. In other words, they would have difficulty thinking about and discussing possible answers to the question, "If people could know the future, would they be happier than they are now?" (Siegler, 1986).

The Formal Operational Period (11 Years Onward)

Propositional logic is the hallmark of formal operations. That is, operations become more abstract so that the individual can reason, not just with objects, but with formally stated premises or propositions. This enables children to not only think hypothetically, but to plan a systematic approach to solving problems. Inhelder and Piaget (1958) presented children and adolescents with a chemistry problem, in which they were to mix clear liquid chemicals from four beakers until they achieved a yellow color. Concrete operational children were rather random in their approach to the problem, sometimes repeating combinations of chemicals they had tried before. In addition, they typically combined only two chemicals at a time, or all four, without considering combinations of three. By contrast, formal operational adolescents generated a systematic plan of testing chemical combinations until they found the solution. Moreover, they kept records of their tests and generated appropriate hypotheses concerning their results.

Finally, the ability to imagine possibilities above and beyond current reality is characteristic of formal operational reasoners. "This leads at least some of them to think about alternative organizations of the world and about deep questions concerning the nature of existence, truth, justice, and morality" (Siegler, 1986, p. 41).

The Processes of Development

If Piaget's description of stages answers the question of psychological states children pass through in development, what mechanism did he propose as responsible for children's progression from one stage to the next? In essence, he considered three processes as being critical to development: assimilation, accommodation, and equilibration.

Assimilation

Assimilation occurs when a child perceives new objects or events in terms of existing schemes or operations. Consider once again the infant who puts things in his mouth. This scheme, and others such as grasping, throwing, or shaking, are means of assimilating information about the objects. Because these schemes are also relatively broad and undifferentiated, they are used without regard to whether an object is appropriate for throwing or putting in one's mouth. Similarly, the children in Scenario 6–2 assimilate different objects into their existing and individual concepts of alive.

It is important to note that Piaget emphasized the functional quality of assimilation (Siegler, 1986). That is, children and adults alike tend to apply any mental structure that is available to assimilate a new event, and they will actively seek to use a newly acquired structure. Children learning to talk, for example, have been observed to talk endlessly to themselves, whether or not anyone else is there to listen. Even adults who have learned a new skill (such as how to use a word processor) will seek to apply their knowledge in as many situations as possible thereafter. Piaget has compared this apparent self-motivation to the external reinforcers for behavior that behaviorists such as Skinner emphasize.

Accommodation

When existing schemes or operations must be modified to account for a new experience, accommodation has occurred. It is likely, for example, that Nan in Scenario 6–2 will encounter experiences that will cause her to shift her conception of alive to exclude button and table as examples of things that are alive. Solving a conservation task also requires a shift in thinking for all salient aspects of the task to be accommodated.

Obviously, accommodation influences assimilation and vice versa. An inadequate attempt to assimilate some new event into existing schemes or operations may result in some adjustment of those schemes or operations (thus accommodating the event). Such accommodation, however, affects subsequent assimilation, which will now proceed in accord with the new structure.

Equilibration

According to Piaget, equilibration is the master developmental process, encompassing both assimilation and accommodation. Equilibration particularly characterizes the child's transition from one stage of development to the next. Within each stage, children operate from a set of logical structures that, for their purposes, work quite well. But toward the end of a stage, they may become aware of shortcomings in their way of thinking. Anomalies of experience create a state of disequilibrium which can only be resolved when a more adaptive, more sophisticated mode of thought is adopted. When Bernard in Scenario 6–2, for example, hears plants being referred to as alive, he will experience disequilibrium. At that point, he is likely to be unsure of what it means to be alive. Eventually, however, he will discover that plants grow and reproduce just as animals do, and with that knowledge, will attain a new equilibrium at a more sophisticated level of thought.

Criticisms of Genetic Epistemology

Piaget's genetic epistemology has been widely influential, attracting both devoted adherents and outspoken critics. There can be no argument regarding Piaget's contribution to the field of cognitive development. His theory is notable first for its exceptional breadth, covering a broad age span and bringing together a large variety of children's achievements at any given age. Piaget also offers a wealth of observations, and the stages he describes "appeal to our intuitions and to our memories of childhood" (Siegler, 1986, p. 22). Finally, Piaget's theory addresses in an integrated fashion issues of interest to scientists and philosophers, parents, and teachers.

Despite its virtues, Piaget's theory has faced serious challenges, especially in recent years. The question we must consider, then, is: How well have the theory's specific claims about children's thinking held up in the face of contemporary research?

Claim 1: The Sequence of Stages is Invariant

Piaget believed that all children, regardless of culture, progress through the four stages of sensorimotor to formal operations. Moreover, once a particular stage is reached, regression to an earlier stage cannot occur, and all children are expected to eventually reach formal operations. These comprise an easily testable claim, and many replications of Piaget's experiments have been conducted. For the most part, results have shown that children in different cultures do pass through the same types of reasoning as did Piaget's children (Dasen, 1972). However, the ages at which children reached certain stages varied from culture to culture, and reaching formal operations was by no means assured. Even in advanced societies, only a minority of adolescents exhibited formal operational reasoning (Siegler, 1986), and Leahey and Harris (1989) go so far as to argue that scientists do not routinely reason at that level.

Imagine, for example, pouring the liquid from a partly filled bottle into a glass (Figure 6–1). On a separate sheet of paper, draw what you think the bottle would look like being held over the glass. If your picture matches that shown at the end of the chapter, you have exhibited formal operational reasoning. If not, you have performed much like the adults who partici-

FIGURE   6–1   An Exercise in Formal Operational Thinking: Imagine
Pouring the Liquid from the Bottle into the Glass. What
would it look like? (Answer shown at the end of the
chapter in Figure 6–3.)

pated in Piaget's study (reported in Piaget & Inhelder, 1967), whose results
are taken as evidence for that fact that, most of the time, people operate at
concrete, rather than formal operational thinking.

As for the question of regression, Inhelder, Sinclair, and Bovet (1974)
observed temporary regression in the reasoning of early concrete
operational children. These results may mean that cognitive restructuring
occurring at stage transitions is not particularly stable for a brief time. Or,
they may be evidence against the stage concept altogether. In other words,
perhaps cognitive development occurs in steady, incremental changes
rather than discontinuous stages. This suggestion brings us to the next
claim of Piaget's theory.

Claim 2: The Stages Represent Qualitative Changes in Cognition

This claim carries two implications: (1) that development is discontinuous,
and (2) that reasoning on different problems is consistent within a given
stage. Whether the cognitive changes that occur during development are
continuous or discontinous is difficult to judge. Siegler (1986) offered the
analogy of a bridge collapsing to suggest that development might be reasonably viewed as either continous or discontinuous. The forces that cause
a bridge to give way, for example, build up over a long period of time. But
the collapse itself is sudden. Perhaps, then, what appear to be sudden
changes in children's thinking are actually part of a gradual progression.

The question of continuity/discontinuity raises the related issue of
whether development can be accelerated, which Piaget has called the

"American question" (Gruber & Voneche, 1977). A discontinuity in stages suggests that such acceleration would be difficult to achieve. Teaching a nonconserver to conserve number, for example, should be virtually impossible while the child is squarely within the preoperational stage. Success at this training task, however, would undermine the concept of discontinuous stages.

Studies attempting to train children on Piagetian tasks have shown that children can learn more than Piaget thought they could. A number of studies provide convincing demonstrations of children benefiting from a variety of instructional techniques (Siegler, 1986), but these should be taken cautiously. "Although young children can learn to solve these problems, they often find doing so exceptionally difficult" (Siegler, 1986, p. 56).

Results of training studies are also somewhat difficult to interpret because their findings can usually be assimilated to Piagetian theory (Cromer, 1981). Although most training techniques appeared to result in changes to the reasoning of preoperational children, these changes were often short-lived or superficial. Many children, in other words, verbally agreed with the experimenter but quickly reverted to nonconservation reasoning. Training is likely to be most successful when children are nearing a transition between stages anyway and when the training task induces disequilibrium (Inhelder et al., 1974).

Finally, with respect to unity of reasoning within a given stage, children should learn to solve, at the same time, a variety of problems that share a dependence on the logical structures developed during that stage. However, "it is increasingly apparent that this view does not accurately characterize children's thinking" (Siegler, 1986, p. 54). In other words, conservation tasks that require similar reasoning are not all mastered at the same time. "Differing amounts of experience with the problems, differences in the ease of drawing analogies to other, better-understood problems, and differences in the complexity of the most advanced solution formulas contribute to [the differences in children's reasoning within a stage]" (Siegler, 1986, p. 55).

To confound the issue, researchers using non-Piagetian tasks have discovered that children sometimes demonstrate unsuspected cognitive strengths. Very young children, for example, seem to have at least some sense of number conservation, even though they may fail the Piagetian task for number conservation. In her experiments, Gelman (1972) discovered that children knew when a penny was secretly removed from a small pile of coins if it caused them to lose a game with the experimenter. Likewise, most parents and many early childhood education teachers will attest to children's sense of number when they are asked to share cookies or crackers with a sibling or peer. In her research, Gelman (1978, 1983) also found similar effects for other Piagetian concepts, suggesting that Piaget's discrete stages might be an artifact of the particular tasks used in Piagetian experiments (cf. Donaldson, 1978).

Claim 3: Children Exhibit the Characteristics of Each Stage

Whether Piaget's stages form a hierarchy of structured wholes that integrate all characteristics of a previous stage (criteria 3 and 4) is difficult to test. But one can examine the traits purported to characterize children's thinking at each stage and ask whether these traits are an adequate description. Do children consistently behave in these ways? Here again, the answer is somewhat mixed. The evidence of unexpected cognitive strengths and the inability of children to master, at the same time, a variety of tasks based on the same underlying reasoning both suggest problems with Piaget's stage descriptions. The problem, however, lies not so much with Piaget's observations of children's behavior, but in his account of stages and their constraints.

With respect to egocentrism in preoperational children, for example, "Piaget's work . . . records a deep insight: for every task where point of view is an issue, one can find an age such that children younger than that age usually err by failing to see the other person's viewpoint" (Carey, 1985a, pp. 13–14). This suggests that children are egocentric, but the nature of the task rather than the stage of development appears to be the critical factor determining when they are egocentric.

There is ample support in the research literature for this conclusion. Flavell (1985) argued that children well beyond the preoperational period continue to be at risk for egocentrism in particular types of tasks. For example, Siegler (1986) cited the classic demonstration in which children are to describe selected pictures from a set in such a way that another child can determine which picture is being described. Although older children are better at this task than younger children, they still cannot overcome their own perspective sufficiently well to generate a description that will allow another child to select the right picture.

Finally, preoperational children are not egocentric all the time. In some situations they will communicate nonegocentrically. "If you ask 3-year-olds to show you their drawings, they hold the side with the artwork toward you. If they were completely egocentric, they would do the opposite, since they would assume that what they see is what you see" (Siegler, 1986, p. 57).

Claim 4: Global Restructuring Characterizes the Shift from Stage to Stage

In part, this claim results from Piaget's requirement that stages represent qualitative changes in children's cognition. But more than that, for children to make the transition between stages, cognitive restructuring (i.e., accommodation in response to disequilibrium) must occur. Carey (1985b) called this global restructuring since it is assumed, in Piaget's theory, to constrain children's ability to acquire knowledge in all domains. In other words, the logical structures available to the child are dependent upon his or her stage of development, and these set limits to thinking within any given domain.

As with other aspects of Piaget's theory, global restructuring has come into question as an adequate mechanism for explaining conceptual changes in children's thinking (Carey 1985a, 1985b; Gelman & Baillargeon, 1983). "In much of their research, Piaget and his colleagues confounded the child's problems with domain-specific scientific concepts . . . and domain-general inferential abilities" (Carey, 1985a, p. 191). Like Piaget's children, the children in Carey's studies had similar ideas about the concept of alive and shifted their concepts at similar ages. But rather than appeal to changes in overall logical abilities to account for these conceptual changes, Carey (1985a) presented a convincing case for children's increased knowledge of biology being the cause. Thus, Carey's results showed that children like Billy in Scenario 6–2, for example, knew considerably more about basic biological functions and bodily processes shared by animals than did younger children.

Views based on domain-specific restructuring have also been proposed to account for supposed concrete versus formal operational reasoning (Carey, 1985a; Gelman & Baillargeon, 1983; cf. Driver & Easley, 1978; Novak, 1977; Vosniadou & Brewer, 1987). These will be discussed in more detail in the next section.

Conclusion

Piaget's theory of cognitive development was certainly ground-breaking in its recognition that children are not just mini-adults. Radical behaviorism, by virtue of its emphasis on behavior, presumed no special principles of development. Children, like adults, were thought to acquire behaviors through their reinforcement contingencies. But Piaget's observations established that children do not see the world quite like adults do. Piaget also raised the right questions: What mental processes lead children to think differently from adults, and how do they represent what they see?

There is evidence now, however, to suggest that Piaget's answers to these questions were not always correct. According to Sternberg (1984a), the Piagetian view "is in need of more microscopic psychological analysis to supplement its useful macroscopic description of cognitive development" (p. viii). To find this microscopic analysis, Sternberg and others (e.g., Case, 1984; Klahr & Wallace, 1976; Siegler, 1986; Siegler & Crowley, 1991; Carey, 1985a) turn to a cognitive information-processing approach.

COGNITIVE ALTERNATIVES TO GENETIC EPISTEMOLOGY

One advantage to stage theories is that the assumption of general shifts in development brings order to a multitude of "bewilderingly diverse developments" (Carey, 1985a). Giving up stages means giving up some of this order. The result is a proliferation of more limited theories to account for these diverse observations. Perhaps for this reason no generally accepted theory of development has yet emerged from the information processing perspective (Leahey & Harris, 1989). Instead, several lines of inquiry have been undertaken by cognitive information processing theorists to understand how children think.

Information processing researchers ask the same questions as Piaget about cognitive development. What are children's cognitive capabilities and limits at various points in development? How do they acquire these capabilities, and how do advanced understandings grow out of more primitive ones? The difference between the two approaches lies in the information processing researcher's assumption that thinking is information processing (see chapter 3 for a review of information processing theories of cognition). Thus, researchers from this perspective focus on "the information that children represent, the processes they use to transform the information, and the memory limits that constrain the amount of information they can represent and process" (Siegler, 1986, p. 63). In some cases, investigators attempt to explain Piagetian phenomena in terms of information processing concepts. In others, researchers study typical information processing topics, such as attention and memory, with the additional aim of modeling developmental change. As a result, current information processing accounts of development differ in the degree to which they incorporate Piagetian concepts.

Siegler (1986) characterized recent efforts of information processing theorists to understand development in terms of four developmental mechanisms on which they focus: automatization, encoding, generalization, and strategy construction. Case (1978, 1984) represents a neo-Piagetian view; like Piaget, he adopted a general stage framework, but he looked to automatization as a process enabling children to overcome memory limits. Klahr and Wallace (1976; Klahr, 1984), on the other hand, shared Piaget's emphasis on the self-modifying nature of assimilation in development, but they focused on children's ability to generalize as the key to self-modification. Siegler (1983, 1986) emphasized the interaction between children's knowledge and their ability to learn, with a particular focus on the process of encoding. Sternberg (1984b, 1985) adopted an exclusively information processing framework to investigate children's thinking in terms of strategy construction. Finally, the works of Carey (1985a, 1985b, 1986), Vosniadou (1988) Vosniadou & Brewer (1987), and Posner (Posner, Strike, Hewson, & Gertzog, 1982) suggest a fifth mechanism on which information processing theorists are focusing: knowledge restructuring. Let us consider each of these approaches in more detail.

Case: A Neo-Piagetian View

Case has described his view as consistent with Piaget's in the assumption of developmental stages and increasingly sophisticated mental structures within each stage. Unlike Piaget, however, he believes that "children's mental structures can best be modeled by using the sorts of concepts developed in the field of information processing and computer simulation, rather than those developed in the field of symbolic logic" (Case, 1984, p. 20). Accordingly, Case has examined children's problem solving in terms of short-term memory capacity and the proportion of that capacity devoted to operating space or storage space. He argues that developmental shifts can be explained by the automatization of problem solving operations. That is, as processing becomes more automatic, the requirements for operating space diminish, allowing for more storage space. This means that older children can solve problems containing more operations, since the others can be held in storage while one is being performed. Younger children, on the other hand, must devote all their memory capacity to performing

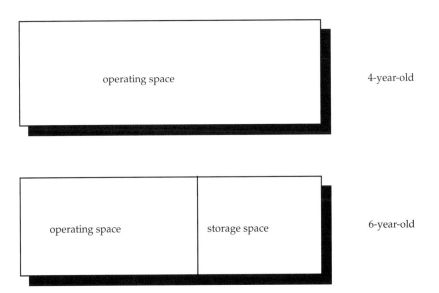

FIGURE   6–2   Case's Model of the Utilization of Memory Capacity in Two Stages of Development

a single operation. See Figure 6–2 for a visual representation of Case's model.

To illustrate the implications of Case's proposal, consider the juice problem presented to young children (Case, 1984). During a warming up period, children watch as the experimenter pours various combinations of small cups of juice and water into pitchers. They are told that some of the resulting mixtures will taste juicier than others. Then the children are shown two rows of cups, each having the same number of water cups but one having more cups of juice. The problem is to determine which row will result in a juicier mixture.

According to Case, solving this problem requires essentially one operation—to scan the two rows and pick the set where the line of juice cups is longest. As a result, both 4-year-olds and 6–year-olds have little difficulty deciding which line will produce a juicier mixture. Now, however, the task is changed slightly. The lines are made approximately the same length, but the proportion of juice cups to water cups is altered. The problem now requires two operations: to count the number of juice cups in each line, noting which has the bigger number, and to assume that a bigger number will result in a juicier mixture. Four-year-olds fail to solve this problem, but 6–year-olds solve it easily. The reason, says Case, is that 4-year-olds cannot keep in mind which line has more juice cups while they think about the relationship between the number of juice cups and resulting juiciness. All short-term memory capacity is used to perform a single operation at a time.

What, then, contributes to increases in operational efficiency? What happens to decrease a 6–year-old's requirements for operational space and increase available storage space? One answer, clearly, is that massive practice in basic operations enables them to become automatic, and automatic processes require less memory capacity (see chapter 3 for a more extensive discussion of automaticity). Although Case accepts automaticity as one factor determining increases in operational capacity, he doubts that automaticity is the only factor. Research on the biology of the brain has led Case to speculate that biological maturation will be an important contributor to operational efficiency. In particular, myelinization of nervous tissue apparently proceeds unevenly in neurological development. "Since there is an approximate correspondence between the myelinization that takes place in different areas of the brain at different ages, on the one hand, and the changes in the efficiency of the types of operations that these areas control, on the other, the possibility exists that the degree of myelinization may be the factor that sets the developmental ceiling on operational efficiency at any age" (Case, 1984, p. 40; see chapter 8 for a more extensive discussion of the biological bases of learning).

Klahr and Wallace: A Computer Simulation of Development

In the early 1970s, Klahr and Wallace undertook a research program aimed at uniting Piaget's theory of development with techniques for simulating human cognition. They faced a difficult challenge: to construct a program that would adequately describe children's behavior at a particular stage and to build one that would modify itself to account for children's transitions among stages. Undaunted, Klahr and Wallace (1976) maintained that "Piaget's steadfast insistence on the characterization of the child as an organism functioning under the control of a developing set of central processes" kept them searching for an appropriate computer language by which to simulate those processes. In addition, recognizing the enormity of simulating all aspects of Piaget's theory, Klahr and Wallace concentrated on building a model of one aspect, quantitative development.

In order to model conservation of number, Klahr and Wallace (1973, 1976) began with the proposal that humans mentally represent quantity through one of three quantifiers. These are subitizing, counting, and estimating. Subitizing refers to the rapid recognition of collections of four or fewer objects. That is, shown an array of four objects, most people can immediately and accurately report how many are there and do so in less time than it would take to count the items. When more than four items are present, people resort to counting. Then, when the collection grows large enough that counting is impractical, estimating enables a quantity to be represented.

Along with the quantifiers, Klahr and Wallace assumed basic processes of self-modification and generalization. In other words, over time children experience regularities in quantification. For example, they may subitize three cookies, then three dolls, or three pennies. Repeated experiences of this sort enable generalization across episodes, so that a rule is formed representing subitizing three items. With additional experience, the cognitive system modifies itself to reflect increasingly abstract rules. Thus, conservation can be explained by reference to what rules have been acquired. According to Klahr (1984), nonconservers can count (i.e., produce and order quantitative symbols) and therefore know that five comes after four. But they have not yet acquired the rule that a collection of five things is more than a collection of four things. Hence, nonconservers like Aaron in Scenario 6–1 continue to assert that the longer row has more blocks.

Critics of computer simulations such as Klahr's and Wallace's contend that they may account for learning but do not capture the essence of development. Yet perhaps the very success of these systems argues for a different conception of development. Klahr (1984) noted, for example, that the distinction between global and local restructuring is blurred in his system.

"Changing a few conditions in an existing production (a local change) may radically alter the firing sequence of it and all of its previous successors. . . . Thus, from local changes come global effects, and from incremental modifications come structural reorganizations" (Klahr, 1984, p. 131). What Klahr believes his view shares with Piaget's is the reliance on processes that are self-contained, that seek pattern and regularity and self-modify from within rather than from explicit feedback of right or wrong responses.

Siegler: An Emphasis on Encoding

Like Case and Klahr and Wallace, Siegler (1983, 1984, 1986) took an aspect of Piaget's theory as a starting point and developed his theory utilizing information processing concepts and analyses. Siegler has been particularly interested in children's knowledge and shares Piaget's emphasis on discrete levels of understanding. His theory differs from Piaget's theory, however, in at least two ways. First, he finds the rule to be a useful means for characterizing children's knowledge (Siegler, 1983). This implies a focus on local description and specific task requirements, rather than a reliance on integrated logical structures that cut across domains. Second, Siegler emphasizes the role of encoding in children's construction of more advanced knowledge (Siegler, 1983, 1984, 1986).

In his early work (e.g., Siegler, 1976), Siegler used a variant of Inhelder and Piaget's (1958) balance scale task to investigate children's thinking. This involved placing weights at different points on a two-arm balance and asking children to predict whether the arm would tip right, tip left, or remain level. An analysis of children's performance on this task revealed that they appeared to use one of four rules to solve it, ranging from considering only the amount of weight on each side to computing and comparing the torques on each side (torque = weight x distance from fulcrum).

Siegler reasoned that children who considered only weight on each side when solving the problem did not encode the information about distance from the fulcrum. He demonstrated that, with tutoring, these children could learn to encode and use this information to solve balance scale problems. From his balance scale experiments, Siegler (1984) developed a performance model for solving problems that consists of four components, or steps. First, Siegler contends, children must actively encode the features of a problem likely to be useful in solving it. Then, they must monitor these features and select specific ones to include in their performance rules. Once relevent features are selected, children must know how to combine their dimensions into the rule to be used for solving the problem. Finally, the rule must be executed correctly.

To be successful in solving balance scale problems, then, children must attend to features such as the size and number of weights (as indicators of the overall weight placed on one side of the balance scale), as well as where on the scale the weights are placed (step 1). Then they must select and monitor overall weight and distance from the fulcrum as the features critical to solving a balance problem (step 2). Finally, they must decide how these features relate to one another by constructing the rule for torque (step 3) and successfully calculating this relationship for the given problem to obtain its solution (step 4). At any point in this problem solving process, children may experience difficulty, and in fact, the ability to perform all four steps has been shown to correlate with age.

Because Siegler has demonstrated that young children can learn to encode, monitor, and use features of a problem that they previously ignored, the question is, Why do they not do so spontaneously? Why do there appear to be such developmental differences in problem solving? Siegler believes that the differences are due to both the limited content knowledge of younger children and their relatively strong preferences for the simple rules they have evolved. That is, young children have not had enough experience in many situations to reject simple rules in favor of more complicated (and correct) ones. In addition, they are loath to give up simple rules that have so far served them well, unless specific disconfirming evidence can reveal the deficiencies of these rules.

Sternberg: A Componential Analysis and Strategy Construction

Sternberg (1984b, 1985) differs from the other theorists discussed so far in his almost total lack of reference to Piaget's theory. Instead, Sternberg grounds his research squarely within information processing theory and proposes to account for intellectual development in terms of "changes in the availability, accessibility, and ease of execution of a variety of kinds of information-processing components" (1984b, p. 164). Moreover, Sternberg's work is distinguished by his interest in the measurement of intelligence; he relates his findings to those yielded by traditional intelligence tests.

According to Sternberg, intelligence is made up of three types of information processing components: metacomponents, performance components, and knowledge-acquisition components. "Metacomponents are executive processes used in planning and decision making in task performance" (Sternberg, 1984b, p. 165). So, for example, determining just what problem is to be solved and deciding upon a particular strategy for solving it are types of metacomponents. Performance components are those processes involved in the actual completion of a problem solving task. Encoding relevant features of the task or comparing possible answer options are examples of performance components. Finally, knowledge-acquisition components are those used for learning new information required to solve a problem at hand. Selectively encoding relevant information, meaningfully interpreting this information, and integrating it with previous knowledge comprise the set of knowledge-acquisition components.

To this point, Sternberg's analysis is no different for children's thinking than the thinking of adults. To account for developmental changes, Sternberg proposes several mechanisms on which intellectual change is thought to be based. First is a feedback mechanism stemming from the knowledge-acquisition components. These components lead to increased knowledge, which leads to more effective use of the components, which again increases the knowledge base, and so on. Second, in a similar fashion, self-monitoring provided by the metacomponents enables a self-correcting feedback loop. One can learn from mistakes in using metacomponents and become more efficient in resource allocation.

Finally, besides feedback, automatization within a component set can give rise to improved intellectual performance. In this aspect, Sternberg's approach resembles Case's. As some processes become automatic, processing resources can be directed toward what is new in a problem solving situation.

To a large extent, Sternberg conceives of the developing child as similar to a novice becoming an expert. A novice has limited knowledge of not only a subject matter domain but also processes that are not automatic within that domain. Both characteristics serve to limit temporarily the novice's, or child's, intellectual performance within that domain.

It is in the measurement of intelligent behavior that we can see the influence of traditional psychometric theory on Sternberg's work. He goes beyond the ordinary aspect of children's thinking that has been the focus of others' theories to consider intelligence in the sense of what IQ tests measure. In this sense, he regards intelligence as bifaceted, including the ability to deal with novel tasks and novel situations and the ability to automatize information processing. Sternberg then uses these two facets as criteria against which to judge tasks used to measure IQ. In other words, novel tasks should be solved more easily by more intelligent people than less intelligent people. And more intelligent people should be faster at reaching automatic levels of task performance than less intelligent people. These tasks, then, together with the componential analysis of intelligence, provide a framework for measuring and understanding both giftedness and mental retardation in children (Sternberg and Davidson, 1983; Sternberg and Wagner, 1982).

Knowledge Restructuring in Development

The final set of views to be examined as an alternative to Piaget's theory concerns the question of knowledge restructuring during development.

Piaget believed that the logical structures associated with each stage of development provide the basis for thinking and reasoning across domains. Changes to these structures that occur when a child moves from one stage of development to the next must therefore affect reasoning in all domains. We have already seen this claim of Piaget undermined by evidence that children's reasoning in a given stage is not consistent across subject matter domains. This opens the door to the notion that perhaps domain-specific restructuring better characterizes cognitive development than global restructuring.

The idea of domain-specific restructuring evolved from several lines of research focused on conceptual change. Novice-expert studies (e.g., Chase & Simon, 1973; Chi, Glaser, & Rees, 1982) drew attention to qualitative differences in how experts and novices represent information and solve problems. Mental models researchers (see chapter 5), investigating how knowledge within a domain is represented, noted that learners typically have preconceived (and often inaccurate) conceptions of scientific phenomena. Studies such as those of Posner et al. (1982) exemplified the concern of science educators for how students' "central, organizing concepts change from one set of concepts to another set, incompatible with the first" (p. 211). Initial mental models, that is, are potentially inaccurate and most certainly inadequate. Therefore, they must change over time to become more adequate representations of scientific ideas. The question is, does this change characterize development, and if so, how does it come about?

Based on the results of her extensive case studies, Carey (1985a) suggested that children begin with a very few conceptual structures: "perhaps only a naive mechanics and a naive psychology" (Carey, 1985a, p. 201). Then, through the theory building that is uniquely human, children continually restructure their knowledge as they develop. Because they have only a few theories to begin with, the domains of these theories must include a wide variety of phenomena, which would account for some of the unity that is observed among developmental differences. With experience, however, children's theories are restructured until they eventually resemble those of adults. And these changes, contrary to Piaget's contention, occur within domains relative to the understanding of specific phenomena.

Both Carey (1985a) and Vosniadou and Brewer (1987) further distinguish between two types of domain-specific restructuring: weak restructuring and radical restructuring. The weak restructuring view puts emphasis on overall knowledge differences in explaining the performance of experts versus novices. That is, more knowledge within the domain permits experts to organize what they know in ways not available to novices. This implies that novices' theories are impoverished relative to experts' theories and causes a focus on what the expert has that the novice lacks. The radical restructuring view, on the other hand, claims that novices have entirely different theories from those of experts—different in structure, in what concepts are included, in what phenomena are explained. Posner et al. (1982) characterized this sort of conceptual change as similar to a paradigm shift in the philosophy of science. It implies that attention should be directed to how and what the novice thinks as well as to how and what the expert thinks.

Vosniadou (1988) and Vosniadou and Brewer (1987) presented evidence that children's conceptions in astronomy change in a manner consistent with the predictions of radical restructuring. This can be seen most clearly in students' misconceptions as they attempt to integrate conflicting pieces of evidence. "For example, the information that the earth is round is interpreted by elementary school children—whose phenomenal experience is of a flat earth—to mean that the earth is a flat circle, like a disk" (Vosniadou & Brewer, 1987, p. 55). Only by radically restructuring their theory can children then adopt the adult point of view. Carey (1985a) argued, too, that her results support, if not radical restructuring, at least weak restructuring. For both researchers, however, the implications of their work include an increased role of prior knowledge in cognitive development. Commenting on the possible causes or explanations of knowledge restructuring, Carey (1985a) stated, "I have appealed to learning . . . such learning presumably being the result of instruction, either formal or informal" (p. 199). Vosniadou (1988) and Vosniadou and Brewer (1987), as well, developed specific implications for instruction that will be considered in the next section. No longer, then, can learning and instruction play a minor role in the story of cognitive development.

Conclusion: Comparisons among Theories

Think back, for a moment to the two basic questions with which this chapter began: What are the psychological states children pass through? What develops? What are the mechanisms responsible for development? How does development occur? For the most part, information processing theorists have disagreed minimally with Piaget on what develops (see Table 6–3 for comparisons). Clearly, children acquire knowledge and the ability to act upon that knowledge. Whereas Piaget believed knowledge is represented in logical, operational structures, information processing theorists presume that children's knowledge is most likely represented by the same sorts of semantic networks and memory connections as adults' knowledge. But they also "presuppose, in the Piagetian spirit, that children are active, self-directing cognitive entrepreneurs who develop their minds through a great many spontaneously generated information-processing activities" (Flavell,1984, pp. 198–99).

TABLE 6–3   Cognitive Alternatives to Piaget

Theorist(s)	Proposed Developmental Mechanism	Similarities to Piaget
Case	Automatization (to reduce operating space in short-term memory)	Assumption of stages Increasingly sophisticated logical structures in each stage Biological maturation assumed to be important
Klahr and Wallace	Generalization (repeated experience enables abstract rules to be generated and used)	Tried to develop computer simulations of Piaget's theory Global restructuring (akin to equilibration) occurs, but unlike equilibration, it can be brought on by local, domain-specific restructuring
Siegler	Encoding (with experience, children encode and use more features of problems to be solved)	Existence of discrete levels of understanding (as evident in Piaget's stages) Disequilibrium is an important concept; children must be shown the deficiencies of their simple rules
Sternberg	Feedback (to provide a self-monitoring, self-correcting function) Automatization (to enable increased resources for processing)	Virtually no reference to Piaget; development is thought to be more or less equivalent to the novice becoming an expert
Carey and others	Knowledge restructuring in specific domains	Qualitative differences in knowledge states (analogous to stages in Piaget's theory)

Where information processing theorists appear to differ most from Piaget is in their conceptions of the mechanisms of development. Only Case retains the Piagetian notion of developmental stages, but he proposes that overcoming short-term memory limits, rather than equilibration, accounts for progress from stage to stage. Moreover, none of the information processing theorists retain Piaget's sense of the biological organism "that has evolved the capability and disposition to acquire some things differently, and with more naive talent or special aptitude, than other things" (Flavell, 1984, p. 192). Again, only Case raises the possibility of a biological factor setting age-dependent limits to cognitive development, and he does so only speculatively.

Flavell (1984) lamented this loss and criticizes information processing theories for their failure to distinguish different mechanisms involved in child and adult cognition. After all, most theorists implicitly agree that development does not continue past young adulthood. Yet, if no biological mechanism operates to set the limits of development, then it should go on throughout life.

Finally, information processing theorists have demonstrated that learning plays a more significant role in development than Piaget supposed. Specifically, "a good deal of human cognitive development can be profitably conceptualized in terms of the acquisition of domain-specific expertise and of the high-quality cognitive functioning that expertise brings with it" (Flavell, 1984, p. 195). Expertise, however, is not to be conceived as simply an accumulation of knowledge. Rather, it implies a process of building rich, conceptual structures—mental models that restructure with experience.

IMPLICATIONS FOR INSTRUCTION OF DEVELOPMENTAL THEORY

Piagetian-Inspired Instruction

Brainerd (1978) wrote of an experience he once had at a school for gifted children. He noted that one of the students there seemed particularly bright compared to the rest, and he asked the teacher how she went about teaching this prodigy. "Surprised that I should ask a question whose answer was so obvious," wrote Brainerd, "she replied, 'I water him and he grows'" (1978, pp. 285–86). This horticultural metaphor is singularly descriptive of most Piagetian-inspired curricula, because it emphasizes a child-centered educational philosophy. "The basic assumption seems to be that children's minds, if planted in fertile soil, will grow quite naturally on their own" (Brainerd, 1978, p. 286).

Consider the implications of this horticultural metaphor for specific instructional techniques. What can teachers and designers of instruction do to ensure fertile soil? According to Wadsworth (1978) and Gruber and Voneche (1977), both of whom make this point rather emphatically, there is no Piagetian dogma about education. There is no set of teaching practices that constitutes a Piagetian approach to instruction. Rather, educators have interpreted Piaget's theory to suggest broad instructional principles. Beyond these, any specific methods depend upon the teacher's understanding of children's thinking. "Piaget has devoted his efforts to changing our understanding of the child; for some this is only a prelude to the development of new educational means, for others it is the new means" (Gruber & Voneche, 1977, p. 691).

There are perhaps three basic instructional principles on which Piagetian theorists generally agree. Let's examine these first, and then take a brief look at several specific curriculum projects, described by Brainerd (1978), that have attempted to implement these principles.

Principle 1: The Learning Environment Should Support the Activity of the Child.

According to Piaget, activity is of paramount importance in the growth of intelligence. Children acquire knowledge through their actions, and thinking is considered to be action-based. Thus, a learning environment should be created that encourages children to initiate and complete their own activities. "Good pedagogy must involve presenting the child with situations in which he himself experiments, in the broadest sense of the term—trying things out to see what happens, manipulating symbols, posing questions and seeking his own answers, reconciling what he finds one time with what he finds at another, comparing his findings with those of other children . . ." (Duckworth, 1964, p. 2).

An active, discovery-oriented environment consistent with Piaget's theory does not mean that children discover what the teacher wants them to discover (Brainerd, 1978). Bruner (e.g., Bruner, Goodnow, and Austin, 1956; see chapter 7) has advocated a form of inquiry teaching in which children are presented with specific examples and carefully questioned in such a way that they discover a general concept or rule. For Piagetian educators, such an approach is fundamentally flawed because it brings children to the teacher's conception instead of allowing them to construct their own conceptions.

Inherent in Piaget's emphasis on activity is the fact that children receive feedback from their own actions. In acquiring physical knowledge, for example, the child learns what characteristics are true about an object by her actions with it. She does not have to be told that blocks can crush softer or more brittle objects; the evidence is there in the thousands of cracker crumbs that resulted from her blow. In the same way, feedback regarding logical-mathematical knowledge is available from the child's actions. Only social-arbitrary knowledge depends upon feedback from other people, who reinforce cultural values and socially appropriate behaviors. To supply feedback for anything but social-arbitrary knowledge is to potentially persuade the child to disregard her natural disequilibrium (Wadsworth, 1978).

Since feedback comes from objects and actions upon objects, concrete, manipulable materials play an important role in a Piagetian-based classroom. To the extent possible, children should be permitted to manipulate materials for themselves. Thus, an experiment to illustrate some scientific principle is likely to mean more when the child conducts it than when the teacher demonstrates it. Although Wadsworth (1978) maintained that pictures are still abstract, Brainerd (1978) argued that their inclusion in textbooks can help to bring some level of concreteness to otherwise exclusively abstract material.

Finally, Piagetian educators encourage play as a pedagogic strategy for active self-discovery (Brainerd, 1978; Gruber & Voneche, 1977). Play effectively represents all of the requisite characteristics of Piagetian-inspired instruction that have been discussed so far. In play, children initiate and control their own activities. They employ concrete objects, either referentially (the object stands for itself) or symbolically (the object represents something other than itself). And they learn from the feedback that is inherent in the play situation. Most of all, they are self-motivated and will persist until the activity has been carried to completion (cf. Wadsworth, 1978).

Principle 2: Children's Interactions with Their Peers Are an Important Source of Cognitive Development

As noted earlier in the chapter, preoperational children are characteristically egocentric in their thinking and language. Piaget believed that peer interactions are essential in helping children move beyond egocentric thought. Other children, thought Piaget, are more likely than adults to have cognitive structures similar to the egocentric child (Piaget, 1951). Therefore, they will be more effective in providing information or feedback to that child about the validity of his or her logical constructions. Thus, instructional strategies are favored that encourage peer teaching and social negotiation during problem solving.

Principle 3: Adopt Instructional Strategies That Make Children Aware of Conflicts and Inconsistencies in Their Thinking

This principle derives largely from Piaget's master developmental process, equilibration. Recall that children must experience disequilibrium, or an imbalance between their current cognitive structures and new information to be assimilated, in order for them to move to a new stage of development. Training studies involving conservation tasks demonstrated that, when confronted with the inadequacy of their reasoning, children learned to adopt more complex and adequate rules. Brainerd (1978) called this confrontation conflict teaching and argued that it serves to induce disequilibrium. Gruber and Voneche (1977) noted that a Socratic dialogue serves much the same function, since the teacher asks questions of the learner that bring out misconceptions and faulty reasoning.

Two important points should be made about this third Piagetian principle. The first is the criticality of diagnosing what children already know and how they think. Obviously, what questions are posed to create conflict or illustrate inconsistency in thinking depend on the teacher's knowing the current state of the child's knowledge. In this way, content is not introduced until the child is cognitively ready to understand it. Piagetian educators also caution that attempts to accelerate learning should be avoided, and this can be ensured through careful diagnosis of existing logical structures.

The second is taking into account the order in which concepts spontaneously emerge in cognitive development for conflict instruction. From a Piagetian perspective, concepts are acquired as a function of the logical structures that underlie them. Thus, questions or experiences designed to induce conflict will only be effective when the logical structures on which they depend have been or are being developed. We will see shortly that this same recommendation will emanate from the information processing perspective, but with a different explanation.

Illustrative Piagetian Curricula
Four curriculum projects were developed in the early to mid-1970s that purported to implement educational practices based on Piaget's theory (Brainerd, 1978). Few attempts have been undertaken to apply this theory; all attempts have been preschool programs focused on the preoperational child. Why so few? and Why the emphasis on preschool children? Reasons are easy to find. Because of the breadth and generality of Piagetian guidelines for education, it is difficult to determine just how they should be implemented and evaluated. In addition, conducting experiments at the elementary and secondary levels is both difficult and expensive. It's not easy to convince school boards that established curricula should be altered to test new, experimental ones. At the preschool level, however, curricular goals are not so well defined, and experimental curricula are more readily accepted.

The four curricula reviewed by Brainerd (1978) differ both in the degree to which they adhere strictly to Piagetian principles and in the extent to which they have been evaluated. It is almost impossible, therefore, to draw any strong conclusions about their effectiveness, either in absolute terms or in comparison to more traditional curricula. Lavatelli (1970), for example, designed the Early Childhood Curriculum to prepare children for the transition from preoperational to concrete operational thinking. Results from pre- to posttest indicated a gain in both standardized IQ and Piaget test scores. This may be an indicator of program effectiveness, but children's scores on these tests typically go up during the period of testing, even without instruction (Brainerd, 1977).

Two other Piagetian-based curricula—the Open Framework Program and the Piagetian Preschool Program—were evaluated using comparison groups of children enrolled in more traditional curricula. In both cases, however, Brainerd (1977) reported that although they were effective in producing gains on various measures, they were no more effective than the comparison curricula. Finally, Kamii (Kamii, 1985a, 1985b; Kamii & DeVries, 1974) has continued to stress the need for Piagetian-based instructional methods, but few results have been forthcoming to support her claims. Brainerd (1977) concluded that "while there are some positive findings, there does not seem to be any evidence to convince a prudent reader that the lofty claims made by the developers of Piagetian curricula are true" (p. 295). He goes further to suggest that it is perhaps the teacher, not the curriculum, that makes the difference (Brainerd, 1977).

Instructional Suggestions from an Information Processing View

Even though Brainerd (1977) was less than optimistic about the promise of Piagetian-based principles for instruction, these principles may yet endure. Despite their different perspectives on development, information processing theorists have suggested implications for instruction that, in a general way, resemble Piaget's. In a sense, information processing theorists have attempted to articulate, in more detail than Piaget, just what activity is beneficial for intellectual growth and how cognitive conflict can be most effectively induced. So far, however, the developmental theorists discussed in this chapter have had little to say about strategies for peer interaction (although researchers from various other learning traditions have provided ample evidence concerning the instructional value of collaborative learning structures).

The Role of Rules in Children's Thinking

Taken together, the work of Case, Klahr and Wallace, Siegler, and Sternberg suggests that rules are a useful means for characterizing children's thinking. Viewing children's thinking in terms of rules yields specific recommendations for instruction.

Case, for example, believes that children's short-term memory places limits on the number of operations (or rules) they can manage at one time. He suggests that these limits lead children to oversimplify problems and ignore important information (Case, 1978). To help children overcome memory limits, Case (1980) recommended that teachers follow a three-step procedure. First, the ways in which children are oversimplifying a given type of problem must be identified. Then students should be shown why their strategy will not work to solve the problem and what information they are ignoring. Finally, they should be taught and given many opportunities to practice a better strategy incorporating all the rules necessary to solve the problem. Throughout this process, Case (1980) cautioned, every means should be taken to reduce overall memory load, including use of familiar terms or objects, small steps, and lots of practice at each step.

While Sternberg (1984b) shares Case's emphasis on rule automatization, Siegler (1983) shares his concern for determining the rules children are currently using to solve problems. Rather than appeal to short-term memory limits to explain children's failure to use certain rules, Siegler argues that children adopt rules based on predictive accuracy. In other words, they will stick with the simplest rule possible that, based on their experience, is most likely to work in a given situation. This implies, however, a corrective procedure similar to that proposed by Case when the rule used by a child is inadequate.

Siegler differs from Case mostly in his emphasis on encoding processes once children have become aware that their rules are faulty. In order to identify the focus of encoding strategies, for example, Siegler recommends analyzing the task for requisite rules along with analyzing the child for the sequence of rule using. In this way, instruction can be effectively designed to facilitate the child's acquisition of new rules.

Promoting Conceptual Change

Like Piaget, theorists from an information processing perspective firmly believe that conceptual change is an integral part of cognitive development. Unlike Piaget, however, they explain this change in terms of domain-specific expertise and changing mental models, as opposed to general logical structures. As a result, they agree with the general Piagetian recommendation that children will learn best from experiences that induce cognitive conflict and indicate inadequacies in their thinking. But what are these experiences and how are they to be arranged?

Posner et al. (1982) contended that useful guidelines for instruction can be found in the metaphor of conceptual change as scientific paradigm shift. New scientific conceptions emerge when (1) there is existing dissatisfaction with the old conception, (2) a new conception can be grasped, (3) the new conception appears plausible, and (4) the new conception opens up new areas of inquiry (Posner et al., 1982, p. 214). Let us examine the implications of these four conditions.

Creating dissatisfaction with an existing conception is partly accom-plished through the existence of anomalies (Posner et al., 1982). These con-sist of experiences or information that cannot be easily assimilated to the existing conception. Vosniadou (1988) gave the example of children hearing an adult say that the earth is "round like a ball" when their mental model is of a flat and stationary earth. But Vosniadou argued that the anomaly alone will not necessarily cause dissatisfaction with the existing conception. Rather, children are apt to be confused or assume that they misunderstood the contradictory statement. After all, the adult could not be wrong, but the experience of a flat earth cannot be reconciled to an earth that is round like a ball. As a consequence, Vosniadou discovered children either remain confused or construct an assimilatory model that in some way makes sense of the new information.

In order to prepare students for conceptual change, then, claimed Vosniadou (1988), teachers must be aware of children's experiential beliefs, point out the contradictions between those beliefs and adult scientific conceptions, and provide persuasive reasons to children for questioning their beliefs. According to Posner et al. (1982), these persuasive reasons may, at least among older students, have already been established as a commitment to consistency between one's beliefs about the world and empirical evidence. Both authors point out, however, that questioning one's beliefs can be threatening and lead to defensive moves for which the teacher should be prepared.

Ensuring the intelligibility of a new conception can be accomplished through analogies, metaphors, and physical models (Vosniadou & Brewer, 1987; Posner et al., 1982). Scientists often notice an analogy to something known when they attempt to make sense of the unknown (e.g., Oppenheimer, 1956). Although such spontaneous reference to analogies does not come easily to students, they can benefit from analogies explicitly taught to establish a new schema or restructure an existing one. The explanatory potential of analogies and metaphors has already been discussed in relation to schema theory and mental models (see chapter 5).

Physical models, too, have been discussed as useful for helping students structure appropriate mental models of concepts (see chapter 5). For example, "physical models are particularly appropriate in a domain like that of planetary mechanics in which the structure of a solar system and its operation can be easily captured in a physical representation" (Vosniadou & Brewer, 1987, p. 62). It should be noted, however, that we still know relatively little about what models are best for what content domains, how these models might best be presented in instruction, and how misrepresentations of models can be most effectively avoided (Vosniadou & Brewer, 1987). This is an area in which more empirical investigation is certainly warranted.

The plausibility of a new conception hinges on its relation to the learner's experiential beliefs and its ability to account for anomalies. Clearly, any new model or theory must account for all previous data as well as the anomalous data that caused its creation in the first place. This consistency with past and present findings should therefore be an area of focus in instruction. But more than that, students' own experiences should be examined relative to the phenomena under study. As discussed earlier, their experiential beliefs can lead them to resist a new conception or to adopt a model that is somewhere between their beliefs and the new conception.

Referring to the earlier example of a round versus flat earth, a teacher might initiate a discussion about the difficulties Christopher Columbus had in finding men willing to sail with him. Since they, like the students, conceived of the earth as flat, they believed ships could fall off the earth if they sailed too far in one direction. Then the teacher could present a physical model of the earth in the solar system and discuss findings and experiences consistent with the representation of the earth as round. Socratic dialogues may also be useful in making students aware of inconsistencies in their current schema relative to the new conception to be acquired (Vosnaidou & Brewer, 1987).

Fruitfulness of a new conception is perhaps best illustrated in the applications to which the new conception may be put. The model of a round earth, for example, led to revolutionary changes in map-making and the planning of explorations. Discussing and illustrating implications of this sort, as well as having students create inventions stemming from a new conception, are ways teachers have found to enhance understanding of the new idea.

Finally, researchers studying conceptual change make two additional pedagogical recommendations. First, interdependencies among concepts within a domain can determine to a great extent the order of acquisition of these concepts (Vosniadou, 1988). Therefore, "instruction that utilizes the information about the order of acquisition of the concepts that comprise a given domain will be much more effective than instruction that does not" (Vosniadou, 1988, p. 10). Yet, when Vosniadou examined the astronomy units of four science text series, she found problems with their organization of concepts. For example, "a unit on the moon at grade one . . . takes the children from a description of the size and shape of the moon to an explanation of the moon's phases (which most of our adult subjects cannot explain), . . . before providing any instruction on the relative size and location of the earth, the sun and the moon in the solar system" (Vosniadou, 1988, p. 10).

Second, teachers should spend a substantial portion of their time diagnosing student misconceptions and guiding them to mental models more consistent with scientific findings (Vosniadou & Brewer, 1987; Roth, Anderson, & Smith, 1986; Posner et al., 1982). This recommendation should sound familiar since it is precisely the same as that proposed by schema theorists and mental models researchers, who investigated learning rather than development. What we might conclude, then, is that the learning and development of children in some ways closely resembles the learning of adults.

This conclusion will receive additional support in the next chapter, where the developmental theories of Bruner and Vygotsky are examined. Although both theorists set out to study cognitive development, many of their ideas appear to apply equally well to adult learning. In addition, what makes Bruner and Vygotsky stand apart from the theorists discussed in this chapter is their emphasis on learning and development within a cultural context.

SUGGESTED READINGS

Brainerd, C. J. (1978). *Piaget's theory of intelligence*. Englewood Cliffs, NJ: Prentice-Hall.

Siegler, R. S. (1986). *Children's thinking*. Englewood Cliffs, NJ: Prentice-Hall.

Gruber, H. E., and Voneche, J. J. (1977). *The essential Piaget*. New York: Basic Books.

REFLECTIVE QUESTIONS AND ACTIVITIES

1. Summarize your understanding of Jean Piaget's genetic epistemology. How does his view of knowledge and knowledge development fit with the epistemological traditions described in chapter 1?

2. As a class project, debate the merits of Piaget's stage theory for explaining cognitive development. What evidence can be amassed to support the theory? What evidence calls it into question?

3. Consider the difference between learning and development. Take a preliminary position on which influences which. That is, must a child be at a certain point in development in order for learning to occur effectively? Or, does learning prompt movement from one stage of development to the next? What evidence would support one position or the other?

4. Researchers who focus on learning through the lifespan have sometimes criticized Piaget's theory because it seems to imply that development is essentially complete once learners enter the formal operational stage. Review literature on lifelong learning or educational gerontology and indicate what evidence there is to suggest that development continues from birth to death. Suppose a new manuscript is discovered in which Piaget proposes a fifth stage of development, beyond formal operations. Speculate on the possible characteristics of this stage and its implications for adult learning.

5. Select a topic that could represent new information to groups of children and adults (one example might be how to operate a personal

computer). From what you have studied of learning theory so far, would you design different instruction for the children than you would for the adults? Why or why not? If you would create different instruction for the two groups, what would these differences entail? Why would you make those instructional decisions?

FIGURE   6–3   An Exercise in Formal Operational Thinking: The Level of the Liquid Should Appear Parallel with the Table Surface and Floor

► 7

Interactional Theories of Cognitive Development

Consider the following scenario.*

Mrs. Bell teaches kindergarten in a school district zoned to increase integration of black children into its predominantly white schools. She has a class of nineteen and begins a lesson with eight students on the concepts of animals with four legs and pets. She draws two overlapping circles on the board, and says, "The blue circle is for all animals that have four legs. The red circle is for pets. Now I want you to start thinking of some animals and where they belong."

As the children make suggestions, Mrs. Bell questions them about where the animals belong (in the blue circle, in the red circle, or in both and thus in their intersection). She also asks the children to justify their selection. Then, with each correct classification, Mrs. Bell hands her chalk to someone, who comes to the board and marks where the animal belongs. During the course of the lesson, the following scene takes place.

Mrs. B: Shannon, have you thought of another animal? (She calls on a petite white girl, who has been waving her hand madly.)

S: Yes, a monkey.

Mrs. B: And where does your monkey belong?

S: (softly) In the red circle.

---

*This scenario was inspired by Emihovich (1981), who studied interaction patterns among kindergarten children as a function of their race and gender.

Mrs. B: In the red circle? Why does it belong there? Is a monkey a pet?

Dean: (a black boy who has been clowning around paying no apparent attention to the lesson) I know someone who had a monkey for a pet!

Mrs. B: (ignores Dean, paces in front of the board holding the chalk close to her chest) But where do you find monkeys?

Chorus: In the circus!

Mrs. B: So is a monkey a pet if it's in the circus? Shannon?

S: (softly) Maybe.

Mrs. B: (tries again) But don't people usually keep pets in their homes? (Shannon nods.) Monkeys aren't usually kept at home, because they don't make very good pets. So where does your monkey belong?

S: In the blue circle. (Mrs. B hands Shannon the chalk to put a mark in the blue circle.)

What is going on in this scenario? How might we explain the events described in terms of the theories of learning discussed so far? Looking from the perspective of behaviorism, we might say that Mrs. Bell rewards correct responses with the chalk and opportunity to write on the blackboard. Thus, Shannon is rewarded only when she acknowledges that a monkey is not a pet and so belongs in the blue circle instead of the red circle. Dean, on the other hand, is ignored by the teacher. This prompts a logical hypothesis that Mrs. Bell considers his behavior disruptive and hopes to extinguish it.

Examining the scenario from a cognitive perspective suggests another interpretation. Through an inductive teaching strategy, Mrs. Bell facilitates the children's schema or concept acquisition. In other words, they are developing separate schemas for four-legged animals and pets by classifying examples of each. In addition, the children are learning rules, or operations (to borrow from Piaget), pertaining to set inclusion and set intersection. For example, a whale goes in neither of the defined sets, whereas a dog goes in both. These rules will undoubtedly serve as prerequisites to other mathematical concepts that the students will encounter when they study set theory.

But have we now understood and explained all the events related to learning that occurred in Scenario 7–1? Some developmental theorists have argued that current theories of learning and development overlook the social and cultural context within which cognitive development occurs. In other words, this scenario did not take place in a vacuum, and so it must be infused with expectations and patterns of interaction that are culturally based. For example, the teacher might be viewed as perpetuating a teacher as chief metaphor. That is, she is the authority, she has knowledge and power, and it is her agenda that prevails in the classroom. Children soon learn, as Shannon appears to in this scenario, that there are right answers and it is the teacher who has them, not other students.

Considering the cultural context of cognitive development also raises sometimes uncomfortable questions about race and gender and how these factors mediate both what and how children learn. Although Scenario 7–1 is too brief to permit valid conclusions about race or gender, one might reasonably wonder to what extent teachers treat boys differently from girls or blacks differently from whites and what effects these differences may have on their learning.

In this chapter, theories of cognitive development will be examined that place an emphasis on the sociocultural context within which the child develops. It is important to note that social and cultural factors in development have not been entirely ignored by the theorists discussed in the previous chapter. Piaget, in particular, included social-arbitrary knowledge as a kind of knowledge that children acquire, and he placed great store on the actions of a child in developing all knowledge. But, Bruner and Bornstein (1989) contended,

> It is our view that developmental psychology [has] been dominated for a decade or two by theories that [seek] primarily to formulate explanations of growth and development in terms of intra-individual factors: processes of accommodation and assimilation, of impulse control, of learning, of genetic predisposition, of cognitive representation, and so forth. When issues of interaction [are] treated in these theoretical accounts, it [is] usually in the spirit of taming them by showing how they [are] simply sources of variance that affect[] such processes as those just mentioned. (p. 1)

Interaction is therefore important to consider in its own right (Bruner & Bornstein, 1989), and it is this focus on interaction that distinguishes the theories discussed in this chapter.

The work of Jerome S. Bruner will be presented first. Although his approach to cognition has changed over the years, Bruner retains a belief that a theory of development should go hand in hand with a theory of instruction. Therefore, implications of his views for instruction will be discussed as his theory of development unfolds.

In the second half of the chapter, the ideas of Lev Semenovich Vygotsky (1896–1934) will be examined. There has been a resurgence of interest in the theories of Vygotsky, a Russian psychologist whose writings were originally published in the late 1920s and early 1930s. Wertsch (1985) described Vygotsky as a brilliant scholar whose interdisciplinary ideas preclude one from considering him only a psychologist. Today, these ideas provide information for theory development in both developmental and educational psychology.

BRUNER: GOING BEYOND THE INFORMATION GIVEN

Recall from chapter 6 that one of the hallmarks of developmental theory is the idea of an endpoint to which all children are assumed to develop. In order to explain how this endpoint is reached, developmental theory must account for the states through which children pass as they develop and the mechanisms by which transition occurs from state to state. Like the theorists discussed in the previous chapter, Bruner proposed answers to these questions.

First and foremost, the outcome of cognitive development, for Bruner, is thinking. That is, the well-developed mind, the intelligent mind, creates from experience "generic coding systems that permit one to go beyond the data to new and possibly fruitful predictions" (Bruner, 1957/1973, p. 234). Moreover, the aim of education is to make the learner "as autonomous and self-propelled a thinker" as possible (Bruner, 1961, p. 23).

The attempt to understand both what it means to know and how one comes to know led Bruner through several phases in his early empirical and conceptual work. These phases can be characterized by interests in public opinion, perception, thought, education, representation in childhood, and skill in infancy (Anglin, 1973). The public opinion research, conducted largely during World War II, centered around the social psychology of attitudes. It is important to mention only because of its influence on Bruner's later work; social and cultural factors came to play a significant role in Bruner's theory of cognitive development.

Taking together the rest of Bruner's work reveals two major themes. The first concerns the sequence of representational systems children acquire through which they understand their worlds. The second pertains to the role of culture in the course of cognitive growth and of schooling as an instrument of culture in the "amplification of human intellectual powers" (Bruner, 1964, p. 13). Let us consider each in some detail.

Three Modes of Representation

"Children, as they grow, must acquire ways of representing the recurrent regularities in their environment" (Bruner, 1964, p. 13). This involves, according to Bruner, an interaction between basic human capabilities that have evolved over a long period of years and culturally invented technologies that serve as amplifiers of these capabilities. "Cognitive growth, then, is in a major way from the outside in as well as from the inside out"

(Bruner, 1964, p. 1). Although it is almost impossible to entirely separate discussion of these two aspects of cognitive development, this section will focus on the inside out and the next section will discuss the outside in.

Based on his study of human evolution, Bruner proposed three systems of processing information by which people understand their world. In particular, he suggested that humans respond to their environment through action or patterned motor acts, through conventionalized imagery and perception, and through language and reason. These capabilities formed the basis for the modes of representation that Bruner called enactive representation, iconic representation, and symbolic representation.

Enactive representation refers to *"a mode of representing past events through appropriate motor responses"* (Bruner, 1964, p. 2). Young children, for example, may not be able to tell you directions to the store from their house, but they can take you there by way of a route previously traveled. Similarly, many adults may not be able to adequately describe or picture the layout of their office complex, but they negotiate its corridors with ease every day. Likewise, pianists have described the need to play a chord on an imaginary piano in order to know how it will sound; their fingers seem to carry the meaning of the chord. Some types of understanding, then, appear to be represented solely within our muscles.

Iconic representation enables the perceiver to *"summarize events by the selective organization of percepts and of images*, by the spatial, temporal, and qualitative structures of the perceptual field and their transformed images"* (Bruner, 1964, p. 2). A child who can draw a map depicting the route from her house to the store now represents her experience and understanding of that route in an iconic mode. Likewise, a person who has experienced a fire might represent his understanding of the experience in images of red-hot flames, black smoke, and charred remains.

Finally, **symbolic representation** comes about with the acquisition of *"a symbol system [which] represents things by design features that include remoteness and arbitrariness"* (Bruner, 1964, p. 2). Language, for example, is the primary symbol system by which humans can encode and represent experience. Not only do words stand as arbitrary designates for objects, events, and ideas, they can be combined to produce "far beyond what can be done with images or acts" (Bruner, 1964, p. 2). The same is true, of course, for other symbol systems, such as the numeric codes used by mathematicians.

The Sequence of Representational Stages

Although Bruner believed that "the usual course of intellectual development moves from enactive through iconic to symbolic representation of the world" (1966, p. 49), he is also famous for the statement that "any subject can be taught effectively in some intellectually honest form to any child at any stage of development" (Bruner, 1960, p. 33). How do we reconcile the two?

Stage theories like Piaget's (see chapter 6) hold that developmental stages proceed in a fixed sequence, transitions among stages occur at certain approximate ages, and certain logical operations develop at each stage. In addition, the operations of each stage are both more complex and adaptive than those of the preceding stage. A Piagetian would consider it futile, therefore, to teach any subject requiring logical operations to a child in a stage where these operations had not yet developed.

Bruner, in contrast to Piaget, believed in the invariant sequence of stages through which children pass but not in their age dependency. He argued instead that influences from the environment play a significant role in amplifying the internal capabilities that learners possess. In other words, the fact that children acquire enactive, iconic, and symbolic modes of representation, in that order, supplies the inside out part of the developmental story. The outside in aspect of development is explained through an examination of how the environment specifically influences the acquisition of these modes. These influences will be discussed more fully in the next section.

There are at least two important implications of this distinction in theory between Bruner and Piaget. First is that it redefines what is meant by readiness for learning. Whereas Piaget might speak of the cognitive readiness of the learner to understand the logical operations inherent in a subject matter, Bruner would ask whether the subject matter is ready for the learner to which it is to be taught. "Any idea can be represented honestly and usefully in the thought forms of children of school age" (Bruner, 1960, p. 33). The task, in Bruner's view, is one of translation, and the challenge is to provide problems in instruction that both fit the manner of children's thinking and tempt them into more powerful modes.

Bruner (1960) described an experienced teacher of elementary mathematics, for example, who recognized the need for presenting material to students in terms they can understand. In the words of the teacher,

> *Given particular subject matter or a particular concept, it is easy to ask trivial questions or to lead the child to ask trivial questions. It is also easy to ask impossibly difficult questions. The trick is to find the medium questions that can be answered and that take you somewhere. This is the big job of teachers and textbooks. (Bruner, 1960, p. 40)*

Consider how this view of readiness compares to that of Ausubel (see chapter 4). Like Bruner, Ausubel believed that instructional materials should be appropriate for the child. But Ausubel defined appropriateness in terms of the child's prior knowledge—i.e., what she knows and how she structures that knowledge in memory—whereas Bruner considers the child's dominant mode of thinking as the basis for appropriateness. As we have seen, the two are certainly related in that more knowledge of a subject correlates with the ability to think symbolically about that subject.

Assuming an invariant sequence of developmental stages and considering learning difficulty to be a function of the interaction between child and subject matter together raise a second important implication. Might not adults, as well as children, pass through the same sequence of enactive to symbolic representation when they learn a subject for which they have no prior experience? "We know little about the conditions necessary for the growth of imagery and iconic representation," wrote Bruner (1964, p. 3). He noted, however, that adults typically require a certain amount of motoric skill and practice before they are able to develop an image representing their actions.

In other cases, as well, adults may require practice with iconic forms before they can understand and use a symbolic mode of representation. For example, in a course taught by a colleague of mine, adults were being introduced for the first time to how a computer works. They became frustrated when they experienced difficulty in comprehending what the instructor thought were simple operations. Even diagrams of a computer's functions proved difficult for the class to understand. Finally, the instructor built a board with slots representing addresses in computer memory and removable cards representing bits of information. Actually moving the cards through input, storage, and output met the students' requirement for learning—they understood through action. Whereas symbolic representation is likely to be used for learning something new in a familiar topic, then, learners of all ages may resort to enactive or iconic representation when they encounter unfamiliar material. Indeed, Bruner (1985) recognized this possibility when he called his theory a "bogus stage theory"; a true stage theory assumes a relationship between age and stage of development.

Sequence and Instruction

The enactive through iconic to symbolic representational sequence of intellectual development implies an optimum sequence for instruction, namely, one that progresses in the same direction (Bruner, 1966). Any domain of knowledge, Bruner contended, can be represented in each of those three modes. "When the learner has a well-developed symbolic system, it may be possible to by-pass the first two stages. But one does so with the risk that the learner may not possess the imagery to fall back on when his symbolic transformations fail to achieve a goal in problem solving" (Bruner, 1966, p. 49). This seems to be precisely what occurred in the computer class described above. Although adults presumably have well developed symbolic systems (i.e., they read and understand language, and they undoubtedly have had the rudiments of mathematics), these systems failed when the instruction was entirely symbolic in nature. Because the students also failed to have corresponding imagery to fall back on, the instructor was forced to begin instruction in the enactive mode.

To determine what mode of representation will be optimal for instruction, then, requires knowing something about the learners' prior knowledge and dominant modes of thinking. Are they capable of symbolically representing the to-be-learned material? Or should the conservative course be followed and instruction developed that follows an enactive to iconic to symbolic sequence?

A second factor should also be considered when this decision is made. Bruner (1966) argued that "optimal sequences. . . cannot be specified independently of the criterion in terms of which final learning is to be judged" (p. 50). In other words, whether speed of learning or transfer of learning is the desirable goal may dictate what representation modes should be included in the instruction. And these, he noted, are sometimes antithetical goals. The ability to transfer what has been learned to new situations may require considerable time to achieve and may depend upon symbolic representation. Conversely, if learning time is short, of necessity, and the to-be-learned material relatively complex, learners may only be able to achieve iconic representation of what they understand.

Let us consider two hypothetical examples. In the learning of mathematics, desirable goals frequently include that learners can apply mathematical concepts to solve a variety of problems. Transferability of knowledge is important and depends upon a true understanding of the concepts. So, for example, suppose the skill of multiplying fractions is being taught. Students are asked to solve word problems such as:

> By the end of the day, Mr. Green had sold 2/3 of the onions he brought to market. He exchanges half of his remaining 1/3 for some corn from the merchant in the stall next to his. What proportion of the onions he brought to sell does he take home?

This problem can certainly be represented symbolically (that is, $1/2 \times 1/3 =$?; the correct answer is 1/6), and students can be taught the procedures for solving this type of problem (multiply the numerators to get the numerator of the answer, multiply the denominators to get the denominator of the answer, then reduce if necessary). However, learning the mathematical procedures does not alone guarantee students an understanding of the concept of fraction. If a computational mistake is made, students may not immediately recognize the error or be able to correct it. Suppose, for example, a student decodes the problem to mean he should divide by 1/2, instead of multiplying, and arrives at an answer of 2/3 by following the procedure invert and multiply. Without understanding that taking 1/2 of something means the result will be smaller than the original amount, he will simply not realize he has made a mistake.

Instead of teaching only mathematical procedures in a symbolic mode, Bruner would recommend that instruction include activities in the enactive and iconic modes for establishing the concept of fractions. These might take the form of games in which students act the part of grocers and customers, buying and selling portions of their wares. Actually making exchanges, such as "I'll take 3/8 of your layer cake," facilitates enactive representation. Similarly, using pie charts and other diagrams to picture fractions will serve to facilitate iconic representation. Although it is time consuming, having students solve many such problems, from enactive to symbolic modes, will ensure a deep understanding of the concept and the ability to apply it appropriately in many contexts.

Now consider an alternative situation in which speed of learning, rather than transfer, is a goal of instruction. Students in a vocational center are learning skills that will enable them to acquire jobs as automobile mechanics. Initially at least, it is more important for them to be able to successfully carry out such procedures as replace spark plugs than to understand the physics underlying what a spark plug does. In this case, then, instruction may never progress beyond the enactive or iconic modes. And the criterion for judging learning may be exclusively enactive, i.e., can the student successfully change a spark plug on an actual engine?

Finally, Bruner (1960) proposed the spiral curriculum as a strategy for translating material into children's modes of thought. It is in this proposal that we see Bruner's beliefs concerning the relations among the three representational modes. Not only can ideas be honestly represented in any mode, but also "these first representations can later be made more powerful and precise the more easily by virtue of this early learning" (Bruner, 1960, p. 33). It makes good instructional sense, then, claimed Bruner, to introduce students "at an early age to the ideas and styles that in later life make an educated man" (1960, p. 52). To accomplish this requires presenting topics consistent with children's forms of thought at an early age and then reintroducing those topics again later in a different form.

The Course of Cognitive Growth

Except to acknowledge the influence of environment on children's acquisition of the three representational systems, little has yet been said about how the transition occurs from stage to stage. In other words, what enables learners to develop the capacity for symbolic thinking when they have been thinking in iconic modes?

It is in answer to this question that we see Bruner's increasing emphasis on interaction. There is interaction between genetic predispositions and experience. Learners may be predisposed, for example, to representing their experience in iconic modes, but with appropriate medium-level questions from a tutor, be brought to a symbolic understanding of some idea. There is also interpersonal interaction; learning is a social enterprise. And there is interaction of the individual with the cultural. Indeed, culture provides the backdrop against which all forms of interaction play (Bruner & Bornstein, 1989). "The growth of intellect," then, ". . . moves forward in spurts as innovations are adopted. Most of the innovations are transmitted to the child in some prototypic form by agents of the culture: ways of responding, ways of looking and imaging, and most important, ways of translating what one has encountered into language" (Bruner, 1964, p. 13).

Just what interactions best transmit innovations that will promote cognitive development? Here we will see how Bruner's proposals for development are interwoven with his ideas about education and schooling.

Learning by Discovery

Bruner defined discovery as "all forms of obtaining knowledge for oneself by the use of one's own mind" (1961, p. 22). In essence, this is a matter of "rearranging or transforming evidence in such a way that one is enabled to go beyond the evidence so assembled to additional new insights" (1961, p. 22). Bruner believed that the process of discovery contributes significantly to intellectual development and that the heuristics of discovery can only be learned through the exercise of problem solving. That being so, he proposed discovery learning as a pedagogic strategy with such important human implications that it must be tested in schools. Before we examine the results of such testing, however, it is important to understand what Bruner had in mind when he proposed discovery learning.

A true act of discovery, Bruner contended, is not a random event. It involves an expectation of finding regularities and relationships in the environment. With this expectation, learners devise strategies for searching and finding out what the regularities and relationships are. Characterizing this searching and finding, however, should also be an attitude of constructionism. In other words, it is not enough to seek information and generate hypotheses without regard to constraints. Bruner (1961) described children who did this (i.e., generated random hypotheses for what information to seek) as "potshotters." Their information gathering lacked connectivity and organization and, as a result, their ability to solve problems was deficient. By contrast, those who demonstrated a connectionist approach were systematic and organized in collecting information that would help solve the problem.

What conditions, then, promote true discovery? For one thing, "discovery, like surprise, favors the well prepared mind" (Bruner, 1961, p. 22). In order to solve any problem, learners must determine what variables are relevant, what information should be sought about those variables, and, when the information is obtained, what should be done with it. In large measure, doing this easily depends on prior knowledge of a range of phenomena, or in Bruner's words, sheer "knowing the stuff"! Learners without such prior knowledge will undoubtedly face frustration and failure in a discovery learning environment.

A second, equally important, condition for discovery concerns the provision of models to help guide discovery. After the publication of "The Act of Discovery" in 1961, the concept of discovery became the basis of a "school of pedagogy" by some educators. Bruner (1973a) wrote,

> *As so frequently happens, the concept of discovery, originally formulated to highlight the importance of self-direction and intentionality, had become detached from its context and made into an end in itself. Discovery was being treated by some educators as if it were valuable in and of itself, no matter what it was a discovery of or in whose service. (p. xv)*

In response to this pedagogical movement, Bruner attempted to clarify "some elements of discovery" in a convention address and later published essay. In particular, he reemphasized that discovery is not haphazard; it proceeds systematically toward a model which is there all the time. "The constant provision of a model, the constant response to the individual's response after response, back and forth between two people, constitute 'invention' learning guided by an accessible model" (Bruner, 1973b, p. 70). Moreover, "discovery teaching generally involves not so much the process of leading students to discover what is 'out there', but rather, their discovering what is in their own heads" (Bruner, 1973b, p. 72).

Bruner, Goodnow, and Austin (1956) proposed a concept attainment model that exemplifies this notion of discovery teaching. Concepts, in essence, are rules for organizing the regularities of experience, and as such, stand as models of the world to be constructed and internalized. In Bruner's view, learners acquire concepts by setting forth tentative hypotheses about the attributes that seem to define a concept and then testing specific instances against these hypotheses (Bruner et al., 1965). Discovery of a concept, then, proceeds from a systematic comparison of instances for what distinguishes examples from nonexamples. To promote concept discovery, the teacher presents the set of instances that will best help learners to develop an appropriate model of the concept.

Note the similarity between the concept attainment model and the discovery teaching demonstrated by Mrs. Bell in Scenario 7–1. In asking for examples and questioning students about those they suggest, Mrs. Bell systematically guides them toward discovery of relationships between animals (a concrete concept) and pets (an abstract concept). She herself is guided by her own mental models of the relationships she hopes they will discover. That is, some four-legged animals are pets, some pets have four legs, and some animals are neither pets nor have four legs. Specific examples also raise issues regarding category definition and who is doing the defining. Mrs. Bell obviously excludes monkeys from her concept of pet, yet people have been known to keep monkeys as pets. Instead of leading Shannon to accept her concept of pet, Mrs. Bell might better have used the opportunity to explore how concepts come to be known. For example, only through the experience of living with the 10-foot Burmese python owned by my husband did my concept of pet come to include snakes.

The provision of models is important for discovery in another aspect. By asking certain kinds of questions or by prompting certain hypotheses during problem solving, the teacher also models the conduct of inquiry. It is necessary, according to Bruner, to teach children how to cut their losses, to pose good testable guesses, to persist in seeking appropriate evidence, and to be concise. In regard to the latter, for example, he described a fifth grader who, when asked what a particular movie was about, responded with a blow-by-blow account instead of giving a synopsis of it. Similarly, Duffield (1990) observed children play a computer game designed to teach problem solving. They were to locate an animal hidden behind "magic squares" by opening one square at a time and posing hypotheses based on the information presented behind each square. Instead of posing guesses that would minimize the number of squares they opened, some children systematically opened every square until they found the animal. The twin goals of hypothesis testing and conciseness were clearly not met in this instance.

Guided practice in inquiry and sufficient prior knowledge, then, constitute minimum conditions for discovery learning to be successful. To these, Bruner later added reflection and contrast (1966, 1973b). The need for reflection occurs when children can accomplish some task but are not able to represent to themselves what they did. In other words, they may successfully solve a problem but have little clue as to why they were successful. Reflecting back on the problem and recasting what occurred in a mode of thought understood by learners may help them to figure it out, to make the knowledge their own.

Finally, contrasts which lead to cognitive conflicts can set the stage for discovery. That is, "readiness to explore contrasts provides a choice among the alternatives that might be relevant" in a discovery learning situation (Bruner, 1973b, p. 81). In science lessons, for example, surprising events can

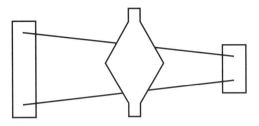

(a) a top view of the funnels as they
are set upon the ramp

(b) the funnels appear to roll uphill
when they sink toward the wider
end of the ramp

**FIGURE   7–1   The "Anti Gravity" Demonstration: A Surprising Event for
Seventh Grade Students in Science Class.**

provide an effective venue for discovery. As part of a unit on space science,
seventh grade science teachers conducted the following demonstration. As
shown in Figure 7–1, two funnels connected together at their wide openings
are placed in the middle of a sloped, triangular ramp. The ramp has been
constructed of two wires such that one end is higher and wider than the
other end. Students are asked to predict which direction the funnels will
roll. Without question, they all indicate that the funnels will roll downhill,
toward the narrow end. When the funnels instead appear to roll uphill, the
students are mystified and ask to see the demonstration done several more
times. To the question of whether this might be an antigravity machine,
most of the students are even willing to say yes.

Eventually, they discover that they have overlooked two important factors: the incline of the funnels is greater than the slope of the ramp, and the ramp is wider at one end. Taken together, these cause the funnels to sink downward into the opening of the ramp. They in fact go downhill, but they appear to go uphill (S. Edwards and R. Driscoll, personal communication, March, 1992; Friedl, 1991, p. 169).

Bruner's recommendation for contrasts that cause cognitive conflict parallels that made by Piaget and the information processing theorists who have focused on restructuring as the major developmental process. Although they have all offered different explanations for why the strategy works, the important point is that it does and can be reliably used in instruction.

Bruner noted in 1973 that by the mid-1960s, educational pedagogy based on discovery learning seemed to have moved far from his intended course. During this time, discovery teaching came to imply providing a rich environment for learning with an accompanying freedom for learners to set their own learning agenda, and there was a surge of popularity for open, unstructured classrooms. The 1970s, however, brought criticism to this pedagogic movement, a new wave of back to basics adherents, and a second look at what inquiry teaching was really about.

Out of this arose a model of inquiry teaching that Collins and Stevens (1982, 1983; see also Collins, Warnock, & Passafiume, 1975; Stevens & Collins, 1980) inductively derived from their observations of effective inquiry teachers. Although no claim is made regarding this model and its relation to Bruner's discovery learning, it nevertheless represents a means by which his ideas may be systematically carried out. According to Collins and Stevens (1983), inquiry teachers pursue two basic goals. The most common is for their students to derive a particular concept, rule, or principle that the teacher has in mind. The second, no less important, is for students to derive general rules or theories, or in other words, learn the conduct of inquiry.

In their model, Collins and Stevens (1983) presented ten of what they considered to be the most important instructional strategies used by inquiry teachers in service of their goals. These strategies are thought to be useful for concept learning and problem solving in any subject matter with any age learner, and numerous and diverse examples are offered to support this claim. For the most part, the examples come from teacher-student dialogues collected by Collins and Stevens during the course of their research. However, other researchers have also conducted studies that demonstrate the effectiveness of these strategies. Moreover, it is important to note that students' more advanced peers, or a well-designed computer-based tutor, may serve in the role of inquiry teacher as effectively as an adult instructor. Listed in Table 7–1, then, are the ten strategies together with examples of how each might be implemented in instruction.

TABLE   7–1   Collins and Stevens (1983) Model of Inquiry Teaching: Instructional Strategies Used by Inquiry Teachers

Strategy	Example in Use
1. Selecting positive and negative exemplars	A teacher presents dog (example), whale (example), and shark (non-example) in a dialogue about mammals.
2. Varying cases systematically	To consider factors that influence average temperature, the teacher offers places that vary in latitude (e.g., Amazon jungle, North Dakota) but not in other factors, such as distance from the ocean.
3. Selecting counterexamples	In a discussion on birds, ostrich is suggested as a counterexample for the attribute "flying."
4. Generating hypothetical cases	To illustrate the unfairness of boys dominating the classroom computer, a teacher asks, "How about a rule that boys can use anything in class except the computer? Would you like that?" (hypothetical case)
5. Forming hypotheses	After considering places where rice is grown, the teacher asks students to suggest what factors influence rice-growing.
6. Testing hypotheses	Students have generated a rule for how sets of 3 numbers (e.g., 2–4–6) relate to one another (e.g., all even numbers, or, $a + b = c$). They are asked for sets to be used to test the rule.
7. Considering alternative predictions	In criminology, students piece together evidence to determine what must have happened at a crime scene. The instructor suggests an alternate explanation that could account for the available evidence.
8. Entrapping students	Students have suggested that a critical feature of fish is that they live in water. The instructor leads them to an incorrect prediction by suggesting that a whale must be a fish.
9. Tracing consequences to a contradiction	In a math lesson, a student suggests doubling the length of a side to double the area of a square. The teacher does what the student suggests, with the result being 4 times the square's area.
10. Questioning authority	An instructor refuses to accept examples of learning theory applications that came from the students' textbooks. She asks students for their own examples, and questions, "Do these principles ever work in practice?"

In addition to the strategies themselves, teachers must have some means for making decisions about which ones to employ and at what point in the instructional dialogue to employ them. Indeed, "the control structure that the teacher uses to allocate time between different goals and subgoals may be the most crucial aspect for effective teaching" (Collins & Stevens, 1983, p. 274).

Based on their analyses, Collins and Stevens proposed four basic parts to this control structure. First is a set of strategies for systematically selecting cases that will facilitate student achievement of a particular, top-level goal. These strategies help to determine the beginning of an instructional dialogue. As it proceeds, however, teachers adjust their questioning according to their model of the student. Students continually reveal errors in reasoning or misconceptions when they respond to the teacher's questions. As teachers identify specific problems, then, they add subgoals to their instructional agenda, using a set of priority rules. Summarized in Table 7–2 are the four parts of an inquiry dialogue control structure.

"By turning learning into problem solving . . . , teachers challenge the students more than by any other teaching method. The students come out of the experience able to attack novel problems by applying these strategies themselves" (Collins & Stevens, 1983, p. 276). Bruner could hardly have said it better.

TABLE 7–2   Collins and Stevens (1983) Model of Inquiry Teaching: A Dialogue Control Structure

1. Strategies for selecting cases	Select cases to illustrate more important factors before less important ones.
	Select cases to move from concrete to abstract factors.
	Select more frequent cases over less frequent ones.
2. A student model	Ask questions to reveal both what students know as well as what gaps exist in their knowledge or reasoning.
3. A teacher's agenda	Begin inquiry according to a top-level goal. Add subgoals as necessary.
4. Priority rules for adding subgoals	Correct errors before omissions
	Correct prior steps before later steps.
	Implement shorter fixes before longer ones.
	Deal with more important factors than less important factors in correcting errors.

Culture and Cognitive Growth

"What does it mean, intellectually, to grow up in one cultural milieu and not another?" (Bruner, 1973c, p. 20). Developmental and cognitive theorists discussed in the previous chapters of this book might reply, "Not much." Their focus has been largely on the search for universal structures of the mind that are presumably unaffected by cultural differences. Bruner, however, found "intrinsic anticulturalism" to be a weakness of context-free approaches to cognitive development. He alluded to the Geneva dilemma (in reference to Piaget): "if the child only takes in what he is 'ready to assimilate,' why bother to teach before he is ready, and since he takes it in naturally when he is ready, why bother afterwards?" (Bruner, 1973d, pp. 153–154). The reason to bother, for Bruner, comes from understanding how culture interacts with human development and biology to define the human condition.

"Intelligence is to a great extent the internalization of 'tools' provided by a given culture" (Bruner, 1973c, p. 22). Members of different cultures, because of the specific and unique demands of living in their societies, make sense of their experiences in different ways. This is similar to the concepts as tools view promulgated by the situated learning theorists discussed in chapter 5. But what determines the particular use or application of concepts is the cultural environment of the user.

Eskimos, for example, depend upon group cooperation to hunt, seal, or fish in order to subsist. Their children, as an apparent consequence, do not exhibit the egocentrism that is characteristic of American and European children (Bruner, Olver, & Greenfield, 1966). Recall that Piaget proposed egocentrism as a universal characteristic of all preoperational children, but he based this proposal on observations of mostly European and American children.

Cole and Bruner (1971) cited another example in which the ability to make estimates of volume or distance was compared between nonliterate rice farmers from Central Africa and Yale University sophomores. Whereas the Yale students were superior in judging distance, the rice farmers were far more accurate in estimating how much rice was contained in different sized bowls. What these results suggest, Cole and Bruner believed, is a cultural influence on the manifestation of inherent competence. Inherently, there must be no difference between the two groups in their ability to make estimates. But demands of their respective cultures have made it more likely for them to develop different manifestations of this ability.

The same argument can be seen in studies of children selling candy in northeastern Brazil (Saxe, 1990). Although all the children studied were from the same culture (in the sense of all being Brazilian), the candy sellers developed different mathematical understandings from their non-candy-selling agemates. Whereas the non-candy sellers learned standard number orthography for manipulating numbers on paper, the candy sellers developed alternative procedures linked to currency exchanges. The candy sellers' understandings were "interwoven with the mathematical and economic problems linked to the practice" of candy selling (Saxe, 1990, p. 99). As in the research discussed in chapter 5, culture here begins to take on a broader meaning.

So what does this influence of culture mean for instruction? For one thing, Bruner sees schooling as an instrument of culture. What goes on in schools should equip students with the cognitive skills required for control and utilization of the resources of the culture (Cole & Bruner, 1971). This implies further that

> To instruct someone in [the] disciplines is not a matter of getting him to commit results to mind. Rather, it is to teach him to participate in the process that makes possible the establishment of knowledge. We teach a subject not to produce living libraries on that subject, but rather to get a student to think mathematically for himself, to consider matters as an historian does, to take part in the process of knowledge-getting. Knowing is a process, not a product. (Bruner, 1966, p. 72)

Bruner also called for a change in the way in which competence and performance are viewed. If performance is treated only as a shallow expression of underlying competence, then achievement differences between, for example, black ghetto children and white middle class children become evidence of underlying capability differences. The black child is then seen as having a deficit in learning caused by cultural deprivation.

Instead, Bruner argued, performance differences evident in the classroom should be viewed in the context of situational differences in how the children have learned to apply their skills outside of school. Surviving in the ghetto, for example, may require verbal negotiation and a show of bravado, but these same skills may be seen by a middle class white teacher as disruptive and counterproductive to learning in the classroom. By understanding how skills are influenced by culture, however, teachers will be in a better position to capitalize on the performances students do exhibit. In other words, teaching new intellectual structures may not be required so much as getting students to transfer skills they already possess to other situations relevant to the school context (Cole & Bruner, 1971).

Summary: Toward a Theory of Instruction

As mentioned earlier, Bruner believed that theories of development and instruction should go hand in hand. Cognitive growth, in his view, is a matter of growing from the outside in as much as from the inside out.

Whereas inherent biological predispositions provide direction to the inside out aspect of cognitive development, the outside in depends upon the mastering of techniques and cognitive tools passed on by agents of the learner's culture. As such, cognitive development can be facilitated and even accelerated through effective instruction. Cross-cultural studies provide evidence that "some environments 'push' cognitive growth better, earlier, and longer than others" (Bruner, 1973c, p. 50). To hold as a goal then, in Bruner's words, "an intellectually more evolved man" is ultimately a question of values.

Assuming that one's curriculum goals stem from a desire to develop self-propelled thinking in learners, Bruner suggested that an adequate theory of instruction must bring together the nature of knowledge, the nature of the knower, and the nature of the knowledge-getting process (Bruner, 1966). Interaction of the first two components influences decisions about what mode of representation should be emphasized in instruction. These decisions affect whether learning proceeds economically or whether learners experience cognitive strain.

Economy relates to how much information must be kept in mind at one time in order to achieve comprehension (Bruner, 1966). It is a function of both the content structure of the material to-be-learned and the preferred processing mode of the learner. Characterizing the Allied Forces' war against Iraq, for example, as a "battle over oil" is an economical means of representing the conflict. But it also overlooks many other factors that are equally important for understanding the event, such as the long history of strife in the Middle East, Iraq's invasion and occupation of Kuwait, and Saddam Hussein's aim to acquire nuclear weapons. Summarizing the conflict in a long sentence which alludes to all these factors, however, is likely to overload a learner's processing capacity, causing cognitive strain. The aim for effective instruction, therefore, is to tread the fine line between economy of representation and power of representation to convey important meanings.

An example where meaning has been sacrificed for economy can be seen in some corporate logos. In the effort to be concise, images or abbreviations are used that fail to convey appropriate or enough information about the organization for which they stand.

The knowledge-getting process dictates the types of instructional strategies that should be employed for instruction to be optimally effective. For reasons already discussed, Bruner recommended strategies that promote discovery in the exercise of problem solving. The activity of problem solving, furthermore, is influenced by the culture in which it is embedded. Because of this, instructors should foster cognitive strategies that will have the greatest likelihood of solving the particular problems faced by the culture.

An illustration of this principle might be seen in a third grade class where students are working in teams to produce instructional videos designed to teach various science concepts to their classmates (G. Stier, personal communication, October, 1992). The teams are multiculturally diverse, as is the overall class (which includes whites, blacks, American Indians, and Hispanics). The students, with help from their teacher, have selected concepts to investigate such as air pollution (which is a significant problem in this urban area). They must research the concept/problem and then determine how their results might be conveyed most effectively through video in order for their classmates to learn what they have discovered.

To accomplish all this, the students must engage in multifaceted problem solving. They must work out differences among team members in order to work collaboratively. They must acquire research skills in order to locate and make use of information related to their topic. They must learn specific roles involved in video production. And they must decide how to illustrate what they have learned in ways to help others learn it as well. All of these are important aspects of learning within a cultural context.

Finally, Bruner spoke to the instructional issues of reinforcement and motivation (1961, 1966, 1973b). Although feedback which can be used for correction is obviously important, Bruner contended that it must be provided in a mode that is both meaningful and within the information processing capacity of the learner. In the example above, for instance, the students can find satisfaction not only in the product of their videotapes but in how well their tapes promote learning in their classmates. Extrinsic reinforcement, on the other hand, can develop a pattern in which children look for cues to the right answer or right way of doing things. Exposing children to discovery learning can therefore promote a sense of self-reward in which students become motivated to learn because of the intrinsic pleasure of discovery.

VYGOTSKY: THE SOCIAL FORMATION OF MIND

Like Piaget, Lev S. Vygotsky was a scholar with broad interests. He graduated from Moscow University in 1917 with a degree in law, having also studied philosophy, psychology, and literature. He began a career teaching literature and psychology, founding a psychological laboratory at a regional teacher training institute. Upon delivering a paper at the Second All-Russian Psychoneurological Congress in 1924, however, Vygotsky's life changed. His brilliant performance led to an invitation to join the Psychological Institute of Moscow University, where he completed a dissertation, "The Psychology of Art," in 1925. From then until his death from tuberculosis in 1934, Vygotsky lectured, conducted research, and published extensively in psychology. Shortly after his death, Vygotsky's work was banned in the USSR for political reasons, and his work was not published again until 1956—a wide ranging impact on psychological theory (Cole & Scriber, 1978; Wertsch, 1985).

Bruner (1962) wrote in an introduction to Vygotsky's *Thought and Language* that "Vygotsky is an original" (p. vi). He "represents still another step forward in the growing effort to understand cognitive processes" (Bruner, 1962, of Vygotsky, p. ix). Like Bruner, Vygotsky attempted to understand the formation of intellect by focusing on its process of development. Also like Bruner, he believed that individual development could not be understood without reference to the social and cultural context within which such development is embedded. But unlike Bruner or Piaget, Vygotsky focused on the mechanisms of development to the exclusion of specific, distinguishable developmental stages. He rejected the idea that a single principle, such as Piaget's equilibration, could account for development. Instead, he suggested that development is much more complex, its very nature changing as it unfolds.

In criticizing developmental stage theories, Vygotsky (1962) wrote,

> *These schemes do not take into account the reorganization of the process of development itself, by virtue of which the importance and significance of any characteristic is continually changing in the transition from one age to another. This excludes the possibility of breaking childhood down into separate epochs by using a single criterion for all ages. Child development is a very complex process which cannot be fully defined in any of its stages solely on the basis of one characteristic. (p. 115)*

So what did Vygotsky propose as an explanation for intellectual development? And what implications does his theory suggest for learning and instruction? These questions provide the focus for the remainder of this chapter. Wertsch (1985) described three themes which appear to form the core of Vygotsky's theoretical framework: "(1) a reliance on a genetic or developmental method; (2) the claim that higher mental processes in the individual have their origin in social processes; and (3) the claim that mental processes can be understood only if we understand the tools and signs that mediate them" (pp. 14–15). Let us begin by examining the first of these three themes. This will provide a foundation for considering the social origins of mental processes, together with the function of signs in mediating their development.

Vygotsky's Developmental Method

Vygotsky took a fundamentally different approach toward development than is typical of other developmental theorists. As we have seen in chapter 6, most researchers interested in cognitive development assume the existence of some endpoint toward which the developmental process is aimed. They frame investigatory questions such as, "By what mechanism does a child become an adult?" or "How are the cognitive abilities of the child transformed into those of the adult?" Vygotsky, on the other hand, maintained a broader perspective. He posed research questions about the process of intellectual development "in all its phases and changes—from birth to death" (Vygotsky, 1978, p. 65). Thus, "by a developmental study of a problem, [Vygotsky meant] the disclosure of its genesis, its causal dynamic basis" (1978, p. 62).

The larger question for Vygotsky, then, had to do with how human beings came to develop higher psychological processes in the first place. A part of this question concerns how individuals, through childhood, come to possess the cognitive functions they exhibit later in life. The answers to either question, in Vygotsky's view, must emanate from a triangulation of multiple sources. He believed it important to study the natural development of cognitive skills in humans, to make cross-species comparisons, and to consider sociohistorical factors that mediate development.

The Natural Process of Development

In order to examine the origin of intellectual skills and their changes through the course of learning and development, Vygotsky believed that experiments should be conducted which provide "maximum opportunity for the subject to engage in a variety of activities that can be observed, not just rigidly controlled" (Cole & Scribner, 1978, p. 12). To achieve this, Vygotsky employed three techniques in his experiments with children. The first involves introducing obstacles which will disrupt normal problem solving. In studying egocentric speech, for example, Vygotsky asked children who spoke different languages to complete a cooperative activity. A second technique is to provide external aids to problem solving that can be used in various ways. Under varying task conditions, children of different ages would be expected to use the materials in systematically different ways. Finally, children may be asked to solve problems that exceed their current knowledge and skills. In this way, Vygotsky sought to discover the rudimentary beginnings of new abilities (Cole and Scribner, 1978).

What all three techniques have in common is their emphasis on illuminating process, rather than product. In other words, the question of interest is not how well did the children perform, but rather, what did they do under varying task conditions? How did they seek to meet task demands?

The findings from his experiments utilizing these techniques provided Vygotsky with evidence supporting a mediational view of development. By **mediation**, Vygotsky meant that "in higher forms of human behavior, *the individual actively modifies the stimulus situation as a part of the process of responding to it*" (Cole & Scribner, 1978, p. 14). The implications of this view will be explored shortly.

Phylogenetic Comparisons

According to Wertsch (1985), Vygotsky drew heavily from Kohler's research on insight (see chapter 1) to propose the use of tools as a prerequisite for the evolution of human cognitive functioning. Recall that Kohler's chimpanzees were observed to use a stick as a tool to reach bananas dangled out of arm's reach. Vygotsky also believed, however, that tool invention and use, although prerequisites to human cognition, were not sufficient conditions. To account for the differences in mental functioning between humans and other animals, then, Vygotsky adopted the Marxian position that socially organized labor activity, which is founded on the use of technical tools, is the basic condition of human existence. In other words, the structure and practices of socially organized labor provide the context for how people act, and subsequently, how they think. But Vygotsky also went beyond this position to consider the emergence of speech to be equally important in distinguishing humans from other animals.

From these phylogenetic comparisons, then, Vygotsky derived a belief very similar to Bruner's discussed earlier. That is, biological and cultural development do not occur in isolation. It is therefore important to consider social and cultural factors as they mediate the development of human intellectual capabilities.

Sociocultural History

Like Bruner, Vygotsky considered the development of intelligence to be the internalization of the tools of one's culture. But tools emerge and change as cultures develop and change. This suggested to Vygotsky that an historical perspective is as important as a cultural perspective in understanding human mental functions. As an example, witness how the concepts that we use to represent and understand the mind have changed through history. Among the tools of Aristotle's day were wax tablets, and he likened memories in the mind to impressions made in the wax on these tablets. Today, however, computers function in many aspects of our lives, and the increasing sophistication of their technology is reflected in increasingly complex computer models of the mind (see chapter 3).

To Vygotsky, cultural and historical perspectives are almost one and the same, because different cultures can be viewed along a continuum of social evolution. For example, Wertsch (1985) wrote of research conducted

---

BOX   7–1   Sociocultural Influences on Cognition

Sort the following words into whatever categories make sense to you, and provide a label or rationale for each category.

males, females, figs, kangaroo, meat, dogs, honey, bees, the moon,

cigarettes, water, sun, spear, wine, wind, fish, mud, fire, birds, rainbow

Now compare your categories to those shown in Box 7–2.

---

by Vygotsky and a colleague in which they investigated subjects' performance on several reasoning tasks. The subjects who participated came from societies in Soviet Central Asia that differed in the degree to which they were literate. Vygotsky argued, in other words, that the literate society represented a later point in social evolution than the nonliterate society, and therefore, should have evolved higher psychological functions.

The results of the research were interesting. On a task requiring them to group familiar objects, nonliterate subjects tended to categorize on the basis of how the objects might go together in a concrete setting. So, for example, *hammer, saw, hatchet,* and *log* were thought to be related. Literate subjects, by contrast, tended to categorize objects by their relationship independent of context. Thus, *hammer, saw,* and *hatchet* were grouped as *tools* (Wertsch, 1985).

BOX   7–2   Classification of Concepts Made by Aboriginal Dyirbal Speakers in Australia

"Research reported in Lakoff (1987) reveals that Dyirbal aborigines possess four basic concept classifications. They are listed below, along with the words presented in Box 7–1

Bayi: *males, kangaroo, the moon, rainbow, fish, spear*
Balan: *females, dogs, birds, fire, water, sun*
Balam: *figs, honey, wine, cigarettes*
Bala: *meat, bees, wind, mud*

Proposed explanations for these classifications include (1) domain of experience (e.g., wine is made from fruit; water extinguishes fire); (2) myths and beliefs (e.g., rainbows are believed to be mythical men; birds are believed to be female spirits); and (3) dangerous and exceptional things are marked by special classification, that is, put in a minimally contrasting category (e.g., dogs are considered to be exceptional animals and so they appear in the second class instead of with men). Consider how different these classifications are from typical Western thinking.

Analogous results can be seen in research reported by Lakoff (1987) concerning the categorization schemes of Dyirbal-speaking aborigines in Australia. Glance at the concepts listed in Box 7–1. How would you categorize them? Now examine the categories shown in Box 7–2. The categories of the aborigines reflect their society—what things go together in their world. Your categories, by contrast, are less likely to be context-bound and more likely to reflect abstract concepts such as things related to romance, for example (males, females, moon, wine, figs; S. Aljabari, personal communication, November 1992). The degree to which thinking is context-bound came to represent, for Vygotsky, an important indicator of intellectual development.

In the section that follows, then, we will see how Vygotsky's developmental method led him to a theory of the social formation of mind.

The Social Origins of Higher Mental Processes

One of the important characteristics distinguishing Vygotsky's theory from the theories of other developmentalists is his premise that "individual development cannot be understood without reference to the social milieu . . . in which the child is embedded" (Tudge & Rogoff, 1989). Social milieu, however, is not just another variable to be explained in the equation of human development (Bruner & Bornstein, 1989). Rather, it causes a shift in how that explanation is derived. The cognitive theorists of chapter 6, for example, focused on the individual as the unit of analysis, but Vygotsky contended that a more appropriate focus is social activity. Development "does not proceed toward socialization"; it is "the conversion of social relations into mental functions" (Vygotsky, 1981, p. 165).

This perspective "highlights the *bi*directional nature of individual and context. . . . Neither organism nor context constitutes the unit of analysis, but rather their interaction does" (Bruner & Bornstein, 1989, p. 9). Bruner and Bornstein go on to suggest that such a view of development is not readily grasped nor easily investigated, but is "decisive to the next step in comprehending human development" (p. 13).

From this interactional perspective, how does the child convert social relations into psychological functions? The answer lies in mediation. We already know that mediation means changing a stimulus situation in the process of responding to it. What this implies is that the conversion from the social to the psychological is not direct. Instead, it is accomplished through some kind of link—a tool, or "sign," as Vygotsky terms it. This can be understood by thinking of what is meant by tool and sign. A tool, for example, is something that can be used in the service of something else; a sign is something that stands for something else. In order to solve the problem of the bananas being out of reach, then, the chimpanzee had to change the situation by using the stick, not as a stick, but as a banana-reaching implement. It used the stick as a tool. Similarly, students learn that an economical way to solve complex word problems is to "let x stand for the unknown quantity which is to be found." They transform the problem into mathematical signs in order to find its solution.

Recall from chapter 3 that the science of signs, or semiotics, concerns how people develop signs and systems of signs (or codes) to interpret and explain their experience. Three types of signs are possible. Indexical signs are those that bear a cause-effect relationship to the objects for which they stand. For example, smoke is a sign of fire; it is caused by fire. Likewise, the reading on a thermometer is an index of temperature, because heat causes it to rise whereas cold causes it to fall.

Iconic signs are images or pictures of the objects for which they stand. Examples of icons can be seen in many computer applications. The trash can on the Macintosh screen, for example, stands for its function; it is used for throwing out or deleting files. Finally, signs that are symbolic in nature bear an abstract relationship with the objects or events for which they stand. Language and mathematics are two examples of symbolic sign systems. (Notice the similarity between these three types of signs and the modes of cognitive representation proposed by Bruner.)

So how do children learn to use signs in the first place? Vygotsky (1978) argued that sign use arises from something that was originally not a sign operation. He gave the example of a child stretching out her hand for an object she cannot quite reach. An adult interprets the gesture as pointing and responds accordingly. Gradually, as the child apprehends the same meaning as the adult, she will deliberately use the gesture as a sign for pointing. The use of signs, according to Vygotsky (1978), "the transition to mediated activity, fundamentally changes all psychological operations just as the use of tools limitlessly broadens the range of activities within which the new psychological functions may operate" (p. 55).

Higher mental processes are created, then, when mediation becomes increasingly internal and symbolic. Two concepts proposed by Vygotsky for understanding this process are internalization and the zone of proximal development.

Internalization

"Any higher mental function necessarily goes through an external stage in its development because it is initially a social function" (Vygotsky, 1981, p. 162). The gesture of pointing, for example, could not have been established as a sign without the reaction of the other person. Until the adult responds, the child is simply grasping, on her own volition, for an object out of reach. With the adult's response, however, the situation has changed to one of social exchange, and it is in that exchange that the act of grasping takes on a shared meaning of pointing. When the child internalizes this meaning and subsequently uses the gesture as pointing, the interpersonal activity has been transformed into an intrapersonal one.

Vygotsky (1962) argued that internalization provides a good explanation for the egocentric speech observed by Piaget in preoperational children. In Piaget's theory, egocentric speech reflects the egocentric thought and reasoning patterns of the preoperational child. It disappears when the logical operations of the next stage are acquired. Vygotsky believed, however, that egocentric speech evolves into inner speech and denotes "a developing abstraction from sound, the child's new faculty to 'think words' instead of pronouncing them" (1962, p. 135). "From the child's own point of view," Vygotsky (1962) argued further, "egocentric speech is not yet separated from social speech" (p. 136).

If he was right about egocentric speech being social speech that is undergoing internalization to inner speech, Vygotsky reasoned that three predictions should hold true. Children should expect their egocentric monologues to be understood by those around them. They should engage in such monologues when they are in a cooperative, social enterprise but not when they are alone. And, their speech should resemble social speech, in that it should be neither inaudible nor whispered.

Vygotsky tested these predictions in a series of experiments. In one, he tried to destroy the illusion of being understood by placing children in cooperative groups with children who were deaf or did not speak their own language. Egocentric speech dropped to nearly zero. In another experiment, Vygotsky observed children working alone; their rate of egocentric speech dropped to one-sixth of what they exhibited when they worked in groups. Finally, he required children to whisper, or conducted the experiment near an orchestra recital so that vocalizations would be difficult to hear. These conditions, too, had the effect of reducing egocentric speech. Vygotsky concluded, therefore, that egocentric speech represents a transition during which children are still isolating their own consciousness from the social world surrounding them. When the transition is complete, egocentric speech will be entirely subvocal and inner-directed.

The Zone of Proximal Development

Consistent with his emphasis on the process of development, Vygotsky sought to understand the beginnings of skill development. As such, he looked for a means to examine "those functions that have not yet matured but are in the process of maturation, functions that will mature tomorrow but are currently in an embryonic state. These functions could be termed the 'buds' or 'flowers' of development rather than the 'fruits' of development" (Vygotsky, 1978, p. 86). The means he discovered consisted of assigning tasks to children that went beyond their current capabilities.

This technique enabled Vygotsky to reveal a gap between a child's "*actual developmental level as determined by independent problem solving*" and the higher level of "*potential development as determined through problem solving under adult guidance or in collaboration with more capable peers*" (1978, p. 86). This gap he called the **zone of proximal development**.

Vygotsky argued that the standard way of assessing a child's mental age reveals only what abilities have developed and provides no information about what will yet develop. To illustrate, he described a hypothetical example:

> *Suppose I investigate two children upon entrance into school, both of whom are ten years old chronologically and eight years old in terms of mental development. Can I say that they are the same age mentally? Of course. What does this mean? It means that they can independently deal with tasks up to the degree of difficulty that has been standardized for the eight-year-old level. If I stop at this point, people would imagine that the subsequent course of mental development and of school learning for these children will be the same, because it depends on their intellect. . . . Now imagine that I do not terminate my study at this point, but only begin it. These children seem to be capable of handling problems up to an eight-year-old's level, but not beyond that. Suppose that I show them various ways of dealing with the problem. Different experimenters might employ different modes of demonstration in different cases: some might run through an entire demonstration and ask the children to repeat it, others might initiate the solution and ask the children to finish it, or offer leading questions. In short, in some way or another I propose that the children solve the problem with my assistance. Under these circumstances it turns out that the first child can deal with problems up to a twelve-year old's level, the second up to a nine-year-old's. Now, are these children mentally the same? (Vygotsky, 1978, pp. 85–86)*

According to Vygotsky (1978), "the zone of proximal development defines those functions that have not yet matured but are in the process of maturation" (p. 86). In this hypothetical example, then, the first child shows evidence of skills that will develop beyond those of which the second child will be capable.

The zone of proximal development, in separating actual development from potential development, suggests rather revolutionary implications for assessment of children's intellectual abilities. It is likely, for example, that children's learning potential is masked by standard IQ or problem solving tests that measure only independent, or intrapsychological, performance. To test this possibility, A. Brown and her colleagues (e.g., Brown & Ferrara, 1985; Campione, Brown, Ferrara, & Bryant, 1984) developed a measure of interpsychological performance. Specifically, they observed the number of standardized prompts children required in order to reach a preset performance criterion on a letter sequencing task.

This index of learning potential, while correlated with IQ and grade level, provided information about students' cognitive levels that went beyond what could be explained by IQ or grade level. For instance, Brown and Ferrara (1985) reported:

> *Overall, the IQ of almost 50 percent of the children did not predict learning speed and/or degree of transfer. Thus, from this wide range of "normal"-ability children (IQ range 88–150) a number of different learning profiles have emerged, including (1) slow learners, narrow transferrers, low IQ (slow); (2) fast learners, wide transferrers, high IQ (fast); (3) fast learners, narrow transferrers (context-bound); (4) slow learners, wide transferrers (reflective); and (5) fast learners, wide transferrers, low IQ (somewhat analogous to Budoff's high scorers). All of these profiles are hidden when one considers only the child's initial unaided performance. (p. 293)*

A second, equally important, implication of the zone of proximal development concerns the role of social interaction in determining its precise boundaries. Its lower limit is obviously fixed by the actual level of development that a child demonstrates. But what about its upper limit? This, Vygotsky believed, is set by processes of instruction that can occur in play, in formal instruction, or in work (Vygotsky, 1978; Wertsch, 1985). What is essential, regardless of the setting, is that "the child is interacting with people in his environment and in cooperation with his peers" (Vygotsky, 1978, p. 90). When we consider the nature of this interaction, we encounter Vygotsky's views on learning and instruction.

Learning, Instruction, and Development

"The only good kind of instruction is that which marches ahead of development and leads it" (Vygotsky, 1962, p. 104). "The only 'good learning' is that which is in advance of development" (Vygotsky, 1978, p. 89). From these statements, it is clear that Vygotsky viewed the processes of learning and development to be separate, in that learning is not the same thing as development, but linked, in that learning can set developmental processes in motion. The lagging behind of development from learning is what results in zones of proximal development. Moreover, "each school subject has its own specific relation to the course of child development, a relation that varies as the child goes from one stage to another" (Vygotsky, 1978, p. 91). When we also take into consideration the impact of social interaction on zones of proximal development, a rather complex picture emerges of just what "good instruction" should be. Let us examine some possibilities.

Teaching Thinking versus Content-Specific Skills

Vygotsky (1978) considered and rejected three views of how development and learning may interact. The first, that development is a precondition for learning, he attributed primarily to Piaget. The logical implication for instruction based on this view is that concepts or problems in any subject should not be taught until children have developed the necessary logical operations to understand them. Furthermore, since logical operations cut across subject matter areas, "instruction in certain subjects [should] develop[] the mental faculties in general" (Vygotsky, 1962, p. 96). This is the basic idea behind instruction in formal disciplines and amounts to instruction in how to think.

The second perspective, that development is learning, is more characteristic of behaviorist and cognitive information processing theories. In describing this view, Vygotsky wrote, "Learning is more than the acquisition of the ability to think; it is the acquisition of many specialized abilities for thinking about a variety of things" (1978, p. 83). For the design of instruction, this suggests attention to specific prerequisites within content domains. And only to the extent that content domains have skills and knowledge in common should we expect a transfer of abilities developed in one to problems in the other. Recall from chapter 6 the current emphasis of cognitive developmentalists on differential development within content domains.

A third view merely combines the first two, and Vygotsky found it equally unsatisfactory. Instead, he proposed a more complex view of the interaction between learning and development, which Wertsch (1985) criticized as being unclear in its implications for instruction. On the one hand, learning—and therefore, instruction—precedes development and, in fact, draws it along. As such, demonstrated ability within a subject area must necessarily depend upon organized instruction within that area. On the other hand, development must also occur in part because of its own internal dynamic. How else can we explain differences among children's zones of proximal development when their learning histories are similar? How else can we account for the changing relation that Vygotsky proposed between the subject and the child during development? Unfortunately, it is not entirely clear what this means for instruction.

Perhaps we may draw a parallel between Vygotsky's views of learning and development and Bruner's. Acquiring specific prerequisite skills and knowledge within a content discipline is obviously important. But so is solving problems that require learners to go beyond their current skill and knowledge levels. As Vygotsky noted, "learning which is oriented toward developmental levels that have already been reached is ineffective from the viewpoint of the child's overall development. It does not aim for a new stage of the developmental process but rather lags behind this process"

(1978, p. 89). We may conclude from his statement that Vygotsky agrees with Bruner about the need for those "medium-level questions" in instruction, the ones that will "take you somewhere."

Vygotsky's acceptance of Marxian philosophy offers another clue to what he regarded as effective instruction. If socially organized labor activity provides the context for how people act and think, it also provides an appropriate context for learning. That is, "cognition is constituted in dialectical relations among people acting, the contexts of their activity, and the activity itself" (Lave, 1988, p. 148; cf, Leontiev, 1981). And learning involves solving problems that arise out of conflict-generating dilemmas in everyday situations. Shoppers learn certain arithmetic practices, for example, because living within a limited budget requires that they calculate the best buys. This suggests that instruction should supply similarly relevant situations in which students are called upon to resolve dilemmas.

Situationally relevant contexts for problem solving are taking shape these days in interactive videodisk and other computer-based learning environments. Largely developing under the rubric of constructivist instructional theory, they will be discussed in detail in chapter 11.

Interaction in the Zone of Proximal Development

For instruction to precede development implies that certain types of interaction will be more effective than others in the child's zone of proximal development. In other words, "children learn to use the tools and skills they practice with their social partners" (Tudge & Rogoff, 1989, p. 25). This means that the social interactions they encounter could lead to developmental delays or abnormal development as well as to normal or accelerated development. Contrast this position to Piaget's, whose theory assumes that development is unidirectional, with all normal children expected to reach the last stage at approximately the same time.

Given that the role of a child's social partner is critical to the zone of proximal development, what can be said about it? For one thing, Vygotsky's theory "requires not only a difference in level of expertise but an understanding on the part of the more advanced partner of the requirements of the less advanced child, for information presented at a level too far in advance of the child would not be helpful" (Tudge & Rogoff, 1989, p. 24). Ideal partners in an instructional enterprise, then, should not be equal in terms of their present level of knowledge and skill. The more advanced partner, whether adult or peer, will function to bring about cognitive development in the less advanced partner.

This is consistent with the notion of scaffolding, where the instructor or more advanced peer operates as a supportive tool for learners as they construct knowledge (Greenfield, 1984; Wood, Bruner & Ross, 1976). "The scaffold, as it is known in building construction, has five characteristics: it provides a support; it functions as a tool; it extends the range of the worker; it allows the worker to accomplish a task not otherwise possible; and it is used selectively to aid the worker where needed . . . a scaffold would not be used, for example, when a carpenter is working five feet from the ground" (Greenfield, 1984, p. 118).

The characteristics of a scaffold define the characteristics of an ideal instructor. An instructor should neither present information in a one-sided way nor shape successive approximations to some goal behavior. Rather, an instructor should provide the guidance required for learners to bridge the gap between their current skill levels and a desired skill level. As learners become more proficient, able to complete tasks on their own that they could not initially do without assistance, the guidance can be withdrawn (Greenfield, 1984).

A second requirement of the social interaction between partners is that their relationship be one of intersubjectivity. By this Vygotsky meant that partners must come to some degree of joint understanding about the task at hand (Wertsch, 1984). It is not enough, in other words, for the partners to simply work together or for one partner to dominate and demonstrate solutions to the other. They must co-construct the solution to a problem or share in joint decision-making about the activities to be coordinated in solving the problem. It should be apparent that the requirement of intersubjectivity denotes a different relationship between social partners in instruction than is typical between a teacher and student or between a tutor and tutee. Intersubjectivity implies shared power and shared authority, where inequality between partners resides only in their respective levels of understanding.

Think back to the scenario with which this chapter began, and consider the teacher's relation to the students from a Vygotskian perspective. Is there evidence of intersubjectivity among partners in instruction? Quite the contrary, there are clear signs that the teacher is in power, making all the instructional decisions. She is evidently standing near the board, for example, while the children are seated, only coming to the board with permission when she hands them a piece of chalk. Moreover, Dean offers information that pertains to the discussion and could be useful in exploring various meanings of pet. But the proffered information is ignored, as the teacher maintains her own instructional agenda.

If the scenario does not represent a good example of instruction as Vygotsky would propose, how might it otherwise be imagined? What could the teacher have done to promote intersubjectivity among herself (the more advanced partner) and the students (the less advanced partners)? There are undoubtedly a number of possibilities. To share authority and thus reduce the subjective difference between herself and the students, the teacher might have sat with them at the table instead of standing while they sat. In that way, access to the board would be equal for all members of the group. With regard to the lesson itself, she, as well as the children, could suggest examples of animals to consider. This might be a particularly effective way of operating in the children's zone of proximal development. She can suggest examples that may be difficult to classify and provide appropriate prompts to assist the students in the task.

Whereas this example is obviously hypothetical, there have been studies conducted that investigate, from a Vygotskian perspective, the effects of social interaction on learning. A number of these studies examined age trends and the nature of interaction between social partners with the conclusion first, that it is useful to distinguish between learning of skills and adopting new perspectives (Tudge & Rogoff, 1989). In the learning of skills, adults were more effective as partners than children's peers. They tended to promote more advanced planning strategies (e.g., Radziszewska & Rogoff, 1988), provide more verbal instruction, and elicit greater participation (e.g., Ellis & Rogoff, 1986) than the child partners. By contrast, "the child teachers appeared relatively unskilled at guiding instruction within the learner's region of sensitivity to instruction" (Ellis & Rogoff, 1986, p. 323).

In learning to consider another's perspective, however, child partners were more effective than adult partners, provided there was a free and active exchange of ideas without one child dominating the conversation. It is likely that peer interaction may provide for a more open forum for discussing issues than is available in adult-child interaction (Tudge & Rogoff, 1989).

Finally, research findings seem to converge in support of the requirement for intersubjectivity between social partners during instruction. Advances in development occurred when partners collaborated to arrive at a solution to a problem (e.g., Forman, 1987). But interaction was less successful when one partner dominated, or when partners argued or engaged in off-task behavior (e.g., Glachan & Light, 1982; Russell, 1982).

An instructional strategy in which intersubjectivity comes together with scaffolding is reciprocal teaching. Developed for reading instruction by Palincsar and Brown (1984; see also Brown & Palincsar, 1982; Palincsar, 1986), reciprocal teaching is designed to improve comprehension of poor readers. In this program poor readers engage in dialogue among themselves and with the teacher, during which they jointly construct meaning from whatever text they are reading. The dialogue is structured to emphasize four comprehension strategies: questioning about the main points in the passage, clarifying to resolve difficulties in understanding, summarizing to capture the gist of the text, and predicting to forecast what might happen next.

Initially, the teacher leads and sustains the discussion, modeling the four comprehension strategies. But as the instruction proceeds, the teacher transfers more and more control of the dialogue to students, who assume the role of instructor. Evaluations of this program have consistently shown significant gains in students' reading comprehension. In addition, they appear to use their newly acquired skills in reading texts in content domains, such as science and social studies.

The Role of Language and Other Sign Systems

A consequence of internalization is the ability to use signs in increasingly elaborative ways that extend the boundaries of children's understanding. In play, for example, young children use whatever resources are available to them to "project themselves into the adult activities of their culture and rehearse their future roles and values" (John-Steiner & Souberman, 1978, p. 129). Although the tools at hand may include sophisticated, prefabricated toys, children are equally successful at creating imaginary situations with sticks and other common objects in their environment. In play, Vygotsky argued, children stretch their conceptual abilities and begin to develop a capacity for abstract thought. The signs they establish in their imaginations, in other words, can make up a very complex symbol system which they communicate through verbal and nonverbal gestures.

The development of language, however, was thought by Vygotsky to have the greatest impact on children's acquisition of higher psychological processes. Vygotsky believed that language constitutes the most important sign-using behavior to occur during cognitive development, because it frees children from the constraints of their immediate environment. It provides for decontextualization, wherein signs (or words, in this case) become more and more removed from a concrete context (Wertsch, 1985). In learning concepts, for example, children initially associate the concept name, such as horse, with a specific animal they have encountered. With experience, however, they learn to abstract the concept from a particular concrete context and so generalize it to other situations and instances of horses.

This process of decontextualization must occur with any symbol system if it is to serve higher mental functions such as reasoning. To illustrate, Wertsch (1985) described the results of Saxe (1977, 1982), who investigated children's understanding of numeration (counting) systems. The children Saxe studied came from New Guinea and counted by employing their body parts in a particular order. Young children, he discovered, focused on the physical characteristics of the body parts, rather than their role in the counting process. Imagine, for example, counting up to four on your fingers, by starting either from the right or left of your hand. The fact that a different finger is reached would mean to the young children of this study that two different numbers must have been counted. Older children, however, were able to abstract the body part from its role in numeration and so would respond that four had been counted in each case.

Although Vygotsky did not address specific implications for instruction of language and other sign systems, other than to suggest that play is important for learning in young children (Vygotsky, 1978), other researchers have begun to pick up the slack. Lemke (1985, 1988) suggested that mastery of a subject entails mastery of its specialized language structures. In one study of a high school class in earth science, for example, Lemke (1988) illustrated how a teacher and his students, with different understandings of what light and heat mean, talked at cross-purposes. He concluded that "meaning relations, in particular, need to be frequently glossed, paraphrased, and made explicit, and students need to be explicitly alerted to the genres of paraphrase and semantic clarification, so that they can use them actively in asking questions, posing problems, and refining their mastery of the thematics of a subject" (Lemke, 1988, p. 97).

Similarly, Emihovich (1981) has demonstrated gender and race differences in discourse structure, not only in teacher-student interactions, but in student-student interactions as well. This reinforces the need for teachers to realize that children's misbehavior may simply stem from misunderstanding rather than willful disobedience. In addition, misunderstanding may be a problem of translation, differences in language structure, rather than a problem of misconception.

CONCLUSION

In this chapter and the preceding one, the concept of human cognitive development has been explored as it relates to learning and instruction. In some respects, the theorists discussed in chapter 6 represent opposing positions. Despite an apparent common focus on interaction between children's native capabilities and their environment to explain development, Piagetian and cognitive information processing theorists diverged in their explanatory emphases. With its proposal of age-based stages and a single develop-ment mechanism (equilibration), Piaget's theory is more nativistic. By contrast, Siegel, Sternberg, and Klahr, and Wallace put more emphasis on environmental factors in development.

In this chapter, Bruner and Vygotsky might be said to offer intermediary positions, with their explicit focus on the role of interaction in development. As John-Steiner and Souberman (1978) suggested, Vygotsky "offers a model for new psychological thought and research to those who are dissatisfied with the tension between traditional behaviorists and nativists" (p. 121). Finally, perhaps recent cognitive developmentalists, and most certainly Bruner and Vygotsky, now recognize a complexity in human development that belies the sufficiency of a single model or theory of development. "The age of global claims appears to be at an end" (Bruner & Bornstein, 1989, p. 13). Instead, many theories may each provide insight into some aspect of learning and development. As we have seen throughout this book, what one theory conceals, another illuminates.

SUGGESTED READINGS

Bruner, J. S. (1986). *Actual minds, possible worlds*. Cambridge, MA: Harvard University Press.

Lave, J. (1988). *Cognition in practice: Mind, mathematics and culture in everyday life*. New York: Cambridge University Press.

Saxe, G. B. (1990). *Culture and cognitive development: Studies in mathematical understanding*. Hillsdale, NJ: Erlbaum.

Vygotsky, L. S. (1978). *Mind in society*. Cambridge, MA: Harvard University Press.

Wertsch, J. V. (1985). *Vygotsky and the social formation of mind*. Cambridge, MA: Harvard University Press.

REFLECTIVE QUESTIONS AND ACTIVITIES

1. Consider the underlying assumptions that Bruner and Vygotsky appear to make about knowledge and its development. With what epistemological position would they most closely align? How are their assumptions similar to or different from those of Piaget or the cognitive information processing theorists?

2. At the end of the last chapter, you took a preliminary position on which comes first, learning or development. Reflect upon your answer and decide whether your opinion has changed or remained the same. In either case, indicate why.

3. Refer back to Scenario 2-1, which described an autistic child. What insights, if any, does developmental theory offer for understanding this child's condition? What recommendations, if any, would a cognitive developmental theorist make for teaching this child? In cases where a child's disability is not so severe, there is some disagreement over whether disruptive behavior should be brought under control before instruction proceeds, or whether the instruction itself can be a mechanism in helping to control the disruptive behavior. Argue one side or the other, being sure to support your arguments with statements consistent with learning and developmental theory.

4. Describe an instructional program (hypothetical or actual) that makes

use of Vygotsky's "zone of proximal development." What is being taught and learned? by whom? and utilizing what instructional strategies?

5. Although Bruner and Vygotsky concerned themselves with the development of knowledge among children, their ideas have been used to apply to adults. What, in your opinion, might be the most likely concepts from their theories to apply to adult learning? Why? Illustrate your answer with specific examples.

▶ Part V

Learning and Biology

▶ 8

Biological Bases of Learning and Behavior

Consider the following scenarios.

Scenario 8–1

Miriam and Mercedes, twins separated from birth, grew up in communities that were different on many counts. Miriam lived with her adoptive family in a small apartment on the east side of a large metropolitan area. She attended a nearby, crowded urban school which, except for math class, she was glad to leave upon graduating. Mercedes, on the other hand, made her home in a rambling farmhouse located far from the nearest neighbors. She routinely rose early to do chores before the school bus picked her up at 7 A.M. She, like her sister, excelled in math at the rural school she attended.

As adults, the twins chose engineering careers, married men named Bob, and enrolled, at the sponsorship of their respective companies, in a management training program where they met for the first time.

Scenario 8–2

Mario was about 4 years old when a severe viral infection irreparably damaged part of his brain. Doctors were unsure whether he would ever recover his speech, much less learn to any normal extent. However, within months, he had begun talking again, and by first grade, no differences in learning were apparent between Mario and his classmates.

What do these scenarios have in common? On the surface, perhaps not much. But they raise similar questions about learning that have not yet been accounted for in detail by any learning theory. That is, to what extent is learning governed by biological factors? Is it just coincidence that Mercedes and Miriam excelled in the same academic subject, chose the same career, and enrolled in the same job-related training program? Can their behavior be satisfactorily explained by reference to contingencies of reinforcement in their respective learning histories? Can similar conditions be found in their environments that would account for particularly well-learned mental models in mathematics? Or is their genetic inheritance responsible to some degree for the way their lives play out?

Similarly, most of us carry an intuitive belief that the brain is somehow implicated in learning. Children with Down's syndrome, for example, never attain the mental functioning of normal children. At the other end of the age continuum, Alzheimer's disease, associated with a severe reduction of a particular neurotransmitter in the brain cortex, can cause extensive memory loss and mental impairment. Yet Mario, in Scenario 8–2, appears to fully overcome the impairment caused by brain injury. (Although this scenario is fictional, it is consistent with the results of neurophysiological studies to be discussed in this chapter.) The question remains, then, What role does the brain play in learning, cognitive development, and memory retention?

Genetic inheritance and brain physiology are the focal points for two basic lines of biological research related to learning. Together with individual development and the adaptive significance of species characteristics, they correspond to the types of causes biologists seek as explanations for behavior (cf. Dewsbury, 1991). Consider, for example, the characteristic of binocular vision in humans. Depth perception can be explained in terms of the structure and placement of human eyes. Our eyes are set relatively close together in our heads, and their anatomical structure permits them to work together in creating the sensation of depth. When biologists provide such physiological explanations of phenomena, they assign proximate causes to behavior. In Mario's case, then, his return to normalcy might be attributed to proximate causes in that other parts of his brain assumed the functions of the damaged part.

Searching for environmental factors thought to influence behavior is also a matter of assigning proximate causes. So, for example, a teenage boy's preference for looking at pictures of pretty women may be attributed to liking the pictures or to peer approval of this behavior. Both are proximate causes. In Scenario 8–1, a reasonable explanation for the girls' mathematical talent might be found in their families' emphasis on and support for learning in math. These, too, would be proximate causes.

Explaining binocular vision only in terms of human anatomy and physiology, however, still leaves open the question of why humans developed the anatomical structures and processes that they have. In other words, why are our eyes set close together in our heads? Asking questions such as this are sociobiologists in search of ultimate causes of human behavior. They look to evolution to provide the answers. With regard to binocular vision, for example, those ancestors who could distinguish depth were undoubtedly more successful at hunting prey and finding their way through a variety of terrains. These behaviors, in turn, proved to be adaptive in the overall struggle for survival. As a result, the genes governing close eye placement gradually dominated through a process of natural selection.

Understanding teenage boys' viewing preferences might also be enlightened by reference to ultimate causes. That is, sexual behavior in general is related to reproductive fitness in ancestral populations. Those behaviors that led to increased fitness are likely to have survived through multitudes of generations, even though they may serve no adaptive function today (cf. Crawford & Anderson, 1989).

In these two branches of biology, then, we see separate and distinct contributions to an overall understanding of the biological bases of human learning and behavior. Both will be examined further in this chapter. In addition, however, the question is addressed as to what, if any, practical implications for instruction may be drawn from these two fields of study. Chipman (1986) noted with concern that educators often adopt uncritically and inappropriately results from neuroscience research. She argued for more multilevel theorizing that will situate neurological interventions within an overall educational enterprise, since, "pills do not, after all, teach reading" (Chipman, 1986, p. 226). In light of these concerns, the intersection between biology and instruction will be examined.

ULTIMATE CAUSES: EVOLUTION AND BEHAVIOR

It goes without saying that Charles Darwin's concept of natural selection in evolution lies at the very heart of sociobiology. The idea of evolution—that present living forms are descendents of long-extinct ancestors—had already been established prior to the publication in 1859 of Darwin's most famous work, *Origin of Species*. What Darwin contributed was a reasonable theory for how evolutionary changes come about. That is, he proposed a process of natural selection. In the struggle for existence, organisms that are perfectly adapted to their environments will survive unchanged. In conditions of less than perfect adaptation, however, those organisms that have traits enabling them to struggle more effectively than other organisms will pass on these genes to more offspring. Over many generations, some traits will be naturally selected over others, with these changes manifested in the genetic makeup and behavior of the organisms.

That organisms evolve to fit ecological niches can be seen from observations of animals everywhere. The finches of the Galapagos Islands, for example, display behaviors that are peculiarly suited to their environment and that are seen among finches nowhere else in the world. Leahey and Harris (1989) described three species of gulls that have evolved behaviors dependent upon their ecological surroundings. The members of one species, for example, nest close to one another and so have developed fine visual discrimination skills for recognizing the differences between their own and a stranger's eggs. Members of another species nest further apart, and the visual discrimination skills of these gulls enable them to distinguish their own chicks rather than their own eggs. Finally, members of a third species nest on cliffs, obviating the need to recognize either eggs or chicks.

The lesson that biologists take from these examples is that evolution is the ultimate determiner of behavior. It predisposes organisms to learning certain things. The gulls, for instance, all possess the capability for fine visual discrimination. This is an obvious conclusion from the fact that such skills are required for both chick and egg recognition. But it is adaptive for the gulls to acquire only the ability to discriminate either eggs or chicks as their ecological environment demands. In this way, sociobiologists provide a view of learning and behavior that integrates common notions of instinctive versus learned behavior. "This distinction [between learned and instinctive behavior]," declared Garcia, Brett, and Rusiniak (1989), "is completely spurious; you cannot have one without the other. . . . Learning itself may be the primary instinct" (p. 200).

Let's take a closer look at the evidence for a sociobiological view and see what implications it holds for current theories of learning and behavior.

Evolution and Conditioning

Reflect back, for a moment, on the discussions in chapters 1 and 2 of classical and operant conditioning. No hint was ever given that the laws of conditioning might be species-specific. Skinner, in fact, held just the opposite view. He believed strongly that learning proceeded in much the same way for all species. Whatever biological constraints could be identified (e.g., animals can hear only certain frequencies of sound and see only certain spectra of light) were assumed to be peripheral to learning.

Despite Skinner's assumption of, and belief in, general learning laws, others have not been so convinced. Students in my learning classes, for example, pose questions every semester about the limits of conditioning principles. Even before we discuss biological factors in learning, they wonder why pigeons learn to peck circles much faster than rats learn to press levers (both undergoing shaping in a Skinner box). Could the differences in performance be attributed to species-specific evolutionary differences?

Pigeons, after all, peck for food so that they may be predisposed toward the behavior of pecking. Rats, on the other hand, have no reason to exhibit the behavior of pressing in their natural environments. Since rats live in underground burrows, however, they may be predisposed to learning spatial layouts, perhaps accounting for the ease with which they take to running mazes in behavioral experiments.

There is evidence now to suggest that both classical and operant conditioning are subject to biological influences. With respect to the former, results of studies on taste aversion indicate that animals are prepared to associate some conditioned stimuli with some unconditioned stimuli, but are not prepared to associate other conditioned stimuli with those unconditioned stimuli (Mowrer and Klein, 1989). Garcia and Koelling (1966) conducted the now-classic study in which this phenomenon was discovered.

In a 2 x 2 factorial design, Garcia and Koelling (1966) paired two conditioned stimuli (flavor and noise) with two unconditioned stimuli (a drug producing illness and a shock producing pain). Under the standard classical conditioning paradigm, the researchers expected the subjects (rats in this case) to avoid any conditioned stimulus that was associated with the consequences of illness or pain. What they found instead is summarized in Figure 8–1. The rats developed a strong aversion to saccharin-flavored water only when it coincided with illness. They continued to drink it when pain was the consequence. Likewise, rats who were shocked attempted to avoid the associated noise, but rats who were sickened paid no attention to it.

Varied replications of this study (e.g., Domjon, 1980; Garcia, Clarke, & Hankins, 1973) strengthened the conclusions that rats are genetically predisposed to these associations. Upon becoming sick, the rat is likely to attribute the cause of its distress to the most recent, novel substance ingested. In other words, "it must be something I ate," but since familiar foods had not previously caused illness, that something must be the most recent, unfamiliar food. Pet owners may recognize this same phenomenon in their animals. Shortly after eating a new kind of dog food I had purchased, my dog became ill. Although a kind of viral infection was later diagnosed, he has since refused to eat that brand of dog food.

Clearly, developing taste aversions to foods that cause illness and avoiding external cues associated with pain are adaptive mechanisms that increase an animal's fitness for survival. Based on the same logic, associations involved in phobias may also be both selective and adaptive (Lohordo & Droungas, 1989). Snakes and spiders were dangerous to pretechnological man. As a result, we may now be predisposed to fear them.

Like classically conditioned associations, operant behaviors appear to be influenced by biological factors. Breland and Breland (1961) coined the

US

	drug (producing illness)	shock (producing pain)
flavor	**strong association**	no results
noise	no results	**strong association**

CS

FIGURE 8–1   **Results of Pairing Two Types of Conditioned Stimuli with Two Types of Unconditioned Stimuli**

Modified from Garcia and Koelling (1966)

term instinctive drift after witnessing a deterioration of operant behavior in trained animals over an extended period of training. As part of an advertising gimmick, they trained pigs and raccoons to deposit coins in a piggy bank. They followed typical shaping and chaining procedures, using food as the reinforcer. At first, the pigs and raccoons demonstrated flawless performance—picking up, on cue, a coin or two and depositing it in the receptacle that served as the piggy bank. With repeated trials, however, the pigs began to root at the coins. The raccoons, after initiating the procedure properly, would not release the coins into the bin, instead rubbing them together and dipping them in and out of the bin.

The Brelands hypothesized that the food reward elicited species-specific feeding patterns which ultimately interfered with the operant response being conditioned. With the notion of instinctive drift, they suggested that instinctive behaviors may eventually dominate operant behavior in many circumstances. Their results have been supported by studies investigating neural substrates of reinforcement (e.g., Vaccarino, Schiff, & Glickman, 1989). That is, significant correlations have been found between stimuli that serve as reinforcers and stimuli that elicit species-characteristic feeding patterns.

Evolution and Cognition

"Even simple organisms, such as scorpionflies and bluegill sunfish, must process information from their environment and make decisions on the basis of it if their interactions with . . . physical aspects of their environment are to be adaptive" (Crawford & Anderson, 1989). This suggests that human information processing mechanisms may have evolved to reflect the types of problems faced by early humans in their ancestral environment.

As a means of studying evolutionary influences on cognition, Cosmides (1989), Cosmides and Tooby (1989) and Tooby and Cosmides (1989) characterized cognitive structures as **Darwinian algorithms**. These are *innate specialized learning mechanisms which adapt cognitive processes to environmental conditions*. Recall from chapter 5 the reasoning task that cognitive researchers have used to investigate context dependency in logical reasoning. Subjects are asked to reason from such rules as, "If there is a vowel on one side of the card, there should be an even number on the other." Results from numerous studies supported a conclusion that such logical reasoning is not content-independent, results which Cosmides and Tooby have taken as evidence for Darwinian algorithms.

For example, subjects performed much better when the rule was, "If a purchase is more than $30, the store manager's signature must be on the back of the receipt." This result may be interpreted in terms of a social exchange that involves detection of cheaters. That is, ancestral humans must have evolved some cognitive mechanism that enabled them to rapidly and accurately detect cheaters on social contracts. This mechanism is then assumed to account for the comparative ease with which problems can be solved using the store manager rule (Cosmides & Tooby, 1989).

A focus on invariant cognitive mechanisms, rather than invariant behavior, highlights two important points. First, not all behavior is assumed to be adaptive under current environmental conditions. This point will be taken up again shortly in more detail. Second, numerous, task-specific mental mechanisms are assumed to account for learning rather than a single, general mechanism. Remember from chapter 3 that Estes (1988) has already cautioned cognitive scientists to expect their models of memory to be proved inadequate, because such models are currently based on a uniform, parallel processing computer metaphor. However, "organisms have not evolved general mechanisms for digestion; they have evolved particular devices for dealing with the particular foods encountered in their ancestral environment. Similarly, from an evolutionary perspective, the human brain/mind can be expected to comprise numerous, specific, complex mechanisms that evolved in response to ancestral environmental conditions, rather than simple, general processes of association and symbol manipulation" (Crawford & Anderson, 1989, p. 1454). By attempting to understand ancestral environmental conditions, then, we may gain clues to the nature of human cognitive mechanisms.

Evolutionary biology has also influenced theories of cognitive development, as we have seen with Piaget's theory in chapter 6. Piaget believed that children's transitions from stage to stage in development resulted in ever more adaptive modes of thinking and reasoning. In this way, he conceived of cognitive development as a process paralleling evolutionary change. Evolutionary concepts, then, served for Piaget as a framework for understanding cognitive development.

Others have suggested that Piaget's genetic epistemology may inform evolutionary biology. For example, the reasons for organisms developing the particular forms they do cannot be attributed solely to genetic factors adapting to particular environments. Certainly that does occur, just as children develop operative schemes adapted to their environments. But children also "spontaneously create new schemes of behavior for which appropriate environments are then realized if possible" (Goodwin, 1985, p. 53). In chapter 6, the example was given of children actively seeking conditions under which to apply some new understanding. Translated into biological terms, this suggests that "spontaneous reorganization within the hereditary constraints can occur, producing organisms with new morphologies and behavior patterns which must then either discover or create appropriate environments" (Goodwin, 1985, p. 54).

This view of evolution has been hailed as insightful but also limited. It draws attention to an overlap in developmental and biological theories in that both attempt to explain the capacity of organisms to internalize aspects of their environment. But the disregard for the impact of social structures on human development is considered a serious oversight (Scaife, 1985), a sentiment in obvious agreement with the theoretical positions of Bruner and Vygotsky that were discussed in chapter 7.

Piaget's theory of cognitive development has also been suggested as a useful framework for understanding the evolution of human intelligence. Taylor-Parker (1985), for example, used Piaget's stages of development as a basis for analyzing the intellectual operations required to invent and produce tools described in the archeological record. Her rationale for doing so is based on the evidence that Piagetian stages appear to be culturally universal (cf. Dasen, 1972). According to Taylor-Parker (1985), *Homo habilis* (about 2 million to 1.3 million years B.C.) and *Homo erectus* (about 1.5 to .5 million years B.C.) must have had intellectual skills characteristic of modern children in the concrete operational stage of development. Their tools were relatively simple and made only of stone. By contrast, *Homo sapiens* (from approximately 100,000 years B.C.) invented hafted tools. Since hafting "entails connecting two dissimilar elements in the construction of a new compound entity," it is thought to be evidence of formal operational reasoning (Taylor-Parker, 1985, p. 94).

Although Gibson (1985) agreed with the general thrust of Taylor-Parker's analysis, she suggested that modern levels of intelligence (i.e., formal operations) have only been recently achieved. Brain size of early humans correlates with the complexity of the tools they invented, but "only by Cro-Magnon times (35,000–10,000 years ago) did the brain achieve both modern shape and size" (Gibson, 1985, p. 105). Moreover, brain size increases coincided with the development of culture which, Gibson speculated, probably came about as an adaptation to the varied and inhospitable habitats into which humankind was expanding.

Parallels of this nature between evolution and development may lend credence to both theories. But recall that Piaget's theory has been criticized for its failure to account for findings that specific intellectual capabilities may be more content-related than age-dependent. Similarly, evidence for formal operational reasoning based on tools in the archeological record in no way guarantees that other abstract systems which should have appeared at the same time actually did (Rutkowska, 1985). Therefore, content dependency in problem solving must be addressed in evolutionary theory as well as in developmental theory.

Implications of Sociobiology for Learning and Instruction

What conclusions can we draw from sociobiology that might inform our study of learning? One, undoubtedly, is that our genetic, evolutionary heritage imposes certain constraints on learning, or determines predispositions to learn certain things in certain ways. Another, however, is that "predispositions and constraints are outcomes, not causes" (Timberlake & Lucas, 1989, p. 260). In other words, what is actually learned and exhibited depends as much on particular environmental stimuli as it does on genetic history. Let us examine these two conclusions more closely.

The role of evolutionary factors in conditioning suggests a more careful analysis of current behavior, desired behavior, and possible reinforcers in light of potential learning predispositions. For example, if humans are predisposed to fear snakes and spiders, such phobias, once acquired, may be extremely resistant to extinction (Lohordo & Droungas, 1985). A program designed to teach people to overcome their fears may therefore be ineffective if it relies solely on cognitive, informational factors (e.g., "spiders are good because they eat other insects"). A learner might agree with such statements intellectually, but find that instinctive reactions prevail when a spider is encountered. Systematic desensitization programs, on the other hand, provide continued and increasing exposure to the feared object in such a way that instinctive reactions can be overcome.

In behavioral interventions, the type of reinforcer chosen may influence the degree to which desired behavior is learned. Breland and Breland (1961) hypothesized that their food reward elicited species-specific feeding patterns that interfered with the animals' acquisition of the desired operant behavior. It is possible that the overuse of primary reinforcers with humans would have a similar effect. Finally, behaviors that are most similar to what proved adaptive in ancestral populations are likely to be the easiest to condition (Timberlake & Lucas, 1989). Likewise, behaviors for which no predisposition to learn has developed are likely to be more difficult to establish. As an example, these might include reactions to people who are different from ourselves. In early human societies, strangers were commonly feared and excluded from participation within the group. However, today's global and multicultural society requires that different races learn to live in harmony. For this to occur, cooperative behaviors must be strengthened with sufficient practice and training to become dominant over more instinctual behaviors (Garcia, Brett, & Rusiniak,1989).

That current environmental conditions are important to the expression of evolutionary predispositions is the primary thesis of Crawford and Anderson (1989). They argued against the notion that traits with evolutionary significance must necessarily appear in all individuals. Similarly, they argued against the idea that all current behavior must be adaptive. Instead, they suggested that evolutionary traits and ecological conditions interact to produce behavior. Moreover, environmental conditions can exert an influence either at the time a behavior is exhibited or during the individual's development.

To understand how these interactions may operate, consider the following examples described by Crawford and Anderson (1989). Three mating tactics can be observed in male scorpionflies: (1) presenting a dead insect to the female as a nuptial gift, (2) generating a salivary mass to offer as a nuptial gift, or (3) forcing copulation without a nuptial gift. Which tactic is followed depends solely on current environmental conditions, namely, how many males are competing for the limited number of females and how abundant are the insects offered as nuptial gifts. When there are few females and many males, for example, forced copulation is the observed tactic. When the numbers are reversed, however, and plenty of insects are available, the male scorpionfly is most likely to offer an insect as a nuptial gift.

Looking at the reproductive tactics of humans reveals an analogous example, except that the tactic pursued later in life appears to depend upon circumstances experienced in childhood. That is, "the child whose father is not involved in the family is 'being prepared' for life in a society where males frequently compete for access to a number of females and do not form enduring bonds or provide much investment in their offspring. The child whose father is deeply involved in the family, on the other hand, is developing attributes enabling it to maximize its reproductive success in a society where males form long-lasting relationships with a single female and provide a high level of investment in their offspring" (Crawford & Anderson, 1989, p. 1452). Thus, whereas genes may control the mechanisms that produce behavioral differences (e.g., three, and only these three, mating patterns are passed on through generations of scorpionflies), environmental and developmental interactions determine which behavior is learned and manifested.

Unraveling the relationship between genetic histories and environmental contingencies is no easy task, especially in humans. For obvious reasons, the study of twins, particularly those reared apart, offers the best hope. Crawford and Anderson (1989) suggested that groups of identical twin pairs be studied on the basis of known genetic differences. Moreover, they recommended a focus on behaviors closely related to reproductive function and sensitive to environmental conditions in a way that would have contributed to fitness in an ancestral population. Similarly, examination of dominance hierarchies and social organizations of groups may prove fruitful for understanding sociobiological influences (Bernhard, 1988). From a single pair of twins, then, as described in Scenario 8–1, we can reach no firm conclusions about the relative impact of genetic history versus environmental conditions on learning. Yet, the striking similarities seen among twins reared apart perhaps precludes an extreme environmentalist interpretation.

Finally, it is important to realize that the human environment has changed dramatically in recent years. This leads to the possibility that previously adaptive behavior may be no longer adaptive or socially acceptable (Crawford & Anderson, 1989). Behaviors related to sexual competition among men for women, for example, probably correlated highly with reproductive fitness in ancestral populations. Today, however, they are more likely to be viewed as sexist. Similarly, behaviors that could have reduced fitness thousands of generations ago may now be culturally accepted or even desirable. The adoption of unrelated children is a possible example. In either case, such behaviors may present problems for learning. No matter what our training, we may occasionally respond negatively to situations once associated with reduced fitness. In the same way, we may find it difficult to eliminate completely ways of thinking, speaking, or acting that have been favored by natural selection in the distant past.

TABLE 8–1   Implications of Sociobiology for Learning and Instruction

Principle	Implication for Instruction
1. Humans may be predisposed to certain fears.	Programs designed to teach people to overcome their fears are likely to be most effective when they include systematic desensitization.
2. Behaviors for which there is no predisposition to learn (e.g., that were either not required or not adaptive for ancestral populations) may be difficult to establish.	Extensive time and practice should be built into teaching programs for these behaviors. For example, computers are an artifact of current culture, so that humans may require extensive practice to become skilled in their use.
3. Previously adaptive behavior, which is no longer useful in today's society, may be difficult to overcome.	Time and practice are again key variables for effective instruction when these behaviors are inadvertently triggered. For example, students in cooperative learning groups may initially experience difficulty working together, because they must work out their differences and establish appropriate social bonds.
4. Actions once associated with decreased fitness in ancestral populations may be difficult to establish.	Attitude learning is at issue here, because learners must be convinced that these actions are now desirable in the context of today's society. For example, learning to work cooperatively with other races may be a matter of perceiving and valuing a common goal.

In schools, one impact of a rapidly changing environment has been the neglect of children's biologically based needs for belonging to and working within a group (Bernhard, 1988). Even in cooperative learning structures, individual achievement and individual accountability are stressed (Slavin, 1991). Yet, in early human societies, "effective defense against predators and the hunting of game were both necessarily cooperative ventures" (Sagan, 1977, p. 104). And "reciprocity in a foraging band [was] ensured by a variety of relationships and conventions that tie[d] individuals together and motivate[d] cooperation. No such relations or traditions exist in the school, except in the most attenuated and abstracted forms" (Bernhard, 1988, pp. 121–122).

What this view suggests for instruction, then, is a greater emphasis on cooperation in learning, which supports the views of Bruner and Vygotsky that were discussed in the previous chapter. Perhaps what a sociobiological perspective adds to the picture thus far created is an emphasis on extended experiences in groups, where students work within the same group for a long time. In that way, children must work out their social differences and develop cooperative behaviors that enable them to reach their goal. Bernhard (1988) argued for multi-age groups, as well, because mixed age groupings occurred naturally in foraging societies and occur naturally in today's adult society. Younger children can learn much from observing and imitating their older peers, and older children gain valuable information about parenting when they interact with younger children (Bernhard, 1988).

Summarized in Table 8–1 are principles for learning that may be derived from a sociobiological perspective and their potential implications for instruction.

PROXIMATE CAUSES: NEUROPHYSIOLOGY OF LEARNING

"One of the great scientific questions of our day is: How is information acquired and stored in the brain?" (Martinez & Kesner, 1991, p. xv). As in sociobiology, no easy answers to this question are forthcoming. Consider the very difficulty of the task. The human brain has some 12 billion neurons and 5000 synapses, all linked together in incredible complexity (Bower & Hilgard, 1981). Moreover, most studies of the brain are aimed at understanding what enables information storage. This means that the physiology of receptors (i.e., our sensory systems for vision, hearing, smell, taste, and feeling) and the physiology of effectors (i.e., different muscle systems) are not considered relevant to study. Even without taking these systems into account, understanding the neurobiology of the brain and its relation to memory and cognition is a formidable enterprise.

Despite the difficulties inherent in studying the brain, neuroscientists have made remarkable progress in understanding its structures and functions. From early beliefs that specific memories and cognitive functions must be located in particular regions of the brain, views about information storage have evolved to implicate brain systems regulating storage and the capacity for storage. In addition, most neuroscience evidence is used together with cognitive analyses in drawing conclusions about the brain and learning (cf. Schacter, 1992). Let us look further at how these views have evolved, as well as the evidence for prevailing views. In addition, brain systems as they relate to processes of attention, cognitive development, and knowledge representation will be discussed.

An Overview of Neural Architecture Implicated in Learning

Perhaps the best way to begin is with a review of the neural architecture of learning and memory as we currently know it. Pictured in Figure 8–2 is a left side view of the human brain, showing the lobes of the cerebral cortex,

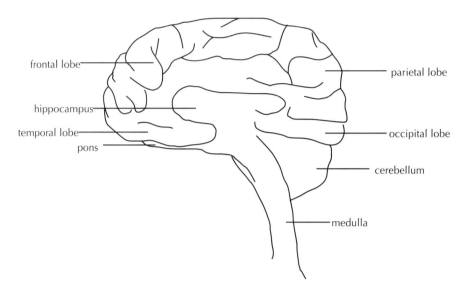

frontal lobe

parietal lobe

hippocampus

temporal lobe

occipital lobe

pons

cerebellum

medulla

FIGURE 8–2 A Left Side View of the Human Brain

the cerebellum, and part of the brain stem. An outline of the hippocampus is also shown. Since it is located on the medial area (or inside) of the temporal lobe, it would not actually be seen from this view.

Which structures in the brain have been specifically implicated in learning? First, the frontal lobe appears to be associated primarily with attention, specifically, the ability to pay attention on cue. The left frontal lobe is also the site of what is known as Broca's area, which seems to be responsible for our ability to speak. The parietal lobe has been associated with the organizing aspects of attention, that is, the ability to attend to specific differences in stimulation, such as different letters in reading. The parietal lobe also seems to be involved in procedural memory, or being able to carry out procedural tasks.

The hippocampus plays perhaps the largest role in learning and memory. On one hand, it appears to subserve our ability to selectively allocate attention and orient us to sudden events which demand attention. In this role, the hippocampus appears to be aided by subcortical mechanisms, probably from the thalamus (in the brain stem structure). A second function of the hippocampus, however, seems to be as mediator of declarative learning, or knowledge of facts and concepts. It is also likely that this role involves organizing memory traces made up of cell assemblies in many areas of the brain. Finally, the left hemisphere (shown in Figure 8–2) is implicated in language and analytic functions, whereas the right hemisphere (the unseen side of Figure 8–2) is implicated in visual-spatial functions.

What is not obvious in the diagram, of course, is that each brain structure is made up of millions of neurons and thousands of synapses. Development causes a differentiation of neurons and synaptic changes. But learning, as well, appears to result in new dendrites and many new temporary synapses (at least in the hippocampus [Rosenzweig, 1986]), some of which remain as stable modifications to the neural architecture. Finally, hormones and neurotransmitters (substances which permit communication between neurons) are certainly involved in memory formation and modulation, but their roles are far from being fully understood.

Let us now consider the evidence for how the brain is involved in learning and memory.

Cerebral Localization and the Search for the Engram

Our intuitive beliefs about the brain as the seat of memory and mind have a long and distinguished history. Early Greek philosophers, including Pythagoras and Plato, subscribed to this view. Medieval physicians, long influenced by the medical pronouncements of Galen in the second century A.D., believed that different parts of the brain were each responsible for different psychological functions. Even Descartes, the father of mind-body dualism, located memories in the brain and not the soul. With the work of Franz Joseph Gall (1758–1828), however, came extended efforts to locate mental faculties in the specific areas of the brain thought to be responsible for them.

Gall was a neuroanatomist who located more than thirty psychological functions in distinct organs of the brain. He assumed that the degree to which certain cerebral parts were developed would be manifested not only in behavior but in the form of the head. Thus, the propensity to steal, for example, corresponded with a well developed "organ of cunning," which was apparent in a long prominence on the skull of thieves (Gall, cited in Herrnstein & Boring, 1968).

Although Gall's phrenology captured the imagination of the populace at the time, it was not held in high regard by his scientific colleagues. One of his harshest critics, an experimental physiologist named Jean Marie Flourens (1794–1867), conducted studies to prove that the brain's functions are distributed throughout rather than localized to a specific region. Flourens removed (ablated) or destroyed (lesioned) parts of animals' brains and observed the behavior changes that resulted. Instead of losing specific abilities or cognitive functions, as phrenology predicted, animals simply became more stupid overall as more of their brain was removed.

Despite Flourens' evidence for a distributionist view of brain function, scientists continued to find appealing the idea of localized centers for brain activity. In 1861, Paul Broca published the clinical findings of a patient who suffered from loss of articulate speech. After the patient's death, an autopsy of his brain revealed lesions in the left front neocortex. Broca argued that this region of the brain, subsequently known as Broca's area, must be responsible for the observed aphasia. A few years later, two German physiologists, Fritsch and Hitzig, conducted a series of studies in which they were able to produce eye movements in a patient by stimulating certain areas of the cerebral cortex (Herrnstein & Boring, 1968). Their findings, together with those of Broca, suggested that the brain does possess some specialized areas for certain functions. Whether specific memories could be traced to regions of the brain, however, was still an open question.

In the early 1900s, while still a graduate student working with John B. Watson, Karl Lashley began the search for the engram, or trace in the brain storing a particular memory. "One has the feeling that then and throughout his life, Lashley wanted to believe in localization of the memory trace, but his own results kept confounding his belief" (Donegan & Thompson, 1991, p. 8). In a series of investigations, Lashley and Franz (1917) had rats learn mazes and systematically ablated or lesioned varying amounts of their frontal cortex before or after learning. Their results forced Lashley to conclude, in his classic 1929 monograph, that memory traces are stored in the cerebral cortex but that they are not localized.

In Lashley's studies, the rats appeared to gradually lose their ability to learn or remember a maze as more and more of their brains was removed or destroyed. But loss in learning ability or memory did not occur as a function of the site of brain tissue destruction. Lashley's results, then, were consistent with those of Flourens, providing additional evidence to support a distributionist view of the brain.

If we accept the proposal that learning and memory are activities of the whole brain, then how are we to account for the findings of Broca, Fritsch, and Hitzig mentioned earlier? At least one answer can be found in the lesion approach to localization adopted by Flourens, Lashley, and others. Given the delicate and complex nature of the brain, it is likely that the destruction of one part will have widespread effects, not confined to a single memory. "It is, in the words of Pavlov, as if one struck a delicate machine with a sledge hammer and then studied the results" (Brogden & Gantt, 1942; cited in Donegan & Thompson, 1991, p. 9).

More modern approaches to localization now include electrical stimulation to parts of the brain, as well as intracranial injections of drugs to block or activate particular neurotransmitter-receptor systems. Although these techniques are admittedly less invasive than removal or destruction of brain tissue, they, too, typically affect more than a single cell or anatomical location in the brain. As a result, for progress to be made in understanding the neural substrates of learning and memory, the problem of localization had to be conceptualized with alternate assumptions. Donald Hebb, a former student of Lashley's, provided the insight when he proposed the concept of cell assembly (Donegan & Thompson, 1991).

According to Hebb, memories are not represented by a single neuron, but by a network of neurons—the cell assembly—in the cerebral cortex. Moreover, these neurons are thought to be distributed and able to participate in more than one memory. This means that a given memory is localized in the sense of it being represented by a particular cell assembly, but it cannot be anatomically located since the neurons making up the assembly are distributed throughout the cortex. Notice the similarity between the cell assembly and the model of memory proposed by the parallel distributed processing theorists (see chapter 3). They, too, argued that networks of subsymbolic units participated in processing and memory. Hebb's theory had the effect not only of renewing interest on the part of researchers in analyzing neurological substrates of learning and memory in the brain, but it also demonstrated that understanding how memories are represented in the brain is no easy or simple matter.

Recently, Donegan and Thompson (1991) have proposed that the neural circuitry essential for the development and expression of a particular form of learning is made up of two parts. The memory trace is the structure or structures—the cell assemblies—responsible for learning a particular behavior. This memory trace is assumed to be plastic in the sense that it must be modifiable through experience and able to retain such modification. The sensory-motor circuit, on the other hand, is the part of the overall memory circuit that represents the peripheral stimulation of the nervous system and the resulting overt response.

This distinction between memory trace and sensory circuits permits several interpretations of localization studies. In such studies, animals are typically trained on some response, and a brain structure is destroyed that is hypothesized to be involved in the learning of that response. Then, post-lesion behavior is compared to pre-lesion behavior. If the lesion abolishes the learned behavior, it is tempting to conclude that the destroyed structure must have contained the memory trace for the behavior. An equally plausible conclusion, however, is that the lesioned structure modulated the sensory circuit involved in the response. In other words, perhaps only the capability of producing the response was destroyed, not the memory for or the ability to cognitively modify the response. Similarly, the fact that a lesion fails to abolish a response can signify that either the lesioned structure is in no way involved in learning that response or that the lesioned structure may be involved in the original learning but not the later expression of the response.

Recent findings support this distinction between the memory trace involved in learning a behavior and the sensory circuits involved in expressing it. For example, animals had difficulty learning simple conditioned responses when electrical stimulation induced seizures of the hippocampus. Yet, animals from which the hippocampus had previously been removed learned the same responses with little problem. "In this case, the simplest inference is that abnormal activation of the hippocampus interferes with development of the memory trace elsewhere in the brain" (Donegan & Thompson, 1991, p. 13).

In order to determine whether learning-induced changes actually develop in a given brain structure (as opposed to being relayed there from elsewhere), more information must be obtained than lesion studies can reveal (Donegan & Thompson, 1991). In other words, the activity of target structures should be compared to the activity of sites peripheral to the target structures. If these rates of activity are in fact different in response to learning, then we may begin to pinpoint which ones are essential to the development and expression of a particular behavior. Once such neuronal structures have been identified, investigations using a variety of recording approaches may determine by what mechanisms these structures cause learning.

The search for the engram, then, continues even in the present day, but what we conceive to be the engram has changed. No longer do researchers assume that a single anatomical structure in the brain changes when learning takes place. Instead, they believe that systems of neurons are implicated in learning. Some systems appear to be more centrally involved in the development and representation of a memory trace, whereas others are peripherally involved in the expression of a learned behavior. Questions that remain to be answered concern just what neuronal systems change with certain types of learning and by what mechanisms they change. These are general questions that can now be examined more closely in the context of learning processes that concern educators.

Attention and the Brain

Cognitive researchers have long recognized the importance of attention in learning. For information to be processed for permanent storage in memory, it must first be noticed. Moreover, learners selectively attend to certain aspects of stimulation that pertain to their learning goals, that are novel and require additional processing resources, or that are distinctive and unconsciously attract notice. Finally, skills that are well-learned and practiced typically require less attention of learners, freeing them to allocate attentional capacity to related, higher level tasks. In reading, for example, decoding of letters and words is more or less automatic as learners concentrate their attention on comprehending the meaning of what is read. (See chapter 3 for an extended discussion of attention.)

Given the importance of attention, what unique contributions may a neurological perspective offer to our overall understanding of the phenomenon? What brain systems underlie attention? What investigations of these systems have been conducted and to what new insights have the investigations led? In reviewing some of the answers researchers offer to these questions, Picton, Stuss, and Marshall (1986) noted that data currently prevail over theories. Many different aspects of attention have been studied, and myriad results make difficult any theoretical synthesis. Researchers have not yet agreed on even so basic an issue as to whether attention is a general or specific system, critical to learning in a wide variety of domains or operating in unique ways within different domains (Posner & Friedrich, 1986). Nonetheless, they do agree that attention, however investigated or conceptualized, involves selectivity.

Characterizing attention as a state, a resource, or a process, provides a useful framework for discussing and evaluating results of studies on attention. All three concepts involve selectivity. Attention as a state occurs when a learner maintains an attitude of expectation, alert to information and heedless of distractions. This is characteristic of learners who are interested in what they study. By contrast, learners who are bored or suffer from an attention deficit disorder are easily distracted from a learning task.

Attention as a resource refers to a learner's capability of selectively allocating more attention to one of several simultaneously occurring events. Although this is often done quite unconsciously, as in driving a car while attending to a program on the radio, it may also occur quite deliberately, as in listening to one conversation at a party while ignoring all others.

Finally, attention as a process involves selecting particular information for further analysis and interpretation over other, available information. For example, the clarinetist in Scenario 3-2 (see chapter 3) paid particular attention to the clarinet part of the symphony performance. This student certainly maintained an attitude of alertness during the performance (a state of attention) and listened to the orchestra while ignoring the whispers of others in the audience (allocating attentional resources), but she also analyzed the overall sound of the orchestra for the specific notes of the clarinet (selectively processing information).

These three aspects of selective attention have been investigated for their neurological substrates in the brain. Studies have typically focused on identifying what parts of the brain and what mechanisms within the brain are responsible for attention. In some studies, the effects of lesions are investigated. In others, electrical signals from the brain, as well as eye movements, are recorded and monitored as attention is systematically varied. Let us now look at the specific evidence related to the state, resource, and process aspects of attention.

Controlling Attentional States

The ability to sustain attention and adapt attention to changing task demands has been extensively studied in patients with varying degrees of brain damage. Lack of attentional control and inattention have been observed frequently among patients with frontal-lobe damage (Picton et al., 1986). In one case, for example, a man with damage to the left frontal lobe had difficulty concentrating on various counting tasks. He was able to count by 3s, but "on subtracting serial 7s, which was completed after counting by 3s, he was unable to stop himself from subtracting (correctly) by 3s. He verbalized that he should subtract by 7s, and yet said, 'Here I go with 3s again'" (Picton et al., 1986, p. 24). This patient simply could not control his attention when multiple tasks required a shift in attention from one task to another.

The syndrome of inattention refers to the failure of a patient to respond to stimuli when such stimuli are presented on the side opposite a cerebral lesion. Thus, individuals fail to attend at all to a task rather than experience difficulty controlling their attention between tasks. This apparently occurs most often with lesions in the right parietal lobe, but has also been reported with lesions to the frontal lobe and elsewhere (Damasio, Damasio, & Chang Chui, 1980; Picton et al., 1986). Other abnormalities of attention (such as wandering attention, delirium, or confusion) have also been associated with frontal lobe damage or frontal lobe dysfunction.

Two attentional disorders for which no specific pathological findings have been identified are schizophrenia and hyperactivity. In both disorders, behavioral symptoms resemble those of patients with frontal lobe damage, causing researchers to speculate that the frontal lobe is in some way involved. One reasonable hypothesis is that, for hyperactive children, maturation of the frontal lobe has been delayed (Stamm & Kreder, 1979). Equally probable, however, is the possibility that attention problems in hyperactive children and schizophrenics are caused by disruptions in catecholamine metabolism.

Catecholamines are neurotransmitters, substances which influence or modulate the electrical activity of neurons. Increased or decreased levels of the cerebral catecholamines appear to result in attentional disorders. In hyperactivity, a depletion of catecholamines is assumed, because the attention deficit symptoms can be successfully treated with amphetamines or amphetamine-like drugs, which increase the release of catecholamines (cf. Margolin, 1978). Take note, however, that people whose catecholamine levels are normal should experience increased attentional problems with administration of amphetamines, because of abnormally increased catecholamine levels. Similarly, an excess of catecholamines in schizophrenics is assumed, because drugs that block the reception of catecholamines by cerebral neurons are effectively used for treatment (Carlsson, 1978).

Unfortunately, not enough is known about the long-term effects of drug treatments to reach firm conclusions about the role of catecholamines in attention. "The prolonged changes in transmitter concentration brought about by chronic drug administration may alter the sensitivity of the receptors and the metabolism of the transmitter" (Picton et al., 1986, p. 38). In other words, over time drugs may significantly change brain metabolism in ways that we cannot yet predict. It is for this reason that other means besides drugs are often chosen in the treatment of hyperactive children.

Finally, results of studies using electroencephalograms to record electrical activity in the brain support the general conclusion that both the frontal lobe and cerebral catecholamines are involved in controlling attention. In typical electroencephalographic studies, brain waves are recorded over a period of time in which subjects selectively attend to different stimuli. One measure of attention is the difference in wave amplitude between what is evoked by a stimulus when it is ignored and when it is attended to. This has been termed processing negativity (Hansen & Hillyard, 1980).

When the brain wave patterns of patients with frontal lobe damage are compared to those of normal subjects for selective attention tasks, their processing negativities are smaller. The same is true for children with hyperactivity, who also show a decreased amplitude of a particular wave known as P3. Drug treatment has been shown to increase the P3 amplitude in hyperactive children, as well as their processing negativities (Picton et al., 1986). From these results, then, it seems likely that the frontal lobe and cerebral neurotransmitters play a critical role in an individual's ability to control his or her attentional state.

Selectively Allocating Attentional Resources

Attention as a matter of allocating resources obviously depends upon the concept of capacity. As we have seen from chapter 3, conceiving of attention in terms of capacity is perhaps the predominant approach currently taken by cognitive theorists. But there is support for this conception from the biological perspective as well. On the one hand, our apparently limited capacity for attention may be viewed as an evolutionary adaptation (Simon, 1986). That is, without some kind of limitation, we would be disposed to processing so many irrelevancies from the wealth of stimulation surrounding us that goal-directed behavior might be impossible. This was the case for a Russian man whose photographic memory produced a flood of remembrances with every interaction, rendering him incapable of living a normal life (Heminway & Tegriti, 1984).

On the other hand, discovering just what biological mechanisms govern attentional limitations may assist us in determining how to make the most of the capacity we have. Until recently, it has been difficult to separate attentional capacity from processing strategy, because both influence overall processing efficiency (Gazzaniga, 1984). However, a series of studies conducted by Holtzman and Gazzaniga (cited in Gazzaniga, 1984) provides neurological evidence of attentional limitations in humans. Furthermore, the evidence points to a subcortical mechanism governing the allocation of attention, rather than the cortical mechanisms already implicated in the control of attentional states.

In one study, Holtzman and Gazzaniga presented subjects with 3 x 3 matrices and the task to detect the location of several xs. These matrices, sometimes the same and sometimes different, were simultaneously presented to both sides of the visual field while subjects fixated on a point between them. Subjects with normal brains could not do the task, but patients whose brains were hemispherically disconnected could do it easily, in effect processing more stimuli at once than is possible for a normal person. Normal brains, then, are limited in attentional capacity that can be allocated to processing stimuli.

Additional studies revealed interactions between the hemispheres in attentional allocation, which suggests a subcortical rather than cortical mechanism at work. That is, if attentional resources are allocated cortically, the hemispheres should operate independently of one another. What Holtzman and Gazzaniga (1982) found, however, was that working on a hard problem in one hemisphere diminished the attention by the other hemisphere on a concurrent task.

Whereas results of studies on cats generally support the proposal of a subcortical system involved in attention allocation, it is questionable whether these results can be applied to humans (Picton et al., 1986). There is evidence that cortical processes, in particular the hippocampus, also influence attention allocation. Animals with hippocampal lesions fail to orient as quickly to novel stimuli introduced into their environments. The orienting response is thought to be a critical means of adapting to the environment, because it enables an organism to suppress ongoing behavioral activity in order to respond to a sudden change in real-time requirements. As Simon (1986) put it, "Because bricks do fly through the air sometimes, it is good to be able to notice and dodge a brick even if you are not scanning the horizon for missiles when it comes flying" (p. 106).

Gazzaniga (1984) also recognized a role for the hippocampus in attention allocation, suggesting that it may regulate the data processing capacity of working memory. It appears, then, that both cortical and subcortical systems may be involved in our ability to selectively allocate attention among competing tasks.

Selectively Organizing Attention

When learners not only allocate attentional resources to a particular task, but then direct those resources to selectively process certain information, they are organizing their attention. This is an important concept for learning, because readers must attend to differences among letters to competently decode words. Orchestral performers must attend to differences among sounds to be sure they are playing in tune. Wine tasters must attend to subtle differences in flavor and bouquet to rate quality of wines. Attentional differences of this sort have been studied primarily in terms of evoked potentials in human brain wave activity, eye movements, and a variety of cognitive measures (such as response times to pattern recognition tasks).

To begin with, promising results have emerged from studies evaluating event-related potentials of children with learning disabilities. Typically, certain types of learning problems, which relate in some way to attention patterns, are diagnosed in children through behavioral techniques. Dyslexic children, for example, may experience difficulty attending differentially to similar letters, such as *b* and *d*. The brain wave patterns of these children are then compared to those of normal children to discover systematic differences that might distinguish between the two groups (cf. Duffy, Burchfiel, & Lombroso, 1979). In addition, children with diagnosed differences in learning abilities may be given specific cognitive tasks and their brain patterns observed while they complete the tasks.

Brain activity mapping has been shown to discriminate between normal and dyslexic children (Duffy, Denckla, Bartels, & Sandini, 1980; Duffy, Denckla, Bartels, Sandini, & Kiessling, 1980; Torello & Duffy, 1985), and among gifted learning disabled, gifted normal, normally achieving, and learning disabled students (Languis, Bireley, & Williamson, 1990; Languis, Miller, & Bertolone, 1990). In the latter study, gifted learning disabled learners were defined as those who score very high on measures of intelligence such as the Wechsler Intelligence Scale for Children, Revised (WISC-R), but who display a discrepancy between their verbal and performance IQ subscores. In general, gifted children demonstrated greater overall activity in brain patterns than their nongifted counterparts, but the gifted learning disabled students also showed some of the same specific patterns as nongifted learning disabled students.

Despite the apparent success of brain mapping in detecting neurological differences between learning disabled and normal children, caution is recommended in the use and interpretation of the technique (cf. Picton et al., 1986). Although the brain patterns of dyslexic children, for example, may indicate abnormalities in the area of the brain important for speech and language, they may also be symptomatic of boredom or drowsiness. Overall, the results of brain mapping studies can be very difficult to interpret. Sometimes, anomalous patterns appear on electroencephalograms that have no clinical significance. Additionally, similar brain patterns may be observed among individuals that cannot be interpreted along a meaningful dimension. In spite of these difficulties, researchers are hopeful that brain patterns may prove useful both in diagnosing learning problems and in finding appropriate interventions for those problems.

Along with brain mapping, researchers have used eye movements to study the organization of attention. This work stems from a basic assumption that orienting of attention plays a critical role in visual processing. It seems obvious that items are more likely to be recognized and processed appropriately within the focus of attention than outside it. Moreover, this focus is extremely limited because only the fovea is capable of detailed pattern vision. In reading, for example, learners can perceive about ten items to the right and three to four items to the left of their fixation point (Rayner, Well, & Pollatsek, 1980). Thus, eye movements represent an important indicator of attentional orienting and subsequent processing.

There is also evidence, however, that a covert attentional mechanism, linked to neural systems in the parietal lobe, operates independently of the eye movement system. Posner and Friedrich (1986) described a study by Chang (1981) which most clearly illustrates this mechanism. Chang presented stories in such a way that subjects could read the words while maintaining a point of fixation. This procedure should eliminate any right-left asymmetry in reading if such asymmetry is a function of the eye movement system. Chang found instead that bias in the visual field remained, and it reflected the internal scan of the words. That is, when words were presented normally, subjects had a larger visual field to the right of fixation. When words were presented upside down, subjects had a larger visual field to the left of fixation. Posner and Friedrich (1986) took these results to mean that attention was covertly driven by some internal semantic operation.

The influence of semantic codes on attention has also been documented by so-called priming studies. When learners are presented with a word from a particular category, their recognition of other words from the same category is facilitated. This effect occurs regardless of the modalities in which the words are presented. That is, both spoken and written words facilitated subjects' recognition of other spoken or written words. Posner and his colleagues contend, therefore, that learners represent meaning in a single semantic code which can be accessed through different sensory pathways (cf. Posner, 1984; Posner & Friedrich, 1986; Sen & Posner, 1979). Assuming this to be true, an important question arises. That is, to what extent do specific intentional strategies influence the ability to shift attention from one kind of code to another in order to accomplish a specific task?

It appears that learners commonly shift attention among different sensory codes, depending upon the nature of the task in which they are engaged, as well as their own abilities and preferences. Beginning spellers, for example, typically rely on phonological codes whereas beginning readers make use of mostly visual codes. With experience, able learners become efficient in coordinating information from several codes and flexible in shifting attention among codes to suit task demands. It is also true, however, that some learners prefer particular codes and may rely on one kind of information when they might better focus on an alternate kind. Good proofreading, for example, probably depends on the ability to isolate and use visual information, to the exclusion of phonological information.

So what should we make of this evidence regarding the organization of attention? As with other aspects of attention, the cerebral cortex is implicated as the neurological basis, but precisely what systems operate and how they operate in attentional organization are not yet fully known. Simon (1986) noted that Posner's discovery of covert attention should call into question the use of eye movements as a primary indicator of attention. Posner (and Friedrich, 1986) suggested that it is too early to make firm prescriptions for instruction from the current neurological evidence on attention. Employing multiple codes during instruction is likely to facilitate learning. But it is not yet clear whether curricula should emphasize one type of code over another or attempt to match learner coding preferences to materials relying upon those preferences. A third alternative is to provide learners with experiences in many types of codes in order to develop their skills in nonpreferred modes. This latter suggestion is consistent with implications of dual-code theory as well as educational semiotics (see chapter 3).

Learning, Memory, and the Brain

In the search for the engram, biological researchers have examined one aspect of learning and memory, namely, information storage. To some degree, these researchers have also tackled the twofold question of how memories are acquired in the first place and how acquired knowledge is used. At least Donegan and Thompson (1991) have suggested two separate systems as responsible for one, acquisition and storage, and two, performance (or use). Interestingly, Donegan and Thompson are far from the only theorists to propose two types of memory systems involved in learning. From the different distinctions to be discussed in this section, we should be able to glean some areas of commonality that may have implications for instruction.

With the exception of Squire (1983, 1986) and Cohen (1984), however, most of these theories proposing dual memory systems have been developed from evidence collected in studies involving animals other than humans. Yet, "language is a paradigm case for understanding how humans represent, acquire, and use a complex cognitive system" (Gleitman, 1986, p. 119). Thus, the biological substrates of language acquisition will be discussed at the end of this section.

Two Types of Memory

The impetus for distinguishing two types of memory came initially from attempts to explain global anterograde amnesia (Mishkin, Malamut, & Bachevalier, 1984). With this type of amnesia, patients suffer memory loss but can retain new experiences of a certain type. They can, for instance, acquire the skills necessary to trace mirror images of words but then cannot later recall what the words were that they traced. Characterizing the lost versus spared abilities of these patients, researchers have used the labels "recognition versus associative memory. . . episodic versus semantic memory. . . working versus reference memory. . . vertical versus horizontal associative memory. . . declarative versus procedural knowledge. . . elaborative versus integrative processing . . . , and automatic versus effortful encoding" (Mishkin et al., 1984, p. 65). At least three distinctions survive as popular frameworks for analyzing the neural systems underlying memory (Kesner, 1991).

First, two types of memory may distinguish between specific contextual aspects of a learning task and general information or general knowledge that is brought to bear on the task (Olton, 1983). In a typical animal learning study, then, trial-unique information would be coded differently than information which remained the same from trial to trial. The specific, temporal, personal information in a learning situation is thought to be coded by working memory. By contrast, general knowledge concerning rules and procedures is coded in reference memory (Olton, 1983). This conception by Olton of two memory systems is similar to the distinction made by Tulving between episodic and semantic memory (see chapter 3).

The neurological basis for Olton's model came from lesion studies of rats running mazes with multiple arms, only some of which contained food. Once the animals had learned which arms contained food, their optimal strategy on subsequent trials was to avoid the unbaited arms and to visit each of the baited arms once. In reference memory should be the general knowledge of what arms were baited or unbaited. But in any given trial, working memory was involved in distinguishing between arms that had been visited or not. Because there are two memory components to the task, Olton reasoned that postlearning lesions should pinpoint which brain system is responsible for which type of memory. He found that lesions to the hippocampus produced deficits in the working memory, but not in reference memory. Rats remembered which arms were unbaited and so avoided them, but they visited baited arms multiple times after having eaten the food on the first visit.

If the hippocampus mediates working memory, what is responsible for reference memory? One possibility is the parietal cortex. In a study conducted by Kesner and DiMattia (cited in Kesner, 1991), rats with lesions to the parietal cortex displayed deficits in reference but not working memory on an eight-arm maze task with four baited and four unbaited arms.

A second perspective on the question of two memory systems came from Mishkin and his associates (Mishkin & Petri, 1984; also Mishkin et al., 1984), who distinguished recognition memories from habits. Working with monkeys, they investigated the neural substates of visual discrimination performance. The task involved learning a win-stay, lose-shift strategy when choosing from pairs of easily discriminable objects. In contrast to normal monkeys, those who had sustained damage to the hippocampus and/or amygdala failed to learn the strategy with only one acquisition trial. But when several trials were given, the operated monkeys performed similarly to normal monkeys.

To explain these results, Mishkin reasoned that two forms of learning took place. First, an object-reward association must be made, a recognition that a previously neutral stimulus now has a reward value; choosing it leads to reinforcement. It is this recognition, normally established in the initial trial, that appears to be impaired with hippocampus/amygdala damage. Independent of this association, however, a connection between the object and an approach response must also be made—a stimulus-response bond. Mishkin called this bond a habit because it strengthened with repeated trials, unaffected by brain lesions.

In essence, Mishkin demonstrated with monkeys the same sort of performance patterns as observed in global amnesiac humans. Building upon this distinction between recognition memory and habits, Mishkin has also elaborated what other researchers acknowledge is the most extensive neural model of memory organization (Kesner, 1991). Mishkin's model is also commonly cited as supporting the third analytic framework for understanding the neurological basis of memory: Squire's and Cohen's proposal of declarative and procedural knowledge.

According to Cohen and Squire (1981; Cohen, 1984; Squire, 1983, 1986), evidence from human amnesic patients suggests that lost or retained abilities are best characterized on a declarative-procedural dimension.

Declarative memory refers to *information concerned with specific facts or data*. **Procedural memory**, on the other hand, refers to *memory for procedures and skills*. Again, it is worth noting that this is much the same distinction as made by cognitive scientists in chapter 3.

The argument for a declarative/procedural distinction comes primarily from studies conducted with H.M., who is perhaps the most well-known and extensively studied amnesic patient. In 1953, at the age of 27, H.M. underwent an operation to relieve epileptic seizures that had become uncontrollable. Although the operation successfully eliminated the seizures, it also unfortunately caused total anterograde amnesia. Thus, although his short-term memory is intact, H.M. can form no new memories (Squire, 1987).

What is interesting about H.M.'s abilities is that he, like other amnesiacs, could perform the mirror drawing task but never remember that he had done it or what the words were. Moreover, he was able to acquire the skills necessary to solve the Tower of Hanoi puzzle (Figure 8–3), but he could not remember any specific facts or experiences related to his performance. Cohen and Squire contended, therefore, that H.M. displays impairment of the declarative memory system while his procedural system remains intact. It logically follows, as well, that the kind of brain damage observed in amnesic patients—namely, to the medial-temporal lobe,

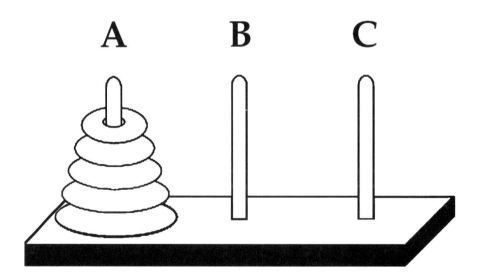

FIGURE   8–3   The Tower of Hanoi Puzzle

The goal is to transfer the rings from A to C without ever placing a larger ring on top of a smaller ring.

including hippocampus and amygdala—must mediate declarative, but not procedural, memory.

Finally, Squire (1986) argued for a particular role of the medial (i.e., inside)-temporal cortex in declarative learning. That is, studies of brain damage leave open the question of whether the affected area causes a problem of storage or a problem of access. In other words, amnesiacs might be able to store data-based information just as normal people do but then fail in their ability to access that information. Antithetically, they may fail to record information in the first place. Squire favors the latter view because he believes that numerous sites are involved in memory representation (much like Hebb's cell assemblies discussed earlier). Multiple memory storage sites imply multiple retrieval routes, not all of which could be affected by damage to one region of the brain. Instead, it seems more reasonable to Squire to postulate that the medial temporal lobe is responsible for organizing and schematizing various sites in the consolidation of memory. Damage to it would then lead to loss of connections and poor memory storage, which is consistent with observed declarative memory deficits.

"At this point any serious student interested in understanding the neural systems that mediate the structure of memory should be totally confused with the multiple distinctions and levels of organization that are made by different theoreticians." So wrote Kesner (1991, p. 524) after reviewing in greater detail the theoretical positions summarized here. Yet he believed integration of various views to be possible and proposed a comprehensive structural model of memory. According to Kesner (1991), there is considerable agreement regarding a data-based memory that is mediated largely by the hippocampus. This corresponds to Olton's working memory, Tulving's episodic memory, Miskin's recognition memory, and Squire and Cohen's declarative memory. It is assumed to be biased toward the coding of facts, data, and personal events.

There is less agreement regarding what Kesner called expectancy-based memory. This includes Olton's reference memory and Tulving's semantic memory, on the one hand, and Mishkin's habit memory and Squire and Cohen's procedural memory, on the other. Expectancy-based memory is assumed to be biased toward previously stored information of a general and procedural nature. Because much less research has been conducted on the neural substrates of expectancy-based memory, and there are greater differences in theorists' conceptions of this memory, Kesner (1991) speculated that multiple regions of the brain may subserve it. Perhaps the research most strongly implicates the posterior parietal lobe.

Finally, to account for the dynamic nature of learning and memory, Kesner (1991) proposed that the two systems—data-based and expectancy-based—operate in parallel, with interaction between them. Obviously, there is considerable room for continued theorizing about the neurological bases of human learning and memory.

A Biological Basis for Language Learning

One approach to the neurophysiology of learning, as we have seen, is to study the capabilities of brain-damaged individuals, whether humans or other animals. The nature and location of the physical damage are then related to the types of impairments observed. Another approach, however, is to study a human capability that has an obvious and unquestioned biological component to it. Language provides such a test case, because "to believe that special biological adaptations are a requirement, it is enough to notice that all children but none of the dogs and cats in the house acquire language" (Gleitman, 1986, p. 119).

The idea that language may be innate is not a new one. Leahey and Harris (1989) observed that Descartes assigned a special role to language as a vehicle for the expression of thought. In more modern times, however, Noam Chomsky (1965, 1972) has been largely responsible for promoting the view that language is an evolved, species-specific organ. Recall from chapter 2 that behaviorists attempted to explain language as just another complex behavior, acquired through processes of operant conditioning. Chomsky was extremely critical of the behaviorist position and argued convincingly for a universal language faculty in humans. At the same time, Eric Lenneberg (1964, 1967) articulated a biological view of language acquisition. He pointed to clinical evidence that language functions are located in the left hemisphere, that language can neither be suppressed (e.g., deaf children will spontaneously invent sign language in the absence of verbal capabilities) nor language learning speeded up, and that certain forms of speech disorders are inheritable.

In the traditions of Chomsky and Lenneberg, Gleitman (1986) proffered three arguments as essential to a case for language being biologically pre-programmed. First is the fact that language learning proceeds uniformly within a linguistic community despite tremendous differences in individuals' experiences. "Isolated words appear at about age 1 year, followed by two-word utterances at about age 2 years. Thereafter, sometime during the third year of life, there is a sudden spurt of vocabulary growth accompanied, coincidentally or not, by elaboration of the sentence structures. By about 4 years of age, the speaker sounds essentially adult" (Gleitman, 1986, pp. 121–122; cf. Lenneberg, 1967).

Second, children do not simply copy what they hear. They make systematic errors that suggest the use of an emerging grammar, of which the rules are never explicitly taught. For example, young speakers will systematically misplace auxiliary verbs in wh-questions, such as "What can I eat?" They will say instead, "What I can eat?"—a form that is never produced by older speakers or adults (cf. Bellugi, 1967; cited in Gleitman, 1986). Similar evidence comes from the order in which children acquire lexical categories. A child's first words are overwhelmingly nouns. Verbs appear slightly later, with adjectives and adverbs appearing still later (Gentner, 1982). These examples are difficult, perhaps impossible, to explain without reference to some sort of innate basis.

Finally, a third argument for the biological preprogramming of language lies in the mistakes that children do not make as they learn to speak. Gleitman provided an illustration with the following two sentences:

1. The man who is a fool is amusing.
2. The man is a fool who is amusing.

Now consider how these are transformed to yield yes/no questions:

1. Is the man who is a fool amusing?
2. Is the man a fool who is amusing?

Children apparently recognize that which *is* moves depends on the structure of the sentence, not the serial position of the word *is*. They never make the mistake of saying, "Is the man who a fool is amusing?" or "Is the man is a fool who amusing?" Yet it is extremely unlikely that children are ever taught the rather abstract rule, "It's the *is* in the higher clause that moves."

If we accept the premise, therefore, that biology plays a significant role in language learning, then we may proceed to the question of just what role it plays. From the studies conducted by Gleitman and others (cf. Feldman, Goldin-Meadow, & Gleitman, 1978; Newport, Gleitman, & Gleitman, 1977; also Fowler, 1986), she reaches the conclusion, first suggested by Lenneberg, that language acquisition is maturationally driven. The progress of normal children was better predicted by their age than by the speech patterns of their mothers. Deaf children learned a gestural language in the same developmental increments that hearing children learned spoken language. Language onset and structural development were the same for blind as for sighted children. Finally, although the onset of language was late for Down's syndrome retardates, its rate and nature of development paralleled that of normal children until a point when learning simply stopped. These results consistently point to the child's neurological age as a critical factor in his or her language learning.

Neurological age may also set limits on language learning in a manner different from what has already been discussed. Anecdotal evidence supports the hypothesis that children are better language learners than adults. They easily manage two languages at a time while adults struggle through second language classes with great difficulty (Gleitman, 1986; cf. Miller, 1981). In addition, findings from studies investigating deaf individuals learning American sign language indicate that final knowledge of the language is best predicted by the age of the learner at first exposure (Newport & Supalla, cited in Gleitman, 1986). Late learners, in other words, failed to acquire all the linguistic structures of American sign language, despite years of subsequent exposure and use. This suggests the possibility of a critical period in language learning, akin to chick imprinting or bird song-learning.

Reflect back, for a moment, on the case of Mario, described at the beginning of this chapter. Although the scenario did not state which part of his brain sustained damage, we might assume that the left cerebral hemisphere was involved because his speech was affected. That Mario regained his speech may be taken as evidence for critical periods in language development. Lenneberg (1967) reported normal language development following damage to the left hemisphere at an early age but loss of linguistic ability when damage occurred after puberty. Recent studies may call Lenneberg's results into question, because more sophisticated psycholinguistic testing has revealed specific competence failures in the language of brain-damaged individuals. "Nevertheless, the clinical impression is that such persons are linguistically normal. The classical conclusion that the young brain is quite flexible in reallocating functions seems to remain valid" (Chipman, 1986, p. 212).

Finally, just as individuals exhibit differences in their preference for processing in certain modes, they also exhibit differences in the areas of the brain that subserve language functions. Females appear different from males, and left-handed persons appear different from right-handed persons. These differences do not, however, result in language deficiencies, which means there is much more to the story of language learning than we currently know.

Cognitive Development and the Brain

In at least one respect, studying cognitive development from a neurophysiological perspective is no different from studying it from a cognitive perspective. The primary question of interest is: To what extent is cognitive development biologically or environmentally determined? Obviously, behaviorists put little stock in biological factors, arguing that development can be fully understood in environmental terms. But cognitive developmentalists have been more open to the possibility of biological determinants in cognitive development. Piaget appealed to a biological model for understanding development, although his ideas never extended to investigations of actual biological processes or substrates of development. And

Case suggested that maturation of certain brain systems may be responsible for limitations to children's working memory compared to adults (see chapter 6).

To characterize the diversity of neuroscience research related to development, four conceptual models are suggested: fixed circuitry, critical periods, plasticity, and modularity (Chall & Peterson, 1986). To some degree, these models integrate much of the research already discussed concerning the neurophysiology of learning. They provide a useful working framework for a look at cognitive development and the brain.

Fixed Circuitry and Critical Periods

In normal prenatal development, what eventually becomes the brain begins as a single layer of cells lining the wall of the neural tube. Cell mitosis results in the genesis of waves of neurons which migrate to destinations in various parts of the developing brain. Elaboration of neuronal dendrites and synapses follows, with the establishment of connections between neurons the ultimate achievement of development (Goldman-Rakic, 1986). What is noteworthy about this process (highly oversimplified here) is the very orchestrated plan it requires. Brain cell generation and migration is virtually complete in humans by the 16th week after gestation. Neurons by then have assumed specific functions in specific regions of the brain. Although dendritic development and synapse formation take longer, generally continuing well into the postnatal period, they form particular patterns of connections that depend upon their location.

What do these fixed circuits and their pattern of development mean for learning and complex cognitive functioning? For one thing, the developing brain will be more or less sensitive to different types of injuries at different times. Dividing cells are now known to be selectively vulnerable to radiation; during the period of cell division, then, subsequent development of the brain can be irreparably harmed if it is exposed to radiation. This helps to explain why many women who survived Hiroshima, and who were 8 to 16 weeks pregnant at the time the atom bomb was dropped, gave birth to mentally retarded children. For children whose gestational age was outside this critical period, however, mental retardation was not common. As Goldman-Rakic (1986) put it, "Toxins, injuries, and stress-induced maternal influences can certainly alter the number of cells generated, their patterns of migration and ultimate synaptic connections" (p. 253). What effects there will be depends upon the critical periods during which the influences are felt.

Critical periods apparently occur not only before birth, but after as well. There is now evidence to believe that the brain may not be fully mature until individuals reach at least 8 to 10 years of age (Heminway & Tegriti, 1984), and a few researchers believe that figure is closer to 18 to 20 (Epstein,

1990). Moreover, data from electroencephalograms show evidence of growth spurts in the brain that some have attempted to correlate with Piaget's stages of cognitive development. This would suggest critical periods for learning that occur around the ages at which children make transitions among stages.

At this point, however, the correlations between brain maturation and Piaget's stages of development are at best weak. For one thing, very global measures of cognitive performance have been used, which are likely to have been insensitive to small increments in brain growth. For another, it has been difficult to reconcile the continuous rate of regional brain maturation with the discrete stage changes that Piaget's theory proposes (Hudspeth & Pribham, 1990). As a consequence, although it may be tempting to draw curricular implications from these data, McCall (1990) has argued that they would be premature.

Eventually, the more that is known about how and when circuits are fixed in the brain, the more likely we will be able to determine neurological causes of certain learning problems. Chall and Peterson (1986) expressed the hope, for example, that reading disabilities may be more accurately detected and treated with knowledge of their neurological origins and potential critical periods.

Plasticity

On the other side of the coin from fixed circuitry is the cortical plasticity of the developing brain. It has already been mentioned that dendritic branching and synaptic formation continue after birth. In fact, although subject to critical periods, "anatomical plasticity during development of the nervous system . . . is the rule rather than the exception" (Crutcher, 1991, pp. 107–108). Yet, there is now ample evidence to suggest that cortical plasticity is characteristic of the brain throughout life. Rosenzweig (1984, 1986) described studies he and others conducted with rodents, investigating brain changes induced by experience. He compared the brain development of rats, mice, ground squirrels, and gerbils raised in standard, enriched, or impoverished environments. The standard environment consisted of a small laboratory cage for three rodents, furnished with food and water. The enriched environment was a larger cage for ten to twelve animals, with food, water, and a variety of objects changed daily (such as shelves and slides). The impoverished environment meant that each animal was raised alone in a small private cage.

Rosenzweig's results were rather astounding. The brains of animals raised in the enriched environment showed increases in weight, dendritic branching, and the size of synaptic contacts relative to the comparison groups. Moreover, the brains of adult rats showed a continued ability to change in response to experience, with these changes related to improvements in learning.

Studying neurological changes in the brain in response to experience is obviously more difficult when it concerns humans rather than rodents. Nonetheless, there is compelling evidence to believe that human brains are also characterized by plasticity. Studies analogous to those of Rosenzwieg have been conducted in which researchers compared the cognitive abilities (as measured by IQ tests) of children raised in different types of environments (Friedman & Cocking, 1986). In general, results suggested the same conclusion. An enriched environment can significantly enhance cognitive development, especially when the enrichment comes at an early age. Additional evidence of neuronal plasticity is provided by Bach-y-Rita (1980, 1982), who taught blind people to interpret tactile information in terms of visual images and stroke victims to regain functions incapacitated by the stroke. In both cases, results suggest that the brain can be taught to modify the functions of its structures.

Although anatomical and behavioral plasticity has been demonstrated in mature brains, there is also evidence that neuronal plasticity declines with age in many species, including humans (Crutcher, 1991). This is thought to be a function of mature individuals committing increasing portions of their nervous system to memory storage. And memory storage, of necessity, must be relatively stable in order for information to be later recalled. It seems likely, then, that older learners are capable of learning new things throughout their lives, but doing so in a flexible manner is somewhat more difficult than it is for younger learners.

Modularity

Conceptualizing memory in terms of modules offers a means for understanding the differences between memories that are lost or retained with brain damage (Chall & Peterson, 1986). This is similar to the declarative-procedural distinction that has already been discussed. Modularity can also refer to differences of another sort. Gardner (1983, 1986) proposed that cognitive development proceeds independently in at least seven relatively autonomous domains, or modules—language, music, logical-mathematical reasoning, spatial processing, bodily-kinesthetic activity, interpersonal knowledge, and intrapersonal knowledge. These make up the sum of one's intelligence.

Evidence for brain modularity comes first from investigations of fixed circuits referred to earlier. Cortical connections associated with visual perception have been found to be arrayed in cellular columns (Hubel & Wiesel, 1962), but so have connections in the frontal cortex that are unrelated to sensory perception. "Modular organization seems to be a universal rule for disposition of connections in the cerebral cortex" (Goldman-Rakic, 1986, p. 249).

As for the different types of intelligences proposed by Gardner, language seems to be predominantly associated with the left cerebral hemisphere, visual-spatial abilities with the right hemisphere, music perception and production with the right anterior lobe, and emotional difficulties with the right temporal lobe (Gardner, 1986). These conclusions have been drawn from observations of mostly brain-damaged patients, but Gardner (1982, 1983) has also examined individuals from what he calls "unusual populations." These included idiot-savants, prodigies in single domains, and retarded individuals who may have a single spared organ of development. From his analyses, Gardner believes that normal individuals possess independent capacities to develop in the seven separate domains mentioned previously. Each domain is subserved by separate neural mechanisms, which can therefore be differentially affected by biological and environmental factors.

Finally, cognitive development in any domain is activated, according to Gardner (1986), within a cultural context. He argued that humans evolved as cultural members just as they evolved as biological creatures. Thus, biological potential is constrained to some extent by cultural factors within the environment. This argument is certainly consistent with the views of sociobiologists and helps to provide a link between the neurophysiology of learning and the sociobiology of learning.

Implications of Neurophysiology for Learning and Instruction

There is likely to be unanimous agreement by this point that the neurophysiology of learning is a complex affair. Is it even possible to integrate the various perspectives described in order to draw sensible and useful implications for instruction? There appear to be at least five areas in which implications emerge, related to (1) modularity, (2) enriched environments, (3) plasticity, (4) language learning, and (5) learning problems. These are explained in the following discussion and summarized in Table 8–2.

Modularity and "Brain-Based" Curricula

Whether humans possess seven distinguishable cognitive capacities, as Gardner proposes, they undoubtedly possess some differentiation of cognitive function that is neurologically based. Both cognitive (see chapter 3) and neurological findings point to differences between general (or procedural) and specific data-based (or declarative) memory. The same is true for different sensory codes that may be activated by attention to establish and access a single semantic memory. These findings, coupled

TABLE 8–2   Implications of Neurophysiology for Learning and Instruction

Principle	Implication for Instruction
1. Cognitive functions are differentiated.	Learners are likely to have preferred modes of processing as well as different capabilities in various modes. This suggests a multimodal approach to instruction: include activities that draw upon different sensory modes.
	For example, Ms. Lilly teaches geography locations using maps and songs. Students learn the locations of countries by singing the names as they locate and touch the countries on the map (personal communication, November 1992).
2. The brain is relatively plastic in nature.	Enriched, active environments are likely to facilitate learning in developing children. As for adults, although plasticity seems to decrease with age, learning can remain flexible if a variety of instructional strategies are offered.
	For example, children's literature serves better to teach reading than primers, and historic literature may be used effectively in social studies instruction.
3. Language may be biologically pre-programmed.	Children have implicit knowledge about language, which should be made explicit during language instruction. In addition, instructors should be aware that language problems could interfere with subject matter learning.
	For example, arithmetic problems should be phrased in language understood by the students.
4. Learning disorders may have a neurobiological basis.	Neurological testing may assist in diagnosing, treating, and evaluating the effectiveness of programs designed to ameliorate various learning problems.

with brain modularity and hemisphere differences that have been observed, suggest two implications.

First, learners are likely to demonstrate considerable variation in their processing preferences and cognitive abilities. If we agree that cognitive competence depends partly upon biological capacity and partly upon experience, then normal variation in both factors should produce extensive observed variability. This certainly comes as no surprise, but Gardner (1986) reminded us that education has routinely placed more emphasis on some types of cognition over others. This means that some learners may be disadvantaged compared to others if their cognitive strengths fall into areas generally overlooked by educators. The challenge to educators, then, is to discover each learner's cognitive profile, so that "we can make more informed decisions about which program of education to follow if we want to play from strength or if we want to shore up weaknesses" (Gardner, 1986, p. 278).

Gardner's statement leads directly to a second implication of modularity for curriculum and instruction. That is, how can educators use this knowledge of differences in memory and processing modes to provide learners with instruction most appropriate to their needs? For one thing, the existence of different memory types and cognitive capabilities implies different instructional strategies suitable for each type. In other words, acquiring a procedural skill in music is likely to demand different learning experiences than acquiring facts about logic. Once we better understand the nature of various cognitive capabilities, we will be in a better position to devise tasks appropriate to help learners progress in a particular domain.

This argument is similar to that which underlies Gagné's (1985) theory of instruction (see chapter 10), as well as many models of instructional design (cf. Reigeluth, 1983). The difference among views appears to concern not whether learners acquire different capabilities but just what these capabilities are. It is hoped that future neurological research may help to sort out the possibilities.

Although domain differences suggest specific instructional strategies, learner differences may do so as well. There may be a problem, however, in the premature application of neuroscience findings to instruction. Educational programs that are designed to exercise both sides of the brain have been popular (Chipman, 1986; Rosenzweig, 1986). Other programs have used appeals to brain research to justify their emphasis on educating the right side of the brain or meeting the needs of predominantly "right-brained" learners. Such programs, however, "are certainly premature and probably misguided" (Rosenzweig, 1986, p. 352). Brain researchers stress the cooperative interaction between the two cerebral hemispheres and argue that their functional roles are only just beginning to be characterized. It would be simplistic to describe hemispheric differences as "analytic-holistic, verbal-spatial, or any others of the popular polar pairs that are often used for this purpose" (Bertelson, 1982, quoted in Rosenzweig, 1986, p. 352).

Although brain-based curricula are not well justified, instructional strategies that appeal to multiple sensory modes and cognitive capabilities probably are. Learners having difficulty understanding an instructional presentation in one mode may benefit from the same presentation in an alternate mode. Exploring how meaning can be conveyed differently in different modes can also be valuable for learning (cf. Tessmer, Wilson, & Driscoll, 1990) and constitutes a central tenet of semiotic (see chapter 3) and constructivist (see chapter 11) approaches to instruction. Not only may different pathways be established to the same memory, that memory may be enhanced and broadened by unique contributions of different codes.

Use It or Lose It: Enriched Environments, Critical Periods, and Plasticity

During the postnatal period of the developing animal, synapses proliferate. Many more are produced by the young brain than are commonly seen in mature or adult brains. This initial overproduction of synapses is then followed by a period of consolidation, in which some synapses will be retracted until adult levels are reached (Goldman-Rakic, 1986). Although behavioral indicators of this sprouting and pruning period are still being determined, many researchers believe that it correlates with critical periods in cognitive development. This may help to explain, for example, why "certain precocious behaviors (like neonatal swimming or imitation) drop out" and why flexibility declines after a certain period (Gardner, 1986, p. 270).

Critical periods for the development of visual perception (cf. Hubel & Wiesel, 1962) are well established, and they are presumed to account for some observed differences in language learning, discussed earlier. There may also be critical periods in each of the seven domains of competence that Gardner has proposed. Whether or not Gardner's proposal is confirmed, what do critical periods in general suggest for instruction? At the least, they imply an important role for environmental events during the period of development deemed critical. Just what this role should be is the question.

In Piaget's view (see chapter 6), equilibration is the major developmental process, implying that whereas environment provides the necessary raw material, the main impetus for development comes from within the learner. Consistent with this view was Piaget's opposition to speeding up development through instructional interventions. Most educators in the Piagetian tradition, then, would consider enriched environments to be those that provide a variety of resources promoting child activity.

By contrast, Bruner and Vygotsky (see chapter 7) accorded the environment a more extensive role, believing that instruction can precede and contribute to development. Similarly, biological evidence from studies of enriched versus impoverished environments supports the influence of environment on development (Friedman & Cocking, 1986). Enrichment can take the form of guided learning or formal, planned instruction. Guided learning includes such tactics as parents, siblings, or peers helping children solve problems, prepare for school tests, or read challenging books. In fact, more challenging textbooks have been associated with higher Scholastic Aptitude Test (SAT) scores, and more difficult books appear to promote language and reading achievement (Chall & Peterson, 1986).

Because critical periods typically occur early in development, with both brain and behavior exhibiting less flexibility over time, a common assumption has been that cortical plasticity may be restricted to early development. However, Rosenzweig's findings effectively debunked this notion. "While acknowledging the importance of the developmental processes that set the stage before birth for later cognitive development and accomplishments, it seems to me that it is equally if not more vital for educators and cognitive scientists to know about the capacity of the nervous system, even in adults, to undergo plastic changes in response to experience" (Rosenzweig, 1986, p. 365).

In clear agreement with Rosenzweig are Friedman and Cocking (1986), who extended their notion of guided learning to include experts helping novices complete a task or generate important questions and therapists helping patients recover functions lost through accident or illness. Their point is that instruction of all sorts can facilitate changes in brain processes. What needs to be better understood, however, are the separate roles of learner motivation and maturity, family support, experience, and patience (Friedman & Cocking, 1986).

Language Learning

What help to educators is offered by knowledge that language may be biologically preprogrammed? Perhaps it comes down to one simple maxim: ". . . much of what is taught—and should be taught—about language to children is already known to the children implicitly. . . . I believe that the best teaching methods will be those that specifically take advantage of this prior knowledge, that call the child's attention to what she or he knows, and build as directly as possible from that knowledge" (Gleitman, 1986, pp. 144–145). This maxim, it seems to me, suggests two related implications for instruction.

First, teachers of multicultural classrooms would be well-advised to consider nonstandard English as a language or languages other than English. In other words, children from predominantly black or other ethnic neighborhoods typically speak English in a way that sounds wrong to most teachers. It is certainly wrong in the sense that it does not conform to the rules of standard English. But neither do other, so-called foreign languages; they have their own internal structure and grammatical rules. The same appears to be true for black English and other forms of nonstandard English. Thus, children of all backgrounds probably speak quite grammatically in the language of their surroundings. Knowing this may help teachers to determine what implicit knowledge children have of their language and to use this to best advantage in teaching standard English.

Second, differential patterns of language development are likely to be reflected in the differential difficulty of various language tasks. For example, "children are able to think about and manipulate word- and syllable-level representations of language much earlier in life than they can do the same for phoneme-segment representations of language" (Gleitman, 1986, p. 145). Thus, to be most effective, language instruction should proceed in the same sequence, helping to draw out and call attention to students' implicit knowledge about language.

This relation between language knowledge and task difficulty is also important to remember in other areas of instruction besides language itself. Recent studies in arithmetic problem solving have shown that the linguistic structure of a word problem can greatly influence its difficulty. For example, consider the two simple problems below.

> Problem A: *John has 5 apples. Mary has 8 apples. How many more apples does Mary have than John?*

> Problem B: *John has 5 apples. Mary has 8 apples. If Mary gives Sally the same number of apples as John, how many will she have left?*

Ostensibly, these two problems are the same, in that they are both solved by subtracting 5 from 8. If subtraction is the skill to be assessed, then either problem presumably should suffice. However, the problems are not linguistically the same, and, in fact, one is more difficult to answer than the other. You are right if you guessed Problem A to be the more difficult one. Concepts of more than and less than appear later in language use than concepts of adding to or taking away. Thus, word problems of this sort can assess linguistic competence and, indeed, mask arithmetic competence. Recall, as well, the influence of schemata on arithmetic problem solving that was discussed in chapter 5 and the conception of language as a sign system that was discussed in chapter 7. It seems likely that different linguistic structures will trigger different problem schemata or sign understandings, which may either enhance or interfere with solving the problem at hand.

Learning Disabilities and their Treatment
There is great hope that neurological testing will some day be sophisticated enough to detect and diagnose a variety of learning problems. However, better diagnosis does not make the problem go away. Rather, the challenge lies in designing effective educational programs to overcome the learning difficulty. The solutions to that challenge are as apt to come from elsewhere as from advances in the neurophysiology of learning (Chipman, 1986).

Perhaps two additional points are salient here. The first concerns how we characterize what neurological causes are discovered for various learning problems. Calling such causes "defects in cerebral architecture" may signify to some people that they are immutable, impossible to alter or fix. Such an assumption might lead to the unwarranted abandonment of efforts to remediate the learning problem. On the other hand, finding neurological bases of cognitive functions does not have to imply that some functioning is normal and some defective. Rather, one might expect the brains of two individuals to be different, with one possessing some skill that the other lacks. Neural indicators of this sort might be helpful as an additional source of information used to evaluate the effectiveness of educational programs (Chipman, 1986).

Finally, it pays us to remember the neurological evidence of brain plasticity. Chall and Peterson (1986) suggested that we adopt the view of the learner as "an active constructor of knowledge, and the brain as a structure that changes physically as well as b ehaviorally with learning" (p. 314). Learners do overcome disabilities, albeit sometimes with great difficulty and prolonged effort.

SUGGESTED READINGS

Crawford, C. B., Smith, M. S., and Krebs, D. (Eds.). (1987). *Sociobiology and psychology: Ideas, issues, and applications.* Hillsdale, NJ: Erlbaum.

Friedman, S. L., Klivington, K. A., and Peterson, R. W. (1986). *The brain, cognition, and education.* Orlando: Academic Press.

Martinez, J. L., and Kesner, R. P. (1991). *Learning and memory: A biological view* (2nd ed.). San Diego: Academic Press.

REFLECTIVE QUESTIONS AND ACTIVITIES

1. What underlying assumptions about knowledge and knowing can be detected in the research presented in chapter 8? Are they different among researchers interested in ultimate causes versus those interested in proximal causes of learning? With what epistemological tradition do these views seem most closely related?

2. Revisit once more your thoughts about learning and development. What do biological theorists add to the discussion? Does the evidence they present better support one position or the other concerning whether development influences learning or the other way around? Is there any evidence to suggest that learning and development might be mutually interactive? What implications would this third position have for instruction?

3. View the movie *Blade Runner*, which was produced in the 1980s, and/or an episode of *Star Trek: The Next Generation*, produced in the 1990s. In the former, replicants are being engineered that are "more human than human itself," whereas in the latter, Data is an android with a "positronic" brain. Discuss the view of the brain that these films present in relation to the neurophysiological research summarized in this chapter. How is learning characterized, and how would these characteristics affect the design of instruction?

4. Review literature on the "nature versus nurture" controversy in education. Using your findings and the research summarized in this chapter to support your arguments, discuss your conclusions with respect to which side of the controversy has the weight of evidence on its side. In particular, consider what implications are suggested for education of ethnic minorities and other special populations.

5. Select an instructional goal that has proven difficult to achieve by some learners. Analyze the goal for the major concepts that must be understood in order for the goal to be attained. Then, brainstorm ways in which these concepts could be presented to or practiced by learners that appeal to different learning modalities. Speculate on what aspects of the goal would be highlighted or obscured in each modality.

▶ Part VI

Learning and Motivation

▶ 9

The Motivation to Learn

Consider the following scenarios.

Scenario 9–1

Sean is a former teacher who has recently accepted the post of field education officer in a developing country. There he is expected to work directly with teachers to help them improve the quality of instruction in their classrooms. In addition, however, he is expected to conduct research to help determine the impact of methods and techniques he suggests. Since he does not have the skills with which to do this job effectively, he attends a one-week training workshop on action research. Although he is anxious to learn these skills quickly, he worries that his current lack of knowledge will put him at a disadvantage in the class. Moreover, despite difficulty in understanding the concepts being presented, Sean asks no questions for fear of looking stupid and holding up the rest of the class. His performance suffers as a result.

Scenario 9–2

Laone is a middle school student who attends a school some 10 miles from where she lives. Her parents own a farm where she is expected to do daily chores after school. This semester, Laone has failed to turn in several assignments in English class, and those she did submit were done hastily and, for the most part, poorly. Mr. Logan, Laone's English teacher, checked with several of her other teachers to see if she was doing poorly in their classes as well as his. He discovered that Laone was also having trouble in social studies, but seemed to be doing fine in math and science, particularly on projects that could be related to farming. A conference with her parents revealed that Laone's father had disliked English in school, since he "weren't very good at it, and never did have much use for it."

Comparing the problems described in the previous two scenarios does not, on the surface of things, suggest that they have much in common. Sean clearly wants to learn the skills and knowledge being covered in the workshop. Laone, on the other hand, appears indifferent to learning in two subjects, English and social studies. Yet in both cases, the result is the same—poor performance. For reasons yet to be determined, learning is failing to occur as intended.

From the perspective of the learning theories discussed so far, we could generate a list of causes potentially responsible for the learning problems presented in the two scenarios. For example, the appropriate contingencies of reinforcement might not be in place (a behavioral hypothesis). Or, Sean and Laone might not possess the prerequisite skills and knowledge with which to process the new information being presented to them (an information processing analysis). Or, Laone might be at a cognitive developmental level slightly below her peers and thus unable to benefit from the same instruction (a developmental conjecture). Closer examination of the scenarios, however, reveals another possible explanation. In both cases, the learners involved appear to be putting forth less effort than is required by the learning situation. Since it is likely that other participants in the workshop have had as little exposure to research methods as Sean, he should perhaps ask more questions to help overcome his confusion. And Laone, having demonstrated good performance in other subjects, probably has the capability of doing as well in English. In order to do this, however, she should be completing more of her English assignments. In both scenarios, then, there are indications of motivational problems which interfere with effective learning and performance.

"Motivation," according to Schunk (1990), "refer[s] to the process whereby goal-directed behavior is instigated and sustained" (p. 3). Motivation is also "a work-related rather than a play-related concept" (Weiner, 1990, p. 621). Teachers say students are not motivated, for example, when they study half-heartedly, complete a task only for the external reward it assures, or spend time on things antithetical to the learning task (e.g., daydreaming about ballet instead of working on fractions). Lack of motivation is also cited when students plainly refuse to become engaged in a learning task or fail to take actions that will assist them in successfully completing it.

The questions of what underlies motivation and how teachers can effectively motivate their students have been the subject of investigation for many years. Although the theories that have emerged from this research cannot strictly be called learning theories, the study of motivation for educators is certainly confounded with the study of learning. As Weiner (1990) put it, "motivation is often inferred from learning, and learning usually is an indicator of motivation for the educational psychologist" (p. 618). The prime issue is, How do we motivate people to engage in new learning?

The purpose of this chapter is to explore issues surrounding the motivation to learn. After a brief look at the history of motivational research in education, sources of motivation to learn will be presented in some detail. These are factors influencing whether learners initiate and persist in learning tasks. As a consequence of these factors and the learners' engagement (successful or not) in learning tasks, they may or may not demonstrate continuing motivation to learn. What determines continuing motivation will therefore be discussed next. Finally, a model of motivational design will be presented, along with suggestions for promoting intrinsic motivation and the self-regulation of learning.

A Brief History of Educational Research on Motivation

"At one time, motivation was the dominant field of study [in psychology]" (Weiner, 1990, p. 616). This was true primarily because psychologists in the 1930s and 1940s conceived of motivation as "what moved a resting organism to a state of activity" (Weiner, 1990, p. 617). You may see already the relationship this concept bears to learning as it was studied in those days. Hull (see chapter 2), for example, developed a theory of learning in which behavior was presumed to come about as a result of drives toward anticipated goals. That is, behavior was motivated toward a goal by the existence of some (usually biological) need—e.g., a need for food, sex, or shelter. Learning occurred when the response was reinforced and the drive that motivated the behavior in the first place was reduced.

Tolman's research on latent learning (see chapter 2), however, had the effect of separating concerns about motivation from concerns about learning (Weiner, 1990). If you recall, Tolman demonstrated that animals appeared to learn a maze simply by exploring it, in the absence of a goal or incentives for drive reduction. Since learning seemed to occur without a clear motivation for it, psychologists began to argue that motivation relates to the use of knowledge, not the development of it.

In the 1960s and 1970s, the shift from a behavioral to cognitive perspective in American psychology (see chapter 3) brought a reintegration of motivation with learning. Psychologists began to examine in new ways the effects of rewards on behavior. Although it had been widely accepted that rewarding a response automatically increased the probability of its reoccurrence, new findings called this into question. In some cases, rewards had little effect on subsequent behavior unless learners generated an expectancy for, or anticipation of, the reward (Estes, 1972). Moreover, some rewards, if perceived by the learners as controlling, tended to reduce their natural interest in the learning task (Deci, 1975). Similarly, rewards for the completion of an easy task tended to signal to learners that they were low in ability (e.g., Meyer et al., 1979). For humans, then, reward can mean a variety of different things, and each meaning can have different motivational—and learning—consequences.

With researchers now concentrating on human behavior, motivational research became dominated by investigations into humans' need for achievement (Weiner, 1990). Also called incentive motivation, effectance, and the urge for mastery, achievement motivation is thought to be a fundamental tendency of humans to manipulate, dominate, or otherwise master their environment (White, 1959). Among the most prominent researchers in achievement motivation were David McClelland and John Atkinson. They sought to understand why some people appear to strive for excellence simply for the sake of achieving while others do not (McClelland, Atkinson, Clark, & Lowell, 1953). It was assumed that a high need for achievement developed in children whose parents stressed achievement and competitiveness at home. But achievement motivation can also be situationally affected. Individuals will work harder under certain conditions, such as particular test instructions, competitive environments, and failure (Atkinson, 1964).

Atkinson's work was paralleled by investigations into other individual difference variables related to motivation. For example, besides having high or low achievement motivation, people can have high or low anxiety (Spielberger, 1966), or high or low internal control (Rotter, 1966). Excessive anxiety can interfere with learning and performance, leading to a reduction in continuing motivation to learn. Conversely, students show greater motivation when they have an internal, as opposed to external, orientation. This means that they tend to perceive learning tasks as skill determined and thus subject to personal control. Externally oriented students tend to believe that their success at a learning task will be determined by chance rather than by means within their control. These students are therefore less likely to be motivated to engage in the learning task.

According to Weiner (1990), the above trends in motivation research have continued to the present day, with an even greater focus on human behavior, particularly the self. As we shall see in the next section, significant attention is being paid to personal goal setting, ways to enhance self-perceptions of control in learning, and strategies to maintain personal beliefs in high ability. Weiner called for more motivational investigations that are not linked with learning, and indeed, there is a growing body of literature demonstrating effects of motivation on variables such as self-esteem, emotions, and so on (Weiner, 1990). However, for educators, the interaction between motivation and learning is what is most important, so that is the specific focus of this chapter. Therefore, the ensuing discussion will be limited to sources and strategies of motivation as they affect and promote learning.

SOURCES OF MOTIVATION TO LEARN

Whereas drive theorists clearly demonstrated that physiological needs (e.g., hunger) motivate organisms to engage in certain behavior (e.g., seek food), cognitive theorists have increasingly shown that cognitive processes are important mediators of motivation. Staying with the food example momentarily, when humans seek food to satisfy hunger, not just any food will do. You might, for example, forego a stop at the nearest hamburger joint to go home and fix a nutritious vegetable salad for lunch. Why might you do this? Perhaps because you value a healthy life-style, to which low-fat, nutritious meals can contribute. Your values, then, have mediated between the drive (hunger) and your response (eating). Likewise, deciding to engage in a learning task and persisting in that task are no simple matters. As we have already seen, motivation can be influenced by one's need for achievement or locus of control (internal versus external orientation). Motivation is also a function of one's cognitions about the task at hand, about the consequences of task completion, and about one's ability to do the task. Each of these sources of motivation is elaborated further in the sections that follow.

Curiosity

When Alice entered the Looking Glass, she remarked at how "curiously [the path] twists," always coming back to the house no matter which route she followed away from it. This made her all the more determined to figure out how to reach the nearby hill so that she could continue her adventures (Carroll, 1946, p. 22). Curiosity, in children and adults alike, is a strong motivator of learning. One type of curiosity, perceptual arousal, is initially stimulated by novel, complex, or incongruous patterns in the environment (Berlyne, 1965), much like what Alice encountered in the Looking Glass and Wonderland. Not only do learners pay greater attention to these unexpected events, but they are also moved to try new ways of perceiving what they are looking at (Gagné & Driscoll, 1988). Alice, for example, puzzled over the many curious things that happened to her, sometimes venturing hypotheses about what they meant.

Teachers, too, can make good use of curious events for motivating students. A history teacher, for example, might don a bit of costume representative of the next era her class will be studying in order to grab the students' attention and activate their curiosity about what is to come.

Since people adapt rather quickly to surprising events, curiosity must be sustained in order for it to be a continuing source of motivation. One way of maintaining attention on a perceptual level is to vary the instructional approaches used in a class period or training session (Keller, 1983, 1987a). Most of you have undoubtedly been bored, at one time or another, by an instructor who did nothing but lecture monotonously and unendingly. To keep learners alert, instructors can employ such strategies as varying their tone of voice, using relevant humor occasionally, and interspersing demonstrations and group activities with lecture.

Another means of sustaining curiosity involves fantasy. "The use of fantasy in learning entails providing learners with a meaningful context for learning that is easy to augment with their imaginations. The context is meaningful to the learner in the sense that it offers a very personal degree of fascination and intrigue" (Rieber, 1991a, p. 320; cf. Malone, 1981). So, for example, learning about longitude and latitude occurs in context and maintains students' attention when a concurrent goal is to locate a "pirate's sunken treasure."

Finally, "a deeper level of curiosity may be activated by creating a problem situation which can be resolved only by knowledge-seeking behavior" (Keller, 1987a, p. 2). Keller (1983) called this inquiry arousal, and it is a factor that researchers in the Cognition and Technology Group at Vanderbilt (CTGV) contend is brought about by the problem complexity inherent in their instructional videos (cf. CTGV, 1990, 1991a, 1991b). They intentionally pose very complex and realistic problems for students to solve, and then provide throughout each video numerous clues and information necessary to solve the problems. The result, they say, is enhanced motivation on the part of learners, who experience the complexity of problems that is characteristic of real life.

A related strategy devised by a long-time teacher is called ambiguous assignments (Woolfolk & McCune-Nicolich, 1984). Students are given a list of possible assignments (e.g., "find a new use for something," "create something that relates to the Civil War," "collect a series of pictures and use them to illustrate, without words, a mathematical principle") and then told to proceed as they see fit. The assignments both stimulate student curiosity and promote prolonged engagement in learning tasks.

Learning Task Relevance

Common sense dictates that students will be more motivated to learn things that are relevant to their interests. How often have we all heard cries like, "What good will spelling do me? All computers have spell-checkers on them!"? Or, a related complaint is heard in the refrain, "I know I should learn to . . . [you fill in the blank] . . . but I'm just not interested in it!"

How to make learning relevant to students, however, is a complicated affair. What makes a subject interesting to learners? How can learners be made to see the future relevance of something when the future seems especially far off? How can teachers help learners both set and attain relevant goals in a subject? How can instruction be designed to meet students' needs for achievement or needs for affiliation? Some of the answers to these questions can be found in the research conducted on goal setting and motive matching. Let us consider each in turn.

Goal Setting

Actively setting goals can be an important source of motivation (Bandura, 1977). When individuals set goals, they determine an external standard to which they will internally evaluate their present level of performance. To the extent that this standard is not met and their goals are not yet achieved, learners will persist in their efforts. Undoubtedly, most of us have had the experience of "sticking with it" until a goal we have set for ourselves has been achieved. This was certainly true some years ago when I decided to take up windsurfing. I already knew how to sail and so thought learning to windsurf would be a snap. Instead, it took teeth-gritting patience and persistence over the better part of one summer.

Not all goals, however, will prompt this persistence in learning. In a review of studies on goal setting and task performance, Locke, Shaw, Saari, and Latham (1981) identified certain properties of goals that are important to the goal setting process. For example, setting explicit goals ("I will be able to connect a circuit to light a lamp") is better than setting general goals ("I will learn about electricity") for motivating persistent behavior. Moreover, as long as the learner is capable of performing the goal, setting more difficult goals tends to lead to greater persistence and better performance (Locke et al., 1981).

There are also differences between setting proximal versus distal goals (Schunk & Gaa, 1981). **Proximal goals** are *those that are close at hand and achievable quickly* (e.g., "I will complete ten extra math problems this week"), whereas **distal goals** are *ones that set criteria to be met in the distant future* (e.g., "I will do one hundred extra math problems this semester"). Not surprisingly, results indicate that setting proximal goals improves self-motivation and performance to a greater extent than setting distal goals. This result may be especially important in the teaching of young children, since they may not be capable of representing distal goals in thought (Schunk and Gaa, 1981).

Finally, Dweck and her colleagues (Dweck, 1986; Dweck & Elliot, 1983; Dweck & Leggett, 1988; Elliot & Dweck, 1988) have conceptualized two types of goals which influence achievement motivation. When learners set performance goals, they "seek to gain favorable judgments of their competence or avoid negative judgments of their competence" (Dweck, 1986, p. 1040). When they set learning goals, on the other hand, learners "seek to increase their competence, to understand or master something new" (Dweck, 1986, p. 1040). The difference between these two types of goals can be seen in statements such as, "I want to get an A on this test" (performance goal) versus "I want to understand why the United States was one of the last countries to enter World War II" (learning goal).

Dweck's studies have provided evidence that different goals promote different motivational patterns. For instance, faced with a performance goal, students who have little confidence in their abilities display helplessness. They avoid challenge and, given the chance, will quit rather than persist in the task. In the same situation, learners who have high confidence in their abilities will seek a challenge and tend to demonstrate high persistence toward the task. Where learning goals are concerned, on the other hand, students' assessments of their present ability is irrelevant. They all display what Leggett and Dweck (1988) called a "mastery-oriented" pattern of motivation. That is, they select challenging tasks, which are believed to benefit learning, and they demonstrate persistence in those tasks (Elliott & Dweck, 1988; Dweck & Leggett, 1988).

The reason for these differences appears to lie in how individuals interpret their failures within the two goal orientations. Performance goals foster the implicit belief that intelligence is fixed. Under this goal orientation, then, learners ask whether their abilities are adequate to the task, and failing is taken to mean that the answer is "no." By contrast, learning goals are associated with the belief that intelligence is malleable and can be developed. Under a learning goal orientation, strategies for task mastery are emphasized, and learners ask themselves how their abilities might best be applied and increased to achieve the goal. Failure in this case signals a problem with the current strategy and the necessity to revise that strategy. An obvious result is that learners will expend more effort to learn in this situation than when they believe they do not have the ability to achieve the goal (Dweck & Leggett , 1988).

What conclusions may we draw for instruction from this research on goal setting? It is apparent that setting challenging, proximal goals contributes to motivation and can lead to enhanced performance. But if we heed Dweck's findings, this is most likely to occur when the goals are oriented toward learning, as opposed to performance. Thus, for instance, Dweck would recommend that an example given earlier in the chapter be reoriented from performance to learning. Instead of, "I will complete ten extra math problems this week," a more effective goal might be, "I will determine the derivation of the principle underlying this week's math problems."

The recommendation to foster a learning goal orientation runs counter to much current educational practice, which attempts to instill learner confidence within a performance goal orientation (Dweck, 1988). Strategies of this sort will, in fact, be discussed later in the chapter. It is likely that the behavioral perspective on learning (specifically, positive reinforcement) contributed to this situation. Recall, for example, the effect of positive reinforcement on learning. How does this relate to motivation? Presumably, behavior that can be described as motivated comes about through its consistent reinforcement. However, "a deeper understanding of the principles of reinforcement would not lead one to expect that frequent praise for short, easy tasks would create a desire for long, challenging ones or promote persistence in the face of failure" (Dweck, 1986, p. 1045).

Motive Matching

Setting goals is one aspect of learners' cognitions about learning tasks that influences their motivation. Another is the degree to which learning tasks meet particular student needs or align with student values. A need can be defined as "any type of deficiency in the human organism or the absence of anything the person requires, or thinks he requires, for his overall well being" (Kolesnik, 1978, p. 149). In this vein, Maslow (1970) proposed a hierarchy of human needs, from lower levels related to survival and safety to higher levels of aesthetic appreciation and self-actualization. Maslow argued that once lower level needs are met, motivation toward satisfying these needs decreases and is refocused toward higher level needs. These, however, can never be totally fulfilled, so that motivation to satisfy them is always present.

Although self-actualization and aesthetic appreciation sound like rather lofty goals for instruction, Martin (1987) contended that they have been long overlooked by teachers and other instructional designers. She believes that attention to the aesthetic appeal of instruction, although not necessarily improving immediate performance, will contribute to the continuing engagement of students in learning. A good example of what she means can be seen in Belland's (1991) description of an audiotutorial laboratory experiment carried out in a freshman biology class at The Ohio State University. Belland wrote,

> Each student was supplied with a work space outfitted with a sink, gas jet, laboratory tools, a transparency viewer, and audiotape playback with both hand and foot controls. Each student was able to spend whatever time she/he needed to work through both the laboratory exercises and the associated curriculum. The laboratory served 12,000 students per year in Biology 100 at a cost of approximately $0.30 per student hour of instruction (an unbelievably

low sum since elementary classroom instruction at the time cost about $0.50).
(1991, p. 24)

In general, [concerning the effectiveness of the course], the finding was
that learners who spent the most time with the materials scored highest on the
tests and received the highest grades. (Belland, 1991, p. 25)

Eventually, the College of Biological Sciences [had to] face [the fact] that
even though several courses in science were required as part of the general
education of all OSU undergraduates, it was a rare student who took a second
course in biology. (Belland, 1991, p. 25)

Why? Among other problems that Belland discovered, the lecturer on the audiotape orated as if speaking to a large class. "His tone of voice, his overcareful enunciation, and his exaggerated emphasis were irritating to me as they surely were to the students," commented Belland (1991, pp. 25–26). Besides being impersonal and noninteractive, the tapes were long (90 minutes), with no obvious breaks in them.

Belland's point was that the audiotutorial program ignored students' affective needs. The consequence was that, although students learned the content of that particular course, they were disinclined to study further in the subject.

Keller (1987a) also suggested that instructors be sensitive to individuals' needs for achievement and for affiliation. Students who have a high need for achievement benefit from setting their own goals and having considerable control over the means of achieving these goals. Students who have a high need for affiliation flourish in noncompetitive situations, such as cooperative groups working together toward the achievement of a goal. To illustrate these differences, consider in what situations you might expect to encounter learners who have a high need for achievement or a high need for affiliation. What about technicians in a high-tech communications firm who must learn about the latest piece of equipment on the market? Or, children with a reading disability who struggle to learn new vocabulary words? There are no correct answers to these questions, but certainly the instructional strategies used in each case would be different.

Finally, Keller (1987a) concurred with Martin and Belland in recommending the use of appealing methods of teaching to promote continuing motivation. Included among his suggestions are instructional games, cooperative activities, positive role models, personal achievement opportunities, and opportunities for leadership (Keller, 1987a).

Self-Efficacy

To this point, the roles in motivation of curiosity and students' cognitions about learning tasks have been explored. But another strong source of

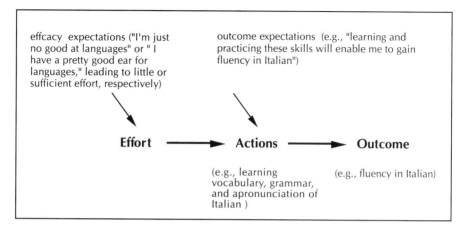

**FIGURE 9-1   Bandura's Theory of Self-Efficacy as a Mediator of
Performance and Achievement**

motivation comes from learners' beliefs about themselves in relation to task difficulty and task outcome. According to Bandura (1977, 1982), self-efficacy involves a belief that one can produce some behavior, independent of whether one actually can or not. Bandura proposed the concept as a mediator of performance and achievement. That is, learners can be sure that certain activities will produce a particular set of outcomes (e.g., Sean in Scenario 9–1 believes that acquiring skills in action research will enable him to perform a job function that he cannot do now). These expectations are what Bandura (1977) referred to as outcome expectations. But, if learners harbor serious doubts as to whether they can perform those required activities, they will not put forth the effort. These self-assessments are called efficacy expectations, and according to Bandura, both outcome and efficacy expectations must be met before a person will enact a behavior that leads to an anticipated outcome (Figure 9–1). In the case of Sean (Scenario 9–1), then, we may surmise that although outcome expectations were met, efficacy expectations were not. He doubted his ability to do the work required to learn research skills.

Influences on Efficacy Expectations

How do learners acquire efficacy expectations initially, and how might these expectations be changed when they prevent learners from undertaking tasks that they have the capability to do? Bandura (1982) suggested four possible sources by which people can gain information to influence their self-efficacy. These are:

1. performance accomplishments
2. vicarious experience
3. verbal persuasion
4. physiological states

Performance accomplishments refer to *learners' own previous success at a task.* An example of how success begets success (and the increased expectation of being successful) can be seen in the following case. Bill was an older student who took a class from me some years ago. I had structured the course so that students had to master a unit quiz before going on to the next unit. They could take each quiz as many as three times in order to achieve an A on it, or they could settle for grades as low as C. One day, early in the semester, Bill took a unit quiz, on which he achieved a B. I asked him, "Bill, do you want to take this quiz over for an A?" He replied, "Oh no, ma'am. I'm not an 'A' kind of guy." Later that day, in proctoring another student's quiz, Bill came back to me and said he thought a mistake might have been made in the scoring of his paper. I checked, and sure enough, one item had been marked wrong that was, in fact, correct. That raised his grade to an A, which I pointed out to him, "You see, Bill, you are an 'A' kind of guy after all." From that day on, Bill nearly always attempted a second try when he achieved less than A on a unit quiz, and on the whole, performed far better than he had ever expected.

Obviously, not all successful experiences occur so easily. A second influence on self-efficacy, then, comes from **vicarious experience**, or *the learner's observation of a role model attaining success at a task.* I frequently witness examples of vicarious experience influencing self-efficacy among the graduate students at my university. Many are convinced that the papers they write, or the research they conduct, will not be good enough for publication or presentation at a conference. This expectation then leads to their failure to complete the work, or their failure to submit it once completed. However, these same students change their self-expectations after attending a conference at which they hear a fellow student present a paper or witness a senior researcher present a boring or flawed paper. Generally, their thoughts run something like, "Gee, I can do at least as well as him (or her)!"

Implied in the story above is the fact that who the role model is affects the extent to which the observer's self-efficacy is enhanced. For example, a graduate student who attends a conference at which he or she is overawed by the presentations is unlikely to modify expectations of not being capable of the same performance. A recent review of studies on the effects of modeling as a function of the model's attributes revealed a number of conclusions (Schunk,1987). First, the role model's age appears to have little effect on whether a learner's self-efficacy is enhanced through his or her observation of the model. The one exception to this general statement occurred in a study by Schunk and Hanson (1985). In their study, elementary school students who had trouble subtracting observed a peer, the teacher, or no model demonstrate regrouping. Observing their peers led to students' reporting greater self-efficacy and achieving greater subtraction skill during the instructional program than observing the teacher, but a teacher model was better than no model.

Second, children are more likely to follow the behavior of those they perceive to be competent in the skill being learned than those they see as less competent. Moreover, when they are fearful about the learning situation, they responded more positively to coping models than mastery models. That is, learners gained confidence and were likely to improve their performance when they observed models who initially showed the same fears but who gradually reached a mastery performance.

Finally, more is better, and peer models can contribute to the self-efficacy of remedial and handicapped students. Presumably, multiple models are superior to one, because chances are greater for the learners to see themselves as similar to at least one of the models. Remedial and handicapped students are among those who have had difficulty learning academic material or coping with stressful situations, both conditions under which peer models can help raise observers' self-efficacy (cf. Bandura, 1986; Schunk, 1987).

Verbal persuasion is a third means by which self-efficacy can be modified, one that is probably most familiar to parents. This refers to *others persuading a learner that he or she is capable of succeeding at a particular task.* "C'mon, you can do it!" is a common exhortation of someone persuading another to attempt a task. This recently occurred to me when my husband and I decided to restain our cedar home, which stands on stilts approximately 20 feet in the air. My self-efficacy for painting from an unstable scaffold that high up was decidedly low, so my husband tried verbal persuasion. "It's easy," he said. "You can do it. Just follow my lead" (vicarious experience). I managed to get to where he was standing before the fourth source of self-efficacy information took over. At that point, out of sheer terror, I froze—unable to look up or down or let go of my tight fisted grip on the bars of the scaffold.

Finally, individuals monitor feelings of self-efficacy on the basis of their **physiological states** (Bandura, 1982). That is, their *"gut feeling" convinces them of probable success or failure.* In my case, my "gut feeling" convinced me that I was about to die! (Obviously, I didn't, but my husband finished the job with me assisting from the ground.) There is probably little a teacher can do to alter a student's physiological state, other than to suggest relaxation exercises or desensitization training (see chapter 2) to overcome fears and anxiety.

There are, then, many ways in which self-efficacy can be enhanced to the point where learners may be willing to expend effort on a learning task. But for action to be taken, their outcome expectations must also be met.

Sources of Outcome Expectations

Outcome expectations relate to both the learner's understanding of what activities are required to reach a learning goal and what consequences reaching the goal will assure. In a sense, this parallels the distinction between learning and performance made by Dweck earlier. On the one hand, students acquire an expectation of what is to be learned by setting goals or being told by the teacher what the goals are. This expectancy has an effect on self-efficacy but also on a number of processes while learning is taking place (Gagné & Driscoll, 1988; see also chapter 3). Students with a learning (as opposed to performance) orientation will then employ whatever learning and study strategies they believe will enable them to be successful in attaining the goals.

On the other hand, students also form an expectation about the consequences of goal achievement, and these consequences must have value for them to initiate and persist in a learning task. Grading contingencies are an example familiar to most learners. In a criterion-referenced system, certain scores must be achieved, or certain objectives mastered to earn an A. Provided students value that A and believe themselves capable of achieving it, they will put forth effort to satisfy the designated criteria. Similarly, achieving course or training goals can lead to such consequences as being accepted to college, getting a promotion, improving job performance, or earning a fellowship. The extent to which learners value these consequences, then, affects their motivation to succeed in the learning task.

Summary

In this section, factors have been considered that influence whether learners will initiate and persist in learning tasks. These have to do with individuals' motivation to learn before the learning has actually begun, and while it is taking place. Most theories of motivation that attempt to account for and explain these factors are classified as expectancy-value theories. As we have seen, for motivation to occur, certain expectancies—about one's abilities, about the task, and about the value of task achievement—must be satisfied.

In the next section, factors are examined that contribute to the overall context of motivation and to continuing motivation. At the end of a learning episode, for example, learners may decide not to continue in further study. This is often caused by expectations that are not met in the original learning situation. In addition, the social milieu surrounding learning can have motivational (or demotivational) influences.

CONSEQUENCES, CONTEXT, AND
CONTINUING MOTIVATION

What happens as a result of past learning determines to a large degree whether students will engage in new learning at some time in the future. At least two factors are important to consider in understanding the continuing motivation to learn. These are (1) whether students' expectations about learning and its consequences have been met, and (2) to what students attribute their failures and successes in learning.

Satisfaction of Expectancies

Imagine that you have just accomplished a challenging goal that you set for yourself. It was a struggle at times, but you remained confident that you would eventually succeed, and so you persisted (this describes me and my windsurfing experience). Now that you have done it, how do you feel? For me, there was an immediate sense of euphoria (I guess I had entertained some doubts that I would not succeed), followed by a feeling of satisfaction and the thought, "I knew I could do it!"

Chances are your reactions were not unlike mine. When learners succeed at a task, two expectations have typically been met. There is the satisfaction of the outcome expectation. That is, I expected that the outcome of my efforts to learn windsurfing would be mastery of the skills involved. Or, similarly, a student may have expected her efforts to result in a course grade of A; when that occurs, her expectation is satisfied.

There is also, however, the satisfaction of efficacy expectations. Recall that a source of information about self-efficacy is one's previous success at the task. Thus, once success is attained, self-efficacy is increased. Having succeeded once in sailing the windsurfer from one end of the bay to the other without falling down, I am more confident in being successful a second time. Moreover, my self-efficacy for learning, in general, has also been increased.

One of the most rewarding (and subsequently, motivating) results of learning is to use the newly acquired skills or knowledge. Keller (1983, 1987a) referred to this as the natural consequences of learning. Natural consequences occur most often when students see the relevance in what they are learning and have the opportunity to apply newly acquired information. Natural consequences are likely, for example, in Scenario 9–1, where Sean is learning skills that are immediately useful to him in his job. In the case of Laone, however, natural consequences may be harder to identify. It is often a challenge for teachers to find some way that students can apply their new knowledge meaningfully. One suggestion for Laone's

English teacher is to allow her to relate her English assignments to farming, which is clearly relevant and interesting to her.

In the event that new knowledge is not immediately useful, outcome expectations may still be satisfied through what Keller (1983, 1987a) called positive consequences. Despite Dweck's concern that extrinsic reinforcement may fail to influence (or may even undermine [Deci, 1975]) intrinsic motivation, there are situations when it is appropriate. It might be useful first, however, to consider when extrinsic rewards are not appropriate for stimulating motivation.

Providing rewards only for participation in an activity has generally led to decreased interest in that activity (Bates, 1979). This is especially true when the activity is itself entertaining or stimulating. So, for example, it would probably be unwise to reward learners for engaging in some task that already interests them. Bates (1979) also concluded that providing rewards may adversely affect motivation when the rewards are not normally regarded as intrinsic to task performance. For example, earning extra wages for more work is salient to tasks performed on an assembly line and therefore might contribute to enhanced motivation. But earning tokens for completed school tasks is not especially intrinsic to performance and may have an effect opposite to that intended.

Positive consequences can be especially useful, on the other hand, when learning tasks are inherently boring or their relevance is not perceived by the learner. Learning to spell might be a good example of this case. Many students find spelling assignments to be sheer drudgery; moreover, they often fail to understand why they should learn to spell in the first place (remember the comment about word processing spell-checkers). In this case, students may find no particular satisfaction in spelling words correctly, but may be satisfied by the attainment of some reward attached to spelling achievement. A fifth grade teacher of my acquaintance gives surprise prizes to students when they achieve certain spelling goals. Although this practice might not interest them in spelling over the long term, it does keep them on task with their spelling assignments by temporarily raising their interest in the subject (cf. Calder & Staw, 1975).

Keller (1987a) also pointed out that "even when people are intrinsically motivated to learn the material, there are likely to be benefits from extrinsic forms of recognition. For example, public acknowledgment of achievement, privileges, student presentations of products, and enthusiastically positive comments are welcome" (p. 6).

In summary, continuing motivation to learn is facilitated through the satisfaction of expectancies in the current learning episode. When learners succeed at a learning goal, their self-efficacy increases and they experience the natural consequences of learning success. Where natural consequences are less likely to occur, positive consequences can serve in some situations to satisfy an outcome expectation.

Attribution Theory

Consider, for a moment, what you think when turning in a test paper on which you know you performed poorly. Do you think, "I didn't study the right things," or "I'm just not feeling up to par today," or "I'm not a good student anyway," or "It's my roommate's fault; he (she) kept me out late so I couldn't study." All of these statements reflect ways in which learners attempt to understand their own performances. Whereas those above pertained to an experience of failure, learners make similar judgments about their successes. For example, "I studied really hard"; "Today is just my lucky day"; "The teacher likes me"; "I'm generally a good student"; "That was an easy test." These attributions about learning and performance constitute an important influence on continuing motivation to learn (Weiner, 1979).

"The central assumption of attribution theory . . . is that the search for understanding is the (or a) basic 'spring of action'" (Weiner, 1979, p. 3). In other words, people attempt to understand the causes for their successes and failures, and their attributions about these causes determine their future actions. Weiner (1985, 1986) postulated three dimensions within which most causal attributions can be categorized. These are: internal versus external, stable versus unstable, and controllable versus uncontrollable.

Internal causes of success or failure are those factors within the person, such as ability, effort, and mood. External causes are those outside the learner, such as task difficulty, the attitude of the teacher, help from other people, and so on. The stability dimension refers to how changeable a factor is over time. Ability tends to be stable, whereas mood or luck is unstable. Finally, controllability refers to the degree to which the individual has control over the causes of success or failure. You alone determine how much time you spend studying for a test, since you can set aside sufficient time and then refuse to be distracted from your appointed task. Whether you suddenly contract a stomach virus on the day of the test is beyond your control.

It should be obvious from the examples given above that most factors fit along a continuum in each of the three dimensions. Ability, for instance, is internal, relatively stable, and controllable only over the long term (high achievement in a subject leads to potential for further achievement in the same subject). Help from another student, on the other hand, is external, unstable, and uncontrollable by the student experiencing learning difficulties. According to Weiner (1979, 1985, 1986), each of these dimensions presents implications for continuing motivation.

Consider the factor of ability, for example. Students tend to perceive this internal factor as uncontrollable. Those who attribute their failure to low ability, then, come to believe that "there is no response in [their] repertoire to alter the course of failure" (Graham & Barker, 1990, p. 7). As a result, a vicious cycle is instigated. Students believe they have failed because they are stupid. Since they are stupid, there is no point in trying hard or studying smarter the next time. Because they are not motivated to apply themselves on the next task, they fail again. And so it goes.

If, on the other hand, students attribute their failures to unstable or controllable causes, they are more likely to believe that they will succeed in the future. Doing poorly this time because of illness or not studying means that doing well next time is still possible. Motivation to succeed next time is likely to be enhanced when students perceive that they have the means within their control to assure goal achievement. Weiner argued, therefore, that instructors should use teaching strategies that help learners to see how learning is a function of their own efforts and effective learning strategies and not a function of low ability.

For most students, failing once is not much cause for concern. Failing repeatedly, however, causes even the most stalwart student to question his or her ability (e.g., Kelley & Michela, 1980). Moreover, indirect cues prompt failure-prone learners to ascribe their failure to low ability (Graham & Barker, 1990). " For example, it has been documented that such seemingly positive teachers' behaviors as praise for success at easy tasks, the absence of blame for failure at such tasks, and affective displays of sympathy or compassion can communicate to the recipients of this feedback that they are low in ability" (Graham & Barker, 1990, p. 7; cf. Barker & Graham, 1987; Graham, 1984).

Graham and Barker (1990) went on to investigate the possibility that the offering of help might be perceived as a low-ability cue. They based their investigation on the observation that help is more likely to be offered when the need for help is perceived to be caused by uncontrollable factors. The following example is illustrative. Joan wants to borrow Mary's class notes to see what she missed when she had to leave school to go to a doctor's appointment (an uncontrollable factor). Tony wants to borrow Mary's notes, too, but he missed class because he skipped school to go to the beach (a controllable factor). Which student, Tony or Joan, would you be more likely to lend your notes to?

When help is offered by the teacher or a peer to less able students, these students are likely to infer from the offer of help that they have low ability. In testing this hypothesis, Graham and Barker (1990) demonstrated that "the targets of unsolicited help are perceived by children as less able students who are less likely than their nonhelped peers to do well in the future and to be desirable work mates" (p. 13). They concluded that some well-intentioned instructional practices (e.g., giving help) can have unexpected negative consequences for perceptions of ability.

What can we conclude, then, regarding the effect of attributions on continuing motivation? For one thing, helping learners to attribute their successes and failures to effort and effective (or ineffective) learning strategies is a procedure likely to facilitate motivation. For learners with a history of failures, however, teachers should be especially alert to cues that might further erode individuals' opinions of their abilities.

To this point, continuing motivation has been discussed in terms of person variables. That is, whether individuals choose to go on in a subject is thought to depend largely on their previous successes and their attributions of success or failure. But learning also takes place in a social context, and this context exerts an influence on motivation that interacts with individual characteristics. Before integrating findings into a model of motivational design, then, let us take a brief look at the role of the social milieu in motivation.

The Social Context of Motivation

"School motivation cannot be divorced from the social fabric in which it is embedded" (Weiner, 1990, p. 621). It "must be considered within the context of social values and the goals of the superordinate culture" (Weiner, 1990, p. 621). What could be meant by these statements?

At the beginning of this chapter, motivation was said to be a work-related rather than play-related concept. In other words, a student practicing his free throws is considered to be unmotivated if he is supposed to be writing a term paper. The same individual, on the other hand, would be considered highly motivated if he is a professional basketball player. Thus, the larger structure of society and the goals associated with particular sub-segments of it have a hand in determining what is or is not motivated behavior.

Motivation is also developed in relation to the values of others. When rats, for example, "do not strive to get food, the other rats are not necessarily unhappy about this and Darwinian principles are likely to prevail" (Weiner, 1990, p. 621). But learning, unlike food, is not a commodity that must be divided. Rather, it might be facilitated by cooperation among learners. This is an implicit assumption of the current trend in education toward cooperative (or collaborative) learning strategies.

Cooperative Learning and Motivation

Johnson and Johnson (1975, 1978, 1979) discovered that students' motivation was greatly influenced by the manner in which they interacted in the achievement of a goal. It is a common tactic, for example, for teachers to group students as they work on some learning task. But the way in which these groups are structured and the way students work with one another to meet the requirements of the task affect individual motivation.

In their investigations, the Johnson brothers defined three types of goal structures that lead to different interpersonal relations among students. Under a cooperative goal structure, learners are motivated to work together, because cooperation is perceived to be the only way for them to attain the goal. This situation is apparent when the learning task is complex and lengthy, and students in the group have unique skills to contribute. Under a competitive goal structure, students are motivated not only to work independently but also to hoard resources and information. They perceive that their own goal attainment depends on others not reaching the goal. For example, students competing for a small number of awards or a few places in a special program are likely to exhibit this behavior. Finally, an individualistic goal structure is one in which students are motivated to work independently, but not competitively, because they perceive goal attainment to be directly related to their own actions and independent of what others do (Johnson & Johnson, 1975, 1978, 1979).

Johnson and Johnson (1975) argued that cooperation is the appropriate goal structure for most learning tasks in school. From the research they reviewed and conducted, they concluded that cooperative learning can lead to both higher achievement and greater motivation to learn. In a recent study, for example, Johnson, Johnson, and Stanne (1985) compared the performance and attitudes of eighth graders under cooperative, competitive, and individualistic goal structures in computer-assisted instruction. They found that the cooperating students completed more daily worksheet items, correctly answered more factual items, and solved more application problems than their counterparts in the competitive and individualistic conditions. Moreover, "cooperation also promoted greater motivation to persist in striving to accomplish learning goals than did competitive and individualistic efforts" (Johnson et al., 1985, p. 675).

Not all studies on cooperative learning have produced such positive findings, particularly where achievement is concerned (Slavin, 1983). Some cooperative teams fail or function much less effectively than other teams (Salomon & Globerson, 1989). One possible reason for this is that students do not always know how to work effectively with one another in a cooperative setting. For example, one team member might, for status reasons, attempt to tell everyone else what to do, whereas another may be content to loaf and freeload off the efforts of his or her teammates (Salomon & Globerson, 1989). Teachers can prepare students for cooperative learning by introducing new norms into the classroom and role-playing these norms through games and exercises (Cohen, 1986). One example of an exercise to teach learners how to be responsive to their group's needs is Broken Circles.

In this activity, "a puzzle cannot be satisfactorily solved unless group members become aware of problems being experienced by others and are willing to give away their pieces of the puzzle in order to attain the group goal" (Cohen, 1986, p. 37).

Webb (1982, 1984) has also been particularly concerned with the interaction patterns among students that are facilitated by cooperative goal structures. She contended that certain interactions (e.g., giving help, receiving help, verbalizing concepts) are what lead to increased performance and motivation, not the cooperative goal structure per se. In a recent review of research on cooperative learning, Webb (1989) found that students who explain or elaborate on concepts during problem-solving learned more than those who either requested help or gave correct answers to other students.

Webb also found that conditions within the cooperative setting can contribute to these interactions. For example, "rewarding students for the achievement of all group members consistently promoted helping behavior" (Webb, 1982, p. 438). And according to Slavin (1978, 1984), because of the group reward structure, group members increase their own individual efforts in order to support each others' efforts.

Although there is still much to be understood about how cooperative learning operates, it appears that cooperative goal structures can establish a social milieu which facilitates motivation. They seem to work best when students must depend on each other to reach a desired goal, when there are rewards for group (rather than individual) performance, and when students know how to work together effectively.

Teacher Efficacy

The final social variable to be examined for its effect on students' continuing motivation concerns the teacher. Obviously, the social environment of the classroom includes the teacher or trainer. And a recent focus of motivation research has been the efficacy felt by teachers regarding their ability to motivate students. Just as students' self-efficacy can affect their motivation to initiate and persist in learning tasks, so can teachers' efficacy determine whether they will employ effective procedures for motivating students.

Ashton and Webb (1986) defined **teaching efficacy** as *the teacher's judgment about the potential influence of teaching on a child's learning*. In other words, low teaching efficacy would be reflected in statements such as, "When it comes right down to it, a teacher can't really do much because most of a student's motivation and performance depends on his/her home environment" (Woolfolk & Hoy, 1990, p. 83). **Personal teaching efficacy** refers to *the teacher's judgment of his or her own ability to motivate students* (Ashton & Webb, 1986). In other words, it is quite possible that teachers might believe, in general, that teaching has potentially powerful effects on student motivation, but lack confidence that they, themselves, can affect their own students' motivation.

Teachers with high personal efficacy tend to encourage student auton-omy and responsibility, structure challenging learning tasks, and help learners succeed on those tasks (Ashton & Webb, 1986). These actions should both promote motivation in students and substantiate the personal efficacy of the teacher. In contrast, teachers with low personal efficacy tend to retain an authoritarian form of control in their classrooms, use punitive management strategies, and avoid planning instruction that might exceed their own capabilities. As a result, they are less likely than high efficacy teachers to help students or find other ways for students to learn who are having difficulty (Ashton & Webb, 1986).

Thus far, the research on teaching efficacy has been confined to obser-vations of teachers' beliefs, with little actual observation of their teaching performance. For the moment, then, we must accept the findings described above as tentative. However, more "motivational research among teachers will contribute to our understanding of how efficacy can affect different aspects of teaching (e.g., planning and evaluating), as well as student out-comes" (Schunk, 1990, p. 5).

Summary

We have seen in this section the influence of context and consequences on students' continuing motivation to learn. Motivation appears to be enhanced when learners' expectancies are satisfied, when they attribute their successes to their own efforts and effective learning strategies, and when the social climate fosters interaction and cooperation among students. With these findings, taken together with those described in the first section, we are ready to consider an integrated model of motivational design. This attempts to answer the question, How can a teacher or instructional designer incorporate into instruction the appropriate motivational condi-tions for all learners?

A MODEL OF MOTIVATIONAL DESIGN

For the last 10 or so years, John M. Keller has been developing and testing an integrated model for understanding motivation and for systematically incorporating motivational concerns into instruction. He combines the vari-ety of inputs to motivation that have already been discussed and suggests strategies for instruction that they imply. As you can see from Figure 9–2, Keller (1983, 1984) assumes that students' motives (or values), together with their expectancies (efficacy and outcome expectations), will influence the

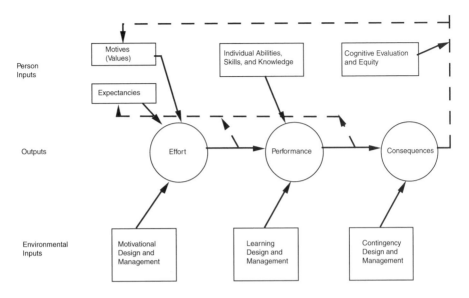

**FIGURE   9–2   A Model of Motivation, Performance, and
Instructional Influence**

From Keller, J. M. A model of motivational design. In *Instructional-design theories and models.*
Edited by C. M. Reigeluth, 1983, Hillsdale, NJ: Lawrence Erlbaum Associates. Copyright 1983
by Laurence Erlbaum Associates. Reprinted by permission.

degree of attention and effort they will supply to a learning task. Although
effort then contributes to performance, so, obviously, do the individual's
current abilities, skills and knowledge. Finally, both the consequences of
achievement (or the failure to achieve) and the learner's attributions
(cognitive evaluation) concerning his or her performance influence motivation in future learning episodes.

In considering the instructional implications of this model, Keller (1983)
proposed four conditions for motivation that must be met to have a
motivated learner. These correspond to each of the four letters in the
acronym, ARCS (Keller, 1984):

A—attention
R—relevance
C—confidence
S—satisfaction

As these are described further in the following section, you will see how
they integrate and build upon the sources of motivation discussed earlier in
the chapter. Then, armed with a repertoire of these strategies, teachers and

instructional designers may use the systematic process described by Keller (1987b) to effectively meet the motivational needs of their learners.

Strategies for Stimulating Motivation

Keller (1987a) appears to view the task of motivating learners as a sequential process. One must first gain the attention of learners and engage them in the learning activity before anything else can take place (*A*). Once involved, however, learners are known to ask the age-old question: "Why must I learn this?" Before instruction can proceed in an optimal way, then, students must believe that it is related to their personal goals and will meet their specific needs (R). Even with attentive learners who see personal relevance in the learning task, motivation can still flag as the activity wears on. Some, like Sean in Scenario 9–1, may have fears about the subject that impede their learning it effectively. This is a problem of confidence (*C*). Others, despite their best efforts, may find their attention wandering if the pace and method of instruction never change (a problem of sustaining *A*). "Finally," Keller wrote, "comes the payoff. Or does it?" (1987a, p. 2). As we have seen earlier in the chapter, learning must result in a sense of satisfaction for students to have a continuing desire to learn (*S*).

What are ways, then, that teachers, trainers or instructional designers can bring about the conditions necessary for motivation? Let's examine Keller's recommendations in each category.

Gaining and Sustaining Attention
Curiosity has already been described as a strong source of motivation, but one that can be fleeting. To make the most of curiosity caused by stimulus changes, teachers can capture students' interest by using novel or unexpected approaches to instruction or injecting personal experiences and humor. Keller himself, for example, often opens a presentation with a funny story that relates in some way to the topic of his talk. Other examples include beginning a class on American literature with a dramatic reading from a book under study, showing visual tricks in a class studying perception, or including a startling picture in the pages of a textbook.

To stimulate more lasting curiosity, or what Keller (1987a) called an attitude of inquiry, instructors should employ techniques that invoke a sense of mystery and involve students in solving problems. The CTGV instructional video series mentioned earlier in the chapter offers a good example. The instructional goal of one series specifically concerns mathematical problem solving, but it is embedded in the context of a story about a kid named Jasper Woodbury. In one episode, Jasper plans a trip downriver to buy a boat and must contend with problems like the tide of the river, inclement weather, not enough gas, and so on. As students learn to solve these problems, they become able to solve analogous ones, such as how long would it take Jasper to reach his intended destination if he could only travel 15 mph, instead of 25 mph? Curiosity in the problem solving process is maintained, however, by the narrative character of the instruction. Not only are students interested in what will happen to Jasper next, they can create their own Jasper adventures (CTGV, 1990, 1991a, 1991b).

Finally, Keller (1983, 1987a) recommended that instructors maintain students' attention by varying the instructional presentation. No matter how interested someone is in the topic of a lecture, movie, demonstration, or audio presentation, that interest will wane in the face of unending sameness. Despite my best efforts and intrinsic interest in many nature specials on television, for example, I find myself nodding off after 15 or 20 minutes of listening to the narrator's well-modulated drone. Similarly, many students will lose interest or find their attention wandering when the instruction is always the same and therefore highly predictable. As a change of pace, lecturers might consider presenting some of their material via some form of media, or alternating lecture with demonstrations, small group discussions, or whole class debates. Likewise, printed text can be varied through different type sizes or fonts or the inclusion of diagrams or pictures. Soundtracks can be made more interesting by the use of two or more narrators and by a variation in format (conversation or interview as opposed to narration).

Enhancing Relevance

"Relevance, in its most general sense, refers to those things which we perceive as instrumental in meeting needs and satisfying personal desires, including the accomplishment of personal goals" (Keller, 1987a, p. 3). What Keller seems to describe with this statement are two aspects of the relevance problem, one which is ends-oriented and one which is means-oriented. To be motivated, learners must first recognize that given instruction has personal utility, i.e., will help them achieve personal goals (or ends). Instructors can assist in this recognition by providing statements of utility along with the goals of instruction, or helping learners to define their own goals and statements of utility. The latter strategy works particularly well in advanced topics with learners who have elected to study those topics. In an advanced research seminar I taught recently, for example, I asked students to determine their own goals and means of assessing progress toward goal attainment. The goals they pursued and the amount of work they completed generally exceeded the expectations I would have set for them.

A particular challenge for teachers arises in situations like the one described in Scenario 9–2, where a student fails to find relevance in a required subject with prescribed instructional goals. Sometimes, motivating these students amounts to persuasion, often with assurances that the students will eventually see the relevance of what they are learning. In the interim, Keller suggests that means-oriented strategies may be useful.

Described earlier in the chapter were the concepts of need for achievement and need for affiliation. In terms of motivation, these needs have less to do with what is taught than how something is taught. Therefore, teachers can help to motivate students by providing opportunities for matching their motives and values. These may include, for example, providing leadership opportunities, occasions for self-study or working in cooperative groups, or allowing friendly competition on individual or group projects. Finding ways to actively engage students in learning can be an effective means of motivating them, irrespective of whether they yet see the relevance of the learning activities.

Finally, Keller includes familiarity as a component of relevance. As he put it, "People enjoy more about things they already believe in or are more interested in" (Keller, 1987a, p. 4). Therefore, to the extent possible, instructors should relate instruction to their learners' experiences by providing concrete examples and analogies. The more familiar something is, the more likely it is to be perceived as relevant to the learner. This recommendation should itself seem familiar. If you recall, the cognitive theories of learning (see chapters 3 to 5) strongly emphasized the importance of a familiar and meaningful context for learning something new. It seems likely, then, that the facilitative effect of context on learning has both cognitive and affective (motivational) components.

Building Confidence

The research on self-efficacy that was reviewed earlier in the chapter established the importance of learners' confidence in their willingness to engage in learning. The question to be addressed here, then, is how to instill confidence in learners who believe they are unable to do, or fear they will fail if they attempt, a given learning task. Keller (1987a) suggested three strategies. First, instructors can create a positive expectation for success by making it clear just what is expected of students. Sometimes, fear of failure is simply fear of the unknown. Because students can be overwhelmed by a detailed discussion of performance requirements and evaluative criteria, Keller recommends progressive disclosure, or telling students what is expected of them as they are ready and able to understand the requirements. In addition, students can be shown how complex, seemingly unreachable goals are made more manageable by their being broken down into subgoals and small steps.

As we have seen from self-efficacy theory, students gain confidence in their own abilities when they actually experience success at challenging tasks. Therefore, a second strategy for building confidence is to provide success opportunities for students. This does not mean that students should never experience failure. Quite the contrary—failure experiences can be constructive, as long as (1) there is a good match between the challenge of the task and the learner's capabilities, (2) the learner's performance is self-initiated, and (3) the learner attributes failure to the poor use of strategies inherent to learning (Clifford, 1984).

Learners are also likely to gain confidence when they are given just enough assistance to perform a task that they are not quite capable of achieving on their own. If you recall from chapter 7, Vygotsky proposed the "zone of proximal development" as that realm between what learners can achieve on their own and what they can achieve given assistance. Any learning task in this zone will be a challenge, but not an insurmountable one. Moreover, the teacher's goal concerning such tasks should be to gradually reduce his or her assistance until the learner is capable of independently performing the task.

Finally, consistent with attribution theory, instructors can build confidence by providing learners with a reasonable degree of control over their own learning and helping learners to recognize that learning is a direct consequence of their own efforts and effective learning strategies. Both Keller (1987a) and Clifford (1984) pointed to the importance of detailed, unambiguous feedback to students to maintain a task orientation and prompt appropriate attributions. A single score on a project or essay assignment, for example, provides little information to the student. The student, in turn, is likely to react with increased anxiety because no way has been provided to learn from his or her mistakes. A better approach would be for the instructor to conduct separate analyses and assign multiple scores for different aspects of the project or essay (e.g., organization, theme, use of resources, grammar, etc.). In this way, students can gain confidence from what they have done well and attribute poor performance to specific problems that can be corrected.

Generating Satisfaction

Keller (1987a) again suggested three categories of strategies for generating learning satisfaction, which correspond with natural consequences, positive consequences, and equity.

Opportunities to use newly acquired skills or knowledge in meaningful ways allow for the natural consequences of learning. So, for example, an arithmetic teacher might suggest to students that they calculate their school team's statistics as a means of practicing newly acquired arithmetic skills. Or, an engineering instructor might provide students with the design specifications called for in a completed contract, and then have students compare their designs to what was actually used. Simulations of all kinds work well to furnish appropriate learning environments within which students can tackle real world problems.

As indicated earlier in the chapter, not all skills or knowledge readily lend themselves to immediate application. Sometimes, component skills or bits of knowledge must accumulate over a long period before they become useful. Alternatively, some students may have no particular interest in the subject but are enrolled to meet some external requirement. In these situations, the use of positive consequences, such as verbal praise, incentives, or real or symbolic awards, may be effective in generating satisfaction. At the conclusion of a training workshop, for example, the sponsoring agency might award participants with certificates of achievement.

"A final and important point," wrote Keller (1987a), "is that people do not look at rewards in isolation" (p. 6). Rather, they tend to make comparisons between themselves and other people going through the learning experience with them. Satisfaction with a particular achievement might be dimmed by the observation that everyone else performed just as well or better. I can remember the first footrace I entered after having taken up running. It was eminently satisfying to actually finish the race, but even more so to finish in the middle of the pack and not last, which I had feared would happen.

Ways to handle equity, according to Keller, include making sure that learning outcomes are consistent with the expectations established at the outset of learning and maintaining consistent standards and consequences for task achievement. To revisit the running example, a colleague of mine did, in fact, finish last in his first footrace. But he derived great satisfaction from this accomplishment anyway because his only goal (and expectation) concerned running the race from start to finish at his own pace. Obviously, maintaining consistent standards throughout a course or training experience is essential for learners to feel that they have been fairly and equitably treated.

Summary

Table 9–1 presents a summary of the components of motivation, as proposed by Keller, along with strategies within each component that can contribute to the process of motivating learners. A recent study of first, year elementary teachers provides some initial data on which of these strategies teachers tend to use in the classroom and the degree to which the strategies related to on- and off-task behavior of students. Newby (1991) observed 30 teachers over a 4-month period who were responsible for a combined total of 770 students. He found that teachers used strategies in all four categories of ARCS, but those pertaining to relevance bore the strongest positive relationship to on-task behavior. In other words, "those classrooms in which there was a higher incidence of giving reasons for the importance of the task or in which students were encouraged to relate the task to their

TABLE   9–1   Instructional Strategies for Stimulating Motivation as Suggested by the ARCS Model

Component of Motivation	Corresponding Strategies
Gaining and sustaining attention	Capture students' attention by using novel or unexpected approaches to instruction
	Stimulate lasting curiosity with problems that invoke mystery
	Maintain students' attention by varying the instructional presentation
Enhancing relevance	Increase the perception of utility by stating (or having learners determine) how instruction relates to personal goals
	Provide opportunities for matching learners' motives and values with occasions for self-study, leadership, and cooperation
	Increase familiarity by building on learners' previous experiences
Building confidence	Create a positive expectation for success by making clear instructional goals and objectives
	Provide opportunities for students to successfully attain challenging goals
	Provide learners with a reasonable degree of control over their own learning
Generating satisfaction	Create natural consequences by providing learners with opportunities to use newly acquired skills
	In the absence of natural consequences, use positive consequences, such as verbal praise, real or symbolic awards
	Ensure equity by maintaining consistent standards and matching outcomes to expectations

personal experiences showed a higher rate of on-task behavior (Newby, 1991, p. 199).

Newby also discovered, however, that satisfaction strategies having to do with rewards and punishments produced a negative correlation with on-task behavior. That is, "students in classrooms in which higher levels of satisfaction strategies, either rewards or punishments, were delivered were observed to have lower levels of on-task behaviors" (Newby, 1991, p. 199). This suggests, perhaps, that such strategies should be used sparingly and only when there are no opportunities to provide for natural consequences of learning.

How particular motivational strategies might be most effectively selected and implemented is discussed in the next section of the chapter.

The Process of Motivational Design

Think back for a moment to the scenarios with which this chapter began. Suppose Sean asked whatever questions would help clarify his confusions, and Laone turned in English assignments on time and well done. Would they be a focus of attention in this chapter? Of course not. Only when there is evidence that motivation is a problem do we become concerned about how to solve it—how to motivate learners. The same holds true when it is suspected that motivation will be a problem, i.e., when learners, for whatever reasons, are expected to be uninterested, fearful, or generally disinclined to learn. The motivational design process, therefore, begins with consideration of learner characteristics, or what Keller (1987b) calls audience analysis.

Step 1: Analyze the Audience

Who are your learners? How likely are they to be interested and ready to learn what you wish to teach? Before you can decide how to go about motivating learners, you must have some idea as to what motivational problems you are likely to face. Keller (1987b) recommended developing an audience profile using the ARCS model in order to identify any gaps in motivation. He noted as well that overmotivation can be as much a problem as undermotivation. For example, a person who claims to know it all already (i.e., is overconfident) is likely to pay little attention in class and make more mistakes as a consequence. Such a person might also prove to be a disruptive influence, diverting other students from assigned tasks.

An audience profile also helps you to determine when motivation is not a likely problem. Where learners are already motivated, it is neither necessary nor desirable to add motivational strategies to the instruction. Imagine your irritation when an instructor spends significant time telling you how valuable the course is and you already know just what you want out of it. Similarly, mediated materials (such as computer software) in which "bells and whistles" are used for motivational purposes may only annoy their users, who want to "get on with it."

Conducting an audience analysis, then, requires rating the attitudes of audience members in each of the categories of ARCS. In many cases, this will involve a "best guess" estimate based on past experience with similar learners. In some cases, however, Keller (1987a) suggested that it may be advisable to conduct interviews with members of the target population.

This might be true, for example, in a situation where one has no knowledge whatever of the learners on which to base an estimate.

In order to acquire a sense of the audience analysis process, consider the following hypothetical cases.

CASEN1

A course in education is required of all persons seeking teacher certification in the state. Most of the students are upper division (junior, senior) and majoring in one of the teacher education areas of concentration. A few students come from disciplines outside education, and a few have already taken and failed the teacher certification test.

Hypothetical Analysis

Attention	Initially low. Education courses have a reputation for being low-level and boring. Also, since the course is required, students are likely to be there because they have to be, not because they want to be.
Relevance	Moderate to high. The goal of the course is to teach skills assessed by the teacher test. Therefore, most students will see the relevance of this course for meeting their certification goals.
Confidence	Variable. The education students will view this course as similar to others in which they have already been successful. They will therefore be quite confident in their ability to do well. Students from other disciplines, or students who have already failed the teacher examination, are likely to have genuine concerns about their ability to learn the skills necessary to pass the certification examination.
Satisfaction Potential	Moderate to high. As long as students find something useful in this course, something that enables them to be effective teachers and makes it likely they will pass the teacher test, they will feel satisfied.

CASE   2

A literacy course is offered to farmers in an underdeveloped nation. The course is offered in the evening and populated by both men and women from the ages of 15 to 61. None of the students knows how to read.

Hypothetical Analysis

Attention	Variable. Because this is a volunteer audience, the fact that they have come at all indicates some level of attentiveness. However, since they are coming from work and are undoubtedly tired, they will require changes of pace and participatory activities to keep them attentive.
Relevance	Initially low. Participants are unlikely to view literacy as something meaningful to their lives, especially the older ones who have survived without knowing how to read.
Confidence	Initially low and probably variable. Most of the participants have probably had little, if any, formal schooling. Thus, they will be uncertain about their ability to learn to read.
Satisfaction Potential	Positive. If participants can be shown that literacy is a means for them to take control of their lives, then they will feel the effort of learning to read is worthwhile.

It should be obvious that both analyses rely upon assumptions made about the learners in each case. If different assumptions are made, or if other characteristics are known about the learners, then the resulting analyses are likely to be different as well. You may find it useful to imagine what sorts of learners would yield high or low ratings in each of the ARCS categories. For example, in what situations might learners have an especially low Satisfaction Potential but adequate ratings in the other three categories? When might they have low Confidence but high ratings in other categories? And so on.

Step 2: Define Motivational Objectives
From the audience profile, a teacher or instructional designer can determine what motivational needs exist and therefore what motivational objectives should be set. In both hypothetical cases, for example, learner attention and confidence are at levels below optimum. These are areas, then, which can be targeted for motivational design. Objectives need not be written, however, for satisfaction, since this showed high potential in both cases.

Like other types of instructional goals, motivational objectives should be written from the learner's perspective. That is, what change in learner performance or attitude is to be expected from achievement of this goal?

So, for example, an objective for confidence that might be written for Case 2 is:

Participants will indicate greater confidence in their ability to read by trying the read-aloud activities in class.

Or, an objective for attention that might be generated for Case 1 is:

Students will indicate a higher degree of attention in class by participating in large group discussion and debate.

As you can see from these examples, the attainment of many motivational objectives can be assessed by direct observation. Most instructors, in fact, can sense whether particular motivational strategies have had the desired effect by the interactions they have with students in class. In some situations, though, self-report measures may be useful for determining whether motivational objectives have been met (Keller, 1987b). For example, participants in a technical training workshop might be asked if their confidence in applying these skills has been increased, or if they found the workshop worthwhile.

Step 3: Design a Motivational Strategy
In this step, specific motivational strategies are selected and integrated into instruction. Keller's ARCS categories serve as an obvious guide to this step, because there are strategies associated with each of the four motivational components of the model. However, these strategies are rather general in nature and must be tailored to the characteristics of the target learners and the subject matter being taught. Under attention, for example, a strategy used to stimulate an attitude of inquiry would be quite different for college students in an education course than for adult learners in a literacy class. Likewise, what tasks might be considered challenging would be quite different in the two cases.

Keller (1987a) recommended brainstorming many different ideas for accomplishing motivational objectives and then selecting those that might best fit the students, the style of the instructor, and the content and format of the instruction. Other factors, such as time and available resources, must also be considered.

Step 4: Try Out and Revise as Necessary
The final step of the motivational design process calls for the teacher or instructional designer to try out the strategies selected in the previous step. This might occur in a field trial of the instruction prior to its actual implementation, as in the formative evaluation of a course, workshop, or set of

TABLE 9–2   Keller's Motivational Design Process

Step 1: Analyze the audience and develop a motivational profile based on ARCS.

> **Example**: A—initially low
> R—moderate to high
> C—variable
> S—moderate to high

Step 2: Define motivational objectives based on the audience profile.

> **Example**: 1. Students will indicate a higher degree
> of attention in class by participating in
> group discussion and debate (**A**).
> 2. Students will exhibit greater confidence
> by setting and pursuing their own goals
> for an application project (**C**).

Step 3: Design a motivational strategy and integrate it into instruction.

> **Example**: 1. Plan debates and discussions to be
> interspersed with lecture. Select
> media to accompany lecture (**A**).
> 2. Set up the structure for a self-study
> project (**C**).

Step 4: Try out and revise the strategy as necessary.

> **Example**: Not enough direction given for the
> self-study project. Students still anxious,
> lack confidence in ability to complete it
> on time. Therefore, provide more
> direction by breaking the project into
> more manageable subparts.

instructional materials. More likely, however, it occurs in the natural implementation of the instruction, as when a teacher meets her class and begins the school term. What is important about this step is that motivation should be thought about separately from other aspects of instruction (Keller, 1987b). The instructor should attempt to be sensitive to what effects the motivational strategies are having, whether desired or undesired. Then, if the strategies are failing to produce intended results, they can be revised or replaced.

In some cases, revision of the motivational design is also warranted because the audience profile is faulty. In hypothetical Case 2, for example, the participants may already be aware of the important role literacy can play in their lives. If that is so, then a comment or two to confirm the relevance of the material can replace exercises or activities designed to establish relevance. Similarly, different instructional methods might be selected, or a different sequence of activities designed, for students who are found to be attentive, when low attention and interest were expected.

Summary
Table 9–2 displays a summary of the steps in the motivational design process which, together with the strategies summarized in Table 9–1, provide teachers and other designers of instruction with an effective means for enhancing motivation. Keller (1987b) also reminded us, however, to draw upon personal experiences while using his model. "After all, we have been consumers of instruction for more years of our lives than we care to remember. We have seen many examples, and nonexamples, of motivating instruction. This personal knowledge combined with some formal knowledge of motivation and a systematic process for motivational design can be powerful tools in improving the motivational appeal of instruction" (p. 7).

SUGGESTED READINGS

Bandura, A. (1986). *Social foundations of thought and action: A social cognitive theory*. Englewood Cliffs, NJ: Prentice-Hall.

Cohen, E. G. (1986). *Designing group work*. New York: Teachers College Press.

Keller, J. M. (1987a, Octoter). Strategies for stimulating the motivation to learn. *Performance and Instruction Journal*, 1–7.

Keller, J. M. (1987b, November/ December). The systematic process of motivational design. *Performance and Instruction Journal*, 1–8.

Weiner, B. (1985). *An attributional theory of motivation and emotion*. New York: Springer-Verlag.

REFLECTIVE QUESTIONS AND ACTIVITIES

1. Consider what assumptions about knowledge and knowing may underlie the conceptions of learner motivation that are discussed in this chapter. With what epistemological tradition do they seem to be most closely associated? What evidence supports your choice?

2. At the conclusion of several other chapters (i.e., chapters 2, 3, 5, and 8), you generated plans for facilitating learning of some difficult goal, involving yourself or other learners. Reflect back on those situations from the perspective of motivation. How much of the learning difficulty might be attributable to a lack of motivation, as opposed to lack of prerequisite skill or poor instruction? How might you now add a motivational design to your instructional plan?

3. Review your answer to Question 5 of chapter 6, in which you discussed instructional strategies suitable for adults versus children. Add a motivational component to your instruction. What would be important to consider in motivating children versus adults?

4. Select a scenario from any previous chapter. Using the ARCS model, analyze the situation for its probable motivational characteristics. Determine a set of motivational objectives, and then suggest strategies you think would be effective for stimulating motivation. Provide a rationale for each of your decisions.

5. Describe a learning situation in which you expect to find learners with low self-efficacy. First, how would you determine that they in fact have low self-efficacy? What behaviors and attitudes would you expect these learners to exhibit? Then, generate an instructional plan that would help learners become more efficacious.

► Part VII

Learning and
Instruction

▶ 10

Gagné's Theory of Instruction

Consider the following scenarios.

Scenario 10–1

At the University of Anywhere Medical School, instructors routinely face the problem of biomedical misconceptions among students. That is, medical students, despite exposure to appropriate information, continue to make diagnostic errors in many of the clinical cases that they study. Instructors have found that students, in their diagnoses, tend to oversimplify, overrely on general theories, and disregard unique or puzzling symptoms. How to best deal with these problems is of major concern, particularly in light of the spiraling costs of medical school education. The instructors want to know how they should revise their instruction or devise new learning experiences, so that students will avoid making so many errors.

Scenario 10–2

Mr. Humphries, who teaches fifth grade math, worries about his students' difficulties solving simple word problems. They perform reasonably well on tests of basic calculations, but cannot seem to transfer these skills to more complex and realistic problems. What makes matters worse is that many of the students see no value in trying to solve complex math problems. They insist that such problems "never happen in real life."

Scenario 10–3

The president and executive vice-presidents of ABC Corporation believe that the future of their company depends upon improved customer relations. Simply put, people will go elsewhere for the goods and services they want if treated badly by ABC employees. To avoid such an occurrence, the Training Department of ABC has begun the design and development of a workshop on customer relations for all staff who have any contact with customers. No more than 15 or 20 employees can be taken away from their jobs at one time, so the workshop will be repeated until all affected employees have been trained.

Think back for a moment to the scenarios with which the other chapters in this book began. How do the three scenarios differ from those? All of the scenarios are in some way concerned with a learning problem, which is used to illustrate the theories discussed in each chapter. But whereas the scenarios from previous chapters described the problem from the perspective of a learner (or learners), the ones in this chapter focus on the problem from the vantage point of an instructor. For you to think about learning from the instructor's perspective is, in a sense, a goal of every chapter. After all, a major purpose for reading this book is to acquire a sufficient understanding of learning in order to teach effectively or to design effective instruction. But in this chapter and the next, explicit theories of instruction will be discussed, as opposed to theories of learning.

It is important to note that several theories (or partial theories) of instruction have already been suggested in some of the other chapters as they have derived from particular views of learning. Radical behaviorism (chapter 2), for example, spawned principles of behavior modification. Ausubel's meaningful reception learning (chapter 4) provided a basis for Reigeluth's (1983) Elaboration Theory as well as Ausubel's own principles of progressive differentiation and integrative reconciliation. Bruner himself (chapter 7) articulated features of an instructional theory, and his work bears significant similarity to the Inquiry Models developed by Collins and Stevens (1983), Taba (in Joyce & Weil, 1986), and Suchman (in Gunter, Estes, & Schwab, 1990). Finally, Keller's (1983) model of motivational design (chapter 9) integrated a variety of perspectives and findings on motivation to learn.

What these theories all have in common, with the possible exception of behaviorism, is a limitation of scope. That is, each proposes instructional methods thought to provide the necessary learning conditions for a particular type of learning goal. Ausubel, for example, was largely concerned with how learners acquire bodies of information as knowledge. Bruner, along with Collins and Stevens, Taba, and Suchman, addressed himself to the attainment of concepts and inquiry skills. Keller obviously confined his attention to the engagement of students in learning. As for behaviorism, Skinner would probably have argued that its principles serve equally well for promoting any kind of learning. However, with its emphasis on observable behavior, it has not always served educators well who want to engender skills and knowledge in learners that are not easily observed.

In this chapter and the next, two theories that their proponents claim are significantly broader in scope than those mentioned earlier will be discussed. The first, Gagné's (1985) conditions for learning, has undergone development and revision for 20 or more years. With behaviorist roots, it now brings together a cognitive information processing perspective on learning with empirical findings of what good teachers do in their classrooms. Gagné's theory also serves as the basic framework for a prominent instructional design theory (Gagné, Briggs, & Wager, 1992).

In contrast to Gagné's theory is the constructivist approach to instruction. Rather than a single theory, constructivism represents a collection of similar approaches which are gaining currency in education and training. They stem from a view of learning more compatible with the ideas of Piaget, Bruner, and Vygotsky than with information processing. Since constructivism is still developing, it remains to be seen whether a single instructional theory will emerge. At present, then, we can only examine the similarities among approaches as they collectively differ from Gagné's theory.

Before proceeding to the specific instructional theories of Gagné and constructivism, let us take a brief look at instructional theory in general.

INSTRUCTIONAL PSYCHOLOGY, INSTRUCTIONAL THEORIES, INSTRUCTIONAL MODELS

Instructional psychology is essentially what this book is about. "Instructional psychologists . . . are concerned with how best to enhance learning" (Dillon & Sternberg, 1986, p. ix). Therefore, they rely on the findings of psychological and instructional research to solve instructional problems and make decisions about instructional practice (Gagné & Dick, 1983; Gagné & Rohwer, 1969; Resnick, 1981). Instructional theory results when instructional psychologists deductively derive principles of instruction from existing learning theory or inductively develop such principles from empirical studies.

Reigeluth (1983) defined **instructional theory** as *identifying methods that will best provide the conditions under which learning goals will most likely be attained*. He stated further that, for an instructional theory to be effective, it must either build on or be compatible with existing learning theory. In other words, learning theory specifies the link between what is learned and the conditions under which learning occurs. Instructional theory, as

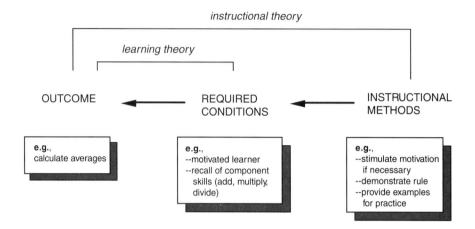

FIGURE   10–1   The Relationship between Instructional Theory and Learning Theory

depicted in Figure 10–1, adds the component of instructional method to the existing equation. What should also be noted about instructional theory is that it involves intentional learning goals. That is, learning will occur when-ever conditions are ripe, and in fact, learning goes on all the time. **Instruction**, however, refers to *the deliberate arrangement of learning conditions to promote the attainment of some intended goal*. Therefore, the purpose of instructional theory is to be prescriptive, to provide principles by which teachers and instructional designers can assure learning. Perhaps an example will be illustrative.

Suppose we are interested in students learning how to calculate averages of groups of numbers. From our knowledge of motivation, we know that for students to acquire this skill, they must have some confidence in their ability to learn it, and they must see some value in learning it. Information processing theory suggests additional conditions required for learning. Students must already know how to add, multiply, and divide, because these skills are components of the rule for calculating averages. Furthermore, the new information (i.e., the rule itself) should be presented to learners in a way that facilitates encoding.

How, then, should we implement these learning conditions? On the basis of instructional theory, effective methods might include demon-strating the rule, followed by providing as practice meaningful examples for students to solve. But even these simple methods can be put into effect in a variety of ways. The practice problems might appear in a textbook, on a worksheet devised by the teacher, or embedded in a problem scenario about the average performance of stocks in an investment portfolio. To guide a teacher's actions, then, are **instructional models**, or *"step-by-step procedure[s] that lead[] to specific learning outcomes"* (Gunter et al., 1990, p. 67). Such models are typically articulated as the principles of instructional theories are tested and validated. Any comprehensive instructional theory, then, that pertains to multiple learning outcomes will provide multiple instructional models. Because Gagné's theory is perhaps a clearer demonstration of this than constructivism, let us consider it first. Then, the collective approaches to constructivism will be discussed in chapter 11.

ROBERT M. GAGNÉ AND THE CONDITIONS OF LEARNING

Robert M. Gagné published the first edition of *The Conditions of Learning* in 1965 and the fourth edition in 1985. In that time, the theory evolved significantly from one that was extensively behavioral to one that is now predominantly cognitive in nature. Much of Gagné's early experience as an instructional psychologist was spent tackling practical problems of training air force personnel. He dealt particularly with problems in determining just what skills and knowledge are required for someone to be an effective performer at a given job. Once job requirements were identified, the task then became one of determining how those requirements might best be learned by a person in training for the job.

Briggs (1980), who was a long-term collaborator of Gagné's, wrote, "I have never asked Gagné about this, but I believe that his early work in the Air Force must have been an important factor in his later derivation of his (a) taxonomy of learning outcomes, (b) concept of learning hierarchies, and (c) related concepts of instructional events and conditions of learning" (pp. 45–46). As it has evolved, Gagné's theory incorporates three major components: a taxonomy of learning outcomes, specific learning conditions required for the attainment of each outcome, and the nine events of instruction. Because Gagné has adopted information processing theory as a foundation for his theory, the conditions for learning include both internal events (such as previously encoded information) and external events (such as methods of elaboration to facilitate encoding). Additionally, the events of instruction refer to methods or procedures designed to facilitate the specific processes (such as encoding, retention, retrieval, etc.) thought to occur during learning.

A Taxonomy of Learning Outcomes

If you recall from chapters 3 and 8, cognitive psychologists and neuroscientists both provided evidence supporting a distinction between declarative and procedural knowledge. Declarative knowledge refers to factual knowledge, or knowing that (e.g., "I know that Shakespeare lived in the sixteenth century"). Procedural knowledge, by contrast, refers to cognitive skills, such as knowing how (and therefore being able to demonstrate how), for example, to conjugate Latin verbs or balance a budget. Cognitive psychologists have also investigated conditional knowledge, the metacognitive knowledge that enables learners to determine when and how to apply declarative or procedural knowledge. For example, I know to look for major headings to organize my learning from textbooks.

All of these types of knowledge are undetectable in the learner purely by observation. That is, I cannot tell by looking at you whether you know when Shakespeare lived, whether you can balance a budget, or whether you pay attention to headings when you study from a textbook. Such knowledge must be inferred from some behavior that is observable. You could tell me the dates Shakespeare lived, or write down the conjugations of certain Latin verbs, or construct an outline of some text chapter.

Telling and writing are behaviors that imply another kind of knowledge. For instance, to write anything, a learner must be able to form the appropriate letters with a writing device. This type of performance is fundamentally different from declarative, procedural, or conditional knowledge in that it involves the use and movement of muscles. Generally called motor skills, these capabilities must also have a psychological component, because they do not have to be relearned with every performance. Despite long periods of nonuse, people generally do not forget completely how to ride a bicycle, shift a car, or swim the breaststroke.

In addition to cognitive and motor types of knowledge, humans appear to have the capacity for affective knowledge. Why, for example, do you listen to a certain type of music or participate in a certain sport or physical activity? Because you like it, it makes you feel good. These internal states of feeling predispose learners to engaging in some activities over others. This helps to explain why an individual who knows perfectly well what to do ("stop when the light turns red") may choose not to do it ("I'm worried that my pay will be docked if I'm late").

In their search for ways to facilitate learning, then, instructional theorists have found it useful to distinguish the variety of capabilities humans can acquire. In doing so, they make a fundamental assumption that different capabilities require different conditions for learning. Helping someone learn to operate a piece of machinery, in other words, is assumed to demand different types of assistance than helping someone memorize lines to a play.

Benjamin Bloom, a contemporary of Gagné's, was among the first to accept the notion that humans' learned capabilities comprise three major domains: cognitive, affective, and psychomotor. Furthermore, he proposed

TABLE 10–1   Bloom's Taxonomy of Cognitive Outcomes

Knowledge	Remembering previously learned material, including facts, vocabulary, concepts, and principles
Comprehension	Grasping the meaning of material
Application	Using abstractions, rules, principles, ideas, and other information in concrete situations
Analysis	Breaking down material into its constituent elements or parts
Synthesis	Combining elements, pieces, or parts to form a whole or constitute a new pattern or structure
Evaluation	Making judgments about the extent to which methods or materials satisfy extant criteria

a taxonomy of levels within the cognitive domain that is still in wide use today (Bloom, Engelhart, Furst, Hill, & Krathwohl, 1956; see Table 10–1). Extending this work, Krathwohl, Bloom, & Masia (1964) developed a taxonomy of outcomes within the affective domain (Table 10–2). Finally, Simpson (1966–1967) prepared a plan for a taxonomy of psychomotor outcomes (Table 10–3). Gagné, however, was the first to propose an integrated taxonomy of learning outcomes which included all three domains.

According to Gagné (1972), there are five major categories of learning outcomes. These include: (1) verbal information, (2) intellectual skills, (3) cognitive strategies, (4) attitudes, and (5) motor skills. The five categories are also summarized in Table 10–4, along with examples of each.

TABLE 10–2   A Taxonomy of Affective Outcomes

Receiving	Becoming sensitized to or willing to receive certain information
Responding	Becoming involved or doing something
Valuing	Displaying a commitment to something because of its inherent worth
Organization	Organizing a set of values and determining their relationships, including which should dominate
Characterization by Value	Integrating values into a total philosophy and acting consistently in accord with that philosophy

TABLE   10–3   Simpson's Plan for a Taxonomy of Psychomotor Outcomes

Perception	Become aware of stimulation and the need for action
Set	Preparing for action
Guided Response	Responding with assistance from a teacher or coach
Mechanism	Responding habitually
Complex Response	Resolving uncertainty and performing difficult tasks automatically
Adaptation	Altering responses to fit new situations
Origination	Creating new acts or expressions

TABLE   10–4   Gagné's Taxonomy of Learning Outcomes with Examples

Verbal Information	Stating previously learned material such as facts, concepts, principles, and procedures, e.g., listing the seven major symptoms of cancer
Intellectual Skills	
Discriminations	Distinguishing objects, features, or symbols, e.g., hearing different pitches played on a musical instrument
Concrete concepts	Identifying classes of concrete objects, features, or events, e.g., picking out all the green M&Ms from the candy jar
Defined concepts	Classifying new examples of events or ideas by their definition, e.g., noting "she sells sea shells" as alliteration
Rules	Applying a single relationship to solve a class of problems, e.g., calculating the earned run averages (ERA) of the Atlanta Braves
Higher order rules	Applying a new combination of rules to solve a complex problem, e.g., generating a balanced budget for a state organization
Cognitive Strategies	Employing personal ways to guide learning, thinking, acting, and feeling, e.g., devising a corporate plan to improve customer relations

TABLE 10–4 *Continued*

Attitudes	Choosing personal actions based on internal states of understanding and feeling, e.g., deciding to exercise daily as a part of preventive health care
Motor Skills	Executing performances involving the use of muscles, e.g., doing a triple somersault dive off the high board

Verbal Information

Verbal information is Gagné's category in the cognitive domain for *declarative knowledge*. It refers to the vast bodies of organized knowledge that learners acquire through formal schooling, books, television, and many other means (Gagné, 1985; Gagné & Driscoll, 1988). Verbal information is what individuals recall when playing such popular games as *Jeopardy*™ and *Trivial Pursuit*™. Examples include stating the capital city of Botswana, reciting Hamlet's famous soliloquy, and, as might be required in Scenario 10–1, listing the symptoms typical of a heart attack.

It should be obvious by now that researchers have been interested for a long time in understanding how information is acquired and what functions it serves for the learner. Gagné's view is consistent with the views of Ausubel, information processing theorists, and schema theorists in accepting that learners organize their knowledge in themes or schemata. These then provide the necessary foundation for acquiring related information as well as solving problems. Problem solving is not itself verbal information, but its success depends upon the learner being able to apply relevant information to the problem. For example, to assist your learning about a particular tribe in Africa, you would call to mind anything else you knew about the region in question—its geography, weather, or form of government. Likewise, in order to diagnose the probable cause of a particular patient's distress (an example of problem solving), a doctor would rely on his or her knowledge of symptoms associated with particular diseases.

Gagné's conception of verbal information appears to incorporate the first two levels of Bloom's taxonomy, knowledge and comprehension. Sometimes, for instance, learners memorize information without regard to its meaning. Although they may then be able to recite what was learned, they probably cannot give an adequate account of it in their own words. On the other hand, when comprehension has occurred, learners can paraphrase or otherwise explain the information that was acquired. In this case, the information no longer remains isolated in memory but becomes integrated within a larger context of related ideas. For obvious reasons, comprehension is usually considered to be a more desirable educational goal than inert, memorized knowledge.

Intellectual Skills

A second category in the cognitive domain of Gagné's taxonomy is that referred to as intellectual skills (Gagné, 1985). **Intellectual skills** are the equivalent of *procedural knowledge* and are divided into five, hierarchically ordered subcategories. These are: discriminations, concrete concepts, defined concepts, rules, and higher order rules.

Gagné's proposal to subdivide the intellectual skill category grew out of his work with learning hierarchies (e.g., Gagné, 1968, 1977). A **learning hierarchy** refers to *a set of component skills that must be learned before the complex skill of which they are a part can be learned* (Gagné, 1985). The hierarchy itself results from an analysis of the desired terminal skill in terms of its prerequisites. Moreover, the relationship between each skill in the hierarchy and its immediate prerequisite is one of "necessary, whether or not sufficient." Consider the example shown in Figure 10–2.

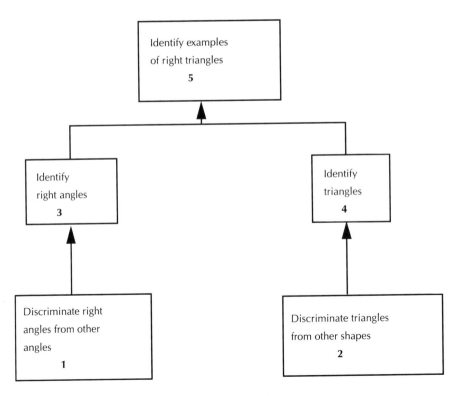

FIGURE   10–2   A Simple Learning Hierarchy

According to the assumptions of learning hierarchies, students must already be able to distinguish triangles from other shapes (Box 2) before they will be able to learn the identifying characteristics of triangles (Box 4). In other words, if they cannot see a perceptual difference between triangles and, say, squares, they will be unable to identify examples of triangles. Thus, the discrimination skill is a necessary (and sufficient) prerequisite to the identification skill. Similarly, identification of right triangles (Box 5) requires identification of triangles and right angles. These two identifications are each necessary and together sufficient for the final skill to be acquired.

Based on the types of relationships that could result from an instructional analysis, Gagné proposed the five levels of intellectual skills. Discrimination is the ability to distinguish, on the basis of perceptual characteristics, one object from another, one feature from another, one symbol from another. Discrimination is also prenominal, which means that some difference is detected without the learner being capable of naming or explaining that difference. In other words, infants can feel and respond to differences in textures of cloth without the words to express *smooth* or *rough* Similarly, my husband can distinguish among different colors quite plainly, but apparently he never learned the same color terms as the rest of us. For instance, he can draw matching socks out of his drawer, but he is likely to call a green dress "purple" or a tan car "brown."

Humans typically acquire many gross discriminations pertaining to the environment at a very young age. Then with experience, these discriminations increase in the fineness of detail to which they refer (Gagné & Driscoll, 1988). Certain environmental circumstances also demand that finer discriminations be developed. Eskimos, for example, can distinguish many more snow conditions than the average person who lives where snow is not common. Likewise, counselors have learned to detect subtle differences in the facial expressions of their clients, microbiologists have learned to see tiny irregularities in the shape and makeup of cells, and sailors have learned to feel almost imperceptible changes in wind direction or velocity.

Once prerequisite discriminations have been acquired, concept learning can occur. According to Gagné (1985), concrete concepts are classes of objects, features, and events, distinguishable by their perceptual characteristics and identifiable by name. So, for example, young children learn such concrete concepts as colors, shapes, and letters of the alphabet. At a more advanced level, a home carpenter must learn to identify wood screws and toggle bolts, whereas a mechanic should know engine oil and brake fluid.

Many concepts, however, cannot be pointed out directly but must be identified by means of a definition. Gagné (1985) called these defined concepts and argued that for learners to have truly acquired defined concepts, they must use the definitions for classifying new instances. It is not enough, therefore, to say that "positive reinforcement means increasing the occurrence of some behavior by rewarding it." One must recognize examples such as a child speaking up in class more often following encouragement by the teacher.

Tessmer, Wilson, and Driscoll (1990) agreed with Gagné that defined concepts make up a significant part of school learning. They suggested, however, that classification of new examples is not the only desirable outcome of defined concept learning. Some defined concepts, such as perestroika or beauty, do not always yield clear or unambiguous examples. A learner's understanding of such terms might be better assessed in other ways. Tessmer et al. (1990) suggested, as alternatives to concept classification, asking learners to generate inferences or reason through some problem involving the concept in question.

Although a defined concept is arguably the simplest type of rule, rule learning typically involves the use of symbols to represent and interact with the environment in generalized ways (Gagné & Driscoll, 1988). There are rules for decoding words, for constructing grammatical sentences, for calculating averages, and for factoring equations. What is particularly important about rule learning is not whether students can verbalize, or state, the rule. Rather, it is whether they can demonstrate the rule by applying it appropriately to a class of problems, even problems that have not been encountered before.

Finally, higher order rules represent combinations of simpler rules for the solving of complex problems. "A higher-order rule is still a rule and differs only in complexity from the simpler rules that compose it" (Gagné & Driscoll, 1988, p. 52). Higher order rules are thought to develop when learners must apply a new combination of rules already known and used individually. This would occur, for example, when a carpet layer must determine how much carpet is required to cover an irregularly shaped room. This is a novel problem, because the carpet layer has not encountered a room with quite this shape before, but it is a solvable one using standard rules of geometry. Similarly, when a nutritionist devises meal plans for a given client, he or she applies standard rules in a unique way to meet the particular needs of that person.

Altogether, Gagné's intellectual skills incorporate reasonably well the remaining four levels of Bloom's taxonomy. Application is demonstrated in concept and rule use, whereas analysis, synthesis, and evaluation are all, to some degree, present in higher order rule using (or problem solving). In order to determine what rules are likely to be effective for solving a given problem, the learner must analyze it, generating subproblems or taking note of important constraints. Applying some combination of rules to solve the problem represents a synthesis. Evaluation occurs when the learner monitors the success of the selected rules for effecting a solution. It also seems likely, however, that analysis, synthesis, and evaluation would also be present in the next category of Gagné's taxonomy.

Cognitive Strategies

Cognitive strategies consist of *numerous ways by which learners guide their own learning, thinking, acting, and feeling.* Gagné (1985) conceived of cognitive strategies as representing the executive control functions of information processing, and they comprise what others have called conditional knowledge. As such, learners employ cognitive strategies to monitor their own attention, to help themselves better encode new information, and to improve their success at remembering critical information at test time. Learners may arrive at these strategies through their own trial and error experiences, or they may be explicitly taught strategies that have proven effective with other learners.

Developing unique as well as effective cognitive strategies is typically considered a part of learning to learn and learning to think independently. Unfortunately, a difficulty with cognitive strategies as desirable learning outcomes is that they are not particularly amenable to assessment. Frequently, because cognitive strategies are employed in the service of other learning goals, it is the attainment (or not) of those goals which is noticed. What cognitive strategies were used is often not immediately evident.

Another aspect of learning to think independently, however, is learning to think creatively, and it is creative thinking where we may detect better evidence of effective cognitive strategies. What constitutes creative thinking is certainly a matter of some debate, but most would agree that it involves originality, seeing problems in new and insightful ways, or finding a solution to what others did not recognize as a problem. Bruner (1973b) perhaps put it best when he distinguished between problem solving and problem finding. In problem solving, the learner tackles a problem defined by someone else. Moreover, the existing parameters of the problem generally constrain its solution, so that all solvers will arrive at more or less the same outcome. The carpet example described earlier illustrates this well. There are only so many ways to determine how much carpet is required, and all carpet layers (if they want to remain in business) will generate similar estimates for the same room.

By contrast, learners generate their own problems in problem finding and bring to bear upon them both previously acquired rules and their own personal ways of thinking (Gagné & Driscoll, 1988). As an example, consider the long, lamented decline in Scholastic Aptitude Test (SAT) scores that has been seen in the United States over the last 20 years. Some statisticians do not perceive this to be a problem, claiming the observed decline is merely an artifact of test construction procedures and statistical regression effects. Other educational researchers, however, perceive the decline in scores to be a symptom of some educational problem. How they define what the problem is determines what actions they take to generate solutions. As a result, many different solutions are offered to what is thought to be wrong with the American education system. These solutions, then, are the outcomes, or evidence, of cognitive strategies.

Attitudes

Whereas verbal information, intellectual skills, and cognitive strategies are all part of the cognitive domain, attitudes are considered to be in affective domain. Gagné (1985) defined **attitudes** as *acquired internal states that influence the choice of personal action* toward some class of things, persons, or events. For example, one's attitudes toward pollution and ecology will affect the purchasing of substances in aerosol spray cans, which have been shown to have a deleterious effect on the earth's ozone layer. Likewise, choosing to save part of one's income every month reflects attitudes toward money and the future. Finally, attitude learning is likely to be involved in Scenario 10–3, because any employee, despite knowing how to interact well with customers, can choose to treat them rudely.

When attitudes are organized into a consistent set, philosophy, or world view that governs subsequent personal action, then they are typically referred to as values. According to taxonomy of affective outcomes (cf. Krathwohl et al. [1964]), we may consider Gagné's definition of attitudes to incorporate the first two levels of receiving and responding. These two levels also highlight two of the three accepted components of attitude formation: the informational component and the behavioral component. That is, information pertaining to an attitude must be known to a learner before he or she can choose to respond in a particular way. The response itself constitutes the behavioral component. The third, or emotional, component of attitude formation refers to the feelings that frequently accompany the choice of personal action. As we shall see later in the chapter, all three components are important to consider when designing instruction to teach or influence attitudes.

Finally, notice the similarity between Gagné's concept of attitude and motivation as discussed in the previous chapter. Clearly, attitudes can serve as motivating forces, and motivating learners is, to some extent, a matter of attempting to instill certain attitudes in them. Motivation, however, is probably a more transitory state than that typically associated with attitudes. For example, a student who is interested in a particular subject may be motivated to attend class regularly. Given a different class, however, the same student may choose to come irregularly if at all. By contrast, a student with a positive attitude toward school (including obedience to its rules and regulations) is likely to attend all classes regularly, regardless of how interesting or boring they may be.

Motor Skills

The fifth type of outcome in Gagné's taxonomy, corresponding to the psychomotor domain, is motor skills. By **motor skills**, Gagné means the *"precise, smooth and accurately timed execution of performances involving the use of muscles"* (Gagné & Driscoll, 1988, p. 59). Examples of motor skills include serving a tennis ball, executing a triple axle jump in ice skating, dribbling a basketball, and lifting a barbell with weights. These are performances all associated with sports and all continuous in nature. That is, although each skill can be roughly subdivided into component movements (e.g., a tennis serve consists of the toss, contact, and follow-through), it is intended to be performed in a single fluid motion.

Other examples of motor skills, however, are complex procedures made up of discrete subskills. For example, a dance may call for a series of discrete steps to be performed. Rounding a mark in a sailboat regatta requires raising one sail, lowering another, resetting the positions of the sails, and moving the tiller to change the direction of the boat. Taking a blood sample from a patient requires putting a cuff around the patient's arm, locating a vein, sterilizing the point of injection, and so on. These examples, along with those above, also illustrate that motor skills are generally acquired in combination with various cognitive skills. To play tennis competitively, for instance, one must know the rules of the game and play strategically, in addition to executing the shots with precision. Therefore, not only motor skills, but also intellectual skills and cognitive strategies, are involved.

As indicated previously, Gagné, like other instructional theorists, proposed his taxonomy with the assumption that different outcomes call for different learning conditions. Thus, during the design of instruction, complex learning goals like those cited above must be considered for their multiple types of outcomes and learning conditions provided that will support the attainment of all components. Just what learning conditions should be provided is the subject of the next section.

Conditions for Learning

In order to plan what learning conditions should be present in instruction, Gagné, Briggs, and Wager (1992) recommended categorizing learning goals according to the type of outcome they represent. From the standpoint of the teacher or instructional designer, this means some very careful consideration of just what ends or results are desired. It may also mean making reasonably concrete what are otherwise fuzzy, vague, or unspecified goals. For example, the goal of a social studies teacher might be that her students "really understand the Bill of Rights." Undoubtedly, most of us have some sense as to what "really understands" might mean to this teacher. It probably does not mean being able to recite the Bill of Rights word for word, nor is it likely to suggest that students render decisions about cases of the sort found on the Supreme Court docket. But between these two extremes are many other outcomes that could be associated with understanding the Bill of Rights. Therefore, to provide effective instruction, the teacher should decide more precisely what she expects of students.

There has been considerable controversy over the use and effectiveness of instructional objectives in facilitating learning. Objectives obviously spring from a behavioral tradition, because they are intended to specify the learned behavior that is desired of students (see chapter 2). Most studies investigating their use, however, have shown either a small positive or no effect on intentional learning (i.e., that related directly to the objectives) and a deleterious effect on incidental learning (i.e., information unrelated to the objectives) (Klauer, 1984). Despite these results, objectives have gained and maintained a solid footing in education and training. Why?

To begin with, investigations on objectives can be faulted on several grounds, so that findings of no effect may not be true. First, most researchers defined objectives for the recall of information only. Second, the instruction used in the studies was typically very short, not more than a few pages. As a result, the objectives in some cases bore a one to one correspondence with the sentences in the experimental text. Third, objectives were frequently employed with no regard for whether students knew how to use them, and, in fact, students are likely to disregard objectives unless they are shown how objectives can help them learn. Finally, the only outcome examined by most studies was some measure of student learning. Therefore, the potential benefit of objectives for anyone other than learners (e.g., teachers or designers) remained in question.

Although objectives may indeed be of limited benefit to learners, they can be extremely useful to teachers and other designers of instruction as a plan both for instruction and for testing. A central tenet of most instructional design models (e.g., Dick & Reiser, 1989; Gagné, Briggs, & Wager, 1992) and many texts on criterion-referenced testing (e.g., Gronlund, 1988; Tuckman, 1988) is that there should be congruence between instructional goals, lessons, and assessment measures. The only way to determine such congruence is from an initial statement of goals.

Once instructional goals have been categorized into types of learning outcomes, then, planning for instruction can proceed systematically. A teacher or instructional designer can determine just what unique conditions are required for learners to acquire each desired skill, knowledge, or attitude. Summarized in Table 10–5 are the external conditions that Gagné proposed as essential for learning the different varieties of outcomes. Recall that internal conditions are specified by the information processing model and research conducted on human cognition.

TABLE 10–5   A Summary of External Conditions Which Can Critically Influence Learning of the Five Major Varieties of Learning Outcomes

Type of Learning Outcome	Critical Learning Conditions
Verbal Information	1. Draw attention to distinctive features by variations in print or speech.
	2. Present information so that it can be made into chunks.
	3. Provide a meaningful context for effective encoding of information.
	4. Provide cues for effective recall and generalization of information.
Intellectual Skills	1. Call attention to distinctive features.
	2. Stay within the limits of working memory.
	3. Stimulate the recall of previously learned component skills.
	4. Present verbal cues to the ordering or combination of component skills.
	5. Schedule occasions for practice and spaced review.
	6. Use a variety of contexts to promote transfer.
Cognitive Strategies	1. Describe or demonstrate the strategy.
	2. Provide a variety of occasions for practice using the strategy.
	3. Provide informative feedback as to the creativity or originality of the strategy or outcome.
Attitudes	1. Establish an expectancy of success associated with the desired attitude.
	2. Assure student identification with an admired human model.
	3. Arrange for communication or demonstration of choice of personal action.
	4. Give feedback for successful performance; or allow observation of feedback in the human model.

Continued

TABLE 10–5 *Continued*

Type of Learning Outcome	Critical Learning Conditions
Motor Skills	1. Present verbal or other guidance to cue the executive subroutine. 2. Arrange repeated practice. 3. Furnish immediate feedback as to the accuracy of performance. 4. Encourage the use of mental practice.

From Gagné, R. M., & Driscoll, M. P. *Essentials of learning for instruction* (2nd ed.). Englewood Cliffs, NJ: Prentice-Hall, 1988. Reprinted by permission.

Conditions for Learning Verbal Information

Assuming that verbal information is stored in vast, interrelated networks in human memory (see chapters 3 and 4) or in schemata and mental models (see chapter 5), how might instruction be planned to best facilitate learning of new information? To be meaningful, new information must be related in some way to what learners already know. Therefore, important internal conditions include the recall of related material. In addition, learners can process only so much information at one time because of the limitations of short-term memory.

⋅ As for external conditions, then, it is important to present information in meaningful chunks so as not to overload the learner's processing system. And for effective encoding to occur, a meaningful context must be either activated or provided. Techniques such as imagery, organizers (advance or comparative), themes, and mnemonics have proven to be effective for this purpose. Remember from chapter 3 that whatever cues are used for encoding are also likely to be effective retrieval cues. Moreover, a greater variety of cues used during initial learning is likely to ensure better generalization of the information to appropriate but new contexts.

When planning instruction for verbal information outcomes, it is also important to remember that information is typically embedded in some larger context. Not everything a professor says in a lecture must be learned and retained in detail, for example. Similarly, textbooks, computer simulations, movies, and television documentaries present tremendous amounts of information—far more than a learner is expected to remember or use. Therefore, instructional tactics should be used that direct learners' attention to significant points. These include, for example, the use of italics and bold-face print in textbooks or voice inflections and gestures in a lecture.

Conditions for Learning Intellectual Skills

Intellectual skills are similar to verbal information in that it is easy to overload the learner in their instruction. Whereas information had to be associated with previously learned and related ideas, intellectual skills build upon previously learned component skills. Therefore, these must be recalled for learning to proceed effectively. Moreover, multiple steps to a new skill should be presented in increments and at a pace that does not strain the limitations of short-term memory. Imagine the result, for example, if a statistics professor explained a new analysis procedure rather rapidly, in highly complicated steps and without defining terms.

As with information, the learning of intellectual skills requires the learner's attention to be directed, but in this case to distinctive features of the concept or rule to be learned. For example, the three sides of triangles distinguish them from other similar shapes and so should be emphasized to the learner. Likewise, staining slides can highlight features of cells or tissues to which biologists should attend when learning to distinguish normal from abnormal conditions.

When rules require a series of steps to be performed in sequence, instruction in their use should include cues as to the appropriate order of steps. These cues can range from verbal statements listing the steps, as might occur in long division, for example, to reminders of the conceptual basis for the rule. Converting temperatures between the Fahrenheit and Celsius scales, for example, can be cued with a reminder as to which number should be larger. "You're starting with a temperature on the Celsius scale. That's the smaller number. So that must mean...." (thus prompting the rule to multiply by 9/5 and add 32).

Finally, Gagné and Driscoll (1988) pointed out the ease and speed with which intellectual skills may be initially acquired, but the apparent difficulty with their being retained and widely applied in new situations. For example, students who appeared to understand the new statistical analysis procedure when the instructor went over it in class may experience problems trying to use it on new sets of data outside of class. They may also fail to recognize instances where the use of the procedure would be appropriate. Therefore, practice with a variety of examples and problems is an essential external condition to facilitate the internal processes of retention and transfer (or generalization).

Conditions for Learning Cognitive Strategies

Internal conditions necessary for the acquisition of cognitive strategies include prior knowledge of the simple concepts and rules that make up highly general strategies, such as "break the problem down into parts" (Gagné, 1985). But they may also include task-relevant concepts, rules, and information. In the case, for example, of developing a strategy to research the decline of SAT scores (a task-specific, undoubtedly complex strategy), learners must have prior research skills, know facts related to the SAT, and understand certain concepts of education.

What external conditions will facilitate the development of cognitive strategies is a matter of some debate. Certainly, many simple and task-oriented strategies are discovered by learners in their attempts to solve a problem or remember something for a test (Gagné, 1985). Other such strategies can apparently be established through demonstration or verbal instructions to the learner (Gagné & Driscoll, 1988). Teachers frequently remind learners to paraphrase, for example, when they say, "Tell me in your own words what _____ [you fill in the blank] means," or "Don't just copy the definitions in your book; write them in your own words." More complex or difficult strategies may also require demonstration. The main idea of a textbook or lecture is not always self-evident to learners but identification can be easily modeled by a teacher who constructs outlines of important information.

Whether strategies are taught or discovered, learners must have ample opportunities to practice them, particularly in novel situations. The Cognition and Technology Group at Vanderbilt (1991a) lamented their students' inability to generate relevant plans for solving problems, which they attributed to a curricular emphasis on memorization of facts and practice on isolated subskills. They suggested as a solution more in-context practice on complex problems. Derry and Murphy (1986) also recommended that teachers of different subjects coordinate their efforts for developing strategies useful across disciplines. They stated, for example:

> One form of coordination is through the use of a common planning model, or metastrategy, called the Four C's Learning Plan. The four C's are as follows: clarify the learning situation; come up with a plan, carry out the plan, and check your results. Thus language arts teachers explain how reading and memorization tactics fit into the four C's, while math teachers explain problem-solving, and physical education teachers explain mood control tactics using the same framework. (p. 18)

Finally, Gagné and Driscoll (1988) considered the provision of informative feedback to be as important as the setting of problem situations. Learners must have some notion as to whether their strategic efforts are effective, creative, or efficient. In some situations, it may also be desirable to explicitly encourage learners to be systematic and efficient in their use of strategy. Duffield (1990) and Atkins and Blissett (1992), in separate studies investigating what children learn from instructional software that purports to teach problem solving strategies, showed that learners most often used trial and error, despite feedback providing clues, which could be used systematically to solve the problem at hand. In neither case, however, were learners encouraged to adopt a systematic strategy or one that would help them solve the problem quickly. Indeed, reflection of any sort concerning strategy effectiveness was generally absent and not nurtured. Yet, such reflection may well be essential to cognitive strategy learning and so should be facilitated by relevant external conditions.

Conditions for Learning Attitudes

For any attitude to be learned and expressed, learners must already possess a variety of related concepts and information. If the attitude to be acquired is "Just say no to drugs," for instance, learners must know something about drugs and their effects. According to Gagné (1985), they must also understand the source of the attitudinal message, the situations in which drugs are likely to be encountered, and the actions likely to be involved in "just saying no." With these prerequisite internal conditions in place, attitudes may be established through a variety of external learning conditions.

Consistent with Skinner's views on the establishment of any behavior, some attitudes are likely to be acquired because they have been consistently reinforced over time. Consider, for example, the enjoyment of reading as a pastime activity. Individuals who like to read probably had parents who reinforced this activity at a young age, perhaps by reading to the child, discussing what was read, and ensuring that many interesting books were available to be read. Undoubtedly, the experience of being successful at the task also had a hand in establishing a positive attitude toward reading. As Gagné (1985) noted, repeated experiences of failure will tend to engender attitudes of dislike. Moreover, when these experiences occur in association with events that produce fear or other unpleasant feelings (as in a teacher, parent or peers berating a person for failing), then the negative attitude that results may persist for years, changing only with great effort and difficulty.

An equally effective set of external conditions for altering or establishing attitudes can be found in human modeling (Bandura, 1969; Gagné, 1985). As we have already seen in the previous chapter, learners modified expectations of themselves and their own behavior after observing the behavior of models with whom they could identify. Because attitudes are a matter of choice, learning attitudes from models involves learning to make the same choices of action that they do. This occurs because people tend to want to "be like" those whom they respect or with whom they identify.

For modeling (or reinforcement) to be most effective in establishing attitudes, instructional conditions should (a) create an expectation in learners that they will be successful in the chosen activity, (b) provide for the activity associated with the attitude to be performed (by the model or the learner), and (c) give feedback for successful performance (Gagné & Driscoll, 1988). In the case of modeling, the latter is often communicated in a testimonial given by the model, as in a sports figure describing during a school visit the improvements in his life since getting off drugs.

Conditions for Learning Motor Skills

Whether a particular motor skill is made up of discrete subskills (e.g., a pattern dance) or continuous part-skills (e.g., a tennis serve), it nonetheless has component skills that must be mastered separately before they can be assembled into the single, terminal performance. These, then, comprise important internal conditions for the learning of motor skills. Also an essential prerequisite, however, is recall of the executive subroutine (Fitts & Posner, 1967), or procedure which dictates the sequence of movements.

As for external conditions, Gagné, along with many motor learning theorists (e.g., Singer & Dick, 1980) incorporated the three phases Fitts and Posner (1967) proposed for motor learning. These are: (1) the early cognitive phase, in which learners attempt to understand the executive subroutine, (2) the intermediate phase, during which learners alternate practice of the subskills with practice of the total skill, and (3) the final autonomous phase, in which skill performance becomes virtually automatic. Corresponding instructional conditions require, therefore, methods for cuing the subroutine (such as verbal directions or demonstrations of the skill), repeated practice, and immediate feedback to correct errors and avert the possibility of bad habits developing. When learners reach the autonomous phase of skill development, mental practice may be useful in helping them reach their peak for competition (Singer, 1980). World class athletes, for example, report benefits of imagining their entire performance before they take their turn to compete. It is useful to remember, however, that only perfect practice makes perfect; imperfect practice simply leads to bad habits that may become nearly impossible to break.

Summary

The learning conditions described in this section appear to critically influence the learning of various outcomes. For this reason, Gagné and Driscoll (1988) referred to them as the building blocks for instruction. At the least, instruction should provide for these conditions, and when multiple outcomes are desired, all types of goals with their corresponding conditions should be considered. But planning instruction also requires taking care to support, throughout a lesson or course, all of the internal processes presumed to occur during learning regardless of what is being learned. Gagné (1985) referred to these external conditions as the events of instruction.

The Nine Events of Instruction

Recall from chapter 3 that information is presumed to undergo a series of transformations as it passes through the stages of memory. Processes thought to be responsible for these transformations include attention, pattern recognition, retrieval, rehearsal, encoding, retention, and so on. Modifying the information flow, as well as setting processing priorities, are executive control processes. Because learning takes place only when these processes are activated, the goal of instruction, according to Gagné (1985), should be to facilitate this activation. And he proposed the events of instruction to do just that.

Listed in Table 10–6 are the nine events of instruction together with the internal processes that they support. Although Gagné believes that most lessons should follow the sequence of events as shown, he recognized that this order is not absolute (Gagné & Driscoll, 1988). Moreover, the manner in which the events are implemented may vary greatly depending upon the instructional delivery system that is chosen. What a teacher will do in the classroom, for example, is likely to differ markedly from activities embedded in a computer-based tutorial. But the effects of the two types of activities, in terms of learning, should be similar if both are designed to implement the same event of instruction. This point should become clearer as the instructional events are illustrated with specific examples. Let us now turn to an examination of these events.

Event 1: Gaining Attention
Since learning cannot occur unless the learner is in some way oriented and receptive to incoming information, gaining attention is the obvious first event that must occur in instruction. The importance of attention was also discussed in the previous chapter, where it played a prominent role in

TABLE 10–6   Gagné's Nine Events of Instruction Associated with the Internal Learning Processes They Support

Event of Instruction	Learning Processes
1. Gaining attention	Attention
2. Informing the learner of the objective	Expectancy
3. Stimulating recall of prior learning	Retrieval to working memory
4. Presenting the stimulus	Pattern recognition; selective perception
5. Providing learner guidance	Chunking, rehearsal, encoding
6. Eliciting performance	Retrieval, responding
7. Providing feedback	Reinforcement, error correction
8. Assessing performance	Responding, retention
9. Enhancing retention and transfer	Retention, retrieval, generalization

Keller's model of motivational design. Typically, gaining attention is accomplished by some sort of stimulus change, which may be repeated in various forms throughout a lesson to regain students' attention when they appear to be off-task. Examples include the teacher calling out particular students' names, using verbal signals such as "Listen up, everybody," or turning the lights on and off. In mediated instruction, gaining attention might take the form of flashing signals on the screen or the sound of beeps indicating "look for a message on the screen."

Event 2: Informing the Learner of the Objective
We saw in the previous chapter the effect that self-expectations can have on motivation. A similar case is holding an expectancy about what one is to learn will influence subsequent processing of information related to that expectancy. If, for example, learners are aware and prepared to learn certain information, they will be more alert to any stimuli related to that goal. Expectancies are easily established by simple statements of instructional goals, references to what students will be able to do after instruction, or demonstrations of anticipated learning outcomes. It should be noted that all students, whether young or mature, will develop expectations about what they are supposed to learn in any instructional situation. When the teacher or instructional material is not explicit about learning goals (or they are in conflict with one another), students are likely to take their cues from what happens in class and what appears on tests (Driscoll, Dick, Johnson, & Flynn, 1990).

Event 3: Stimulating Recall of Prior Learning
Although new learning depends to a large extent on what has been learned before, students do not always call to mind and use relevant information when faced with a new learning task. This is perhaps truer of younger learners than older learners, simply because younger learners have not yet built a broad base of knowledge. However, as discussed in chapter 5, the transfer of knowledge, i.e., the application of something previously learned to a new problem or in a new context, is difficult at any age. Therefore, to prepare learners for encoding or transfer, instructors should assist them in recalling relevant and prerequisite information.

Stimulating recall of prior learning can be as simple as reminding learners of what was studied the day before, or last week, in class. This is often observed in the quick reviews with which many teachers begin each day's activities. In some instances, however, simple reminders are not enough. It then becomes necessary to reinstate the prerequisite knowledge or skills by some practice activity (Gagné & Driscoll, 1988). An example can be seen in the following protocol, taken from Driscoll and Dick's (1991) observations of an eighth grade science teacher about halfway through an instructional unit on light and lenses.

> *MLH is circulating about the classroom, helping individual kids as they ask questions. Then she goes to the board, puts up the formula—*t = d/r *(*t *is time,* d *is distance,* r *is the speed of light)—and says, "Listen up, everybody. Remember how we do these problems. We're given the distance, which is what? 3.8 times 10 to the eighth meters. Right! And we know the speed of light through a vacuum. Remember, it's in your book. Yes, it's 3.0 times 10 to the eighth meters per second. So what do we do to figure out how long it will take for the light to go this far? Righhhht! That's good! Divide. . . ." MLH goes on to give several more examples. The kids are apparently having difficulty with Question 1 under READING CRITICALLY. Several seem to have asked her a question about it, so she goes over the procedures again for everyone.*

Considerable effort is often required for learners to transfer prior knowledge to new situations, even when they are aware that they have such relevant knowledge (Salomon & Perkins, 1989) . Moreover, learners may simply find it easier to ask someone else for the answer than to figure it out for themselves. In situations where the process of solving problems is an important goal of instruction, then, students should be prompted in ways that promote their persistence in "sticking with it."

Event 4: Presenting the Stimulus

This event of instruction depends upon what is to be learned. If the goal of instruction is information acquisition, then the stimulus may consist of a textbook chapter, lecture, or film containing the content. If, on the other hand, the desired outcome is intellectual skill learning, then the most effective stimulus is one which prominantly displays distinctive features of the concept or rule to be learned. In Driscoll and Dick's (1991) observations, for example, the concept of focus was presented by the textbook in a diagram highlighting its essential features and by the teacher using a light box, lenses, and chalk dust. In the latter case, the teacher emphasized essential features of the concept through gestures and verbal explanations as she conducted the demonstration.

Presenting the stimulus for motor skill or cognitive strategy learning consists of demonstrating the desired outcome or giving verbal directions. For attitude learning, the stimulus is a demonstration of the desired action or choice, generally by a model. For all types of outcomes, the stimulus presentation should emphasize distinctive features or essential elements of the desired outcome in order to facilitate the processes of pattern recognition and selective perception.

Event 5: Providing Learning Guidance

How or what learning guidance is provided in instruction also depends upon the desired outcome, but the primary process to be facilitated is semantic encoding. Specifically, instructional activities should promote the entry of what is to be learned into long-term memory in a meaningful way. Here is where a teacher or instructional designer should refer to the learning conditions that are critical and unique to each type of learning outcome.

How much learning guidance to provide is a separate question and one which depends upon several factors, including the ability and sophistication of the learners, the amount of time available for instruction, and the presence of multiple learning goals. Very able or sophisticated learners probably require less guidance than not so able students. For example, highly educated communications technicians who attend training to learn the latest developments in technology typically approach the situation with very focused goals. "Just tell me what I should know or where I can find the required information," they say, indicating a need for mostly stimulus presentation and little learning guidance. By contrast, third grade children having difficulty reading are likely to require considerable learning guidance.

When the process or experience of learning and problem solving is to be emphasized, then instructors may find it desirable to provide minimal learning guidance of a highly directive nature. Rather, discovery learning is stressed. Hints or cues are provided, but learners are expected to figure things out for themselves without being told just what to do. Because discovery learning can also be quite time consuming, instructors generally must weigh its benefits (e.g., facilitating long-term retention and transfer) against its costs (e.g., need for extensive resources and time). Remember as well that Ausubel argued against using discovery learning for most school situations because he believed that meaningful reception learning was as cognitively active and much more efficient. Bruner, however, would be more likely to argue that, although active cognition might be possible under conditions of receiving information, it does not occur very often that way. Certainly, instructor beliefs will also play a part in the decision to use discovery learning methods.

Event 6: Eliciting Performance

Instructional Events 1 through 5 presumably assure that learning has occurred, i.e., that what was to be learned has been sufficiently encoded and stored in long-term memory. Event 6, then, enables the learners to confirm their learning—to themselves, their teachers, and others. It requires the learner to produce a performance, something that is an appropriate indicator of what was learned. Remember that learning must be inferred from behavior, so for this event, an important question to answer concerns what behavior will serve as the best index of the desired learning goal.

The intent of eliciting performance is for learners to demonstrate what they have learned without penalty. In other words, this event provides an opportunity to gauge progress, with the assumption that errors are still undergoing correction and performance is still being improved. The next event, then, provides the learners with information useful for effecting performance improvement.

Event 7: Providing Feedback

Having shown what they can do, learners should be provided informative feedback on their performance. This implies, for knowledge and skills that call for discrete answers, telling the learners whether or not their answers are correct. If incorrect, feedback should assist learners in detecting and cor-recting their errors.

Kulhavy and Stock (1989) developed a feedback model from their research that explains how feedback works as a function of learners' confi-dence in their initial responses. Consider, for example, any test you have taken recently. You get the test back and discover marked wrong a question that you were really sure you had answered correctly. What would you do? According to Kulhavy and Stock's model, you would most likely pay care-ful attention to what the teacher says about that item when she goes over the test. Or, you might carefully search through your notes or the textbook to determine what your mistake had been. In either case, the feedback plays an important role in your correcting the error, and you will pay close atten-tion to it.

By contrast, when learners get test items wrong that they were most unsure about anyway, feedback plays a different role. In this case, error cor-rection is not so much the issue as learning better what the question was intended to assess. Instead of a definite misconception, the learner has only a vague conception. Feedback, then, should consist of reteaching or extended elaboration on the knowledge or skill in question.

Obviously, not all material to be learned consists of right and wrong answers. Motor skills, for example, may be performed correctly, but inex-pertly or clumsily. Feedback, then, should be aimed at showing learners how to improve their current skill. Similarly, feedback for cognitive strategy learning may inform learners as to how their performance might become more strategic or more creative.

Event 8: Assessing Performance

Remember that learning was defined in terms of a change in behavior or performance that persists over time. In other words, a new skill must be performed dependably before most teachers will agree that it has been well learned. Therefore, after learners have had opportunities to demonstrate and refine their knowledge, it may be formally assessed. This event is typically carried out through unit or chapter tests, projects, portfolios, skill demonstrations, and so on. It also tends to be the basis on which student grades are assigned. Even with this event occurring so late in a lesson, however, Gagné and Driscoll (1988) stated that it is desirable for each correct performance to be given suitable feedback.

Event 9: Enhancing Retention and Transfer

Although this is the last event in the series, instructional activities to enhance retention and transfer are frequently built into the instruction at a much earlier phase. It has already been suggested, for instance, that a variety of examples and contexts are critical learning conditions for learners to be able to transfer intellectual skills appropriately. These would most likely be planned during Event 5, providing learning guidance. Similarly, spaced reviews facilitate retention of intellectual and motor skills and could be planned as several iterations of Events 6 and 7, eliciting performance and providing feedback.

Attitude learning perhaps has unique requirements for retention and transfer. Many attitudes, such as that pertaining to drug use, are unlikely to be performed in the context of the original instruction. That is, it would be unethical, not to mention illegal, for a teacher to offer drugs to students in the hope that they would say no and that behavior would be appropriately reinforced. Therefore, activities should be used, such as role plays or discussions centered around scenarios and questions of "What would you do if . . . ?". The point of these activities is to encourage students to reflect upon their own knowledge and belief systems as they are exposed to those of other people. Finally, computer-based simulations, albeit still in their infancy, are likely to prove useful in helping students to examine their own attitudes in a wide variety of situations. Simulations can show students what the consequences of their decisions can be, thus making more personal the information associated with attitudes.

Summary: Planning Instructional Events

Does effective instruction depend upon the inclusion of all nine events of instruction? Is the teacher or instructional designer always responsible for planning the instructional events? Cannot learners sometimes be held responsible for their own instruction? In answer to these questions, the choice of instructional events, and who makes that choice, should depend upon the nature of the learning situation (Gagné & Driscoll, 1988). For example, in the classroom that Driscoll et al. (1990) studied, the teacher reviewed material frequently (Events 3 and 9), perhaps because the textbook did a poor job of it. Using cooperative learning structures, however, she often relied on the students to provide each other with both learning guidance and feedback. Finally, "including more instructional events than are necessary is likely to lead to boredom on the part of the students. Providing fewer than are needed, however, has the serious consequence of inadequate learning, misdirected learning, or no learning at all" (Gagné & Driscoll, 1988, p. 131). The best guide to planning instructional events, then, is the students themselves.

CONCLUSION

Gagné's instructional theory is widely used in the design of instruction by instructional designers in many settings, and its continuing influence in the field of educational technology can be seen in the more than 130 times that Gagné has been cited in prominent journals in the field during the period from 1985 through 1990 (Anglin & Towers, 1992). The increasing interest in constructivism, however, has caused researchers to question theories like Gagné's and to examine whether they are compatible with the goals and assumptions of constructivist epistemology.

In a case study investigating a particular teacher's implementation of cooperative learning, for example, Flynn (1992) attempted to determine if and how Gagné's events of instruction are carried out in a cooperative learning structure. He concluded that the two approaches—cooperative learning and the events of instruction—each brought something valuable to the understanding of what went on in that classroom. More such studies are necessary, however, to determine just what is illuminated or obscured by each perspective about learning.

In the next chapter, the various approaches to constructivism are discussed, with contrasts drawn to the theory discussed in this chapter.

SUGGESTED READINGS

Gagné, R. M. (1985). *The conditions of learning.* (4th ed.). New York: Holt, Rinehart & Winston.

Gagné, R. M., Briggs, L. J., and Wager, W. W. (1992). *Principles of instructional design.* (4th ed.). Fort Worth: Harcourt Brace Jovanovich.

Gagné, R. M., and Driscoll, M. P. (1988). *Essentials of learning for instruction*, (2nd ed.). Englewood Cliffs, NJ: Prentice-Hall.

REFLECTIVE QUESTIONS AND ACTIVITIES

1. Apply Gagné's taxonomy to a subject you expect to teach and generate examples in each category. Give your examples (randomly ordered) to a fellow student and ask him or her to sort the examples into the same categories. Do your categorizations agree? Discuss any disagreements. Try to reach consensus on the usefulness of Gagné's conception of learning outcomes.

2. Select a unit of instruction, such as a single topic in a course syllabus or a stand-alone, independent study module. Examine this instruction (and its accompanying materials, such as textbooks, lectures, handouts, and the like) from the perspective of Gagné's theory. What features would be considered well designed, and what features does it lack to be "good instruction"? Predict what effects this instruction is likely to have on learners. If it is possible, observe learners going through the instruction and compare its actual effects to those you predicted.

3. Rewrite one of the instructional plans you have already generated in the course of reading this book. Apply Gagné's instructional theory. Evaluate the results in terms of the probable effects on learning. What has Gagné's theory added to the plan that was lacking before?

► 11

Constructivism

Recall (or reread) the scenarios that opened chapter 10. Medical school instructors wish to revise their instruction in diagnostic medicine to reduce the number of diagnostic errors made by students. A fifth grade teacher struggles with how best to teach problem solving to his students. And corporate executives plan training in customer relations for their employees. Imagine what instructional strategies might be proposed for them given a different view of the learning process than was evident in Gagné's instructional theory.

In this chapter, potential answers will be discussed that arise from constructivist theory. As you read the chapter, you may also find it worthwhile to look back at chapters 3, 5, 6, and 7 in order to review some of the concepts that underpin constructivist theory.

CONSTRUCTIVISM: A CONTRASTING THEORY

"Constructivism has multiple roots in the psychology and philosophy of this century" (Perkins, 1991a, p. 20). Among those already discussed in this book are the constructive theory of memory (see chapter 3), the cognitive and developmental perspectives of Piaget (see chapter 6), the interactional and cultural emphases of Bruner and Vygotsky (see chapter 7), and the contextual nature of learning emphasized in chapter 5. In addition to these, constructivist researchers acknowledge the philosophies of Dewey (1933) and Goodman (1984), and the ecological psychology of Gibson (1977) as important influences on their work.

As mentioned in chapter 10, there is no single constructivist theory of instruction. Rather, there are researchers in fields from science education to educational psychology and instructional technology who are articulating various aspects of a constructivist theory. Moreover, constructivism is only one of the labels used to describe these efforts. Its use probably stems from Piaget's reference to his views as "constructivist" (see chapter 6) and Bruner's conception of discovery learning as "constructionist" (see chapter 7). Other labels include generative learning (CTGV, 1991a, 1991b; Wittrock, 1985a, 1985b), embodied cognition (Johnson, 1987; Lakoff, 1987) cognitive flexibility theory (Spiro, Feltovich, Jacobson, & Coulson, 1991), situated learning and authentic instruction (Brown, Collins, & Duguid, 1989; CTGV, 1990), postmodern and poststructural curricula (Hlynka, 1991; Culler, 1990), and educational semiotic (Cunningham, 1992). In this chapter, then, no single constructivist approach will be described. Instead, the assumptions common to the collection of approaches will be examined, together with the learning conditions and instructional methods being proposed as consistent with these assumptions.

Constructivist Assumptions about Learning

Theorists who write in the emerging constructivist tradition often contrast their ideas with the epistemological assumptions of the objectivist tradition. Objectivism is the view that knowledge of the world comes about through an individual's experience of it. As this experience grows broader and deeper, knowledge is represented in the individual's mind as an ever-closer approximation of how the world really is (see chapter 1). In a sense, then, knowledge is thought to exist independently of learners, and learning consists of transferring that knowledge from outside to within the learner.

Both behavioral and cognitive information processing theories of learning emerged from the objectivist tradition. Consider, for example, the emphasis on universal laws of learning that is one of the hallmarks of behaviorism. Behaviorists define desired learning goals independent of any learner and then proceed to arrange reinforcement contingencies that are presumed to be effective with any learner; only the type of reinforcer is assumed to vary according to the individual. Although information processing theorists put mind back into the learning equation, they, too, appear to assume that knowledge is "out there" to be transferred into the learner. The computer metaphor itself suggests that knowledge is input to be processed and stored by learners.

In contrast to the objectivist view, then, constructivist theory rests on the assumption that knowledge is constructed by learners as they attempt to make sense of their experiences. Learners, therefore, are not empty vessels waiting to be filled, but rather active organisms seeking meaning. Regardless of what is being learned, constructive processes operate and learners form, elaborate, and test candidate mental structures until a satisfactory one emerges (Perkins, 1991a). Moreover, new, particularly conflicting experiences will cause perturbations in these structures, so that they must be constructed anew in order to make sense of the new information. This should sound much like the development and revision of mental models, as discussed in chapter 5. In chapter 6, Piaget referred to a similar process as schema accommodation, and other developmental theorists called it knowledge restructuring. Both Bruner and Vygotsky, as well, devised similar concepts to account for the changes in children's knowledge as they develop (see chapter 7).

What constructivists argue strongly, however, is that knowledge constructions do not necessarily bear any correspondence to external reality. That is, they do not have to reflect the world as it really is to be useful and viable. This is consistent with the idealist or interpretist epistemology that was discussed in chapter 1. Perhaps an example would help to illustrate this idea.

Recall from chapter 6 the research revealing children's conceptions of the earth in relation to the sun. Because children's experience is that of a flat earth with the sun moving across the sky during the day, they typically believe that the earth is flat and that the sun revolves around it. In the constructivist view, they have constructed a perfectly viable model, which accounts well for their own experience. We know in this case that, for most people, this model is revised to reflect current understanding of the earth's relationship to the sun. As a pragmatist (see chapter 1) would suggest, however, the current model will prevail for only as long as the collective experience of scientists supports it. Therefore, the model should not be assumed to reflect reality; instead, it should be construed as the best construction of humankind's experience of its world.

If no correspondence is presumed between reality and the learner's cognitive constructions of it, does this mean that all constructions are equally viable? Those subscribing to an idealist philosophy might say yes (see chapter 1), but most constructivist theorists would say no. There must be limits to what sense learners make of their environment and their experience. Limits are imposed by human biological characteristics as well as by what is possible in reality. Moreover, many constructivist theorists adhere to Vygotsky's notions about the social negotiation of meaning (see chapter 7). That is, learners test their own understandings against those of others, notably those of teachers or more advanced peers.

Although constructivists have described, often in detail, the epistemological assumptions underlying their work, they have been less clear about what models of memory arise from these assumptions. Cunningham (1988) has begun to explore the implications of Eco's rhizome metaphor (see chapter 3) for a model of memory. Likewise, Bereiter (1991) has seen promise in the new connectionist models, also described in chapter 3. He argued that concepts, for example, "are much more like perceptions than they are like rule-defined categories" (p. 13), and that, in fact, it seems likely students do not learn rules at all. What they learn instead are connections, which, to satisfy constraints of experience and environment, come to resemble rule-based performance.

Finally, John R. Anderson, known for his ACT model of memory (see chapter 3), is exploring new directions for the study of human cognition that seem increasingly compatible with the assumptions of constructivism. Rather than continue the atomistic analysis of cognitive mechanisms which characterized his earlier work, Anderson (1990) has proposed an approach to building a theory of cognition that focuses on the adaptation of human behavior in terms of achieving human goals. That is, Anderson assumes that "the cognitive system operates at all times to optimize the adaptation of the behavior of the organism" (1990, p. 28). This is similar to the view espoused by Bruner (1986), who stated that "meaning . . . is an enterprise that reflects human intentionality and cannot be judged for its rightness independently of it" (p. 158). It remains to be seen, of course, whether Anderson's approach will yield a model consistent with both existing data about memory and whatever new data are generated from constructivist investigations.

Let us now turn to an examination of the instructional recommendations emanating from constructivism. Because any theory of instruction must deal with learning goals, conditions of learning, and instructional methods to bring about these conditions, it makes sense to consider what constructivist approaches propose in each of these categories.

Constructivist Learning Goals

Unlike the "objectivist approach . . . that focuses on identifying the entities, relations, and attributes that the learner must 'know'" (Duffy & Jonassen, 1991, p. 8), the constructivist approach to identifying learning goals emphasizes learning in context. Brown et al. (1989), for example, argued that knowledge that learners can usefully deploy should be developed. Moreover, this can only be done in the context of meaningful activity. It is not enough, in other words, for students to acquire concepts or routines that lie inert, never to be called upon even in the face of relevant problems to be solved. Instead, knowledge must develop and continue to change with the activity of the learner. "Learning [is] a continuous, life-long process resulting from acting in situations" (Brown et al., 1989, p. 33).

In this statement, we see from the start how constructivist ideas have emerged from or are consistent with theories discussed in previous chapters. That knowledge develops in context is central to the notions of situated learning (see chapter 5), Bruner's discovery learning (see chapter 7), and the dialectics of Vygotsky's theory (see chapter 7).

As a start to articulating what is meant by "deployable knowledge learned in context," the CTGV (1991a) defined thinking activities to be the primary goals of concern to constructivists. Specifically, they named: "the ability to write persuasive essays, engage in informal reasoning, explain how data relate to theory in scientific investigations, and formulate and solve moderately complex problems that require mathematical reasoning" (CTGV, 1991a, p. 34). Virtually agreeing with these sentiments, Perkins (1991a) declared, "The basic goals of education are deceptively simple. To mention three, education strives for the retention, understanding, and active use of knowledge and skills" (p. 18).

Other authors have offered variations of these goals. Spiro et al. (1991) described the need for learners to acquire cognitive flexibility, whereas Culler (1990) spoke of the need to foster poststructuralist thinking, a kind of reflective criticism. Critical thinking and mindful consideration are also among those goals thought to be fostered by constructivist pedagogy.

If we consider this constructivist collection of goals in light of a taxonomy such as Gagné's, what would we conclude? Are the authors cited above defining educational goals that Gagné would categorize as higher order rule using (problem solving) and cognitive strategies? Dick (1991) clearly thought so when he discussed, from an instructional designer's perspective, research and development efforts of the Cognition and Technology Group at Vanderbilt and others. Goals that instructional designers might define for the scenarios at the beginning of chapter 10, for example, include diagnose hypertension (Scenario 10-1), solve realistic word problems (Scenario 10-2), or conduct a sales transaction efficiently and pleasantly (Scenario 10-3). These seem to be virtually no different from goals that constructivists might define for those situations. But, as we shall see, how constructivists would proceed to design instruction to meet those goals differs in fundamental ways from how someone following Gagné's theory would proceed.

Dick (1991) raised a concern, for instance, about the lack of attention paid by constructivists to the entry behaviors of students. He stated, "Designers use analytic techniques to determine what a student must know or be able to do before beginning instruction, because without these skills research shows they will not be able to learn new skills. Why are constructivists not concerned that the gap will be too great between the schema of some students and the tools and information that they are provided?" (Dick, 1991, p. 43).

In Dick's view, achievement of a goal such as diagnosing hypertension must depend upon prior knowledge of hypertensive symptoms, as well as the ability to distinguish those from similar conditions that might be attributable to some other disease. An instructional analysis would reveal not only what these prior skills are that must be acquired before the end goal can be reached, but also whether students have actually acquired the identified skills. If they have not, then remediation would be prescribed before students engaged in solving problems dependent upon those skills.

In response to Dick's concerns, Perkins (1991b) acknowledged the cognitive demands that constructivist learning goals and instruction typically place on learners. Learners must deal with complex problems, and they must "play more of the task management role than in conventional instruction" (Perkins, 1991b, p. 20). According to Perkins, however, this simply implies that teachers must coach individual students who lack adequate entry skills. "It is the job of the constructivist teacher . . . to hold learners in their 'zone of proximal development' by providing just enough help and guidance, but not too much" (Perkins, 1991b, p. 20). Similarly, Cunningham (1992) commented that teachers must not only coach students who lack prerequisite skills, but persuade those who are unwilling or unmotivated to engage in instruction. Just how teachers can best coach unable students and coax unwilling ones remains an open question (Driscoll & Lebow, 1992).

One possible way to deal with the lack of prerequisite knowledge and skills is to identify and ameliorate gaps within the context of the desired problem solving (CTGV, 1992). In other words, a part of solving complex problems involves determining what skills or information a learner needs to know. And learners who discover that, to solve a problem at hand, they must acquire some other skill or piece of information will be more motivated to do just that. Consider, for example, your own knowledge of the word processor or other computer software that you use regularly. Chances are that you do not know all of its possible functions and routines. Chances are even greater that to learn some of those that you do not know will require learning one or two other routines first. But it is unlikely that you will take the time to learn any of these unknown routines until you encounter a need for them. Once that need is present, however, you will learn whatever prerequisites are necessary to acquire the skill that meets your needs.

The same is probably true for learners involved in solving a complex problem like those presented by the CTGV. As students determine what subproblems must be solved in order to solve the challenge presented in an instructional video (e.g., what is the fastest way to rescue an injured eagle from a meadow to which there are no passable roads?), they discover needs for further learning (e.g., how do we determine how much fuel would be needed if an ultralight aircraft is used to fly to the meadow?). "Once these insights about need occur, then it is appropriate and beneficial to let students find environments (e.g., drill-and-practice programs) that can help them master specific types of information more efficiently" (CTGV, 1992,

p. 77). Thus, the medical student who realizes, in the course of a clinical interview, that she or he cannot call to mind the symptoms of hypertension with which to compare an observed symptom will be motivated to restudy that information.

Prerequisite skills or entry learning goals, then, are not necessarily ignored by constructivists, but they are attended to largely in the context of higher order goals. Moreover, detailed analyses of learning goals, of the sort intended to yield specific instructional objectives, are likely to be viewed by many constructivists as destroying the essence, or holistic nature, of the goal. This is because such analyses tend to result in "decontextualized" skills and knowledge where the very reason for learning them is lost or forgotten. Instead, constructivists prefer to retain their focus on higher order goals and just make sure the necessary scaffolding is there for support when, and if, learners require it.

It seems clear from the remarks of both Perkins and the CTGV that constructivist learning goals are best met through a variety of instructional conditions that differ from any proposed by theorists like Gagné. Let us now consider what these might be.

Constructivist Conditions for Learning

If problem-solving, reasoning, critical thinking, and the active use of knowledge constitute the goals of constructivist instruction, what are the learning conditions likely to bring these goals about? Again we see a variety of recommendations from the numerous researchers attempting to articulate constructivist theory. Moreover, many of these recommendations embody instructional principles that were originally derived from theories already discussed. Finally, as we shall also see, they largely emphasize the process of learning, rather than the products of learning. Collectively, these recommendations include:

1. Provide complex learning environments that incorporate authentic activity (e.g., CTGV, 1991a, 1992; Hannafin, 1992; Honebein, Duffy, & Fishman, in press; Levin & Waugh, 1987; cf. mental models in chapter 5 and Piaget's theory in chapter 6; Perkins, 1991a; Spiro et al., 1991);

2. Provide for social negotiation as an integral part of learning (e.g., CTGV, 1990; Culler, 1990; also Piaget in chapter 6; Vygotsky in chapter 7; reciprocal teaching in chapter 7; cooperative learning in chapter 9; Cunningham, 1992; Language Development & Hypermedia Research Group, 1992a, 1992b);

3. Juxtapose instructional content and include access to multiple modes of representation (e.g., Cunningham, 1992; Spiro et al., 1991; also semiotic theory in chapter 3);

4. Nurture reflexivity (e.g., Cunningham, 1987, 1992; Language Development & Hypermedia Group, 1992a, 1992b; cf. Bruner in chapter 7); and

5. Emphasize student-centered instruction (e.g., Hannafin, 1992; Perkins, 1991a).

Complex Learning Environments

"Students cannot be expected to learn to deal with complexity unless they have the opportunity to do so" (CTGV, 1991a, p. 36, emphasis theirs). This bold statement undoubtedly reflects the opinions of most constructivist authors, who further believe that simplifying tasks for learners will prevent them from learning how to solve the complex problems they will face in real life. For problem solving skills to be maximally facilitated, they argue, learners must cope with very complex situations. Remember from chapter 5 that Schoenfeld's students believed math problems were virtually unsolvable if they could not be solved in 5 minutes or less (Schoenfeld, 1988). Experience with only simple problems can lead to such beliefs, whereas experience with more complicated and realistic problems can prevent such erroneous ideas.

What complex problems entail seems to depend largely upon the subject matter within which problem solving and reasoning are being learned. To a somewhat lesser extent, perhaps, they also depend upon the ages and characteristics of the targeted learners. The video-based learning environments that the CTGV (1990, 1991a) developed for mathematical problem solving, for example, contain problems of more than 15 interrelated steps. All of the information required to solve these problems is incorporated into each video, but the students must decide what information is relevant and how various pieces fit together. Initially used with fifth and sixth grade students, the videos have apparently been adapted successfully for use with first and second graders (CTGV, 1991b).

Learning environment complexity can also be conceived in terms of both the tools and the content of learning (Perkins, 1991a, 1991b). With respect to content, much constructivist instruction aims to debunk students' naive conceptions or misconceptions, particularly in the areas of science and mathematics. To do this, situations must make plain the inconsistencies and inadequacies of the learners' models and "challenge [them] either to construct better models or at least to ponder the merits of alternative models presented by the teacher" (Perkins, 1991b, p. 19). But what should such situations look like?

This is where the tools of a rich learning environment come in. Specifically, Perkins proposed that "construction kits" and "phenomenaria" be widely used in the classroom (1991a). Construction kits enable learners to assemble "not just things, such as TinkerToys, but more abstract entities, such as commands in a program language, creatures in a simulated ecology, or equations in an environment supporting mathematical manipulations" (p. 19). Similarly, phenomenaria include such things as simulation games and computer-based microworlds that allow students to observe various phenomena and to manipulate concepts and assumptions within those phenomena.

An alternative argument for complex learning environments comes from research on how people learn to solve problems in "ill-structured domains" (Spiro et al., 1991; see also Spiro and Jehng, 1990). Unlike solving an algebraic problem, for example, diagnosing a medical problem depends more on heuristics than on well-formed rules. Furthermore, a doctor (unlike a mathematician) has no proven means for determining whether a diagnosis is correct. Although a prescribed treatment may appear to be suc-cessful in curing the patient, at least two other possibilities are often equally plausible. The treatment may be ineffective and the patient got better on his or her own, or the treatment effectively cured the problem, but the problem was not what was originally diagnosed. Doctors must be prepared to accept either of these possibilities if additional evidence seems to warrant it.

Spiro and his colleagues documented the tendency of medical students to oversimplify the concepts and principles comprising diagnostic medicine. They argued that "instructional focus on general principles with wide scope of application across cases or examples" (Spiro et al., 1991, p. 27) was the cause. Part of the solution, therefore, should be to retain, in medical instruction, the complexity inherent in this ill-structured domain. In order to do this, cases should be studied as they really occurred, "not as stripped down 'textbook examples' that conveniently illustrate some principle" (Spiro, Vispoel, Schmitz, Samarapungavan, & Boerger, 1987, p. 181). In learning about hypertension, then, medical students might best examine multiple case histories of hypertensive patients, so that the full range of their symptoms might be illustrated.

Although Gagné does not appear to incorporate the notion of complex learning environments in the conditions for learning, he has written recently about the importance of teaching multiple goals within a context that meaningfully relates them. This larger scale activity, or enterprise, gives meaning and purpose to the individual learning objectives. Then when these individual objectives become integrated during learning, they comprise a schema in the mind of the learner (Gagné & Merrill, 1990). According to Gagné and Merrill (1990), designers of instruction should make provision for this enterprise schema by communicating the purpose of instruction to learners. This is not unlike Keller's motivational category of enhancing relevance (see chapter 9), but it probably falls short of the constructivist's call for learning environments in which learners can experience the full complexity and authenticity of real world problems.

Finally, the concept of authenticity in learning environments bears additional scrutiny. The inclusion of complex problems is one way in which authentic learning environments can be established. Another tactic is to build in ownership of the task by the learners (Honebein et al., in press). As an example, consider the following report of a project with elementary school students:

> In Harel and Papert's [1992] work, elementary school students who displayed a great dislike for fractions tackled the task of learning about fractions with great enthusiasm when their role was changed from students to software designers. They were asked to design a computer program in LOGO (software they were already familiar with) that would teach the basics of fractions to children one year younger than themselves. In order to do this, they first had to teach themselves what was important to know about fractions. When the project was complete, the students had learned not only about fractions, but also about software design and instructional design. (Honebein et al., in press, p. 9)

This example is remarkably similar to one cited in an earlier chapter in which an elementary school teacher had students produce videotapes to teach their peers about topics in science. In both cases, the students have an investment in the project, making their own decisions and evaluating their own progress. The teacher is there to serve as coach and resource, sharing in the learning process rather than controlling it.

Social Negotiation

". . . learning in most settings is a communal activity, a sharing of the culture" (Bruner, 1986, p. 127). Or, to paraphrase Vygotsky, higher mental processes in humans develop through social interaction. Because constructivists hold to these beliefs about learning and thinking, they emphasize collaboration as a critical feature in the learning environment. Collaboration is not just a matter of asking students to work together in groups or to share their individual knowledge with one another. Rather, collaboration enables insights and solutions to arise synergistically (Brown et al., 1989) that would not otherwise come about. For example, can you recall a situation in which, but for the efforts of a group, some problem would have gone unsolved? No single member of the group would have had the wherewithall to independently generate an effective solution, but the members together had the necessary knowledge.

Another important function of collaboration in learning environments is to provide a means for individuals to understand perspectives other than their own. Cunningham (1992), for example, argued that dialogue in a social setting is required for students to come to understand another's view. Listening, or reading privately, is not sufficient to challenge the individual's egocentric thinking. Echoing Cunningham's view, the Language Development & Hypermedia Group (1992a, 1992b) described instruction as a matter of nurturing processes by which learners develop and defend individual perspectives while recognizing those of others. What happens in learning, then, is the transmission or sharing of cultural knowledge, i.e., how concepts in a particular culture are understood and applied by its members.

As an example, consider how medical interns can be brought together to discuss symptoms noticed in a particular case. Having taken note of different things, they may propose alternative treatments, which they must then justify to their peers. Similarly, students involved in solving a challenge such as those proposed in the CTGV's instructional videodisks may propose alternative solutions and then justify the reasoning behind their proposals. Hearing a variety of other perspectives helps learners to judge the quality of their own solutions and to learn perhaps more effective strategies for problem solving.

Juxtaposition of Instructional Content
Characteristic of ill-structured content domains are cases or examples that are diverse, irregular, and complex (Spiro et al., 1991). General principles do not apply widely across cases, nor is it possible to use a single analogy or model to represent all cases or content in the domain. When learners attempt to apply, to ill-structured domains, the strategies they have used effectively for understanding well-structured domains, they make errors of oversimplification, overgeneralization, and overreliance on context-independent representations (Spiro, Coulson, Feltovich, & Anderson, 1988).

In the biomedical domain, for example, which Spiro and his colleagues have contended is ill-structured, students who use only the metaphor of the machine to help them understand how the body functions tend to analyze cases only partially. The same is true among students who understand bodily functions only in terms of organicist metaphors. The point Spiro makes is that neither metaphor is wrong, but neither metaphor captures all aspects of body functions.

Remember the difficulties inherent in selecting pedagogical models for helping students to develop mental models of complex phenomena (see chapter 5). Whereas mental models researchers proposed the use of one model, pointing out its limitations, or a series of models to illustrate different aspects of the phenomenon, Spiro and his colleagues have proposed the notion of **multiple juxtapositions of instructional content**. That is, the only way to avoid partial understandings, is to *examine the same* *material from multiple perspectives or multiple metaphors* (Spiro et al., 1988, 1991). "Revisiting the same material, at different times, in rearranged contexts, for different purposes, and from different conceptual perspectives is essential for attaining the goals of advanced knowledge acquisition" (Spiro et al., 1991, p. 28).

Cunningham (1992) advanced a similar argument when he suggested that hypermedia could be effectively used to encourage students to think about ideas, theories, literary works, or whatever from a variety of perspectives. In a sense, books such as this one about theories of learning are written with much the same goal in mind. Many of the same questions about learning are tackled by different theorists from different perspectives, and different metaphors for learning function to highlight different aspects of the same content. The actual juxtaposition of ideas, however, is largely in your hands as the reader. It would be unwieldy for me, as the author, to revisit content to the extent that you, as the reader, can do very easily. For this reason, perhaps, many constructivist theorists have turned to emerging technologies as the most promising means by which to implement essential learning conditions.

Finally, using multiple modes of representation can serve as a means of juxtaposition. That is, viewing the same content through different sensory modes (such as visual, auditory, or tactile) again enables different aspects of it to be seen. It is also worth noting that multiple modes of representation have now received support as an instructional strategy from cognitive information processing theory, educational semiotics, and biological theories, as well as from constructivism.

Nurturance of Reflexivity

Reflexivity, as Cunningham defined it (Cunningham, 1987, 1992; Language Development & Hypermedia Group, 1992a, 1992b), is *the ability of students to be aware of their own role in the knowledge construction process."* Awareness of one's own thinking and learning processes is a capability cognitive information processing theorists have commonly called metacognition (see chapter 3). Helping learners to become more aware of their thinking processes is thought by many, including Gagné, to be essential in the development of mindful, strategic behavior or cognitive strategies. Although constructivists might well agree with cognitive information processing theorists on the definition and importance of metacognition, they mean something more by reflexivity.

With reflexivity, a critical attitude exists in learners, an attitude that prompts them to be aware of how and what structures create meaning. With this awareness comes the ability to invent and explore new structures or new interpretive contexts. In other words, when learners come to realize how a particular set of assumptions or world view shapes their knowledge, they are free to explore what may result from an alternate set of assumptions or a different world view.

The goal of reflexivity is partly supported by the juxtaposition of instructional content and the resulting emphasis on multiple perspectives. It is also very much related to ownership in instruction and the learner's subsequent commitment to a particular perspective.

Consider, for example, the different views of learning that are presented in this book. What do they each imply about your own learning of their assumptions and principles? From a cognitive information processing point of view, you might be expected to treat the book as declarative knowledge to be acquired, with different schemata about the various theories constituting the result of your learning efforts. By contrast, from a constructivist point of view, you might be expected to recognize that all these theories are constructed to make sense of the phenomenon of learning. Their different assumptions lead to different pictures of learning, and consequently, of instruction. From discussion with your classmates and others, you might develop a personal view as to what theory (or theories) is the most right or useful. Or you may reject the assumptions upon which all these theories have been built in order to pose a new set of assumptions and explore a potentially new theory of learning.

It should be noted that this contrast between constructivist and information processing theory has been drawn rather sharply to illustrate the point of reflexivity. Not everyone would agree with my distinctions, but the very debate that would be prompted by such disagreement would serve to further illuminate both positions.

Nurturing reflexivity, then, is a learning condition that constructivists assert is essential to the acquisition of goals such as reasoning, understanding multiple perspectives, and committing to a particular position for beliefs that can be articulated and defended.

Student-Centered Instruction

Arranging instruction to meet individual student needs is not an idea new to constructivism. It has been a recurring theme throughout not only this book but also learning theory development in general. What distinguishes the constructivist perspective on student-centered instruction is the placement of the student as "the principal arbiter in making judgments as to what, when, and how learning will occur" (Hannafin, 1992). In other words, students are not passive recipients of instruction that has been designed for them. Instead, they are actively involved in determining what their own learning needs are and how those needs can best be satisfied. As Perkins (1991b) put it, "students are not likely to become autonomous thinkers and learners if they lack an opportunity to manage their own learning" (p. 20). Once again, the notion of student ownership in learning arises.

Whether students are prepared to manage their own learning is another question altogether. Clark (1982) reviewed research on student attitudes toward and preferences for particular instructional strategies and concluded that students are not the best judges of their own learning needs. For the most part, they preferred methods that were not well suited for facilitating their individual achievement. Many investigators of learner control in computer-based instruction have reached much the same conclusion (Steinberg, 1989). When given options, learners apparently choose the quickest route through the instruction, whether or not that route best meets their learning needs.

Two issues are raised by these findings. The first concerns whether students are capable of making effective judgments about their own learning needs and how to satisfy them, whereas the second concerns whether they are willing to do so. A tacit assumption of student-centered learning environments is that students possess whatever metacognitive skills are necessary to successfully navigate in those environments (Hannafin, 1992). If they do not, then designers of these environments should embed aids to students that will help them navigate lessons. These might include, for example, an organizing theme, various forms of help, advice, hints, or guided reflection.

Perkins (1991b) agreed that students must often be assisted in managing learning tasks and referred to the classic solution of scaffolding, or coaching, mentioned earlier. Exactly how to do this, particularly by one teacher with a number of students, is less clear and is indicated by Driscoll and Lebow (1992) as a pressing problem for constructivist researchers to solve.

As for the concern that students do not all "buy into" the notion of managing their own learning, it has already been suggested that teachers must persuade them. To do this requires that a "teacher or instructional designer approach the double agenda as such, engaging students constructively in thinking both about X [the content] and about the learning process reflectively" (Perkins, 1991b, p. 20).

Finally, perhaps one of the reasons that students have difficulty navigating a learning environment or try not to do so on their own accord is that such environments have typically been decontextualized. Without a meaningful context to guide them, learners are left to figure out "what the teacher wants" or "what will be on the test." When that happens, learning tasks become tests of endurance, something "to be gotten through." On the other hand, "tasks that are thought to be difficult when attempted in a decontextualized environment become intuitive when situated in a larger framework" (Honebein et al., in press), that is, a more authentic context. The reasons become clear as to why information and skills should be learned, and their learning advances the students toward the achievement

**TABLE   11–1   A Summary of Goals, Conditions of Learning, and
Instructional Methods Consistent with Constructivism**

Instructional Goals	Conditions of Learning	Methods of Instruction
Reasoning Critical thinking Problem solving	Complex, rich learning environments that incorporate authentic activity	Microworlds, construction kits, phenomenaria, cognitive apprenticeships
Retention, understanding, and use	Social negotiation	Collaborative learning, Bubble Dialogue, Cognitive apprenticeships
Cognitive flexibility Mindful reflection	Juxtaposition of instructional content	Microworlds, hypermedia
	Nurturance of reflexivity	Bubble Dialogue, role plays, debates, collaborative learning
	Student-centered instruction	Microworlds, Bubble Dialogue, collaborative learning, hypermedia

of some larger goal, like the production of videotapes to teach peers what they have learned.

Summary

Displayed as a summary in Table 11–1 are the learning goals associated with constructivism, together with the learning conditions presumed to bring about those goals. We are now ready to consider the third element in constructivist instructional theory: specific methods of instruction. Suggested methods are also presented in Table 11–1.

Constructivist Methods of Instruction

Some methods have already been suggested that are shown or likely to be effective in implementing the conditions constructivists believe are essential for learning. Others, such as microworlds and hypermedia designs, cognitive apprenticeships, collaborative learning, and open software and authoring tools, serve to implement multiple conditions simultaneously. Each merits a brief discussion.

Microworlds and Hypermedia Designs

As the name implies, microworlds are small but complete subsets of real environments that promote discovery and exploration (Papert, 1981). Their design has been influenced by research on mental models (see chapter 5) as well as theoretical developments leading to the emergence of constructivism. Microworlds have two essential characteristics that distinguish them from similar concepts, such as simulations (Rieber, 1991b). That is, they embody the simplest working model of a domain or system, and they offer a point of entry that matches the learner's cognitive state. LOGO, for example, perhaps the most widely researched microworld currently in existence, permits children to explore and discover the world of computer programming by writing commands that drive a "turtle" (Papert, 1980).

In *ScienceVision*, an interactive videodisk-based microworld, students conduct scientific experiments of the sort that would generally be precluded from middle school instruction because of prohibitive expense, time requirements, or potential danger to the students (Tobin & Dawson, 1992). For example, in the study of ecology, students can investigate what it would take to convert a mining site to farmland. Through simulation, they analyze soil samples, plant and monitor various crops, and conduct cost-benefit analyses based on their findings.

Because interactive videodisk microworlds are themselves expensive to design and produce, some researchers and instructors are turning to hypermedia as a less expensive and more widely available alternative. Hypermedia designs typically run on microcomputers, which can be networked and therefore accessed by several learners at once. Design strategies include representing a vast body of information about the topic of interest, including such types of information as autobiographical data, descriptions, definitions, photographs or graphic designs, interviews or other samples of research data, and the like. For example, in the Lab Design Project (Honebein, Chen, & Brescia, 1992), graduate students investigate the sociology of a building by exploring different aspects of it that are represented in the hypermedia database. They can call up from the database the types of information they would actually collect if they were to do research in a real building (Honebein et al., in press).

At the least, microworlds and hypermedia provide rich, student-centered learning environments in which authentic activity is stressed. Depending upon their use in an instructional context, they may also support conditions of social negotiation (e.g., Emihovich, 1988) and nurturance of reflexivity (Rieber, 1991a, 1991b).

Cognitive Apprenticeships
According to Brown et al. (1989), one means by which students can engage in authentic activity is through cognitive apprenticeships. As an example, they described how apprentice tailors learn about cutting and sewing first by ironing finished garments. By implication, school children should

acquire the knowledge and skills of historians, mathematicians, or scientists by becoming apprentices in those disciplines.

Certainly in higher education, the concept of apprenticeships has long been a part of instructional programs, typically taking the form of an internship in the student's final semester of study. The usual purpose of internships is to provide students with an opportunity to practice the skills and knowledge they have spent (in some cases) years studying. Advantages accrue from the authentic environment in which the student is placed and from the transitional nature of the assignment. In other words, students do the same work as regular employees, but are not yet expected to bear the same responsibilities.

Although school children and learners in other situations cannot become apprentices in quite the same way as interns, they may experience some of the same advantages through projects in which the instructor models desired skills and coaches learners as they attempt to follow suit. Honebein et al. (in press) described an educational research class, for example, designed to engage students in the authentic activities of educational research such as generating researchable ideas, formulating research problems, and designing studies to investigate those problems. The instructor assumed a role similar to that of a research center director—meeting with students individually and collectively throughout each phase of the projects they planned, providing feedback on their decisions, and helping them to refine the process. In this example, we see an emphasis on both authenticity and complexity of experience, which, in the absence of true internships, can be provided to some degree through lengthy, multifaceted projects.

Along with the potential advantages of cognitive apprenticeships—authentic activity, sharing of culture—there may also be disadvantages. Wineburg (1989) commented that, unless well-planned and monitored, apprenticeships can be "tedious, inefficient, repressive, servile, tradition-bound, and in some cases downright mean" (p. 9). The same could be true for lengthy projects. Care should be taken to ensure that each student is involved in a worthwhile educational experience.

Collaborative Learning and Computer-Based Tools

The functions of and strategies for collaborative learning were discussed at length in chapter 9. Constructivists have added little yet to that literature except to emphasize the importance of intragroup dependence. However, another means for facilitating collaboration among learners can be found in a computer-based tool known as Bubble Dialogue, produced by the Language Development & Hypermedia Group (1992a, 1992b).

Bubble Dialogue is a type of computer-based tool referred to by its designers as "open software." Open software is software that is largely empty of content, being instead a "shell" that can be readily adapted to the user's intended application. Through Bubble Dialogue, students create conversations among comic strip characters, including thoughts that would not be said out loud. In this way, they have the opportunity to express "personal (perhaps naive) views of the world, to contemplate multiple perspectives in both public and private domains and to accommodate their own thinking to contrary views" (Language Development & Hypermedia Group, 1992a, p. 44).

The authors of Bubble Dialogue have found the tool useful in facilitating dialogue among grade school children about the longstanding conflict in Northern Ireland and among preservice teachers about teaching strategies. Moreover, the permanent archive created by the program facilitates later editing or reflection and supports the development of literacy.

Summary
It is probably no accident that constructivism is gaining popularity and momentum at the same time interactive, user-friendly computer technologies are becoming widely available. The computer offers an effective means for implementing constructivist strategies that would be difficult to accomplish in other media. However, this is not to imply that other media cannot also be effectively employed within constructivist pedagogy. The discussion that is facilitated by Bubble Dialogue, for example, can also occur in well managed debates and role plays. Moreover, projects need not be situated in hypermedia databases to provide authentic activity and opportunities for apprenticeship. However, it is likely that a variety of resources and time will be required to effectively implement most constructivist principles.

CONCLUSION

Constructivism has taken such a strong hold in many areas of education today that it seemed appropriate to discuss it within its own chapter, despite the fact that it is not yet one theory but a multitude of approaches. As these approaches develop and proliferate, it also becomes less clear as to whether constructivism is a theory or a philosophy (Lebow, in press). As a theory, it may indeed be incommensurable with an instructional theory such as Gagné's, because the two would have been built from opposing assumptions. But as a philosophy, constructivism may be viewed as not competing with other instructional theories, but providing them with an alternative set of values that deserve serious consideration.

These values, according to Lebow (in press), form the basis for five principles which should perhaps be incorporated into any theory of instruction: "(a) maintain a buffer between the learner and the potentially damaging effects of instructional practices in use, (b) provide a context for learning where the needs for both autonomy and belongingness are supported, (c) embed the reasons for learning something into the learning activity itself, (d) support self-regulation through the promotion of skills and attitudes that enable the learner to assume increasing responsibility for the develop-

mental restructuring process, and (e) strengthen the learner's tendency to engage in intentional learning processes" (pp. 4–5).

Much remains to be done to articulate constructivist theory and determine its place in the broader framework of learning and instructional theory. At this point, theory and conjecture far outstrip empirical findings. The next few years should be exciting ones as research in constructivism begins to catch up.

SUGGESTED READINGS

Duffy, T. M., Lowyck, J., and Jonassen, D. (in press). *Designing environments for constructive learning*. Hillsdale, NJ: Erlbaum.

Educational Technology (1991, May). Special issue on constructivism and educational technology.

Educational Technology (1991, September). Continuing the dialogue.

REFLECTIVE QUESTIONS AND ACTIVITIES

1. Contrast the epistemologies underlying Gagne's instructional theory and constructivism, with a view toward determining their compatibility or incompatibility. When Kuhn (1970) described the process of scientific revolution, in which one paradigm (and corresponding epistemology) supplants another, he argued that competing paradigms are incommensurable. In other words, one could not at the same time be an objectivist and a constructivist. Review other points of view on the incommensurability thesis (see, for example, past issues of the *Educational Researcher*). Decide what your own views are on the subject and present arguments to support your case.

2. Using the unit of instruction you analyzed from the perspective of Gagne's theory, examine it again from the perspective of constructivism. What features now would be considered well designed, and what features does it lack to be good instruction? From a constructivist point of view, what effects would this instruction be likely to have on learners? Are these effects

the same or different from those predicted on the basis of Gagne's theory? Explain.

3. Writing and/or using instructional objectives is something that most instructional designers and many teachers take for granted and think little about. Objectives, however, as you have seen in this book, come from a behaviorist tradition and reflect an empiricist perspective on learning. For this reason, the practice of using objectives has been criticized by constructivists. Considering the role that objectives have played in assessment, how should objectives and assessments change to be consistent with constructivism?

4. Locate and view a hypermedia microworld or learning environment. Analyze its features in terms of Gagne's instructional theory and the principles of constructivism, and compare your analyses.

5. Rewrite one of the instructional plans you have already generated in the course of reading this book, this time in terms of constructivism. Compare how this plan differs from its Gagné version, and evaluate the probable effects of the two plans on learning.

▶ 12

Toward a Personal Theory of Learning

Throughout this book, I have tried to emphasize the nature of theories as provisional and limited in their views of learning. That is, any given learning theory accounts for only some of the data that have been amassed about learning phenomena. Moreover, each theory provides a particular picture of learning that highlights some aspects and obscures others. Because learning is such a complex matter, it is perhaps impossible to conceive of a single theory broad enough to encompass all important aspects of learning and yet still specific enough to be useful for instruction. So, like the blind men, each touching a different part of the elephant, we must evaluate each separate theory for what it illuminates about learning and for how it can guide the development of effective instruction.

Evaluating various learning theories for their validity and usefulness ultimately becomes a matter of developing a personal theory of learning and instruction. Before you began reading this book, you already possessed many intuitive theories about learning and instruction. These would have been based on your own experience of schooling and instruction, on any experiences you had as a teacher or designer of instruction, and on any previous knowledge you had acquired about learning and instruction. You may or may not, however, have given much thought to your intuitive theories or their influence on your actions in the classroom or at the design table. An experienced teacher or designer is likely to have been prompted to reflect upon his or her practices by classes that somehow went wrong or by instruction that failed to facilitate learning. But the neophyte's tacit theories have probably not been tested.

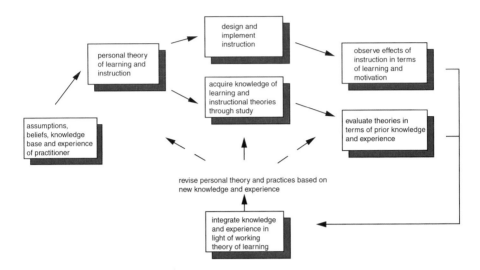

FIGURE   12–1   Building a Personal Theory of Learning and Instruction

Now, however, you are in a position to construct anew your personal theory of learning, with the expectation that it should serve as an improved guide to your own instructional practices. With each chapter, you have encountered concepts and ideas that added to or challenged your previous knowledge about learning and instruction. With each chapter, you have also had practice comparing, criticizing, and applying theories, and then reflecting on the results of those comparisons, criticisms, and applications. In essence, you have conducted much the same process of theory building as any of the theorists discussed in this book, especially if you have had the opportunity to try out some of the ideas presented here. Figure 12–1 illustrates how the systematic and recursive process of theory building that was depicted in Figure 1–1 at the beginning of the book can be revised to represent your personal theory building.

Although this is the end of the book, it is hoped that your reflective theory building has only begun. New findings in diverse fields from neuropsychology to computer-based training continually provide information for theory and practice in psychology and education. And as you gain experience, your practical knowledge will serve to temper your theoretical understandings to enable you to make instruction as good as it can be.

References

Allocco, L., Coffey, J., Dalton, A. M., Dariano, J., Dioguardi, J. E., Galterio, L., & Monahan, B. (1992, August). To teach or not to teach Logo: Reflecting on Logo's use as a problem-solving tool. *Educational Technology*, *32*, 23–27.

Anderson, J. R. (1976). *Language, memory and thought*. Hillsdale, NJ: Erlbaum.

Anderson, J. R. (1983). *The architecture of cognition*. Cambridge, MA: Harvard University Press.

Anderson, J. R. (1990). *The adaptive character of thought*. Hillsdale: Erlbaum.

Anderson, J. R. & Bower, G. H. (1973). *Human associative memory*. Washington, DC: Winston.

Anderson, R. C. (1977). The notion of schemata and the educational enterprise. In R. C. Anderson, R. J. Spiro, and W. E. Montague (Eds.), *Schooling and the acquisition of knowledge*. Hillsdale, NJ: Erlbaum.

Anderson, R. C. (1982). Allocation of attention during reading. In A. Flammer and W. Kintsch (Eds.), *Discourse processing*. Amsterdam: North Holland.

Anderson, R. C., & Faust, G. W. (1973). *Educational psychology: The science of instruction and learning*. New York: Dodd, Mead.

Anderson, R. C., & Ortony, A. (1975). On putting apples into bottles—A problem of polysemy. *Cognitive Psychology*, *7*, 167–180.

Anderson, R. C., & Pichert, J. W. (1978). Recall of previously unrecallable information following a shift in perspective. *Journal of Verbal Learning and Verbal Behavior*, *17*, 1–12.

Anderson, R. C., Spiro, R. J., & Anderson, M. C. (1978). Schemata as scaffolding for the representation of information in connected discourse. *American Educational Research Journal*, *15*, 433–440.

Andre, T. (1979). Does answering higher-level questions while reading facilitate productive learning? *Review of Educational Research*, *49*, 280–318.

Andre, T., & Phye, G. D. (1986). Cognition, learning, and education. In G. D. Phye and T. Andre (Eds.), *Cognitive classroom learning*. Orlando: Academic Press.

Anglin, G. J., & Towers, R. L. (1992). Reference citations in selected instructional design and technology journals, 1985–1990. *Educational Technology Research and Development*, *40*(1), 40–46.

Anglin, J. M. (Ed.). (1973). *Jerome S. Bruner: Beyond the information given*. New York: Norton.

Armbruster, B. B. (1986). Schema theory and the design of content-area textbooks. *Educational Psychologist*, *21*, 253–267.

Ashton, P. T., & Webb, R. B. (1986). *Making a difference: Teachers' sense of efficacy and student achievement*. New York: Longman.

Atkins, M., & Blissett, G. (1992, January). Interactive video and cognitive problem-solving skills. *Educational Technology*, *32*, 44–54.

Atkinson, J. W. (1964). *An introduction to motivation*. Princeton, NJ: Van Nostrand.

Atkinson, R. C., & Shiffrin, R. M. (1968). Human memory: A proposed system and its control processes. In K. Spence and J. Spence (Eds.), *The psychology of learning and motivation* (Vol. 2). New York: Academic Press.

Atkinson, R. C., & Shiffrin, R. M. (1971). The control of short-term memory. *Scientific American*, 225, 82–90.

Ausubel, D. P. (1960). The use of advance organizers in the learning and retention of meaningful verbal material. *Journal of Educational Psychology*, 51, 267–272.

Ausubel, D. P. (1961). In defense of verbal learning. *Educational Theory*, 11, 15–25.

Ausubel, D. P. (1962). A subsumption theory of meaningful verbal learning. *Journal of General Psychology*, 66, 213–224.

Ausubel, D. P. (1963a). *The psychology of meaningful verbal learning*. New York: Grune & Stratton.

Ausubel, D. P. (1963b). Cognitive structure and the facilitation of meaningful verbal learning. *Journal of Teacher Education*, 14, 217–221.

Ausubel, D. P. (1965). A cognitive structure view of word and concept meaning. In R. C. Anderson and D. P. Ausubel (Eds.), *Readings in the psychology of cognition*. New York: Holt, Rinehart and Winston.

Ausubel, D. P. (1968). *Educational psychology: A cognitive view*. New York: Holt, Rinehart and Winston.

Ausubel, D. P. (1980). Schemata, cognitive structure, and advance organizers: A reply to Anderson, Spiro, and Anderson. *American Educational Research Journal*, 17, 400–404.

Ausubel, D. P., & Fitzgerald, D. (1961). The role of discriminability in meaningful verbal learning. *Journal of Educational Psychology*, 52, 266–274.

Ausubel, D. P., & Fitzgerald, D. (1962). Organizer, general background, and antecedent learning variables in sequential verbal learning. *Journal of Educational Psychology*, 53, 243–249.

Ausubel, D. P., Novak, J. D., & Hanesian, H. (1978). *Educational psychology: A cognitive view* (2nd ed.). New York: Holt, Rinehart and Winston.

Ausubel, D. P., & Youssef, M. (1963). The role of discriminability in meaningful parallel learning. *Journal of Educational Psychology*, 54, 331–336.

Ayllon, T., & Azrin, N. H. (1968). *The token economy*. New York: Appleton-Century-Crofts.

Azrin, N. H. (1967, May). Pain and aggression. *Psychology Today*, 1, 27–33.

Azrin, N. H., & Holz, W. C. (1966). Punishment. In W. A. Honig (Ed.) *Operant behavior: Areas of research and application*. New York: Appleton-Century-Crofts.

Bach-y-Rita, P. (1980). Brain plasticity as a basis for therapeutic procedures. In   P. Bach-y-Rita (Ed.), *Recovery of function: Theoretical considerations for brain injury rehabilitation*. Baltimore: University Park Press.

Bach-y-Rita, P. (1982). The relationship between motor processes and cognition in tactile vision substitution. In W. Prinz and A. Sanders (Eds.), *Cognition and motor processes*. New York: Springer-Verlag.

Baddeley, A. D. (1978). The trouble with levels: A reexamination of Craik and Lockhart's framework for memory research. *Psychological Review*, 85, 139–152.

Bandura, A. (1969). *Principles of behavior modification*. New York: Holt, Rinehart and Winston.

Bandura, A. (1977). Self-efficacy: Toward a unifying theory of behavioral change. *Psychological Review*, 84, 195–215.

Bandura, A. (1982). Self-efficacy mechanism in human agency. *American Psychologist*, 37, 122–147.

Bandura, A. (1986). *Social foundations of thought and action: A social-cognitive theory*. Englewood Cliffs, NJ: Prentice-Hall.

Bandura, A., Ross, D., & Ross, S. A. (1961). Transmission of aggression through imitation of aggressive models. *Journal of Abnormal and Social Psychology*, 63, 575–582.

Bandura, A., Ross, D., & Ross, S. A. (1963). Imitation of film-mediated aggressive models. *Journal of Abnormal and Social Psychology*, 66, 3–11.

Barclay, J. R., Bransford, J. D., Franks, J. J., McCarrell, N. S., & Nitsch, K. (1974). Comprehension and semantic flexibility. *Journal of Verbal Learning and Verbal Behavior*, 13, 471–481.

Barker, S., & Graham, G. P. (1987). Developmental study of praise and blame as attributional cues. *Journal of Educational Psychology*, 79, 62–66.

Barnes, B., & Clawson, E. U. (1975). Do advance organizers facilitate learning? Recommendations for further research based on the analysis of thirty-two studies. *Review of Educational Research*, 45, 637–659.

Barron, R. F. & Schwartz, R. M. (1984). Graphic postorganizers: A spatial learning strategy. In C. D. Holley and D. F. Dansereau (Eds.), *Spatial learning strategies*. Orlando: Academic Press.

Bartlett, F. C. (1932). *Remembering: A study in experimental and social psychology*. Cambridge, England: Cambridge University Press.

Bates, J. A. (1979). Extrinsic reward and intrinsic motivation: A review with implications for the classroom. *Review of Educational Research*, *49*, 557–576.

Bean, T. W., Singer, H., Sorter, J., & Frazee, C. (1986). The effect of metacognitive instruction in outlining and graphic organizer construction on students' comprehension in a tenth grade world history class. *Journal of Reading Behavior*, *18*, 153–169.

Beck, I. L. (1981). Reading problems and instructional practice. In T. G. Waller and G. E. MacKennon (Eds.), *Reading research: Advances in theory and practice* (Vol. 2). New York: Academic Press.

Beck, I. L. (1983). Developing comprehension: The impact of the directed reading lesson. In R. Anderson, R. Tierney, & J. Osborn (Eds.), *Learning to read in American schools*. Hillsdale, NJ: Erlbaum.

Belland, J. C. (1991). Developing connoisseurship in educational technology. In   D. Hlynka and J. C. Belland (Eds.), *Paradigms regained: The uses of illuminative, semiotic and post-modern criticism as modes of inquiry in educational technology*. Englewood Cliffs, NJ: Educational Technology Publications.

Bellezza, F. S. (1981). Mnemonic devices: Classification, characteristics, and criteria. *Review of Educational Research*, *51*, 247–275.

Bellugi, U. (1967). *The acquisition of negation*. Unpublished doctoral dissertation, Harvard University.

Bereiter, C. (1991, April). Implications of connectionism for thinking about rules. *Educational Researcher*, *20*, 10–16.

Berlyne, D. E. (1965). *Structure and direction in thinking*. New York: Wiley.

Bernhard, J. G. (1988). *Primates in the classroom: An evolutionary perspective on children's education*. Amherst, MA: The University of Massachusetts Press.

Bertelson, P. (1982). Lateral differences in normal man and lateralization of brain function. *International Journal of Psychology*, *17*, 173–210.

Bilodeau, I. M., & Schlosberg, H. (1951). Similarity in stimulating conditions as a variable in retroactive inhibition. *Journal of Experimental Psychology*, *41*, 199–204.

Bloom, B. S. (1986, February). "The hands and feet of genius." Automaticity. *Educational Leadership*, 70–77.

Bloom, B. S., Engelhart, M. D., Furst, E. J., Hill, W. H., & Krathwohl, D. R. (1956). *Taxonomy of educational objectives, handbook I: Cognitive domain*. New York: McKay.

Bornstein, R. F. (1988). Radical behaviorism, internal states, and the science of psychology: A reply to Skinner. *American Psychologist*, *43*, 819–821.

Bourne, L. E., Dominowski, R. L., Loftus, E. F., & Healy, A. F. (1986). *Cognitive processes* (2nd ed.). Englewood Cliffs, NJ: Prentice-Hall.

Bousfield, W. A. (1953). The occurrence of clustering in the recall of randomly arranged associates. *Journal of General Psychology*, *49*, 229–240.

Bower, G. H. (1981). Mood and memory. *American Psychologist*, *36*, 129–148.

Bower, G. H., Black, J. B., & Turner, T. J. (1979). Scripts in memory for text. *Cognitive Psychology*, *11*, 177–220.

Bower, G. H., & Clark, M. C. (1969). Narrative stories as mediators for serial learning. *Psychonomic Science*, *14*, 181–182.

Bower, G. H., Clark, M. C., Lesgold, A. M., & Winzenz, D. (1969). Hierarchical retrieval schemes in recall of categorized word lists. *Journal of Verbal Learning and Verbal Behavior*, *8*, 323–343.

Bower, G. H., & Hilgard, E. R. (1981). *Theories of learning* (5th ed.). Englewood Cliffs, NJ: Prentice-Hall.

Bower, G. H., Karlin, M. B., & Dueck, A. (1975). Comprehension and memory for pictures. *Memory and Cognition*, *3*, 216–220.

Brainerd, C. S. (1978). *Piaget's theory of intelligence*. Englewood Cliffs, NJ: Prentice-Hall.

Bransford, J. D. (1979). *Human cognition: Learning, understanding, remembering*. Belmont, CA: Wadsworth.

Bransford, J. D., & Franks, J. J. (1971). The abstraction of linguistic ideas. *Cognitive Psychology*, *2*, 331–350.

Bransford, J. D., & Johnson, M. K. (1972). Contextual prerequisites for understanding: Some investigations of comprehension and recall. *Journal of Verbal Learning and Verbal Behavior*, *11*, 717–726.

Bransford, J. D., & Johnson, M. K. (1973). Considerations of some problems of comprehension. In W. G. Chase (Ed.), *Visual information processing*. New York: Academic Press.

Breland, K., & Breland, M. (1961). The misbehavior of organisms. *American Psychologist*, *16*, 681–684.

Brewer, W. F. (1974). There is no convincing evidence for operant or classical conditioning in adult humans. In W. Weimer and D. Palermo (Eds.), *Cognition and the symbolic processes*. Hillsdale, NJ: Erlbaum.

Briggs, L. J. (1980, February). Thirty years of instructional design: One man's experience. *Educational Technology*, *20*, 45–50.

Broadbent, D. E. (1957). A mechanical model for human attention and immediate memory. *Psychological Review*, *64*, 205–215.

Brooks, L. W., & Dansereau, D. F. (1983). Effects of structural schema training and text organization on expository prose processing. *Journal of Educational Psychology*, *75*, 811–820.

Brown, A. L. (1980). Metacognitive development and reading. In R. J. Spiro, B. C. Bruce, & W. F. Brewer (Eds.), *Theoretical issues in reading comprehension*. Hillsdale, NJ: Erlbaum.

Brown, A. L., & Ferrara, R. (1985). Diagnosing zones of proximal development. In J. V. Wertsch (Ed.), *Culture, communication, and cognition: Vygotskian perspectives*. New York: Cambridge University Press.

Brown, A. L., & Palincsar, A. S. (1982). Inducing strategic learning from texts by means of informal, self-control training. *Topics in Learning and Learning Disabilities*, *2*, 1–17.

Brown, J. (1958). Some tests of the decay theory of immediate memory. *Quarterly Journal of Experimental Psychology*, *10*, 12–21.

Brown, J. S., Collins, A., & Duguid, P. (1989, January/February). Situated cognition and the culture of learning. *Educational Researcher*, *18*, 32–42.

Bruner, J. S. (1957/1973). Going beyond the information given. Originally published in *Contemporary approaches to cognition*, and reprinted in J. M. Anglin (Ed.), *Jerome S. Bruner: Going beyond the information given*. New York: Norton.

Bruner, J. S. (1960). Readiness for learning. In J. S. Bruner, *The process of education*. Cambridge, MA: Harvard University Press.

Bruner, J. S. (1961). The act of discovery. *Harvard Educational Review*, *31*(1), 21–32.

Bruner, J. S. (1962). Introduction. In L. S. Vygotsky, *Thought and language*. Cambridge, MA: The MIT Press.

Bruner, J. S. (1964). The course of cognitive growth. *American Psychologist*, *19*, 1–15.

Bruner, J. S. (1965). The growth of mind. *American Psychologist*, *20*, 1007–1017.

Bruner, J. S. (1966). *Toward a theory of instruction*. Cambridge, MA: Belknap.

Bruner, J. S. (1973a). Preface. In J. S. Bruner, *The relevance of education*. New York: Norton.

Bruner, J. S. (1973b). Some elements of discovery. In J. S. Bruner, *The relevance of education*. New York: Norton.

Bruner, J. S. (1973c). Culture and cognitive growth. In J. S. Bruner, *The relevance of education*. New York: Norton.

Bruner, J. S. (1973d). Poverty and childhood. In J. S. Bruner, *The relevance of education*. New York: Norton.

Bruner, J. S. (1985). On teaching thinking: An afterthought. In S. F. Chipman, J. W. Segal & R. Glaser (Eds.), *Thinking and learning skills* (Vol. 2). Hillsdale, NJ: Erlbaum.

Bruner, J. S. (1986). *Actual minds, possible worlds*. Cambridge, MA: Harvard University Press.

Bruner, J. S. & Bornstein, M. H. (1989). *Interaction in human development*. Hillsdale, NJ: Erlbaum.

Bruner, J. S., Goodnow, J., & Austin, G. A. (1956). *A study of thinking*. New York: Wiley.

Bruner, J. S., Olver, R., & Greenfield, P. M. (1966). *Studies in cognitive growth*. New York: Wiley.

Bushell, D., Wrobel, P., & Michaelis, M. (1968). Applying "group" contingencies to the classroom study behavior of pre-school children. *Journal of Applied Behavior Analysis*, *1*, 55–61.

Calder, B. J., & Staw, B. M. (1975). Self-perception of intrinsic and extrinsic motivation. *Journal of Personality and Social Psychology*, *31*, 599–605.

Campbell, A., & Sulzer, B. (1971, February). *Naturally available reinforcers as motivators towards reading and spelling achievement by educable mentally handicapped students*. Paper presented at the American Educational Research Association Annual Meeting, New York.

Campione, J. C., Brown, A. L., Ferrara, R. A., & Bryant, N. R. (1984). The zone of proximal development: Implications for individual differences and learning. In B. Rogoff and J. V. Wertsch (Eds.), *New Directions for Child Development: No. 23. Children's learning in the "zone of proximal development*," San Francisco: Jossey-Bass.

Carey, S. (1985a). *Conceptual change in childhood*. Cambridge, MA: The MIT Press.

Carey, S. (1985b). Are children fundamentally different kinds of thinkers and learners than adults? In S. F. Chipman, J. W. Segal, & R. Glaser (Eds.), *Thinking and learning skills* (Vol. 2). Hillsdale, NJ: Erlbaum.

Carey, S. (1986). Cognitive science and science education. *American Psychologist*, *41*, 1123–1130.

Carlsson, A. (1978). Antipsychotic drugs, neurotransmitters, and schizophrenia. *American Journal of Psychiatry*, *135*, 164–173.

Carroll, L. (1946). *Through the looking glass* (special ed.). New York: Random House.

Case, R. (1978). Piaget and beyond: Toward a developmentally-based theory and technology of instruction. In R. Glaser (Ed.), *Advances in instructional technology*, (Vol. 1). Hillsdale, NJ: Erlbaum.

Case, R. (1980). Intellectual development: A systematic reinterpretation. In F. Farley and N. J. Gordon (Eds.), *Psychology and education: The state of the union*. Berkeley, CA: McCutchan.

Case, R. (1984). The process of stage transition: A neo-Piagetian view. In R. J. Sternberg (Ed.), *Mechanisms of cognitive development*. New York: Freeman.

Chall, J. S., & Peterson, R. W. (1986). The influence of neuroscience upon educational practice. In S. L. Friedman, K. A. Klivington, & R. W. Peterson (Eds.), *The brain, cognition, and education*. Orlando: Academic Press.

Chang, F. R. (1981). *Distribution of attention within a single fixation in reading: Studies of the perceptual span*. Unpublished doctoral dissertation, University of Oregon, Eugene.

Champagne, A. B., Klopfer, L. E., & Anderson, J. H. (1980). Factors influencing the learning of classical mechanics. *American Journal of Physics*, 48, 1074–1079.

Champagne, A. B., Klopfer, L. E., Fox, J., & Scheuerman, K. (1982). *Laws of motion: Computer-simulated experiments in mechanics (the a-machine and the inclined plane)*. New Rochelle, NY: Educational Materials & Equipment.

Chase, W. G., & Simon, H. A. (1973a). Perception in chess. *Cognitive Psychology*, 4, 55–81.

Chase, W. G., & Simon, H. A. (1973b). The mind's eye in chess. In W. G. Chase (Ed.), *Visual information processing*. New York: Academic Press.

Cheng, P. W., Holyoak, K. J., Nisbett, R. E., & Oliver, L. M. (1986). Pragmatic versus syntactic approaches to training deductive reasoning. *Cognitive Psychology*, 18, 293–328.

Chi, M. T. H. (1978). Knowledge structures and memory development. In R. Siegler (Ed.), *Children's thinking: What develops?* Hillsdale, NJ: Erlbaum.

Chi, M. T. H., Glaser, R., & Rees, E. (1982). Expertise in problem solving. In   R. Sternberg (Ed.), *Advances in the psychology of human intelligence*. Hillsdale, NJ: Erlbaum.

Chiesi, H. L., Spilich, G. J., & Voss, J. F. (1979). Acquisition of domain-related information in relation to high and low domain knowledge. *Journal of Verbal Learning and Verbal Behavior*, 18, 257–273.

Chipman, S. F. (1986). Integrating three perspectives on learning. In S. L. Friedman, K. A. Klivington, & R. W. Peterson (Eds.), *The brain, cognition and education*. Orlando: Academic Press.

Chomsky, N. (1959). Review of Skinner's *Verbal Behavior*. *Language*, 35, 26–58.

Chomsky, N. (1965). *Aspects of a theory of syntax*. Cambridge, MA: MIT Press.

Chomsky, N. (1972). *Language and mind* (enlarged ed.). New York: Harcourt Brace Jovanovich.

Clark, R. E. (1982). Antagonism between achievement and enjoyment in ATI studies. *Educational Psychologist*, 17, 92–101.

Clement, J. (1982). Analogical reasoning patterns in expert problem solving. *Proceedings of the Fourth Annual Conference of the Cognitive Science Society*. Ann Arbor, MI: University of Michigan.

Clifford, M. M. (1984). Thoughts on a theory of constructive failure. *Educational Psychologist*, 19, 108–120.

Cognition and Technology Group at Vanderbilt (1990, April). Anchored instruction and its relationship to situated cognition. *Educational Researcher*, 19(3), 2–10.

Cognition and Technology Group at Vanderbilt (1991a, May). Technology and the design of generative learning environments. *Educational Technology*, 31, 34–40.

Cognition and Technology Group at Vanderbilt. (1991b, September). Some thoughts about constructivism and instructional design. *Educational Technology*, 31, 16–18.

Cognition and Technology Group at Vanderbilt. (1992). The Jasper experiment: An exploration of issues in learning and instructional design. *Educational Technology Research and Development*, 40(1), 65–80.

Cohen, E. G. (1986). *Designing groupwork*. New York: Teachers College Press.

Cohen, N. (1984). Preserved learning capacity in amnesia: Evidence for multiple memory systems. In L. R. Squire & N. Butters (Eds.), *Neuropsychology of memory*. New York: Guilford Press.

Cohen, N., & Squire, L. R. (1981). Preserved learning and retention of pattern-analyzing skill in amnesia. *Science*, 210, 207–210.

Cole, M., & Bruner, J. S. (1971). Cultural differences and inferences about psychological processes. *American Psychologist*, 26, 867–876.

Cole, M., & Scribner, S. (1978). Introduction. In L. S. Vygotsky, *Mind in Society*. Cambridge, MA: Harvard University Press.

Collins, A. M., & Quillian, M. R. (1969). Retrieval time from semantic memory. *Journal of Verbal Learning and Verbal Behavior*, 8, 240–247.

Collins, A., & Stevens, A. L. (1982). Goals and strategies of effective teachers. In R. Glaser (Ed.), *Advances in instructional psychology* (Vol. 2). Hillsdale, NJ: Erlbaum.

Collins, A., & Stevens, A. L. (1983). A cognitive theory in inquiry teaching. In C. M. Reigeluth (Ed.), *Instructional-design theories and models*. Hillsdale, NJ: Erlbaum.

Collins, A., Warnock, E. H., & Passafiume, J. J. (1975). Analysis and synthesis of tutorial dialogues. In G. H. Bower (Ed.), *The psychology of learning and motivation* (Vol. 9). New York: Academic Press.

Cooper, G., & Sweller, J. (1987). The effects of schema acquisition and rule automation on mathematical problem-solving transfer. *Journal of Educational Psychology*, 79, 347–362.

Corte, H. E., Wolf, M. E., & Locke, B. J. (1971). A comparison of procedures for eliminating self-injurious behavior of retarded adolescents. *Journal of Applied Behavior Analysis*, 4, 201–214.

Cosmides, L. (1989). The logic of social exchange: Has natural selection shaped how we reason? *Cognition*, 31, 187–276.

Cosmides, L., & Tooby, J. (1989). Evolutionary psychology and the generation of culture, Part II: Case study: A computational theory of social exchange. *Ethology and Sociobiology*, 10, 51–98.

Craik, F. I. M., & Lockhart, R. S. (1972). Levels of processing: A framework for memory research. *Journal of Verbal Learning and Verbal Behavior*, 11, 671–684.

Craik, F. I. M., & Tulving, E. (1975). Depth of processing and retention of words in episodic memory. *Journal of Experimental Psychology: General*, 104, 268–294.

Crawford, C. B., & Anderson, J. L. (1989). Sociobiology: An environmentalist discipline? *American Psychologist*, 44, 1449–1459.

Cromer, R. F. (1981). Reconceptualizing language acquisition and cognitive development. In R. L. Scheifelbusch & D. D. Bricker (Eds.). *Early language: Acquisition and intervention*. Baltimore: University Park Press.

Crowder, N. A. (1960). Automatic tutoring by intrinsic programming. In A. A. Lumsdaine & R. Glaser (Eds.). *Teaching machines and programmed learning*. Washington, DC: National Education Association.

Crutcher, K. A. (1991). Anatomical correlates of neuronal plasticity. In J. L. Martinez, Jr. & R. P. Kesner (Eds.), *Learning and memory: A biological view* (2nd ed.). San Diego: Academic Press.

Culler, J. (1990, April). *Fostering post-structuralist thinking*. Paper presented at the Annual Meeting of the American Educational Research Association, Boston.

Cunningham, D. J. (1987). Outline of an education semiotic. *American Journal of Semiotics*, 5, 201–216.

Cunningham, D. J. (1988, April). *Abduction and affordance: A semiotic view of cognition*. Paper presented at the Annual Meeting of the American Educational Research Association, New Orleans.

Cunningham, D. J. (1992). Beyond educational psychology: Steps toward an educational semiotic. *Educational Psychology Review*, 4, 165–194.

Cunningham, D. J., & Shank, G. (1984). Semiotics: A new foundation for education? *Contemporary Education Review*, 3, 411–421.

Damasio, A. R., Damasio, H., & Chang Chui, H. (1980). Neglect following damage to frontal lobe or basal ganglia. *Neuropsychologia*, 18, 123–132.

Dansereau, D. F., Collins, K. W., McDonald, B. A., Holley, C. D., Garland, J. C., Dickhoff, G., & Evans, S. H. (1979). Development and evaluation of a learning strategy program. *Journal of Educational Psychology*, 71, 64–73.

Darwin, C. J., Turvey, M. T., & Crowder, R. G. (1972). The auditory analogue of the Sperling partial report procedure: Evidence for brief auditory storage. *Cognitive Psychology*, 3, 225–267.

Dasen, P. R. (1972). Cross-cultural Piagetian research: A summary. *Journal of Cross-Cultural Psychology*, 3, 23–39. Reprinted in J. Berry & P. Dasen (Eds.) (1974). *Culture and cognition: Readings in cross-cultural psychology*. London: Methuen, 1974.

De Bono, E. (1985). The CORT thinking program. In J. W. Segal, S. F. Chipman, & R. Glaser (Eds.) *Thinking and learning skills: Relating instruction to basic research* (Vol. 1). Hillsdale, NJ: Erlbaum.

Deci, E. L. (1975). *Intrinsic motivation*. New York: Plenum Press.

DeCorte, E., Verschaffel, L., & De Win, L. (1985). Influence of rewording verbal problems on children's problem representations and solutions. *Journal of Educational Psychology*, 77, 460–470.

deKleer, J., & Brown, J. S. (1983). Assumptions and ambiguities in mechanistic mental models. In D. Gentner & A. L. Stevens (Eds.), *Mental models*. Hillsdale, NJ: Erlbaum.

Dempsey, J. V. (1986, April). Using the rational set generator with computer-based instruction for creating concept examples: A template for instructors. *Educational Technology*, 26, 43–46.

Dempsey, J. V., Driscoll, M. P., & Litchfield, B. Feedback complexity, retention, discrimination error and feedback study time in computer-based instruction. *Journal of Research in Educational Computing*.

Derry, S. J., & Murphy, D. A. (1986). Designing systems that train learning ability: From theory to practice. *Review of Educational Research*, *56*, 1–39.

Derry, S. J., Hawkes, L. W., & Tsai, C-j. (1987). A theory for remediating problem-solving skills for older children and adults. *Educational Psychologist*, *22*, 55–87.

Dewey, J. (1933). *How we think: Restatement of the relation of reflective thinking to the educative process*. Boston: Heath.

Dewsbury, D. A. (1991). "Psychobiology." *American Psychologist*, *46*, 198–205.

Dick, W. (1991, May). An instructional designer's view of constructivism. *Educational Technology*, *31*, 31–44.

Dick, W., & Reiser, R. A. (1989). *Planning effective instruction*. Englewood Cliffs, NJ: Prentice-Hall.

Dillon, R. F., & Sternberg, R. J. (1986). *Cognition and instruction*. Orlando: Academic Press.

diSessa, A. A. (1982). Unlearning Aristotelian physics: A study of knowledge-based learning. *Cognitive Science*, *6*, 37–75.

diSessa, A. A. (1983). Phenomenology and the evolution of intuition. In D. Gentner and A. Stevens (Eds.), *Mental models*. Hillsdale, NJ: Erlbaum.

Domjon, M. (1980). Ingestional aversion learning: Unique and general processes. *Advances in the study of behavior* (Vol. 11). New York: Academic Press.

Donaldson, M. (1978). *Children's minds*. New York: Norton.

Donegan, N. H., & Thompson, R. F. (1991). The search for the engram. In J. L. Martinez, Jr., & R. P. Kesner (Eds.), *Learning and memory: A biological view* (2nd ed.). San Diego: Academic Press.

Dooling, D. J., & Lachman, R. (1971). Effects of comprehension on retention of prose. *Journal of Experimental Psychology*, *88*, 216–222.

Doyle, W. (1988). Work in mathematics classes: The context of students' thinking during instruction. *Educational Psychologist*, *23*, 167–180.

Driscoll, M. P. (1984, Winter). Alternative paradigms for research in instructional systems. *Journal of Instructional Development*, *7*, 2–5.

Driscoll, M. P. (1985). Measures of cognitive structure: Do they assess learning at the level of comprehension? *Contemporary Educational Psychology*, *10*, 38–51.

Driscoll, M. P., & Dick, W. (1991). What do textbooks contribute to learning. Unpublished raw data.

Driscoll, M. P., & Lebow, D. (1992). Making it happen: Possibilities and pitfalls of Cunningham's educational semiotic. *Educational Psychology Review*, *4*, 211–221.

Driscoll, M. P., & Tessmer, M. (1985, February). The rational set generator: A method for creating concept examples for teaching and testing. *Educational Technology*, *25*, 29–32.

Driscoll, M. P., Dick, W., Johnson, M., & Flynn, J. (1990, April). *Textbooks in schools: What part do they play in effective instruction?* Paper presented at the Annual Meeting of the American Educational Research Association, Boston.

Driver, R., & Easley, J. (1978). Pupils and paradigms: A review of literature related to concept development in adolescent science students. *Studies in Science Education*, *5*, 61–84.

Duckworth, E. (1964). Piaget rediscovered. In R. E. Ripple and V. N. Rockcastle (Eds.), *Piaget rediscovered*. Ithaca, NY: Cornell University Press.

Duell, O. K. (1986). Metacognitive skills. In G. D. Phye and T. Andre (Eds.), *Cognitive classroom learning*. Orlando: Academic Press.

Duffield, J. A. (1990, April). *Problem-solving software: What does it teach?* Paper presented at the Annual Meeting of the American Educational Research Association, Boston.

Duffy, F. H., Burchfiel, J. L., & Lombroso, C. T. (1979). Brain electrical activity mapping (BEAM): A method of extending the clinical utility of EEG and evoked potential data. *Annals of Neurology*, *5*, 309–321.

Duffy, F. H., Denckla, M. B., Bartels, P. H., & Sandini, G. (1980). Dyslexia: Regional differences in brain electrical activity by topographic mapping. *Annals of Neurology*, *7*, 412–420.

Duffy, F. H., Denckla, M. B., Bartels, P. H., Sandini, G., & Kiessling, L. D. (1980). Dyslexia: Automated diagnosis by computerized classification of brain electrical activity. *Annals of Neurology*, *7*, 421–428.

Duffy T. M., & Jonassen, D. H. (1991, May). Constructivism: New implications for instructional technology? *Educational Technology*, *31*, 7–12.

Dweck, C. S. (1986). Motivational processes affecting learning. *American Psychologist*, *41*, 1040–1048.

Dweck, C. S., & Elliott, E. S. (1983). Achievement motivation. In P. H. Mussen (Gen. Ed.) & E. M. Hetherington (Vol. Ed.), *Handbook of child psychology: Vol. IV. Social and personality development* (pp. 643–691). New York: Wiley.

Dweck, C. S., & Leggett, E. L. (1988). A social-cognitive approach to motivation and personality. *Psychological Review*, *95*, 256–273.

Ebbinghaus, H. (1885). *Memory: A contribution to experimental psychology*. (H. A. Ruger & C. Bussenius, trans.). (1913). New York: Columbia University, Teacher's College Press.

Eco, U. (1976). *A theory of semiotics*. Bloomington: Indiana University Press.

Eco, U. (1984). *Semiotics and the philosophy of language*. London: Macmillan Press.

Elliott, E. S., & Dweck, C. S. (1988). Goals: An approach to motivation and achievement. *Journal of Personality and Social Psychology*, *54*, 5–12.

Ellis, S., & Rogoff, B. (1982). The strategies and efficacy of child versus adult teachers. *Child Development*, *43*, 730–735.

Emihovich, C. E. (1981, May–December). Social interaction in two integrated kindergartens. *Integrated Education*, *19*, 72–78.

Epstein, H. T. (1990). Stages in human mental growth. *Journal of Educational Psychology*, *82*, 876–880.

Estes, W. K. (1972). Reinforcement in human behavior. *American Scientist, 60*, 723–729.

Estes, W. K. (1988). Toward a framework for combining connectionist and symbol-processing models. *Journal of Memory and Language*, *27*, 196–212.

Falmagne, R. J. (1980). The development of logical competence: A psycholinguistic perspective. In R. H. Kluwe and H. Spada (Eds.), *Developmental models of thinking*. New York: Academic Press.

Feldman, H., Goldin-Meadow, S., & Gleitman, L. (1978). Beyond Herodotus: The creation of language by linguistically deprived deaf children. In A. Lock (Ed.), *Action, symbol and gesture: The emergence of language*. New York: Academic Press.

Ferster, C. B., & Skinner, B. F. (1957). *Schedules of reinforcement*. Englewood Cliffs, NJ: Prentice-Hall.

Feuerstein, R., Rand, Y., Hoffman, M.B., & Miller, R. (1980). *Instrumental enrichment: An intervention program for cognitive modifiability*. Baltimore: University Park Press.

Fitts, P. M., & Posner, M. I. (1967). *Human performance*. Belmont, CA: Brooks/Cole.

Fitzgerald, D., & Ausubel, D. P. (1963). Cognitive versus affective factors in the learning and retention of controversial materials. *Journal of Educational Psychology*, *54*, 73–84.

Flavell, J. H. (1979). Metacognition and cognitive monitoring: A new area of cognitive developmental inquiry. *American Psychologist*, *34*, 906–911.

Flavell, J. H. (1984). Discussion. In R. J. Sternberg (Ed.) *Mechanisms of cognitive development*. New York: Freeman.

Flavell, J. H. (1985). *Cognitive development*. Englewood Cliffs, NJ: Prentice-Hall.

Flynn, J. L. (1992, October). Cooperative learning and Gagné's events of instruction: A syncretic view. *Educational Technology*, *32*, 53–60.

Forman, E. A. (1987). Learning through peer interaction: A Vygotskian perspective. *The Genetic Epistemologist*, *15*, 6–15.

Fowler, A. (1986). Down's syndrome language: Syntax and morphology. In D. Cicchetti & M. Beeghley (Eds.), *Down's Syndrome: The developmental perspective*. New York: Cambridge University Press.

Friedl, A. E. (1991). *Teaching science to children: An integrated approach*. New York: McGraw-Hill.

Friedman, S. L., & Cocking, R. R. (1986). Instructional influences on cognition and on the brain. In S. L. Friedman, K. A. Klivington, & R. W. Peterson (Eds.), *The brain, cognition and education*. Orlando: Academic Press.

Fry, P. S. (1992). A consideration of cognitive factors in the learning and education of older adults. *International Review of Education*, *38*(4), 303–325.

Fuson, K. C., & Willis, G. B. (1989). Second graders' use of schematic drawings in solving addition and subtraction problems. *Journal of Educational Psychology*, *81*, 514–520.

Gagné, E. D. (1985). *The cognitive psychology of school learning*. Boston: Little, Brown.

Gagné, R. M. (1968). Learning hierarchies. *Educational Psychologist*, *6*, 1–9.

Gagné, R. M. (1972). Domains of learning. *Interchange*, *3*, 1–8.

Gagné, R. M. (1977). Task analysis. In L. J. Briggs (Ed.), *Instructional design: Principles and application*. Englewood Cliffs, NJ: Educational Technology Publications.

Gagné, R. M. (1983). Some issues in the psychology of mathematics instruction. *Journal of Research in Mathematics Education*, *14*, 7–18.

Gagné, R. M. (1985). *The conditions of learning* (4th ed.). New York: Holt, Rinehart & Winston.

Gagné, R. M., Briggs, L. J., & Wager, W. (1992). *Principles of instructional design* (4th ed.). Fort Worth: Harcourt Brace Jovanovich.

Gagné, R. M., & Dick, W. (1983). Instructional psychology. *Annual Review of Psychology*, *34*, 261–295.

Gagné, R. M., & Driscoll, M. P. (1988). *Essentials of learning for instruction* (2nd ed.). Englewood Cliffs, NJ: Prentice-Hall.

Gagné, R. M., & Glaser, R. (1987). Foundations in learning research. In R. M. Gagné (Ed.), *Instructional technology: Foundations*. Hillsdale, NJ: Erlbaum.

Gagné, R. M., & Merrill, M. D. (1990). Integrative goals for instructional design. *Educational Technology Research and Development*, *38*, 23–30.

Gagné, R. M., & Rohwer, W. D., Jr. (1969). Instructional psychology. *Annual Review of Psychology*, *20*, 381–418.

Garcia, J., Brett, L. P., & Rusiniak, K. W. (1989). Limits of Darwinian conditioning. In S. B. Klein, & R. R. Mowrer (Eds.), *Contemporary learning theories: Instrumental conditioning theory and the impact of biological constraints on learning*. Hillsdale, NJ: Erlbaum.

Garcia, J., Clark, J., & Hankins, W. (1973). Natural responses to schedule rewards. In P. Bateson and P. Klopfer (Eds.), *Perspectives in ethology*. New York: Plenum Press.

Garcia, J., & Koelling, P. A. (1966). Relation of cue to consequence in avoidance learning. *Psychonomic Science*, *4*, 123–124.

Gardner, H. (1982). Giftedness: A biological perspective. In D. Feldman (Ed.), *Developmental approaches to giftedness and creativity: New directions for child development*. San Francisco: Jossey Bass.

Gardner, H. (1983). *Frames of mind: The theory of multiple intelligences*. New York: Basic Books.

Gardner, H. (1986). Notes on cognitive development: Recent trends, new directions. In S. L. Friedman, K. A. Klivington, & R. W. Peterson (Eds.), *The brain, cognition, and education*. Orlando: Academic Press.

Gazzaniga, M. S. (1984). Advances in cognitive neurosciences: The problem of information storage in the human brain. In G. Lynch, J. L. McGaugh, & N. M. Weinberger (Eds.), *Neurobiology of learning and memory*. New York: The Guilford Press.

Gelman, R. (1972). The nature and development of early number concepts. In H. Reese (Ed.), *Advances in child development and behavior* (Vol. 7). New York: Academic Press.

Gelman, R. (1978). Cognitive development. In M. R. Rosenzweig & L. W. Porter (Eds.). *Annual Review of Psychology* (Vol. 29). Palo Alto, CA: Annual Reviews, Inc.

Gelman, R. (1983). Recent trends in cognitive development. In G. Scherrer and A. M. Robers (Eds.), *The G. Stanley Hall Lecture Series* (Vol. 3). Washington, DC: American Psychological Association.

Gelman, R., & Baillargeon, R. (1983). A review of some Piagetian concepts. In P. Mussen (Ed.), *Manual of child psychology* (4th ed.). *Vol.: 3. Cognitive development* (J. H. Flavell & E. M. Markman, Eds.). New York: Wiley.

Gentner, D. (1982). Why nouns are learned before verbs: Linguistic relativity vs. natural partitioning. In S. Kuczaj (Ed.), *Language development: Language, culture, and cognition*. Hillsdale, NJ: Erlbaum.

Gibson, J. J. (1977). The theory of affordance. In R. Shaw & J. Bransord (Eds.), *Perceiving, acting, and knowing*. Hillsdale, NJ: Erlbaum.

Gibson, K. (1985). Has the evolution of intelligence stagnated since Neanderthal Man? In G. Butterworth, J. Rutkowska, & M. Scaife (Eds.), *Evolution and developmental psychology*. Great Britain: The Harvester Press.

Glachan, M., & Light, P. (1982). Peer interaction and learning: Can two ways make a right? In G. Butterworth and P. Light (Eds.), *Social cognition: Studies of the development of understanding*. Brighton: Harvester Press.

Glaser, R. (1984). Education and thinking: The role of knowledge. *American Psychologist*, *39*, 93–104.

Gleitman, L. (1986). Biological preprogramming for language learning? In S. L. Friedman, K. A. Klivington, & R. W. Peterson (Eds.), *The brain, cognition and education*. Orlando: Academic Press.

Glynn, S. M., & Divesta, F. J. (1977). Outline and hierarchical organization as aids for study and retrieval. *Journal of Educational Psychology*, *69*, 9–14.

Glynn, S. M., & Divesta, F. J. (1979). Control of prose processing via instructional and typographical cues. *Journal of Educational Psychology*, *71*, 595–603.

Goldenberg, C. N. (1992). The limits of expectations: A case for case knowledge about teacher expectancy effects. *American Educational Research Journal*, *29*, 517–544.

Goldman-Rakic, P. S. (1986). Setting the stage: Neural development before birth. In S. L. Friedman, K. A. Klivington, & R. W. Peterson (Eds.), *The brain, cognition and education*. Orlando: Academic Press.

Good, T. L. (1987). Two decades of research on teacher expectations: Findings and future directions. *Journal of Teacher Education*, *38*, 32–47.

Good, T. L., & Brophy, J. E. (1984). *Looking in classrooms*. New York: Harper & Row.

Goodman, N. (1984). *Of mind and other matters*. Cambridge, MA: Harvard University Press.

Goodwin, B. (1985). Constructional biology. In G. Butterworth, J. Rutkowska, &   M. Scaife (Eds.), *Evolution and developmental psychology*. Great Britain: The Harvester Press Limited.

Goodwin, D. W., Powell, B., Bremer, D., Hoine, H., & Stern, J. (1969). Alcohol and recall: State-dependent effects in man. *Science*, *163*, 1358.

Grabe, M. (1986). Attentional processes in education. In G. D. Phye & T. Andre (Eds.), *Cognitive classroom learning*. Orlando: Academic Press.

Graham, S. (1984). Communicating sympathy and anger to black and white children: The cognitive (attributional) consequences of affective cues. *Journal of Personality and Social Psychology*, *3*, 71–88.

Graham, S. & Barker, G. P. (1990). The down side of help: An attributional-developmental analysis of helping behavior as a low-ability cue. *Journal of Educational Psychology*, *82*, 7–14.

Greenfield, P. M. (1984). A theory of the teacher in the learning activities of everyday life. In B. Rogoff & J. Lave (Eds.), *Everyday cognition*. Cambridge, MA: Harvard University Press.

Greeno, J. (1980). Trends in the theory of knowledge for problem solving. In D. Tuma and F. Reif (Eds.), *Problem solving and education: Issues in teaching and research*. Hillsdale, NJ: Erlbaum.

Gronlund, N. E. (1988). *How to construct achievement tests* (4th ed.). Englewood Cliffs, NJ: Prentice-Hall.

Gruber, H. E., & Voneche, J. J. (1977). *The essential Piaget*. New York: Basic Books.

Gunter, M. A., Estes, T. H., & Schwab, J. H. (1990). *Instruction: A models approach*. Boston: Allyn & Bacon.

Guthrie, E. R. (1933). Association as a function of the time interval. *Psychological Review*, *37*, 412–428.

Hannafin, M. J. (1992). Emerging technologies, ISD, and learning environments: Critical perspectives. *Educational Technology Research and Development*, *40*, 49–64.

Hansen, J. C., & Hillyard, S. A. (1980). Endogenous brain potentials associated with selective auditory attention. *Electroencephalography and Clinical Neuropsychology*, *49*, 277–290.

Harris, F. R., Wolf, M. M., & Baer, D. M. (1967). Effects of adult social reinforcement on child behavior. In S. W. Bijou & D. M. Baer (Eds.), *Child development: Readings in experimental analysis*. New York: Appleton-Century-Crofts.

Harris, R. J., Schoen, L. M., and Lee, D. J. (1986). Culture-based distortion in memory for stories. In J. L. Armagost (Ed.), *Papers from the 1985 Mid-America Linguistics Conference*. Manhattan: Kansas State University Department of Speech.

Hartley, J., & Davies, I. K. (1976). Pre-instructional strategies: The role of pretests, behavioral objectives, overviews, and advance organizers. *Review of Educational Research*, *46*, 239–265.

Heminway, J. (Producer, Director, and Author) & Tegriti, A. (Author). (1984). *The brain: Learning and memory*. WNET New York: Educational Broadcasting.

Herrnstein, R. J. & Boring, E. G. (1968). *A sourcebook in the history of psychology*. Cambridge, MA: Harvard University Press.

Higbee, K. L. (1979). Recent research on visual mnemonics. Historical roots and educational fruits. *Review of Educational Research*, *49*, 611–630.

Hlynka, D. (1991, June). Postmodern excursions into educational technology. *Educational Technology*, *31*, 27–30.

Holland, J., & Skinner, B. F. (1961). *The analysis of behavior*. New York: McGraw-Hill.

Holtzman, J. D., & Gazzaniga, M. S. (1982). Dual task interaction due exclusively to limits in processing resources. *Science*, *218*, 1325–1327.

Honebein, P. C., Duffy, T. M., & Fishman, B. J. (in press). Constructivism and the design of authentic learning environments: Context and authentic activities for learning. In T. M. Duffy, J. Lowyck, & D. Jonassen (Eds.), *Designing environments for constructive learning*. Hillsdale, NJ: Erlbaum.

Honebein, P. C., Chen, P., & Brescia, W. (1992). Hypermedia and sociology: A simulation for developing research skills. *Liberal Arts Computing*, *1*(1), 9–15.

Hong, E. S., & O'Neil, H. F. (1992). Instructional strategies to help learners build relevant mental models in inferential statistics. *Journal of Educational Psychology*, *84*, 150–159.

Hubel, D., & Wiesel, T. (1962). Receptive fields, binocular interaction, and functional architecture in the cat's visual cortex. *Journal of Physiology*, *160*, 106–154.

Hudspeth, W. J., & Pribham, K. H. (1990). Stages of brain and cognitive maturation. *Journal of Educational Psychology*, *82*, 881–884.

Hutchins, E. (1983). Understanding Micronesian navigation. In D. Gentner & A. L. Stevens (Eds.), *Mental models*. Hillsdale, NJ: Erlbaum.

Inhelder, B., & Piaget, J. (1958). *The growth of logical thinking*. New York: Basic Books.

Inhelder, B., Sinclair, H., & Bovet, M. (1974). *Learning and the development of cognition.* Cambridge, MA: Harvard University Press.

Jacoby, L. L., & Craik, F.I.M. (1979). Effects of elaboration of processing at encoding and retrieval: Trace distinctiveness and recovery of initial context. In L. S. Cermak & F. I. M. Craik (Eds.), *Levels of processing in human memory .* Hillsdale, NJ: Erlbaum.

Jacoby, L. L., Levy, B. A., & Steinbach, K. (1992). Episodic transfer and automaticity: Integration of data-driven and conceptually-driven processing in reading. *Journal of Experimental Psychology: Learning, Memory and Cognition , 18,* 15–24.

Jih, H. J., & Reeves, T. C. (1992). Mental models: A research focus for interactive learning systems. *Educational Technology Research and Development ,* 40, 1042–1629.

John-Steiner, V., & Souberman, E. (1978). Afterword. In L. S. Vygotsky, *Mind in society.* Cambridge, MA: Harvard University Press.

Johnson, D. W., & Johnson, R. (1975). *Learning together and alone: Cooperation, competition, and individualization.* Englewood Cliffs, NJ: Prentice-Hall.

Johnson, D. W., & Johnson, R. T. (1978). Many teachers wonder . . . will the special needs child ever really belong? *Instructor , 87,* 152–154.

Johnson, D. W. and Johnson, R. T. (1979). Conflict in the classroom: Controversy and learning. *Review of Educational Research , 49,* 51–70.

Johnson, K. R., & Perkins, M. R. (1976). *Mastery workbook for educational psychology.* Dubuque, IA: Kendall-Hunt.

Johnson, M. J. (1987). *The body in the mind: The bodily basis of meaning.* Chicago: University of Chicago Press.

Johnson, R. T., Johnson, D. W., & Stanne, M. B. (1985). Effects of cooperative, competitive, and individualistic goal structures on computer-assisted instruction. *Journal of Educational Psychology , 77,* 668–677.

Johnson-Laird, P. N. (1983). *Mental models.* Cambridge, MA: Harvard University Press.

Johnson-Laird, P. N. (1988). How is meaning mentally represented? In U. Eco, M. Santambrogio, & P. Violi (Eds.), *Meaning and mental representations.* Bloomington: Indiana University Press.

Jones, B. H. (1988). Learning computer systems by analogy: Mental models research. *International Journal of Instructional Media , 15,* 59–65.

Joyce, B., & Weil, M. (1986). *Models of teaching* (3rd ed.). Englewood Cliffs, NJ: Prentice-Hall.

Kahneman, D. (1973). *Attention and effort .* Englewood Cliffs, NJ: Prentice-Hall.

Kamii, C. (1985a). Leading primary education toward excellence: Beyond worksheets and drill. *Young Children ,* 40(6), 3–9.

Kamii, C. (1985b). Reading in kindergarten: Direct vs. indirect teaching. *Young Children ,* 40(4), 3–9.

Kamii, C., & DeVries, R. (1974). Piaget for early education program. In R. K. Parker (Ed.), *The preschool in action* (2nd ed.). Boston: Allyn & Bacon.

Kant, I. (1787/1963). *Critique of pure reason* (N. K. Smith trans.). London: Macmillan.

Kaplan, B. (1967). Meditations on genesis. *Human Development , 10,* 65–87.

Keller, F. S. (1968). "Goodbye, teacher. . ." *Journal of Applied Behavior Analysis , 1,* 79–89.

Keller, J. M. (1983). Motivational design of instruction. In C. M. Reigeluth (Ed.), *Instructional - design theories and models .* Hillsdale, NJ: Erlbaum.

Keller, J. M. (1984). Use of the ARCS model of motivation in teacher training. In K. E. Shaw (Ed.), *Aspects of educational technology XVII: Staff development and career updating.* New York: Nichols.

Keller, J. M. (1987a, October). Strategies for stimulating the motivation to learn. *Performance and Instruction Journal ,* 1–7.

Keller, J. M. (1987b, November/December). The systematic process of motivational design. *Performance and Instruction Journal,* 1–8.

Kelley, H. H., & Michela, J. (1980). Attribution theory and research. In M. Rosenzweig & L. Porter (Eds.), *Annual Review of Psychology* (Vol. 31, pp. 457–501). Palo Alto, CA: Annual Reviews.

Kesner, R. P. (1991). Neurobiological views of memory. In J. L. Martinez, Jr. & R. P. Kesner (Eds.), *Learning and memory: A biological view* (2nd ed.). San Diego: Academic Press.

Kessen, W. (1984). Introduction: The end of the age of development. In R. J. Sternberg (Ed.), *Mechanisms of cognitive development .* New York: Freeman.

Kiewra, K. A. (1985). Investigating notetaking and review: A depth of processing alternative. *Educational Psychologist , 20,* 23–32

Kiewra, K. A., DuBois, N. F., Christian, D., McShane, A., Meyerhoffer, M., & Roskelley, D. (1991). Note-taking functions and techniques. *Journal of Educational Psychology, 83,* 240 – 245.

Kiewra, K. A., & Frank, B. M. (1988). Encoding and external-storage effects of personal lecture notes, skeletal notes and detailed notes for field independent and field dependent learners. *Journal of Educational Research*, 81, 142–148.

Kintsch, W. (1974). *The representation of meaning in memory*. Hillsdale, NJ: Erlbaum.

Kintsch, W. (1976). Memory for prose. In C. N. Cofer (Ed.), *The structure of human memory*. San Francisco: Freeman.

Kintsch, W. (1977). *Memory and cognition* (2nd ed.). New York: Wiley.

Kintsch, W. (1988) The role of knowledge in discourse comprehension: A construction-integration model. *Psychological Review*, 95, 163–182.

Kintsch, W., & van Dijk, T. (1978). Toward a model of text comprehension and production. *Psychological Review*, 85, 363–394.

Klahr, D. (1984). Transition processes in quantitative development. In R. J. Sternberg (Ed.), *Mechanisms of cognitive development*. New York: Freeman.

Klahr, D., & Wallace, J. G. (1973). The role of quantification operators in the development of conservation of quantity. *Cognitive Psychology*, 4, 301–327.

Klahr, D., & Wallace, J. G. (1976). *Cognitive development: An information-processing view*. Hillsdale, NJ: Erlbaum.

Klatzky, R. L. (1980). *Human memory* (2nd ed.). New York: Freeman.

Klauer, K. J. (1984). Intentional and incidental learning with instructional texts: A meta-analysis for 1970–1980. *American Educational Research Journal*, 21, 323–340.

Kohler, W. (1917). On the insight of apes. (Trans. E. G. Boring) In R. J. Herrnstein and E. G. Boring (Eds.), *A sourcebook in the history of psychology*. Cambridge, MA: Harvard University Press, 1961.

Kohler, W. (1925). *The mentality of apes*. London: Routledge & Kegan Paul.

Kolesnik, W. B. (1978). *Motivation: Understanding and influencing human behavior*. Boston: Allyn & Bacon.

Kosslyn, S. M. (1980). *Image and mind*. Cambridge, MA: Harvard University Press.

Kozminsky, E. (1977). Altering comprehension: The effect of biasing titles on text comprehension. *Memory and Cognition*, 5, 482–490.

Krathwohl, D. R., Bloom, B. S., & Masia, B. B. (1964). *Taxonomy of educational objectives, handbook II: Affective domain*. New York: McKay.

Kuhn, D. J., & Novak, J. D. (1971). A study of cognitive subsumption in the life sciences. *Science Education*, 55, 309–320.

Kuhn, T. S. (1970). *The structure of scientific revolutions* (2nd ed.). Chicago: University of Chicago Press.

Kulhavy, R. W., & Stock, W. A. (1989). Feedback in written instruction: The place of response certitude. *Educational Psychology Review*, 1, 279–308.

Kulhavy, R. W., & Swenson, I. (1975). Imagery instructions and the comprehension of text. *British Journal of Educational Psychology*, 45, 47–51.

Kulik, J. A., Kulik, C. C., & Cohen, P. A. (1979). A meta-analysis of outcome studies of Keller's Personalized System of Instruction. *American Psychologist*, 34, 307–318.

LaBerge, D., & Samuels, S. J. (1974). Toward a theory of automatic information processing in reading. *Cognitive Psychology*, 6, 293–323.

Lakoff, G. (1987). *Women, fire and dangerous things: What categories reveal about the mind*. Chicago: University of Chicago Press.

Lampert, M. (1986) Knowing, doing, and teaching multiplication. *Cognition and Instruction, 3*, 305–342.

Language Development and Hypermedia Group. (1992a, February). "Open" software design: A case study. *Educational Technology*, 32, 43–55.

Language Development and Hypermedia Group. (1992b). Bubble dialogue: A new tool for instruction and assessment. *Educational Technology Research and Development*, 40(2), 59–67.

Languis, M. L., Bireley, M., & Williamson, T. (1990, April). *Brain mapping assessment of information processing patterns in gifted/learning disabled students*. Paper presented at the Annual Meeting of the American Educational Research Association, Boston.

Languis, M. L., Miller, D., & Bertoline, G. (1990, April) *Spatial visualization skill: Topographic brain mapping assessment; Influence of cognitive intervention*. Paper presented at the Annual Meeting of the American Educational Research Association, Boston.

Larken, J. H., McDermott, J., Simon, D. P., & Simon, H. A. (1980) Models of competence in solving physics problems. *Cognitive Science*, 4, 317–345.

Lashley, K. S. (1929). *Brain mechanisms and intelligence*. Chicago: University of Chicago Press.

Lashley, K. S., & Franz, S. I. (1917). The effects of cerebral destruction upon habit-formation and retention in the albino rat. *Psychobiology*, 71–139.

Lavatelli, C. S. (1970). *Early childhood curriculum, a Piagetian program*. Boston: American Science and Engineering.

Lave, J. (1988). *Cognition in practice: Mind, mathematics and culture in everyday life.*. New York: Cambridge University Press.

Leahey, T. H., & Harris, R. J. (1989). *Human learning* (2nd ed.). Englewood Cliffs, NJ: Prentice-Hall.

Lebow, D. Constructivist values for instructional systems design: Five principles toward a new mindset. *Educational Technology Research and Development*.

Lemke, J. L. (1985). *Using language in the classroom*. Geelong, Victoria, Australia: Deakin University Press.

Lemke, J. L. (1988). Genres, semantics, and classroom education. *Linguistics and Education*, 1(1), 81–99.

Lenneberg, E. H. (1964). A biological perspective of language. In E. H. Lenneberg (Ed.), *New directions in the study of language*. Cambridge, MA: MIT Press.

Lenneberg, E. H. (1967). *Biological foundations of language*. New York: Wiley.

Leontiev, A. N. (1981). The problem of activity in psychology. In J. V. Wertsch (Ed.), *The concept of activity in Soviet psychology*. Armonk, NY: Sharpe.

Levin, J. R. (1983). Pictorial strategies for school learning: Practical illustrations. In M. Pressley & J. R. Levin (Eds.), *Cognitive strategy research: Educational applications*. New York: Springer-Verlag.

Levin, J. R., & Kaplan, S. A. (1972). Imaginal facilitation of paired-associate learning: A limited generalization? *Journal of Educational Psychology*, 63, 429–432.

Levin, J. R., & Pressley, M. (Eds.). (1986). Learning strategies (Special issue). *Educational Psychologist*, 21 (1&2).

Levin, J. R., & Waugh, M. (1987). Educational simulations, tools, games, and microworlds: Computer-based environments for learning. *International Journal of Educational Research*, 12, 71–79.

Lewis, A. B. (1989). Training students to represent arithmetic word problems. *Journal of Educational Psychology*, 81, 521–531.

Lewis, D. (1972). *We the navigators*. Honolulu: The University Press of Hawaii.

Lewis, E. L., Stern, J. L., & Linn, M. C. 1993, January. The effect of computer simulations on introductory thermodynamics understanding. *Educational Technology*, 45–58.

Light, L. L., & Berger, D. E. (1976). Are there long-term "literal copies" of visually presented words? *Journal of Experimental Psychology: Human Learning and Memory*, 2, 654–662.

Litchfield, B. C., Driscoll, M. P., & Dempsey, J. V. (1990). Presentation sequence and example difficulty: Their effect on concept and rule learning in computer-based instruction. *Journal of Computer-Based Instruction*, 17, 35–40.

Locke, E. A., Shaw, K. N., Saari, L. M., & Latham, G. P. (1981). Goal setting and task performance: 1969–1980. *Psychological Bulletin*, 90, 125–152.

Loftus, E. F. (1979). *Eyewitness testimony*. Cambridge, MA: Harvard University Press.

Loftus, E. F., & Palmer, J. C. (1974). Reconstruction of automobile destruction: An example of the interaction between language and memory. *Journal of Verbal Learning and Verbal Behavior*, 13, 585–589.

Lohordo, V. M., & Droungas, A. (1989). Selective associations and adaptive specializations: Taste aversions and phobias. In S. B. Klein & R. R. Mowrer (Eds.), *Contemporary learning theories: Instrumental conditioning theory and the impact of biological constraints on learning*. Hillsdale, NJ: Erlbaum.

Ludwig, P. J., & Maehr, M. L. (1967). Changes in self-concepts in stated behavioral preferences. *Child Development*, 38, 453–469.

McCall, R. B. (1990). The neuroscience of education: More research is needed before application. *Journal of Educational Psychology*, 82, 885–888.

Mager, R. F. (1962). *Preparing instructional objectives*. Belmont, CA: Fearon.

Malcolm, N. (1964). Behaviorism as a philosophy of psychology. In T. W. Wann (Ed.), *Behaviorism and phenomenology*. Chicago: University of Chicago Press.

Malone, T. (1981). Toward a theory of intrinsically motivating instruction. *Cognitive Science*, 4, 333–369.

Mandler, J. M., Johnson, N. S., & DeForest, M. (1976, April) *A structural analysis of stories and their recall: From "once upon a time" to "happily ever after."* Center for Human Information Processing Technical Report.

Mannes, S. M., & Kintsch, W. (1987). Knowledge organization and text organization. *Cognition and Instruction*, 4, 91–115.

Margolin, D. (1978). The hyperkinetic child syndrome and brain monoamines: Pharmacology and therapeutic implications. *Journal of Clinical Psychiatry*, 39, 130–140.

Martin, B. L. (1987, June). Aesthetics and media: Implications for the design of instruction. *Educational Technology*, 26, 15–21.

Martinez, J. L., & Kesner, R. P. (1991). *Learning and memory: A biological view* (2nd ed.). San Diego: Academic Press.

Maslow, A. H. (1970). *Motivation and personality*. New York: Harper & Row.

A mathematician's research on math instruction . (1987, December). Research news and comment. *Educational Researcher*, 16(9), 9–12.

Matlin, M. (1983). *Cognition* . New York: Holt, Rinehart & Winston.

Mayer, R. E. (1977). The sequencing of instruction and the concept of assimilation-to-schema. *Instructional Science*, 6, 369–388.

Mayer, R. E. (1979a). Can advance organizers influence meaningful learning? *Review of Educational Research* , 49, 371–383.

Mayer, R. E. (1979b). Twenty years of research on advance organizers: Assimilation theory is still the best predictor of results. *Instructional Science*, 8, 133–167.

Mayer, R. E., & Gallini, J. K. (1990). When is an illustration worth ten thousand words? *Journal of Educational Psychology* , 82, 715–726.

Mayer, R. E., & Greeno, J. G. (1972). Structurally different learning outcomes produced by different instructional methods. *Journal of Educational Psychology* , 63, 165–173.

McClelland, D., Atkinson, J. W., Clark, R. W., & Lowell, E. L. (1953). *The achievement motive*. New York: Appleton-Century-Crofts.

McClelland, J. L. (1988). Connectionist models and psychological evidence. *Journal of Memory and Language* , 27, 107–123.

McClelland, J. L., Rumelhart, D. E., & the PDP Research Group (1986) *Parallel distributed processing: Explorations in the microstructure of cognition* (Vol. II). Cambridge, MA: Bradford Books.

McCloskey, M. (1983). Naive theories of motion. In D. Gentner & A. L. Stevens (Eds.), *Mental models* . Hillsdale, NJ: Erlbaum.

McCloskey, M., Caramazza, A., & Green, B. (1980). Curvilinear motion in the absence of external forces: Naive beliefs about the motion of objects. *Science*, 210, 1139–1141.

McGeoch, J. A. (1932). Forgetting and the law of disuse. *Psychological Review* , 39, 352–370.

Merrill, M. D. (1983). Component display theory. In C. M. Reigeluth (Ed.), *Instructional-design theories and models* . Hillsdale, NJ: Erlbaum.

Miller, G. A. (1956). The magical number, seven, plus or minus two: Some limits on our capacity for processing information. In G. A. Miller (1967). *Psychological Review 63*, 81–97.

Miller, G. A. (1967). *The psychology of communication* . Baltimore, MD: Penguin Books.

Miller, G. A. (1981). *Language and speech*. San Francisco: Freeman.

Minsky, M. (1975). A framework for representing knowledge. In P.H. Winston (Ed.), *The psychology of computer vision* . New York: McGraw-Hill.

Mishkin, M., Malamut, B., & Bachevalier, J. (1984). Memories and habits: Two neural systems. In G. Lynch, J. L. McGaugh, & N. M. Weinberger (Eds.), *Neurobiology of learning and memory* . New York: The Guilford Press.

Mishkin, M., & Petri, H. L. (1984). Memories and habits: Some implications for the analysis of learning and retention. In N. Butters & L. R. Squire (Eds.), *Neuropsychology of memory* . New York: The Guilford Press.

Morrisett, L., & Hovland, C. I. (1959). A comparison of three kinds of training in human problem solving. *Journal of Experimental Psychology* , 58, 52–55.

Mowrer, R. R., & Klein, S. B. (1989). A contrast between traditional and contemporary learning theory. In S. B. Klein and R. R. Mowrer (Eds.), *Contemporary learning theories: Instrumental conditioning theory and the impact of biological constraints on learning* . Hillsdale, NJ: Erlbaum.

Mulligan, J., Oglesby, S., & Perkins, M. R. (1980). *The status of on-site rehabilitation in private proprietary homes for adults: Issues, problems, and recommendations regarding program standards, guidelines, and training* . Report prepared for the Office of Mental Health, Albany, NY.

Neisser, U. (1967). *Cognitive psychology* . New York: Appleton-Century-Crofts.

Nelson, T. O. (1977). Repetition and depth of processing. *Journal of Verbal Learning and Verbal Behavior*, 16, 151–171.

Newby, T. J. (1991). Classroom motivation strategies of first-year teachers. *Journal of Educational Psychology*, 83 , 195–200.

Newell, A., & Simon, H. A. (1972). *Human problem solving* . Englewood Cliffs, NJ: Prentice-Hall.

Newell, A., Simon, H. A., & Shaw, J. C. (1958). Elements of a theory of human problem solving. *Psychological Review* , 65, 151–166.

Newport, E. L., Gleitman, H., & Gleitman, L. R. (1977). Mother, I'd rather do it myself: Some effects and noneffects of maternal speech style. In C. E. Snow & C. A. Ferguson (Eds.), *Talking to children: Language input and acquisition.* New York: Cambridge University Press.

Norman, D. A. (1982). *Learning and memory*. San Francisco: Freeman.

Norman, D. A. (1983). Some observations on mental models. In D. Gentner & A. L. Stevens (Eds.), *Mental models*. Hillsdale, NJ: Erlbaum.

Norman, D. A., Gentner, D. R., & Stevens, A. L. (1976). Comments on learning schemata and memory representation. In D. Klahr (Ed.), *Cognition and Instruction*. Hillsdale, NJ: Erlbaum.

Novak, J. D. (1977). An alternative to Piagetian psychology for science and mathematics education. *Science Education*, 61, 453–477.

Olton, D. S. (1983). Memory functions and the hippocampus. In W. Seifert (Ed.), *Neurobiology of the hippocampus*. New York: Academic Press.

Oppenheimer, R. (1956). Analogy in science. *American Psychologist*, 11, 127–135.

Ormrod, J. E. (1990). *Human learning: Theories, principles, and educational applications*. Columbus, OH: Merrill.

Paivio, A. (1971). *Imagery and verbal processes*. New York: Holt, Rinehart & Winston.

Paivio, A., Yuille, J. C., & Rogers, T. B. (1969). Noun imagery and meaningfulness in free and serial recall. *Journal of Experimental Psychology*, 79, 509–514.

Palincsar, A. S. (1986). The role of dialogue in scaffolded instruction. *Educational Psychologist*, 21, 73–98.

Palincsar, A. S., & Brown, A. L. (1984). Reciprocal teaching of comprehension-fostering and monitoring activities. *Cognition and Instruction*, 1, 117–175.

Papert, S. (1980). *Mindstorms: Children, computers, and powerful ideas*. New York: Basic Books.

Papert, S. (1981). Computer-based microworlds as incubators for powerful ideas. In R. Taylor (Ed.), *The computer in the school: Tutor, tool, tutee*. New York: Teacher's College Press.

Peper, R. J., & Mayer, R. E. (1978). Notetaking as a generative activity. *Journal of Educational Psychology*, 70, 514–522.

Perfetti, C. A., & Curtis, M. E. (1986). Reading. In R. F. Dillon & R. J. Sternberg (Eds.), *Cognition and instruction*. Orlando: Academic Press.

Perkins, D. N. (1991a, May). Technology meets constructivism: Do they make a marriage? *Educational Technology*, 31, 18–23.

Perkins, D. N. (1991b, September). What constructivism demands of the learner. *Educational Technology*, 31, 19–21.

Perkins, D. N., & Salomon, G. (1989, January/February). Are cognitive skills context-bound? *Educational Researcher*, 18, 16–25.

Peterson, L. R., & Peterson, M. (1959). Short-term retention of individual items. *Journal of Experimental Psychology*, 58, 193–198.

Peterson, P. L., Carpenter, T., & Fennema, E. (1989). Teachers' knowledge of students' knowledge in mathematics problem solving: Correlational and case analyses. *Journal of Educational Psychology*, 81, 558–569.

Phillips, D. C. (1983, September/October). After the wake: Post-positivistic educational thought. *Educational Researcher*, 12, 4–12.

Phillips, D. C. (1987). *Philosophy, science, and social inquiry*. Oxford: Pergamon Press.

Phye, G. D., & Andre, T. (Eds.). (1986). *Cognitive classroom learning*. Orlando: Academic Press.

Piaget, J. (1951). *Play, dreams, and imitation in childhood*. New York: Norton.

Piaget, J. (1969). *Science of education and the psychology of the child*. New York: Viking.

Piaget, J., & Inhelder, B. (1967). *The child's conception of space*. New York: Norton.

Piaget, J., & Inhelder, B. (1969). *The psychology of the child*. New York: Basic Books.

Pichert, J. W., & Anderson, R. C. (1977). Taking different perspectives on a story. *Journal of Educational Psychology*, 69, 309–315.

Picton, T. W., Stuss, D. T., & Marshall, K. C. (1986). Attention and the brain. In S.L. Friedman, K.A. Klivington, & R. W. Peterson (Eds.), *The brain, cognition and education*. Orlando: Academic Press.

Popham, W. J. (1988). *Educational evaluation* (2nd ed.). Englewood Cliffs, NJ: Prentice-Hall.

Posner, G. J., Strike, K. A., Hewson, P. W., & Gertzog, W. A. (1982). Accommodation of a scientific conception: Toward a theory of conceptual change. *Science Education*, 66(2), 211 – 227.

Posner, M. I. (1984). Selective attention and the storage of information. In G. Lynch, J. L. McGaugh, & N. M. Weinberger (Eds.), *Neurobiology of learning and memory*. New York: The Guilford Press.

Posner, M. I., & Friedrich, F. J. (1986). Attention and the control of cognition. In S.L. Friedman, K.A. Klivington, & R. W. Peterson (Eds.), *The brain, cognition and education*. Orlando: Academic Press.

Prawatt, R. S. (1989). Promoting access to knowledge strategy and disposition in students. *Review of Educational Research*, 59, 1–41.

Premack, D. (1959). Toward empirical behavior laws: I. Positive reinforcement. *Psychological Review*, 66, 219–233.

Pressey, S. L. (1926). A simple apparatus which gives tests and scores—and teaches. *School and Society*, *23*, 373–376.

Pressey, S. L. (1927). A machine for automatic teaching of drill material. *School and Society*, *25*, 549–552.

Pressey, S. L. (1964), Autoinstruction: Perspectives, problems, potentials. In E. R. Hilgard (Ed.), *Theories of learning and instruction*. Chicago, IL: National Society for the Study of Education and University of Chicago Press.

Pressley, M., Borkowski, J. G., & O'Sullivan, J. R. (1984). Memory strategy instruction is made of this: Metamemory and durable strategy use. *Educational Psychologist*, *19*, 94–107.

Pressley, M. & Levin, J. R. (1983). *Cognitive strategy research: Educational applications*. New York: Springer-Verlag.

Pressley, M., Snyder, B. L., & Cariglia-Bull, T. (1987). How can good strategy use be taught to children? Evaluation of six alternative approaches. In S. M. Cormier and J. D. Hagman (Eds.), *Transfer of learning*. New York: Academic Press.

Pylyshyn, Z. W. (1973). What the mind's eye tells the mind's brain: A critique of mental imagery. *Psychological Bulletin*, *80*, 1–24.

Radziszewska, B., & Rogoff, B. (1988). The influence of collaboration with parents versus peers in learning to plan. *Developmental Psychology*, *24*, 840–848.

Rayner, K., Well, A. D., & Pollatsek, A. (1980). Asymmetry of the effective visual field in reading. *Perception and Psychophysics*, *27*, 537–544.

Reigeluth, C. M. (1979). In search of a better way to organize instruction: The elaboration theory. *Journal of Instructional Development*, *2*(3), 8–15.

Reigeluth, C. M. (1983). Instructional design: What is it and why is it? In C. M. Reigeluth (Ed.), *Instructional-design theories and models*. Hillsdale, NJ: Erlbaum.

Reigeluth, C. M., & Stein, F. (1983). The elaboration theory of instruction. In C. M. Reigeluth (Ed.), *Instructional-design theories and models*. Hillsdale, NJ: Erlbaum.

Reiser, R. A., Driscoll, M. P., & Vergara, A. (1987). The effects of ascending, descending, and fixed criteria on student performance and attitude in a mastery-oriented course. *Educational Communications and Technology Journal*, *35*, 195–202.

Resnick, L. B. (1981). Instructional psychology. *Annual Review of Psychology*, *32*, 659–704.

Reynolds, G. S. (1968). *A primer of operant conditioning*. Glenview, IL: Scott-Foresman.

Rice, G. E., & Meyer, B. J. F. (1985). Reading behavior and prose recall performance of young and older adults with high and average verbal ability. *Educational Gerontology*, *11*, 57–72.

Rieber, L. P. (1991a). Animation, incidental learning, and continuing motivation. *Journal of Educational Psychology*, *83*, 318–328.

Rieber, L. P. (1991b, February). *Computer-based microworlds: A bridge between constructivism and direct instruction*. Paper presented at the Annual Meeting of the Association of Educational Communications and Technology, Orlando

Roediger, H. L., III (1980). Memory metaphors in cognitive psychology. *Memory and Cognition*, *8*, 231–246.

Rogoff, B. (1984). Introduction: Thinking and learning in social context. In B. Rogoff & J. Lave (Eds.), *Everyday cognition*. Cambridge, MA: Harvard University Press.

Rosch, E. H. (1973). Natural categories. *Cognitive Psychology*, *4*, 328–350.

Rosch, E. H. (1975). Cognitive representations of semantic categories. *Journal of Experimental Psychology: General*, *104*, 192–233.

Rosch, E. H. (1978). Principles of categorization. In E. Rosch & B. Lloyd (Eds.), *Cognition and categorization*. Hillsdale, NJ: Erlbaum.

Rosenthal, R., & Jacobson, L. (1968). *Pygmalion in the classroom: Teacher expectation and pupils' intellectual development*. New York: Holt, Rinehart & Winston.

Rosenzweig, M. R. (1984). Experience, memory, and the brain. *American Psychologist*, *39*, 365–376.

Rosenzweig, M. R. (1986). Multiple models of memory. In S. L. Friedman, K. A. Klivington, & R. W. Peterson (Eds.), *The brain, cognition and education*. Orlando: Academic Press.

Roth, K. T., Anderson, C. W., & Smith, E. L. (1986, February). *Curriculum materials, teacher talk, and student learning: Case studies in fifth-grade science teaching*. East Lansing: Michigan State University, The Institute for Research on Teaching.

Roth, M. (1990). *Collaboration and constructivism in the science classroom*. Paper presented at the Annual Meeting of the American Educational Research Association, Boston.

Rotter, J. B. (1966). Generalized expectancies for internal versus external control of reinforcements. *Psychological Monographs*, *80*, 1–28.

Royer, J. M., & Cable, G. W. (1975). Facilitated learning in connected discourse. *Journal of Educational Psychology*, *67*, 116–123.

Royer, J. M., Lynch, D. J., Hambleton, R. K., & Bulgareli, C. (1984). Using the sentence verification technique to assess the comprehension of technical text as a function of subject matter expertise. *American Educational Research Journal*, 21, 839–869.

Royer, J. M., & Perkins, M. R. (1977). Facilitative transfer in prose learning over an extended time period. *Journal of Reading Behavior*, 9, 185–188.

Royer, J. M., Perkins, M. R., & Konold, C. E. (1978). Evidence for a selective storage mechanism in prose learning. *Journal of Educational Psychology*, 70, 457–462.

Rumelhart, D. E. (1975). Notes on a schema for stories. In D. G. Bobrow & A. M. Collins (Eds.), *Representation and understanding: Studies in cognitive science*. New York: Academic Press.

Rumelhart, D. E. (1980). Schemata: The building blocks of cognition. In R. J. Spiro, B. C. Bruce, & W. F. Brewer (Eds.), *Theoretical issues in reading comprehension*. Hillsdale, NJ: Erlbaum.

Rumelhart, D. E., & Norman, D. A. (1978). Accretion, tuning, and restructuring: Three modes of learning. In J. W. Cotton & R. L. Klatzky (Eds.), *Semantic factors in cognition*. Hillsdale, NJ: Erlbaum.

Rumelhart, D. E., & Norman, D. A. (1981). Analogical processes in learning. In J. R. Anderson (Ed.), *Cognitive skills and their acquisition*. Hillsdale, NJ: Erlbaum.

Russell, J. (1982). Cognitive conflict, transmission, and justification: Conservation attainment through dyadic interaction. *Journal of Genetic Psychology*, 140, 287–297.

Rutkowska, J. (1985). Does the phylogeny of conceptual development increase our understanding of concepts or of development? In G. Butterworth, J. Rutkowska, & M. Scaife (Eds.), *Evolution and developmental psychology*. Great Britain: The Harvester Press.

Sagan, C. (1977). *The dragons of Eden: Speculations on the evolution of human intelligence*. New York: Ballantine Books.

Salomon, G., & Globerson, T. (1989). When teams do not function the way they ought to. *International Journal of Educational Research*, 13, 89–99.

Salomon, G., & Perkins, D. N. (1987). Transfer of cognitive skills from programming: When and how? *Journal of Educational Computing Research*, 3, 149–169.

Salomon, G., & Perkins, D. N. (1989). Rocky roads to transfer: Rethinking mechanisms of a neglected phenomenon. *Educational Psychologist*, 24, 113–142.

Sawyer, R. J., Graham, S., & Harris, K. R. (1992). Direct teaching, strategy instruction, and strategy instruction with explicit self-regulation: Effects on the composition skills and self-efficacy of students with learning disabilities. *Journal of Educational Research*, 84, 340–352.

Saxe, G. B. (1977). A developmental analysis of notational counting. *Child Development*, 48, 1512–1520.

Saxe, G. B. (1982). Developing forms of arithmetical thought among Oksapmin of Papua, New Guinea. *Developmental Psychology*, 18, 583–594.

Saxe, G. B. (1990). *Culture and cognitive development: Studies in mathematical understanding*. Hillsdale, NJ: Erlbaum.

Scaife, M. (1985). The implications of a structuralist biology for developmental psychology. In G. Butterworth, J. Rutkowska, & M. Scaife (Eds.), *Evolution and developmental psychology*. Great Britain: The Harvester Press.

Schacter, D. L. (1992). Understanding implicit memory: A cognitive neuroscience approach. *American Psychologist*, 47, 559–569.

Schank, R. C., & Abelson, R. P. (1975). Scripts, plans, and knowledge. *Advance Papers of the Fourth International Joint Conference on Artificial Intelligence*. Tbilisi, Georgia, USSR.

Schank, R. C., & Abelson, R. P. (1977). *Scripts, plans, goals, and understanding*. Hillsdale, NJ: Erlbaum.

Schoenfeld, A. H. (1982). Measures of problem-solving performance and of problem-solving instruction. *Journal of Research in Mathematics Education*, 13, 31–49.

Schoenfeld, A. H. (1985). *Mathematical problem solving*. New York: Academic Press.

Schoenfeld, A. H. (1988). When good teaching leads to bad results: The disasters of "well-taught" mathematics courses. *Educational Psychologist*, 23, 145–166.

Schoenfeld, A. H., & Herrmann, D. J. (1982). Problem perception and knowledge structure in expert and novice mathematical problem solvers. *Journal of Experimental Psychology: Learning, Memory and Cognition*, 8, 484–494.

Schunk, D. H. (1987). Peer models and children's behavioral change. *Review of Educational Research*, 57, 149–174.

Schunk, D. H. (1990). Introduction to the special section on motivation and efficacy. *Journal of Educational Psychology*, 82, 3–6.

Schunk, D. H., & Gaa, J. P. (1981). Goal-setting influence on learning and self-evaluation. *Journal of Classroom Interaction*, 16(2), 38–44.

Schunk, D. H., & Hanson, A. R. (1985). Peer models: Influence on children's self-efficacy and achievement. *Journal of Educational Psychology*, 77, 313–322.

Segal, J. W., Chipman, S. F., & Glaser, R. (1985). *Thinking and learning skills: Relating instruction to research* (Vol. 1). Hillsdale, NJ: Erlbaum.

Seligman, M. E. P., & Maier, S. F. (1967). Failure to escape traumatic shock. *Journal of Experimental Psychology, 74*, 1–9.

Sen, A., & Posner, M. I. (1979). The effect of unattended visual and auditory words on cross modal naming. *Bulletin of the Psychonomic Society, 13*, 405–408.

Shank, G. (1988). Three into two will go: Juxtapositional strategies for empirical research in semiotics. In J. Deely (Ed.). *Semiotics 1987.* New York: University Press of America.

Shepard, R. N. (1978). The mental image. *American Psychologist, 33*, 125–137.

Shiffrin, R. M., & Schneider, W. (1977). Controlled and automatic human information processing. II. Perceptual learning, automatic attending, and a general theory. *Psychological Review, 84*, 127–190.

Shulman, L. S. (1988). Disciplines of inquiry in education: An overview. In R. M. Jaeger (Ed.), *Complementary methods for research in education.* Washington, DC: American Educational Research Association.

Siegler, R. S. (1976). Three aspects of cognitive development. *Cognitive Psychology, 8*, 481–520.

Siegler, R. S. (1983). Five generalizations about cognitive development. *American Psychologist, 38*, 263–277.

Siegler, R. S. (1984). Mechanisms of cognitive growth: Variation and selection. In   R. J. Sternberg (Ed.), *Mechanisms of cognitive development.* New York: Freeman.

Siegler, R. S. (1986). *Children's thinking.* Englewood Cliffs, NJ: Prentice-Hall.

Siegler, R. S., & Crowley, K. (1991). The microgenetic method: A direct means for studying cognitive development. *American Psychologist, 46* 606–620.

Siegler, R. S., & Klahr, D. (1982). What do children learn? The relationship between existing knowledge and the acquisition of new knowledge. In R. Glaser (Ed.), *Advances in instructional psychology.* Hillsdale, NJ: Erlbaum.

Siegler, R. S., & Richards, D. (1982). The development of intelligence. In R. J. Sternberg (Ed.), *Handbook of human intelligence.* Cambridge, England: Cambridge University Press.

Simon, H. (1986). The role of attention in cognition. In S. L. Friedman, K. A. Klivington, & R. W. Peterson (Eds.), *The brain, cognition and education.* Orlando: Academic Press.

Simpson, E. J. (1966–67). The classification of educational objectives, psychomotor domain. *Illinois Teacher of Home Economics, 10*, 110–144.

Singer, R. N. (1980). *Motor learning and human performance* (3rd ed.). New York: Macmillan.

Singer, R. N., & Dick, W. (1980). *Teaching physical education* (2nd ed.). Boston: Houghton Mifflin.

Singley, M. K.. & Anderson, J. R. (1989). *The transfer of cognitive skill.* Cambridge, MA: Harvard University Press.

Skinner, B. F. (1938). *The behavior of organisms: An experimental analysis.* Englewood Cliffs, NJ: Prentice-Hall.

Skinner, B. F. (1948). Superstition in the pigeon. *Journal of Experimental Psychology, 38*, 168–172.

Skinner, B. F. (1950). Are theories of learning necessary? *Psychological Review, 57*, 193–216.

Skinner, B. F. (1957). *Verbal behavior.* Englewood Cliffs, NJ: Prentice-Hall.

Skinner, B. F. (1958). Reinforcement today. *American Psychologist, 13*, 94–99.

Skinner, B. F. (1969). *Contingencies of reinforcement.* Englewood Cliffs, NJ: Prentice-Hall.

Skinner, B. F. (1974). *About behaviorism.* New York: Knopf.

Skinner, B. F. (1987). Whatever happened to psychology as the science of behavior? *American Psychologist, 42*, 780–786.

Skinner, B. F., & Krakower, S. (1968). *Handwriting with write and see.* Chicago: Lyons & Carnahan.

Slavin, R. E. (1978). Student teams and achievement divisions. *Journal of Research and Development in Education, 12*, 39–49.

Slavin, R. E. (1983). *Cooperative learning.* New York: Longman.

Slavin, R. E. (1984). Students motivating students to excel: Cooperative incentive tasks and student achievement. *The Elementary School Journal, 85*, 53–64.

Slavin, R. E. (1991, February). Synthesis of research on cooperative learning. *Educational Leadership, 48*, 71–77.

Smith, E. E., Shoben, E. J., & Rips, L. J. (1974). Structure and process in semantic memory: A featural model for semantic decision. *Psychological Review, 81*, 214–241.

Snowman, J. (1986). Learning tactics and strategies. In G. D. Phye & T. Andre (Eds.), *Cognitive classroom learning.* Orlando: Academic Press.

Solnick, J. V., Rincover, A., & Peterson, C. R. (1977). Some determinants of the reinforcing and punishing effects of timeout. *Journal of Applied Behavior Analysis, 10*, 415–424.

Sperling, G. (1960). The information available in brief visual presentations. *Psychological Monographs, 74* (Whole No. 498).

Spielberger, C. D. (Ed.). (1966). *Anxiety and behavior*. New York: Academic Press.

Spilich, G. J., Vesonder, G. T., Chiesi, H. L., & Voss, J. F. (1979). Text processing of domain-related information for individuals with high and low domain knowledge. *Journal of Verbal Learning and Verbal Behavior*, *18*, 275–290.

Spiro, R. J. (1977). Remembering information from text: Theoretical and empirical issues concerning the "State of Schema" reconstruction hypothesis. In R. C. Anderson, R. J. Spiro, & W. E. Montague (Eds.), *Schooling and the acquisition of knowledge*. Hillsdale, NJ: Erlbaum.

Spiro, R. J. (1980). Constructive processes in prose comprehension and recall. In R. J. Spiro, B. C. Bruce, & W. F. Brewer (Eds.), *Theoretical issues in reading comprehension*. Hillsdale, NJ: Erlbaum.

Spiro, R. J., Coulson, R. L., Feltovich, P. J., & Anderson, D. K. (1988). Cognitive flexibility theory: Advanced knowledge acquisition in ill-structured domains. In *Tenth Annual Conference of the Cognitive Science Society*. Hillsdale, MJ: Erlbaum.

Spiro, R. J., Feltovich, P. J., Jacobson, M. J., & Coulson, R. L. (1991, May). Cognitive flexibility, constructivism, and hypertext: Random access instruction for advanced knowledge acquisition in ill-structured domains. *Educational Technology*, *31*, 24–33.

Spiro, R. J., & Jehng, J. C. (1990). Cognitive flexibility and hypertext: Theory and technology for the nonlinear and multidimensional traversal of complex subject matter. In D. Nix & R. J. Spiro (Eds.), *Cognition, education and multimedia*. Hillsdale, NJ: Erlbaum.

Spiro, R. J., Vispoel, W., Schmitz, J., Samarapungavan, A., & Boerger, A. (1987). Knowledge acquisition for application: Cognitive flexibility and transfer in complex content domains. In B. C. Britton (Ed.), *Executive control processes*. Hillsdale, NJ: Erlbaum.

Squire, L. R. (1983). The hippocampus and the neuropsychology of memory. In   W. Seifert (Ed.), *Neurobiology of the hippocampus*. New York: Academic Press.

Squire, L. R. (1986). Memory and the brain. In S. L. Friedman, K. A. Klivington, &   R. W. Peterson (Eds.), *The brain, cognition and education*. Orlando: Academic Press.

Squire, L. R. (1987). *Memory and brain*. New York: Oxford University Press.

Stamm, J. S., & Kreder, S. V. (1979). Minimal brain dysfunction: Psychological and neurophysiological disorders in hyperkinetic children. In M. Gazzaniga (Ed.), *Handbook of behavioral neurobiology. Vol. 2: Neuropsychology*. New York: Plenum Press.

Steinberg, E. (1989). Cognition and learner control: A literature review, 1977–1988. *Journal of Computer-Based Instruction*, *16*, 117–121.

Steinmetz, S. K. (1977). *The cycle of violence*. New York: Praeger.

Sternberg, R. J. (1984a) Preface. *Mechanisms of cognitive development*. New York: Freeman.

Sternberg, R. J. (1984b). Mechanisms of cognitive development: A componential approach. In R. J. Sternberg (Ed.) *Mechanisms of cognitive development*. New York: Freeman.

Sternberg, R. J. (1985). *Beyond IQ: A triarchic theory of human intelligence*. New York: Cambridge University Press.

Sternberg, R. J., & Davidson, J. E. (1983). Insight in the gifted. *Educational Psychologist*, *18*, 52–58.

Sternberg, R. J., & Wagner, R. K. (1982). Automatization failure in learning disabilities. *Topics in Learning Disabilities*, *2*, 1–11.

Stevens, A. L., & Collins, A. (1980). Multiple conceptual models of a complex system. In R. Snow, P. Federico, & W. Montague (Eds.), *Aptitude, learning and instruction: Cognitive process analysis*. Hillsdale, NJ: Erlbaum.

Stevens, A. L., & Gentner, D. (1983). Introduction. In D. Gentner & A. L. Stevens (Eds.), *Mental models*. Hillsdale, NJ: Erlbaum.

Strauss, M. A., Gelles, R. J. & Steinmetz, S. K. (1980). *Behind closed doors: Violence in the American family*. Garden City, NY: Doubleday.

Sui, P. K. (1986). Understanding Chinese prose: Effects of number of ideas, metaphor, and advance organizers on comprehension. *Journal of Educational Psychology*, *78*, 417–423.

Sulin, R. A., & Dooling, D. J. (1974). Intrusion of a thematic idea in retention of prose. *Journal of Experimental Psychology*, *103*, 255–262.

Sulzer, B. & Mayer, G. F. (1972). *Behavior modification procedures for school personnel*. New York: Holt, Rinehart & Winston.

Sussman, D. M. (1981). PSI: Variations on a theme. In S.W. Bijou & R. Ruiz (Eds.), *Behavior modification: Contributions to education*. Hillsdale, NJ: Erlbaum.

Sweller, J., Mawer, R. F., & Ward, M. R. (1983). Development of expertise in mathematical problem solving. *Journal of Experimental Psychology: General*, *112*, 639–661.

Sweller, J. (1989). Cognitive technology: Some procedures for facilitating learning and problem solving in mathematics and science. *Journal of Educational Psychology*, *81*, 457–466.

Taylor-Parker, S. (1985). Higher intelligence as adaptation for social and technological strategies in early *Homo sapiens*. In G. Butterworth, J. Rutkowska, & M. Scaife (Eds.), *Evolution and developmental psychology*. Great Britain: The Harvester Press.

Tennyson, R. D., & Cocchiarella, M. J. (1986). An empirically based instructional design theory for teaching concepts. *Review of Educational Research*, 56, 40–71.

Terrace, H. (1963a). Discrimination learning with and without errors. *Journal of Experimental Analysis of Behavior*, 6, 1–27.

Terrace, H. (1963b). Errorless transfer of a discrimination across two continua. *Journal of Experimental Analysis of Behavior*, 6, 223–232.

Tessmer, M., & Driscoll, M. P. (1986). Effects of a diagrammatic display of concept definitions on classification performance. *Educational Communications and Technology Journal*, 34, 195–205.

Tessmer, M., Wilson, B., & Driscoll, M. (1990). A new model of concept teaching and learning. *Educational Technology Research and Development*, 38 (1), 45–54.

Thomson, D. M., & Tulving, E. (1970). Associative encoding and retrieval: Weak and strong cues. *Journal of Experimental Psychology*, 86, 255–262.

Thorndike, E. L. (1913). *Educational psychology. Vol. II. The psychology of learning*. New York: Teachers College, Columbia University.

Timberlake, W., & Lucas, G. A. (1989). Behavior systems and learning: From misbehavior to general principles. In S. B. Klein & R. R. Mowrer (Eds.), *Contemporary learning theories: Instrumental conditioning theory and the impact of biological constraints on learning*. Hillsdale, NJ: Erlbaum.

Tobias, S. (1976). Achievement-treatment interaction. *Review of Educational Research*, 46, 61–74.

Tobin, K., & Dawson, G. (1992). Constraints to curriculum reform: Teachers and the myths of schooling. *Educational Technology Research and Development*, 40(1), 81–92.

Tooby, J. & Cosmides, L. (1989). Evolutionary psychology and the generation of culture, Part I: Theoretical considerations. *Ethology and Sociobiology*, 10, 29–49.

Torello, M. W., & Duffy, F.H. (1985). Using brain electrical activity mapping to diagnose learning disabilities. *Theory into Practice*, 25, 95–99.

Torgeson, J. K. (1977). The role of nonspecific factors in the task performance of learning disabled children: A theoretical assessment. *Journal of Learning Disabilities*, 10, 27–34.

Treisman, A. M. (1960). Contextual cues in selective listening. *Quarterly Journal of Experimental Psychology*, 12, 242–248.

Tuckman, B. (1988). *Testing for teachers*. San Diego: Harcourt Brace Jovanovich.

Tudge, J., & Rogoff, B. (1989). Peer influences on cognitive development: Piagetian and Vygotskian perspectives. In M. H. Bornstein & J. S. Bruner (Eds.), *Interaction in human development*. Hillsdale, NJ: Erlbaum.

Tulving, E. (1962). Subjective organization in free recall of "unrelated" words. *Psychological Review*, 69, 344–354.

Tulving, E. (1972). Episodic and semantic memory. In E. Tulving & W. Donaldson (Eds.), *Organization and memory*. New York: Academic Press.

Tulving, E., & Thomson, D. M. (1973). Encoding specificity and retrieval processes in episodic memory. *Psychological Review*, 80, 352–373.

Vaccarino, F. J., Schiff, B. B., & Glickman, S. E. (1989). Biological view of reinforcement. In S. B. Klein & R. R. Mowrer (Eds.), *Contemporary learning theories: Instrumental conditioning theory and the impact of biological constraints on learning*. Hillsdale, NJ: Erlbaum.

van Dijk, T. A., & Kintsch, W. (1983). *Strategies of discourse comprehension*. New York: Academic Press.

Varnhagen, C. K., & Goldman, S. R. (1986). Improving comprehension: Causal relations instruction for learning handicapped learners. *The Reading Teacher*, 39, 896–904.

Vosniadou, S. (1988, April). *Knowledge restructuring and science instruction*. Paper presented at the Annual Meeting of the American Educational Research Association, New Orleans.

Vosniadou, S., & Brewer, W. F. (1987). Theories of knowledge restructuring in development. *Review of Educational Research*, 57, 51–67.

Vygotsky, L. S. (1962). *Thought and language*. Cambridge, MA: The MIT Press.

Vygotsky, L. S. (1978). *Mind in society*. Cambridge, MA: Harvard University Press.

Vygotsky, L. S. (1981). The genesis of higher mental functions. In J. V. Wertsch (Ed.), *The concept of activity in Soviet psychology*. Armonk, New York: Sharpe.

Wadsworth, B. J. (1978). *Piaget for the classroom teacher*. New York: Longman.

Walters, G. C., & Grusec, J. E. (1977). *Punishment*. San Francisco, CA: Freeman.

Wang, M. C., & Palincsar, A. S. (1989). Teaching students to assume an active role in their learning. In M. C. Reynolds (Ed.), *Knowledge base for the beginning teacher*. New York: Pergamon Press for the American Association of Colleges for Teacher Education.

Watson, J. B. (1913). Psychology as the behaviorist views it. *Psychological Review*, 20, 158–177.

Watson, J. B., & Rayner, R. (1920). Conditioned emotional reactions. *Journal of Experimental Psychology*, 3, 1–14.

Webb, N. M. (1982). Student interaction and learning in small groups. *Review of Educational Research*, 53, 421–445.

Webb, N. M. (1984). Microcomputer learning in small groups: Cognitive requirements and group processes. *Journal of Educational Psychology*, 74, 475–484.

Webb, N. M. (1989). Peer interaction and learning in small groups. *International Journal of Educational Research*, 13, 21–39.

Weiner, B. (1979). A theory of motivation for some classroom experiences. *Journal of Educational Psychology*, 71, 3–25.

Weiner, B. (1985). An attributional theory of achievement motivation and emotion. *Psychological Review*, 92, 548–573.

Weiner, B. (1986). *An attributional theory of motivation and emotion*. New York: Springer-Verlag.

Weiner, B. (1990). History of motivational research in education. *Journal of Educational Psychology*, 82, 616–622.

Weiner, H. (1969). Controlling human fixed-interval performance. *Journal of Experimental Analysis of Behavior*, 12, 349–373.

Weinstein, C. E. (1982). A metacurriculum for remediating learning strategy deficits in academically unprepared students. In L. Noel & R. Levitz (Eds.), *How to succeed with academically unprepared students*. Iowa City, IA: American College Testing Service.

Weinstein, C. E., & Mayer, R. E. (1986). The teaching of learning strategies. In M. C. Wittrock (Ed.), *Handbook of research on teaching* (3rd ed.). New York: Harper & Row.

Werner, H. (1957). The concept of development from a comparative and organismic point of view. In D. Harris (Ed.), *The concept of development*. Minneapolis: The University of Minnesota Press.

Wertsch, J. V. (1984). The zone of proximal development: Some conceptual issues. In B. Rogoff and J. V. Wertsch (Eds.), *New Directions for Child Development*. No. 23: *Children's learning in the "zone of proximal development."* San Francisco: Jossey-Bass.

Wertsch, J. V. (1985). *Vygotsky and the social formation of mind*. Cambridge, MA: Harvard University Press.

West, C. K., Farmer, J. A., & Wolff, P. M. (1991). *Instructional design: Implications from cognitive science*. Englewood Cliffs, NJ: Prentice-Hall.

West, L. H. T., & Fensham, P. J. (1976). Prior knowledge or advance organizers as effective variables in chemical learning. *Journal of Research in Science Teaching*, 13, 297–306.

White, R. W. (1959). Motivation reconsidered: The concept of competence. *Psychological Review*, 66, 297–333.

Wilcox, W. C., Merrill, M. D., & Black, H. B. (1981). Effect of teaching a conceptual hierarchy on concept classification performance. *Journal of Instructional Development*, 5, 8–13.

Wineburg, S. S. (1989, May). Remembrance of theories past. *Educational Researcher*, 18, 7–10.

Wittrock, M. C. (1985a). Teaching learners generative strategies for enhancing reading comprehension. *Theory into Practice*, 24, 123–126.

Wittrock, M. C. (1985b). The generative learning model and its implications for science education. *Studies in Science Education*, 12, 59–87.

Wolf, M. M., Risley, T. R., & Mees, H. L. (1964). Application of operant conditioning procedures to the behavior problems of an autistic child. *Behavior Research and Therapy*, 1, 305–312.

Wolpe, J. (1958). *Psychotherapy by reciprocal inhibition*. Stanford, CA: Stanford University Press.

Wolpe, J. (1969). *The practice of behavior therapy*. Oxford: Pergamon Press.

Wood, D., Bruner, J. S., & Ross, G. (1976). The role of tutoring in problem solving. *Journal of Child Psychology and Psychiatry*, 17, 89–100.

Woolfolk, A. E., & Hoy, W. K. (1990). Prospective teachers' sense of efficacy and beliefs about control. *Journal of Educational Psychology*, 82, 81–91.

Woolfolk, A. E., & McCune-Nicholich, L. (1984). *Educational psychology for teachers* (2nd ed.). Englewood Cliffs, NJ: Prentice-Hall.

Yuille, J. C., & Cutshall, J. L. (1986). A case study of eyewitness memory of a crime. *Journal of Applied Psychology*, 71, 291–301.

Index

Numbers in italic *indicate illustrations, numbers followed by* t *indicate tables.*

Accommodation in developmental process, 179
Accretion in schema-based processing, 146–147
Achievement motivation, research on, 294
Advance organizers for instruction, 126–131
Ambiguous assignments to enhance motivation, 296
Anchoring ideas for meaningful learning, 114
Arithmetic problem solving, schema theory and, 150–151
Assimilation
  in developmental process, 179
  to schema, meaningful learning as, 135–137
Assimilation theory, 122
Atkinson, John, on achievement motivation, 294
Attention
  brain and, 262–269
  disorders of, 264
  gaining
    in instruction, 351–352
    and sustaining, in stimulating motivation, 314–315
  in information processing, 73
    automatic, 75–76
    selective, 73–75
  organization of, selective, 267–269
  as process, 263
  as resource, 263
    selective allocation of, 265–267
  as state, 263
    control of, 264–265
  Attitudes
    conditions for learning, 349–350
    as learning outcomes, 342–343
Attribution theory, motivation and, 307–309

Audience analysis in motivational design, 320–322, 324
Ausubel, David P., on meaningful learning, 112–137
Automaticity in information processing, 75–76

Behavior(s)
  changing, planning program for, 48–53
    determining appropriate reinforcers in, 49–50
    evaluating progress in, 50–53
    procedure implementation for, 50
    procedure selection for, 50
    recording results in, 50
    revisions in, 51–53
    setting behavioral goals in, 48–49
  contingencies of reinforcement and, 30–32
  evolution and, 247–257
  experimental analysis of, 29–32
  learning and, 25–63
  maintaining, 45–48
  fixed interval schedules of reinforcement in, 47–48
  fixed ratio schedules of reinforcement in, 46
  variable interval schedules of reinforcement in, *47*, 48
  variable ratio schedules of reinforcement in, *47*, 48
  new, teaching, 40–45
    chaining in, 42–43
    discrimination learning in, 43–44
    fading in, 44–45
    shaping in, 40–42
  operant, 30
  reinforcement and, 61–62

Performance accomplishments, self-efficacy
expectations and, 302
Personal teaching efficacy, 311–312
Personalized system of instruction (PSI) in
management of instruction, 57–58
Perspective as antecedent to schema theory,
144
Persuasion, verbal, self-efficacy expectations
and, 303
Phylogenetic comparisons in development,
227
Physical knowledge, 172, *174*
Physiological states, self-efficacy expectations
and, 303
Piaget, Jean
genetic epistemology of, 171–184. *See also*
Genetic epistemology
instruction inspired by, 195–199
Plasticity, cortical, of developing brain,
278–279
implications of, for instruction, 284
Pragmatism, 13–14
Preoperational period of development,
176*t*, 177
Primacy effect of serial position curve,
rehearsal and, 83
Proactive interference, forgetting
and, 98
Procedural learning, 141
Procedural memory, 272
Progressive differentiation for instruction,
133–134
Propositional learning, 116–117
Propositional models of long-term memory,
89–90
Prototype model of pattern recognition, 77
Proximal goals, setting, 297–298
Psychological functions, converting social
relations to, 229–230
Punishment, weakening response with,
35–37
Radical behaviorism, 27–63
behavior management and, 32–53. *See also*
Behavior management
contributions of, to instruction, 53–61
in behavior modification, 53–54
in classroom management, 54–55
computer-based instruction as, 59–61
in management of instruction, 55–58
teaching machines as, 58–59
Rational set generator in organizing
instruction, 100, *102*
Rationalism, 12–13
Recall in information retrieval, 94
Recency in working memory, 82
Reception learning versus discovery learning,
115
Reciprocal teaching, 237–238
Recognition in information retrieval, 95–96
Reconciliation, integrative, for instruction,
131–133
Reconstructive process, cognition as, 106–107
Reference memory, 270

Reflexivity, nurturance of, as constructivist
learning condition, 370–371
Rehearsal in working memory, 83–84
Reinforcement
contingencies of, 30–32
fixed interval schedules of, in maintaining
behavior, 47–48
fixed ratio schedules of, in maintaining
behavior, 46–47
human behavior and, 61–62
intrinsic motivation and, 62–63
negative, strengthening operant behaviors
with, 34–35
positive, strengthening operant behaviors
with, 32–34
variable interval schedules of, in
maintaining behavior, 47, 48
variable ratio schedules of, in maintaining
behavior, 47, 48
Reinforcers
appropriate, determination of, in planning
program for behavior change, 49–50
primary, 33
relativity of, 34
secondary, 33–34
selection of, 34
Relevance
enhancing, in stimulating motivation,
315–316
task, learning, motivation and, 296–300
Representation
enactive, 209
iconic, 209
modes of, 208–213
stages of, sequence of, 209–211
instruction and, 211–213
symbolic, 209
Representational learning, 116, 117
Respondent behavior, 29–30
Response cost, weakening response with, 38
Restructuring in schema-based processing,
147
Retention
enhancing, in instruction, 356
of meaningful learning, 122–123
Retrieval
failure of, forgetting and, 97
of learned information in long-term
memory, 93–97
cues for, 96–97
recall in, 94
recognition in, 95–96
Rhizome metaphor for cognition, 107–109
Rote learning versus meaningful learning,
115–116
Rule learning in learning hierarchy, 340

Satisfaction, generating, in stimulating
motivation, 317–318
Scaffolding in zone of proximal development,
235–236
Schema
cultural knowledge based on, 151